NUMERICAL METHODS
A SOFTWARE APPROACH

NUMERICAL METHODS
A SOFTWARE APPROACH

R. L. Johnston
University of Toronto

John Wiley & Sons
New York • Chichester • Brisbane • Toronto • Singapore

Library of Congress Cataloging in Publication Data:

Johnston, Robert L.
  Numerical methods.

  Includes index.
  1. Numerical analysis—Computer programs.
I. Title.
QA297.J64   519.4′028′5425   81-12974
ISBN 0-471-09397-1   AACR2

Printed in the United States of America

10 9 8 7 6 5 4 3 2 1

PREFACE

This book is intended to serve as a text for an introductory course in numerical methods. It evolved from a set of notes developed for such a course taught to science and engineering students at the University of Toronto.

The purpose of a numerical methods course is to acquaint the student with up-to-date techniques for carrying out scientific computations on an electronic computer. A recent and important tool in this regard is mathematical software—pre-programmed, reliable computer subroutines for solving mathematical problems. As the title implies, this book is oriented toward learning how to use this tool effectively, that is, how to select the most appropriate routine available for solving a particular problem at hand and how to interpret the results that are returned by it. This approach involves more than the usual discussion of numerical methods plus a simple citing of the various software routines that are currently available. In order to be an effective user of a subroutine, one must be aware of its capabilities and limitations and this implies at least an intuitive understanding of how the underlying algorithm is designed and implemented. Hence, while the list of topics covered in the book is more or less standard for a numerical methods text, the treatment is different from most texts in that it emphasizes the software aspects. The aim is to provide an understanding, at the intuitive level, of how and why subroutines work in order to help the reader gain the maximum benefit from them as a computational tool.

The mathematical background assumed is two years of college mathematics including calculus, basic linear algebra, and an introduction to differential equations. Also, the reader should be familiar with programming in a high-level language such as Fortran. In addition, it is assumed that, in order to do the computational exercises, the reader has access to a general-purpose mathematical software package on the local computing system.

In this regard, a package such as TEAPACK (see Appendix), that is designed to facillitate experimentation with algorithms, would be very useful.

v

This particular package was developed, at Toronto, for use in our numerical methods courses, and it has been made available for general distribution.

I am indebted to a number of people for encouragement and assistance during preparation of the manuscript. They are: Uri Ascher, Cliff Addison, Steve Cook, Julio Diaz, Wayne Enright, Graeme Fairweather, Ian Gladwell, Ken Jackson, Steve Ho-Tai, Tom Hull, Pat Keast, Rudi Mathon, Richard Pancer, David Sayers, Pavol Sermer, Bruce Simpson, and Jim Varah. In addition, I wish to thank the many students in my courses who suffered through preliminary versions of the manuscript and, through their criticisms, helped me to improve it.

Robert L. Johnston

CONTENTS

CHAPTER 1
INTRODUCTION

This book deals with the solution of mathematical problems using an electronic computer. There are two aspects to the subject. One is the development and analysis of viable computer methods for solving the various types of problems that arise. Such methods are called *numerical methods* and their study is a field called *numerical analysis.* It is a highly specialized field requiring a rather sophisticated mathematical background. The second aspect is the use of these methods in the course of carrying out scientific computations. The typical "user" of numerical methods is a non-expert (in numerical analysis) who simply wants to apply the product of the numerical analyst as a reliable tool to assist in the pursuit of his or her own field of study. Usually, such a person has no interest in learning all of the intricacies of a method as long as it solves the problem at hand. However, since numerical methods are not infallible, a "black-box" approach to using them can be dangerous. In order to avoid difficulties, a user should acquire a certain level of expertise. For instance, it is desirable to know whether or not a particular method will indeed compute a solution to a given problem. Also, whenever there is a choice of methods, it is useful to be able to choose the most efficient one available. In other words, one should be an *intelligent,* rather than a naive, user of numerical methods. The purpose of this book is to help the reader become an intelligent user.

In order to select a numerical method for solving a particular problem, a user should (1) know what methods are available, (2) how they work, and (3) have an appreciation of their relative advantages and disadvantages. However, instead of the detailed knowledge that a numerical analyst must have, it is sufficient to have an intuitive understanding of the basic principles involved. This is the level at which the material in this book is presented. The mathematical background assumed is that normally acquired in the first two years of university mathematics—differential and integral calculus, elementary linear algebra and an introduction to differential equations—that is, exposure to the various types of mathematical problems treated here.

In recent years, numerical analysts have produced a new product, namely, *mathematical software*—packages of computer subroutines for carrying out the basic computations of science and engineering. A list of some well-known and widely available packages is given in the Appendix at the end of the book. Most computer installations have mathematical software package(s) available in their libraries so that subroutines can easily be called by a user's program. These routines are based on up-to-date numerical methods and their implementations are designed to be as efficient as possible for the particular machine on which they reside. Hence, mathematical software is a computational tool that can be of great benefit to the scientific programmer. Now, it might seem that the availability of preprogrammed, state-of-the-art subroutines would allow a programmer to adopt the black box approach in using them. However, this is not the case. A perusal of the index of any software package will reveal that it contains several subroutines for each type of problem. Hence, one is faced with the question of choosing the most appropriate routine for solving a given problem. In addition, subroutines are not "fail safe," that is, sometimes they may fail to compute a solution. Very often a routine will recognize such a situation itself and return the information. This essentially eliminates the problem of detecting failure but one must still be able to understand what caused the difficulty so that an appropriate remedy can be taken. In other words, one must have an adequate knowledge of the algorithms implemented in a mathematical software package in order to use it intelligently. As its title implies, this book adopts a "software approach" in that it is intended to help the reader become an intelligent user of mathematical software.

In each of Chapters 2 to 6, we discuss the numerical solution of a specific type of mathematical problem. The list of topics is the usual one for a course entitled "Numerical Methods for Scientists" or some variation thereof. By and large, each chapter follows a similar format. We begin with a discussion of the methods that are normally used by software routines for solving the type of problem under consideration. Following this, a discussion of some aspects of typical subroutines is given. Specifically, we consider calling sequences, some ideas concerning design and implementation, and how to interpret the information returned by a routine. The exercises at the end of each chapter are designed, for the most part, to encourage the reader to investigate the properties of whatever software packages are available on the local computer system. This is in keeping with the stated goal of learning about mathematical software in order to prepare the reader for applying it to solve problems in his or her own field of interest.

This chapter deals with some basic ideas about scientific computing. In the next section, we develop the concepts of computer arithmetic and illustrate some of the pitfalls to be avoided. Then, in Section 1.2, we discuss the process of producing mathematical software.

1.1. COMPUTER ARITHMETIC AND ERROR CONTROL

In the course of carrying out a mathematical computation, one has to deal with the problem of errors. There are three ways in which errors can enter a calculation. First, they may be present at the outset in the original data (*inherent* error). Second, they may occur as the result of replacing an infinite process by a finite one (*truncation* error). A typical example is the representation of a function by the first few terms of its Taylor series expansion. The third source of error arises from the finite precision of the numbers that can be represented in a computer (*round-off* error). The latter is a topic which is discussed in Section 1.1.2. Each of these types of error is unavoidable in a calculation. Hence, the "problem of errors" is not one of preventing their occurrence. Instead, it is one of controlling their size in order to obtain a final result that is as accurate as possible. This process is called *error control*. It is concerned with the propagation of errors throughout a computation. For example, we want to be sure that the error that results from performing an arithmetic operation on two numbers, which are themselves in error, is within tolerable limits. In addition, the propagation, or cumulative effects, of this error in subsequent calculations should also be kept under control. These questions are discussed in this section. We remark that there is also a fourth source of error—one caused by doing an arithmetic operation incorrectly (a blunder). However, we view this type of error as avoidable, that is, it need not occur at all, and will not consider it further.

A modern computer is capable of performing arithmetic operations at very high speeds. As a consequence, large scale computations, which are intractable by desk calculation, can be handled routinely. However, while a computer greatly facilities the job of carrying out mathematical calculations, it also introduces a new form of problem with respect to error control. This is due to the fact that intermediate results are not normally seen by the user. Such results are useful because they provide indications of possible large error buildup as the calculation proceeds. In desk computation, all intermediate results are in front of the problem solver. Consequently, error buildup is relatively easy to detect. On the other hand, a computer programmer must be able to detect or anticipate any possible large errors without seeing the warning signals. The examples in this section illustrate some of the ways that this can occur. Before considering them, however, we discuss the source of round-off errors.

The mathematician, in devising a method for solving a problem, assumes that all calculations will be done within the system R of real numbers. This assumption greatly simplifies the mathematical analysis of problems. However, when it comes to actually computing a solution, we must do without the real number system. This is because it is infinite and any set of numbers that is representable on a computer is necessarily finite. Actually, R is infinite in two senses. First, it is infinite in range, that is, it contains arbitrarily large numbers (of both signs). On the other hand, a computer number system can, at best, represent only those real numbers within a given finite interval. Second, it is infinitely dense, that is, the interval between any two real numbers contains infinitely many real numbers. The absence of this property in a computer's number system is the source of round-off error. In order to be more precise, we need to discuss the type of (finite) number systems used in computers.

1.1.1. Computer Number Systems

In a computer memory, each number is stored in a location that consists of a sign ($\pm$) plus a fixed number of digits. One question that confronts the designer of the machine is how to use these digits to represent numbers. One approach is to assign a fixed number of them for the fractional part. This is called a *fixed-point* number system. It can be characterized by three parameters:

β—the number base.
t—the number of digits.
f—the number of digits in the fractional part.

We denote such a system by $P(\beta, t, f)$. As an example, we consider $P(10, 4, 1)$. It contains the 19,999 evenly spaced numbers -999.9, $-999.8, \ldots, 999.8, 999.9$. This set is uniformly dense in $[-1000, 1000]$. As a consequence, any real number x in this interval can be represented by an element $fix(x) \in P(10, 4, 1)$ with an *absolute error* $x - fix(x)$ of, at most, 0.05 in magnitude. For example, if $x = 865.54$, then $fix(x) = 865.5$ and the absolute error is 0.04. However, assuming $x \neq 0$, it is preferable, instead, to look at the *relative error* $(x - fix(x))/x$. In this respect, the set $P(10, 4, 1)$ gives an uneven representation of R. For example, the relative error in the representation of 865.54 is $0.04/865.54 \doteq 0.00005$, or 0.005%. On the other hand, if $x = 0.86554$, then $fix(x) = 000.9$ and the relative error is 4%! Hence, the *relative density* of $P(10, 4, 1)$ is not uniform in $[-1000, 1000]$. This weakness is shared by all fixed-point number systems.

Most computers use a *floating-point* number system, denoted by $F(\beta, t, L, U)$. The four parameters are:

β —the number base.

t —the precision.

L, U—the exponent range.

Any nonzero number $x \in F$ has the form

$$x = \pm \left(\frac{d_1}{\beta} + \frac{d_2}{\beta^2} + \cdots + \frac{d_t}{\beta^t} \right) \times \beta^e$$

written as

$$x = \pm.d_1d_2 \ldots d_t \times \beta^e$$

where the digits $d_1, \ldots, d_t$ in the *fractional part* satisfy

$$1 \le d_1 < \beta$$

$$0 \le d_s < \beta \qquad 2 \le s \le t$$

and the *exponent e* is such that

$$L \le e \le U$$

Also, the number 0 belongs to F. Its representation is

$$0 = +.00 \ldots 0 \times \beta^L$$

As implied, the advantage of a floating point number system is that, within its range of values, the relative density in R is uniform. As an example, consider the system $F(10, 4, -2, 3)$. Its range of values is the two intervals $\pm[.001, 999.9]$ plus 0. Referring to the previous example, the representation of 865.54 is $.8655 \times 10^3$ and, for 0.86554, it is $.8655 \times 10^0$. In each case, the relative error is the same, namely, 0.005%.

To illustrate the comparison between fixed and floating point systems, we display the 33-number sets $P(2, 4, 2)$ and $F(2, 3, -1, 2)$[1] in Figure 1.1.

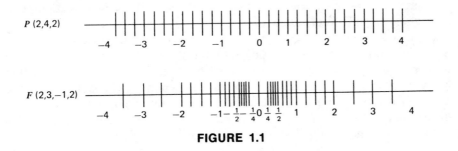

FIGURE 1.1

[1]The representation of the set $F(2, 3, -1, 2)$ is reproduced from [16] with permission.

The difference between absolute and relative density is readily apparent. In effect, the choice between the two types of number systems is one of choosing between absolute and relative error for the purpose of assessing accuracy. Relative error is a measure of the number of correct digits in a number and, as our examples indicate, it is clearly preferable. We remark that this comparison holds in many other contexts as well. As we will see, subroutines usually use relative error as a basis for checking accuracy.

1.1.2. Round-off Errors

Now we consider the differences between performing calculations in F as opposed to R. The source of the differences lies in the fact that F is not closed under the arithmetic operations of addition and multiplication (and the complementary operations of subtraction and division as well). That is, the sum or product of two numbers in F is not necessarily an element of F also. Hence, to stay within the set, we must replace the "true" result of an operation by an element of F and, in the process, incur some error.

There are two ways in which an arithmetic result can lie outside F. First of all, the exponent e in the result may lie outside the range $L \le e \le U$. For example, consider the system $F(2, 3, -1, 2)$ illustrated in Figure 1.1. The product

$$.100 \times 2^2 \times .110 \times 2^2 = .110 \times 2^3 \qquad (2 \times 3 = 6)$$

is not in F because the exponent 3 is too large. This situation is called *overflow*. Similarly, we can have *underflow* when the exponent is too small, as is the case with the product

$$.100 \times 2^0 \times .110 \times 2^{-1} = .110 \times 2^{-2} \qquad (\tfrac{1}{2} \times \tfrac{3}{8} = \tfrac{3}{16})$$

The actual result of trying to represent a number that lies outside the admissible range is highly software and hardware dependent, with little consistency between different computer systems. We will not attempt to define an acceptable criterion here. However, we remark that the occurrence of either overflow or underflow must be considered as an abnormal event in a calculation and the programmer should determine what caused it. Very often, it is an indication of some trouble with the overall algorithm being used, in which case it should be redesigned. Sometimes, however, the difficulty arises from the fact that the range of numbers that has occurred in the computation overlaps one boundary of the admissible range. In this case, a rescaling of the problem will remedy the situation. We will not pursue this topic further. In what follows, we assume that the exponent of a number is within the admissible range.

The second way of obtaining a result outside F is when the fractional part has more than t digits. Consider again the system $F(2, 3, -1, 2)$. The result of the addition

$$.110 \times 2^0 + .111 \times 2^0 = .1101 \times 2^1 \qquad (\tfrac{3}{4} + \tfrac{7}{8} = \tfrac{13}{8})$$

is not in our set because four (binary) digits are required to represent the fractional part. Similarly, the product

$$.111 \times 2^0 \times .110 \times 2^0 = .10101 \times 2^0 \qquad (\tfrac{7}{8} \times \tfrac{3}{4} = \tfrac{21}{32})$$

is not in F. We remark that while this situation does not always arise with addition, it almost invariably does with multiplication. To define a result that can be represented in the machine, we select a nearby element of F. There are two methods for doing this. Suppose that the actual result of an operation is $.d_1 \ldots d_t d_{t+1} \ldots d_u \times \beta^e$. (Recall our assumption that $L \le e \le U$.) Then the two methods are:

1. *Chopping*, whereby the digits beyond d_t are simply dropped.
2. *Rounding*, whereby the fractional part is taken to be the first t digits of $d_1 d_2 \ldots d_t d_{t+1} + \tfrac{1}{2}\beta$.

For example, the number in $F(2, 3, -1, 2)$ corresponding to $.1101 \times 2^1$ is $.110 \times 2^1$ by chopping, and $.111 \times 2^1$ by rounding. For $.10101 \times 2^0$, it is $.101 \times 2^0$ by either method. Briefly, the relative merits of the two methods are that chopping is less expensive whereas rounding produces better accuracy. Both methods are in common usage on present day computers.

No matter which method—chopping or rounding—is used to obtain a result in F, there is some error created in the process. We call this *round-off* error (even when chopping is done). More precisely, let $fl(x)$ denote the machine representation of a real number x (whose exponent is within range). Then round-off error is the difference $x - fl(x)$. For $x \ne 0$, we define the *relative round-off* error $\delta(x)$ in $fl(x)$ by

$$\delta(x) = \frac{x - fl(x)}{x}$$

It can be shown [16, p. 88–9] that

$$(1.1) \qquad |\delta(x)| \le \text{EPS} = \begin{cases} \beta^{1-t} & \text{for chopping} \\ \tfrac{1}{2}\beta^{1-t} & \text{for rounding} \end{cases}$$

Consider, for example, the system $F(10, 4, -50, 50)$ with chopping and suppose $x = 12.467$. Then $fl(x) = .1246 \times 10^2$ and

$$\delta(x) = \frac{0.007}{12.467} \doteq 0.00056 < \text{EPS} = 10^{-3} = 0.001$$

For the same system with rounding, we have $fl(x) = .1247 \times 10^2$ and

$$\delta(x) = \frac{0.003}{12.467} \doteq 0.00024 < \text{EPS} = \frac{1}{2} 10^{-3} = 0.0005$$

The parameter EPS in (1.1) plays an important role in computation in a floating-point number system. It is commonly referred to as *machine epsilon* and is defined to be the smallest positive machine number such that

$$fl(1 + \text{EPS}) > 1$$

that is, the machine representation of the sum $1 + \text{EPS}$ is different from 1. For example, machine epsilon for $F(10, 4, -50, 50)$ with chopping is $10^{-3} = 0.001$ since

$$fl(1 + .001) = .1001 \times 10^1 > 1$$

and this is not true for any smaller positive number within the system. Similarly, machine epsilon for $F(10, 4, -50, 50)$ with rounding is 0.0005. Machine epsilon is an indicator of the attainable accuracy in a floating-point number system. For this reason, it is often used in subroutines to determine if the maximum possible accuracy has been achieved. We discuss this further in Section 1.2.

1.1.3. Control of Round-off Error

So far, we have only considered the round-off error incurred by representing the result of a single arithmetic operation whereas, in the course of carrying out a computer calculation, a very large number of arithmetic operations is performed. Therefore, we must be concerned with the question of how these errors propagate and affect the final result. One of the tasks of the numerical analyst is to provide an answer by performing a "round-off error analysis." This is a highly technical process that will not be pursued here. Instead, we adopt the more pragmatic approach of trying to minimize the error created in each operation with the view that this provides less error to be propagated, making the final result as accurate as possible.

There are several ways in which round-off error in each operation or set of operations can be minimized. They fall into three categories: hardware features, software features and careful programming. We discuss one example of each, using the system $F(10, 4, -50, 50)$, with chopping, to illustrate them.

1. *Hardware feature.* Suppose that we want to subtract 0.5678 from 12.34. Before subtracting, the machine representations of the numbers must be adjusted in order to align the decimal points. In the process, some of the least significant digits of the smaller number will be lost. The provision of a *guard digit*—an extra digit in the fractional part of a number—in the arithmetic unit of a computer can prevent undue loss of accuracy in such situations. To illustrate, we have

No guard digit	*With a guard digit*
$.1234 \times 10^2$	$.12340 \times 10^2$
$.0056 \times 10^2$	$.00567 \times 10^2$
$\overline{.1178 \times 10^2}$	$\overline{.11773 \times 10^2}$

The result with the guard digit is closer to the exact result 11.7722. The slash through the 3 indicates that it is chopped when the result is stored. At first glance, it may seem unimportant to quibble about a difference of only one in the last digit of a number. However, in large-scale computations involving millions of arithmetic operations, there is a potential for round-off error to accumulate significantly. Consequently, it is important to ensure that the result of each individual operation is as accurate as possible. For this reason, the provision of a guard digit in the arithmetic unit is generally regarded as essential in a computer which is designed for scientific computation.

   2. *Software feature.* An expression that appears frequently in scientific calculations is of the form

$$(1.2) \qquad a + b \cdot c$$

This combination of operations is often referred to as a *floating-point operation* or, briefly, a *flop*. It arises, for instance, in the solution of problems in linear algebra (see Chapter 2). Due to the precedence of operations, the multiplication is performed first. This produces a "double-length" result, that is, either $2t - 1$ or $2t$ digits long. Normally, this would be chopped to t digits before doing the addition. However, better accuracy can be assured if the addition is done before chopping. For example, let $a = 0.1462$, $b = 12.34$, and $c = 0.5678$. Then, assuming a guard digit, we have

	Single length	*Double length*
$b \cdot c$	$.70060 \times 10^2$	$.7006652 \times 10^2$
$+a$	$.00146 \times 10^2$	$.00146 \quad \times 10^2$
	$\overline{.70206 \times 10^2}$	$\overline{.70212 \quad \times 10^2}$

Since flops occur so often in scientific calculations, many compilers are designed to recognize them within an arithmetic statement and assemble the appropriate machine code to carry out the addition using the double length product. Here, then, is a software feature for helping to minimize the amount of round-off error created.

3. *Careful programming.* Each of the preceding examples illustrates a method for enhancing accuracy. Moreover, since each can be built into a computer system, one does not have to be conscious of them beyond an initial check to ensure that the features are, indeed, provided. The user should, however, be aware of possible error-reducing methods that can be incorporated into a program. We discuss one example here and leave others to the exercises.

Suppose we want to compute the midpoint c of the interval $[a, b]$. We have the choice of two formulas,

$$\text{(i)} \quad c = \frac{a + b}{2}, \quad \text{or} \quad \text{(ii)} \quad c = a + \frac{b - a}{2}$$

The first is cheaper to compute because it only involves one addition and one division, whereas the second requires two additions and one division. However, on the basis of accuracy, (i) is not necessarily better. Suppose, for example, that $a = 3.483$ and $b = 8.765$. Then the respective formulas give:

$$\text{(i)} \quad c = \frac{a + b}{2} = \frac{.1224 \times 10^2}{2} = .6120 \times 10^1 = 6.120$$

$$\text{(ii)} \quad c = a + \frac{b - a}{2} = .3483 \times 10^1 + \frac{.5282 \times 10^1}{2}$$

$$= .3483 \times 10^1 + .2641 \times 10^1$$

$$= .6124 \times 10^1 = 6.124$$

Since the correct result is 6.124, the second formula is clearly better. On the other hand, suppose $a = -3.483$ and b is the same as before. Then the results are

$$\text{(i)} \quad c = .2641 \times 10^1 = 2.641.$$
$$\text{(ii)} \quad c = .2637 \times 10^1 = 2.637.$$

The correct value is $c = 2.641$, in which case the first formula is better. From these results, we conclude that, to obtain the best accuracy, we should use either (i) or (ii) depending on whether or not a and b differ in sign. Hence, we have a third "formula," which we write in the form of a program segment:

$$\text{(iii)} \quad \text{IF } (\text{sgn}(a) \neq \text{sgn}(b)) \text{ THEN}$$
$$c = (a + b)/2$$
$$\text{ELSE}$$
$$c = a + (b - a)/2$$

On the basis of accuracy, it is clearly the best of the three possible formulas. This illustrates how some care in choosing the correct formula can improve the accuracy of a program.

1.1.4. Pitfalls in Computation

In the previous section, we discussed methods for minimizing the amount of round-off error that can enter at any stage of a computation. However, such measures are not sufficient to guarantee an accurate final result. There are many ways a computation can go awry, as the following examples illustrate. Two of the examples (2 and 3) are taken from a paper entitled "Pitfalls in Computation, or Why a Math Book Isn't Enough," by G. E. Forsythe [15]. Indeed, even the title of this section was taken from this paper. It is recommended reading for further study.

Example 1. We consider the quadratic equation

$$ax^2 + bx + c = 0 \qquad a \neq 0$$

It is well known that the roots of this equation are given by the formulas

$$(1.3) \qquad x_1 = \frac{-b + \sqrt{b^2 - 4ac}}{2a} \quad \text{and} \quad x_2 = \frac{-b - \sqrt{b^2 - 4ac}}{2a}$$

Suppose $a = 1$, $b = -320$, $c = 16$ and that computations are done in $F(10, 4, -50, 50)$ with chopping and one guard digit. For convenience, we adopt the usual "E format" notation for elements of F, namely, $\pm .d_1 d_2 d_3 d_4 E\, e$. For example, the number $-320 = -.3200 \times 10^3 \in F$ is written as $-.3200E\,3$. Then we have

$$x_1 = \frac{.3200E\,3 + \sqrt{.1024E\,6 - .6400E\,2}}{.2000E\,1}$$

$$= \frac{.3200E\,3 + .3198E\,3}{.2000E\,1}$$

$$= \frac{.6398E\,3}{.2000E\,1} = .3199E\,3 = 319.9$$

Similarly,

$$x_2 = \frac{.3200E\,3 - .3198E\,3}{.2000E\,1}$$

$$= \frac{.2000E\,0}{.2000E\,1} = .1000E\,0 = 0.1$$

The underscores indicate the position of the first incorrect digit resulting from round-off error. The correct roots, to six significant digits, are

$$x_1 \doteq 319.950 \quad \text{and} \quad x_2 \doteq 0.0500078$$

Hence, we have obtained a very good value for x_1, but a very bad one for x_2—the relative error is 100%.

It is easy to discover what happened with the calculation for x_2. The two numbers 320.0 and 319.8 in the numerator are almost the same size. Hence, when they are subtracted, the most significant digits cancel, leaving the least significant ones to determine the result. In this particular case, the first three digits cancel and only the last one determines the result. But the last digit of 319.8 contains some round-off error. Therefore, the result of the subtraction operation is completely worthless because its most significant digit is in error. This phenomenon is called *catastrophic cancellation*. It occurs when two numbers of the same sign and approximately the same magnitude are subtracted. Its consequence is to increase the level of error in a computation.

Catastrophic cancellation is, of course, to be avoided. This can be done by careful planning of the algorithm on which the program is based. In the case of the quadratic equation, we can do it by considering the alternative pair of formulas (see Exercise 10) for the roots:

$$(1.4) \qquad x_1 = \frac{-b - \operatorname{sgn}(b)\sqrt{b^2 - 4ac}}{2a} \quad \text{and} \quad x_2 = \frac{-c}{ax_1}$$

where $\operatorname{sgn}(b)$ is the sign ($\pm$) of b. Then, for our example, we would compute x_1 as before, and

$$x_2 = \frac{.1600E\,2}{.3199E\,3} = .5002E - 1 = .05002$$

With (1.4), we have avoided the possibility of catastrophic cancellation by eliminating the need to subtract two numbers of the same sign. In this way, we can ensure that the level of round-off error is not increased significantly. We will see more examples of avoiding cancellation throughout this book.

Example 2. [15] Suppose we want to devise an algorithm to compute the value of the exponential function e^x for any given value of x. Since this function arises very often in scientific computation, it is important to be able to evaluate it accurately and efficiently. We recall that e^x can be represented by the infinite series

$$(1.5) \qquad e^x = 1 + x + \frac{x^2}{2!} + \frac{x^3}{3!} + \cdots$$

which converges for any real (or complex) x. Hence, a possible method on which to base an algorithm is to truncate the series at some point and evaluate the resulting finite series. The point at which to truncate will depend on the size of x and the accuracy desired. Suppose, for example, that we want to compute the value of $e^{-5.5}$ using the floating point system $F(10, 5, -50, 50)$. We obtain

$$
\begin{aligned}
e^{-5.5} = \quad & 1.0000 \\
- \ & 5.5000 \\
+ \ & 15.125 \\
- \ & 27.730 \\
+ \ & 38.129 \\
- \ & 41.942 \\
+ \ & 38.446 \\
- \ & 30.208 \\
+ \ & 20.768 \\
- \ & 12.692 \\
+ \ & 6.9803 \\
- \ & 3.4902 \\
+ \ & 1.5997 \\
& \ \vdots \\
\hline
+ \ & 0.0026363
\end{aligned}
$$

The series was truncated after 25 terms because no subsequent term affects the sum. Hence, we have a value that is as accurate as possible using this method and particular number system. But, in fact, $e^{-5.5} \doteq 0.0408677$! Therefore, something has gone wrong.

It is obvious from the list of terms, that cancellation is once again involved. We see that the least significant digit in each of the terms that is greater than 10 in magnitude, affects the most significant digit in the result. Therefore, since these terms are slightly in error, we should not expect any accuracy in the final result (and, indeed, there is not). One possible remedy for this situation is to carry extra digits, that is, do the computation in $F(10, t, -50, 50)$, $t > 5$. However, this is more costly. A better method is to compute $e^{+5.5}$ and take the reciprocal, that is,

$$
e^{-5.5} = \frac{1}{e^{5.5}}
$$

$$
= \frac{1}{1 + 5.5 + 15.125 + \cdots}
$$

$$
\doteq 0.0040865
$$

There is no cancellation and a good result is obtained. We emphasize that this example is given strictly for illustrative purposes. The rate of convergence of the series (1.5) is very slow, making it necessary to use a large number of terms in order to get good accuracy. Hence, any algorithm that is based on (1.5) will not be very good on grounds of inefficiency. There are much better methods [19] for evaluating e^x.

We remark that this example illustrates the dependence (which is not always stated explicitly) of a mathematical result on the underlying number system. In the case of the series (1.5), it converges for arbitrary $x \in R$ and the proof depends on the closure properties of R. However, when these properties are absent, as they are with a floating-point number system, the proof breaks down. In fact, it is easy to construct counterexamples as we have just seen for the system $F(10, 5, -50, 50)$. Therefore, the series (1.5) does not converge for arbitrary $x \in F$, where F is any floating-point system.

Before continuing, we give another interpretation of the preceding examples. The examples illustrate how a method can sometimes be very sensitive to small changes in a problem. For instance, in the quadratic equation example, suppose the coefficient b is changed from -320.0 to -320.1. Then the formula (1.3) gives a computed root $x_2 = 0.05$. Hence, a change of only 0.03% in one coefficient produces a change of 400% in the computed result. (The true root has only shifted by 0.03% to 0.0499922.) Of course, the formula (1.3) for x_2 is only sensitive for sets of coefficients satisfying $b < 0$ and $b^2 \gg 4ac$. Otherwise, it will give good results. However, the point is that a method may be sensitive to small perturbations in some problems. Since the creation of round-off error can be interpreted as introducing a small perturbation into the problem, it is obviously very dangerous to use a method in situations where it is sensitive to such perturbations. Instead, one should find an alternative method for use in such cases.

Example 3. The previous examples illustrate that a method can be very sensitive to small perturbations in the problem. We now show that it is possible for the problem itself to be very sensitive to such perturbations. A classic example, first given by Wilkinson [32], is the polynomial

$$(1.6) \qquad p(x) = (x - 1)(x - 2) \ldots (x - 20) = x^{20} - 210x^{19} + \cdots$$

Its roots are $1, 2, \ldots, 20$. Suppose we change the coefficient of x^{19} to $-(210 + 2^{-23})$. This gives a new polynomial that is only slightly different from $p(x)$. However, the roots of the new polynomial are, to five decimal places,

1.00000	$10.09527 \pm 0.64350i$
2.00000	$11.79363 \pm 1.65232i$
3.00000	$13.99236 \pm 2.51883i$
4.00000	$16.73074 \pm 2.81262i$
5.00000	$19.50244 \pm 1.94033i$
6.00001	
6.99970	
8.00727	
8.91725	
20.84691	

Clearly, a very small perturbation in the problem has produced significant changes in the solution. (Note that this phenomenon does not happen with the polynomial in Example 1.) We emphasize the distinction between the previous examples and this one. In the former, the methods of solution were sensitive to small perturbations and the remedy was to use an alternative method when necessary. Here, the problem itself is sensitive and, no matter what method of solution is used, round-off error is bound to introduce perturbations that will make significant changes in the solution. There is very little one can do in such cases except to identify that the situation is present and try to reformulate the overall algorithm in order to avoid the need to solve such a sensitive problem. We discuss this example further in Section 4.1.3.

Example 4. Another example [31] of a sensitive problem is the system of linear equations

$$11x_1 + 10x_2 + 4x_3 = 1$$

$$12x_1 + 11x_2 - 13x_3 = 1$$

$$14x_1 + 13x_2 - 66x_3 = 1$$

The solution is easily seen to be

$$x_1 = 1 \qquad x_2 = -1 \qquad x_3 = 0$$

Suppose we perturb each right-hand side element to 1.001, 0.999, 1.001, respectively. Then, the solution of the new system is, to three decimal places,

$$x_1 = -0.683 \qquad x_2 = 0.843 \qquad x_3 = 0.006$$

Hence, by perturbing some elements of the system by only 0.1%, we experience perturbations of about 175% in the larger elements of the solution. It turns out that, up to a certain point, we can deal with sensitivity in linear systems by a process called iterative improvement. This is discussed in Chapter 2.

Example 5. This example illustrates a phenomenon called *instability*. It is concerned with the computation of a sequence of numbers $\{u_n\}_{n=0}^{N}$ using a *difference equation*, that is, a formula that relates the value of u_n to previous terms in the sequence. An important application of difference equations is in the numerical solution of differential equations, a topic which is discussed in Chapter 6. Specifically, we consider the following two difference equations:

$$\text{(a)} \quad u_n = 4u_{n-1} - 3u_{n-2} - 0.2$$

(1.7)

$$\text{(b)} \quad u_n = \tfrac{1}{2}(3u_{n-1} - u_{n-2} + 0.1)$$

If we are given "initial values" for u_0 and u_1, it is clear that either equation can be used as a formula to generate, successively, a sequence of values u_2, u_3, and so on. We remark that each of these formulas was derived as a possible method for computing a numerical solution, at the points $x_n = n/10$, $n = 0, 1, \ldots, N$, of the differential equation

$$(1.8) \quad \frac{dy}{dx} = 1 \quad \text{with} \quad y(0) = 0$$

whose (analytic) solution is easily seen to be the function

$$(1.9) \quad y(x) = x$$

A numerical solution of a problem such as (1.8) is defined to be a sequence of points $\{(x_n, u_n)\}_{n=0}^{N}$, where each u_n is an approximation for the true value $y_n = y(x_n)$ of the solution at $x = x_n$. Hence, from (1.9), each of the formulas (1.7) should generate sequences such that $u_n \doteq y_n = x_n = 0.1n$. It is easily verified that, given the initial values $u_0 = y_0 = 0.0$ and $u_1 = y_1 = 0.1$, each formula produces the correct sequence exactly. Suppose, however, that the initial value u_1 is perturbed slightly to $u_1 = 0.1001$. Then, as we see in Table 1.1, the two formulas give quite different results. The sequence generated by (1.7)(a) is not at all satisfactory, whereas the one computed by (1.7)(b) is quite good.

The previous sources of difficulty are not responsible for the bad results with (1.7)(a) because the computations were done in exact arithmetic so that neither round-off error nor bad cancellation could occur. Consequently, we conclude that the error growth must be entirely due to propagation of the initial error 0.0001 in u_1. Therefore, the question we seek to answer is why formula (1.7)(a) magnifies this error whereas (1.7)(b)

TABLE 1.1

n	x_n	(1.7)(a) u_n	(1.7)(b) u_n
0	0.0	0.0	0.0
1	0.1	0.1001	0.1001
2	0.2	0.2004	0.20015
3	0.3	0.3013	0.300175
4	0.4	0.4040	0.4001875
5	0.5	0.5121	0.50019375
6	0.6	0.6364	.
7	0.7	0.8093	.
8	0.8	1.128	.
9	0.9	1.884	.
10	1.0	3.952	1.0002

does not. To this end, we consider the general solution[2] u_n of the difference equation (1.7)(a):

(1.10) $u_n = 0.1n + c_1 + c_2 3^n$

where c_1, c_2 are constants that are uniquely determined by the initial conditions u_0, u_1. For our example, the initial conditions are $u_0 = 0.0$, $u_1 = 0.1001$ and, substituting these into (1.10) with $n = 0$ and 1, respectively, we obtain the system of equations

$$c_1 + c_2 = 0.0$$
$$c_1 + 3c_2 = 0.0001$$

whose solution is $c_1 = -c_2 = -0.00005$. We observe that the first term on the right in (1.10), that is, $0.1n$ corresponds to the exact value $y(x_n)$ from (1.9). Therefore, the remaining terms must account for the error e_n in u_n, that is,

$$e_n = u_n - y_n = c_1 + c_2 3^n = 0.00005(3^n - 1)$$

From this, we see that the rapid propagation of the initial error is due to the exponential growth factor 3^n. Turning to formula (1.7)(b), its general solution is

$$u_n = 0.1n + c_1 + c_2(0.5)^n$$

---

[2]The equations (1.7) are linear *difference* equations with constant coefficients. The method of solving such equations is analogous to solving linear *differential* equations with constant coefficients. For details, see [5, p. 349].

where $c_1 = -c_2 = 0.0002$ when $u_0 = 0.0$ and $u_1 = 0.1001$. Once again, we see that the error contains an exponential term. However, this time it is a decay factor, rather than a growth factor, so that the error e_n in u_n approaches the constant value c_1. This behavior is verified by the results in Table 1.1.

This example shows us the difference between an *unstable* difference formula such as (1.7)(a) and a *stable* one such as (1.7)(b). With the former, errors are magnified as the computations proceed whereas, with stable formulas, they are damped out. Quite clearly, one should avoid using an unstable difference formula to generate a sequence $\{u_n\}$.

1.2. DEVELOPING MATHEMATICAL SOFTWARE

The task of producing a reliable, efficient subroutine as an item of mathematical software is rather involved. It requires expertise both in numerical analysis and in computer systems design. In this section, we briefly describe the development process, and discuss some criteria that a good software subroutine should satisfy.

1.2.1. Creation of a Software Routine

There are three basic steps in creating a software routine:

- **i** Choosing the underlying method(s) to be used.
- **ii** Designing the algorithm.
- **iii** Producing the subroutine as an item of software.

We define a *method* to be a mathematical formula for finding a solution for the particular problem under study. For example, each of the formula pairs (1.3) and (1.4) defines a possible method for solving the problem of determining the roots of a quadratic equation. In choosing a method, one must first assemble a list of possible ones that could be used. This means searching the literature for existing methods as well as, perhaps, devising new ones. Next, a detailed mathematical analysis of each method must be performed in order to provide a sound theoretical basis on which to compare them. In addition, one should gather sufficient computational experience with each method to support, and even extend, the analytical comparisons. After all this work has been done, the most appropriate method or combination of methods can be determined.

Once it has been decided which method(s) to use, one must make a detailed description of the computational process to be followed. This description is called an *algorithm*. We emphasize the distinction between a method and an algorithm. The former is a mathematical formula, while the latter is a practical, computational formula designed to solve the problem as accurately as possible on a computer.

The final step is to convert the algorithm into an item of mathematical software. Just as we made a distinction between a method and an algorithm, it is important to distinguish between an algorithm and a piece of software. The latter is the physical realization of the algorithm. It is a computer program, and the task of writing it involves numerous important and difficult questions with respect to the arithmetic structure used in the machine, storage allocations, device speeds, and operating software. The objective is to fully utilize the available computational capabilities of the system in the most efficient way possible. In addition to the actual writing of the program, this step includes the testing of it and the provision of documentation. We discuss these aspects in the next section.

From the preceding description, it is clear that the production of a software routine requires a great deal of work, and there is a definite methodology for carrying it out. As part of the development process, one must formulate design criteria and work toward satisfying them. This is our next topic.

1.2.2. Design Criteria

The aim in developing a piece of mathematical software is to provide a useful computational tool for the scientific programmer. In order for a subroutine to satisfy this goal and gain widespread acceptance, it should meet certain criteria that are considered to be essential to good software design. These are accuracy, reliability, robustness, good documentation, ease of use, validation, and portability.

Accuracy, reliability, and robustness are measures of the performance of a subroutine. The first two of these are more or less self-evident. The term *robustness* is an indicator of the scope of the subroutine. To be more precise, a numerical method will very often involve some parameters whose values are determined on the basis of properties of the particular problem at hand. An example is the choice of stepsize in a quadrature formula for evaluating a definite integral (see Chapter 5). If the subroutine is intended for use by nonnumerical analysts, it is preferable (for ease of use) to make it automatic in that the program will select the method parameters itself rather than requiring the user to do it. Therefore, the algorithm should be designed with the capability of analyzing the problem and assigning values to the parameters accordingly. The analysis process is usually based on the behavior of "model" problems, that is, typical problems that generally arise in practical applications. We remark that accuracy and reliability are measures of the performance of an algorithm on all problems that are similar to the model. It is expected, of course, that the behavior of most problems, that arise in practice, will not differ much from the model. Nevertheless, a subroutine should be able to deal with nonmodel problems. It should not necessarily be expected to solve them, that is, obtain a solution to within the requested accuracy. However, there should not be a precipitous decline in performance as the problem deviates more and more from the underlying model. Instead, the performance should deteriorate slowly and gracefully with such deviation. The extent to which this happens is a measure of an algorithm's robustness.

The next two criteria—good documentation and ease of use—need little explanation. The documentation of a subroutine should give a concise, easy-to-understand explanation of how it works and how to use it. This is helpful not only in deciding whether or not to use the routine in the first place, but it can also be of assistance in diagnosing any difficulties arising from its use. Clearly, one part of the ease of use criterion is good documentation, but a more important aspect is the amount of information that the user is required to supply to the subroutine. An easy-to-use subroutine is one that only requires, as input, a straightforward definition of the problem to be solved. Any analysis of the problem for the purpose of setting method parameters is done automatically by the subroutine rather than the user.

Validation is a very important phase in the production of a piece of mathematical software. The purpose of it is to establish that the routine will, in fact, achieve its intended goal. To begin, we need a clear statement of this goal, that is, a definition of the class of problems that can be solved and what is meant by a "solution." For the example of a quadratic equation having exact roots r_1 and r_2, a solution would be defined as any pair of numbers s_1, s_2 such that $|s_i - r_i| < \epsilon |r_i|$, $i = 1, 2$, for some specified $e > 0$. (Usually, ϵ will be expressed as a small integer multiple of machine epsilon.) Then the goal of a quadratic equation subroutine would be to solve all quadratic equations whose exact solutions are within the range of the particular machine's number system. The process of validation of a subroutine includes a detailed mathematical analysis of the algorithm, a proof that the program is a faithful representation of the algorithm and, finally, extensive testing on a representative set of problems. We remark that, prior to testing, one must construct a "representative" set of problems and this, in itself, requires a good deal of effort.

The last criterion on our list—portability—is concerned with changes in a program's performance whenever the machine environment is changed. This is a very difficult question because there are so many factors which affect performance. To quote from [25],

> *... Actual examples exist in which changing from one FORTRAN compiler to another (both considered good) can increase execution time by 100%, where rewriting $x + 1.0$ as $(x + 0.5) + 0.5$ can preserve accuracy, where multiplying by 1.0 can avoid unnecessary underflow and a program stop.*

Ideally, a software routine should be completely portable but, in view of anomalies such as the ones just cited, it is virtually impossible to attain this goal. There are, however, some measures that can be taken that help a great deal in achieving uniformity of performance. We discuss three of them.

One cause of differences in performance is the wide variety of machine architectures in existence. The usual remedy for this situation is to produce several versions of a subroutine, each of which is designed for use on a specific type of machine. Admittedly, this does not make a subroutine portable in the literal sense of the word. However, it does make the name of the routine portable and this, in turn, contributes to the portability of the user's program.

The second way of helping to eliminate differences in performance is to write the program in a "standard" dialect of the programming language being used. For instance, with the Fortran language, there is a standard set down by the American National Standards Institute (ANSI), and published in [21]. A design criterion for any Fortran compiler is that it must be able to recognize, and process, statements written in ANSI Fortran. Therefore, no matter what local dialect of Fortran is used, a subroutine, written in the ANSI version, will always compile. (Note that the user's program can still be written in the local dialect.) A very useful tool for ensuring that a (Fortran) program conforms strictly to the ANSI standard is the PFORT verifier program [18]. It will accept, as data, a program written in any of the common Fortran dialects and check it for deviations from the ANSI standard.

The third measure for improving portability concerns machine epsilon, EPS. As we have already seen, the value of EPS is useful for making decisions concerning accuracy. Therefore, we need a method for making its value available to a subroutine. Since EPS is machine dependent, we cannot use a constant to define its value within a routine because this would severely hinder portability. Another possibility would be to provide a parameter in the calling sequence so that the user can supply the value. However, from the standpoint of ease of use, this is also unsatisfactory. A better method is for the subroutine itself to determine the value of EPS, that is, it will include some code to compute EPS. A disadvantage of this approach is that the code is executed *every* time the routine is called. However, the extra cost that this incurs is negligible and there is much more to be gained in terms of portability and ease of use. A typical Fortran program segment for computing EPS is

(1.6)
```
    EPS = 1.0
  1 EPS = 0.5*EPS
    EPSP1 = EPS + 1.0
    IF (EPSP1 .GT. 1.0) GO TO 1
```

We observe that this code will not always compute the exact value of EPS (see Exercise 5). However, it produces an approximation which differs from EPS by at most a factor of 2 and this is close enough for all practical purposes.

1.3. NOTATION AND CONVENTIONS

To conclude this chapter, we define some notation and conventions that are used throughout this book.

One of the bases for comparing algorithms is computational cost and, as a measure of this aspect, we use an *operations count*, that is, an estimate of the number of arithmetic operations required to solve a problem. The usual practice is to count additions and multiplications separately since they take different amounts of time—a floating-point multiply is faster because there is no need to align the "fractional" point. A typical operations count will be of the form 10A's and 5M's, meaning that 10 additions and 5 multiplications are required. We use this type of notation throughout. In addition, since flops (1.2) appear so often in linear algebra algorithms, it has become common practice to give operations counts in terms of them. We follow this convention in Chapter 2, and elsewhere.

There are no self-contained computer programs in this book. However, there are several program segments, each of which is presented in order to illustrate some concept. In writing these segments, the primary aim was to give a clear presentation of each point rather than adherence to the conventions of a particular programming language. It is assumed that, if need be, the reader can easily translate these segments into whatever language he or she wishes.

EXERCISES

1. Consider the floating-point number system $F(2, 8, -7, 8)$.
   (a) How many numbers does this system contain?
   (b) Find the representations of the (decimal) numbers 3.625 and 59.6 in this system.

(c) Add (in F) the two numbers from part (b) under each of the following assumptions:

   i   Chopping and no guard digit.
   ii Rounding and no guard digit.
   iii Chopping and one guard digit.
   iv Rounding and one guard digit.

(d) Multiply (in F) the two numbers from part (b) under each of the assumptions in part (c).

2. Repeat Exercise 1 using the floating-point number system $F(16, 2, -7, 8)$. This is an example of a *hexadecimal* (base 16) number system. It is usual to denote the 16 units digits by 0, 1, 2, 3, 4, 5, 6, 7, 8, 9, a, b, c, d, e, f.

3. A hexadecimal digit can be uniquely represented by a sequence of four binary digits. Specifically, we have

$$0 \leftrightarrow 0000$$
$$1 \leftrightarrow 0001$$
$$2 \leftrightarrow 0010$$
$$3 \leftrightarrow 0011$$
$$\vdots$$
$$e \leftrightarrow 1110$$
$$f \leftrightarrow 1111$$

Hence, the digits in a hexadecimal system can be represented by a sequence of binary digits, grouped in sets of four. This is a convention used in computers that employ a hexadecimal system.

(a) Show how each of the systems $F(2, 8, -7, 8)$ and $F(16, 2, -7, 8)$ can be represented on a computer with words consisting of a sign ($\pm$) plus 12 binary bits.

(b) Compare these two number systems with respect to their range and density in R.

4. Determine machine epsilon EPS for each of the systems $F(2, 8, -7, 8)$, $F(2, 8, -50, 50)$, $F(2, 16, -7, 8)$, and $F(16, 2, -7, 8)$ assuming

(a) Chopping.
(b) Rounding.

5. Determine machine epsilon EPS for the local computer system. Verify that the program segment (1.6) gives an estimate for EPS that is within a factor of $\frac{1}{2}$. Will this estimate always be too small or too large? Explain.

6. Consider the following list of numbers:

339.9	567.2	.6848
45.75	4.556	79.93
962.1	67.35	84.40
1.288	821.3	429.2

(a) Working in $F(10, 4, -50, 50)$ with one guard digit and chopping, find the sum of these numbers by adding them in:

    i   Given order (by rows).
    ii   Ascending order.

   Compare your results with the exact sum 3403.6588.

(b) Suppose that the sign of each number in the second column is changed to negative. What is the best algorithm for summing the resulting list? Explain.

(c) Apply the algorithm in part (b) to sum the series for $e^{-5.5}$ in Example 2.

7. We want to find the value of the expression

$$\left[\frac{3-\sqrt{8}}{3+\sqrt{8}}\right]^3$$

In addition to this form, one could use any of the following equivalent forms:

$$(17-6\sqrt{8})^3 \qquad\qquad (17+6\sqrt{8})^{-3}$$

$$(3-\sqrt{8})^6 \qquad\qquad (3+\sqrt{8})^{-6}$$

$$19{,}601-6930\sqrt{8} \qquad (19{,}601+6930\sqrt{8})^{-1}$$

Working in $F(10, 4, -50, 50)$ with one guard digit and chopping, which form(s) would be preferable? Explain.

8. When each of the following expressions is evaluated using floating-point arithmetic, poor results are obtained for a certain range of values of x. In each instance, identify this range and provide an alternate expression that can be used for such values of x.

(a) $\sqrt{1+x} - \sqrt{1-x}$.

(b) $1 - \cos x$.

(c) $e^x - 1$.

(d) $x - \sqrt{x^2 - a}$.

9.   A function $f(x)$ is to be evaluated at each of N equally spaced points in [0, 1], where N is large. Which of the following pieces of (Fortran) code is preferable for this task? Explain.

```
(i)    X = 0.0                    (ii)    H = 1.0/FLOAT(N)
       H = 1.0/FLOAT(N)                   DO 10 I = 1,N
       DO 10 I = 1,N                        X = FLOAT(I)*H
         X = X + H                          WRITE(6,*) F(X)
         WRITE(6,*) F(X)          10 CONTINUE
    10 CONTINUE
```

10.   Show that the formulas (1.4) for solving a quadratic equation are mathematically equivalent to (1.3).

11.   As a project, produce a subroutine for solving quadratic equations. The steps outlined in Section 1.2 should be followed and there should be an accompanying report detailing the development, implementation, and testing of the routine.

CHAPTER 2
NUMERICAL LINEAR ALGEBRA

Numerical linear algebra, as the name implies, consists of the study of computational algorithms for solving problems in linear algebra. It is a very important subject in numerical analysis because linear problems occur so often in applications. It has been estimated, for example, that about 75% of all scientific problems require the solution of a system of linear equations at one stage or another. It is therefore important to be able to solve linear problems efficiently and accurately.

Compared to other areas of numerical analysis, numerical linear algebra is well advanced in that there is general agreement as to which are the best algorithms and why they are best. In addition to the theory, much work has gone into the implementation of algorithms. The result is that packages of very efficient and reliable subroutines for the solution of problems in linear algebra are now widely available. The aim in this chapter is to acquaint the reader with some of the reasoning behind the selection of algorithms and the design of subroutines so that he or she can make the most efficient use of such routines.

We assume familiarity with matrix-vector notation and with the basic notions and results of linear algebra. The types of problems we will consider are:

i   Solve a system $A\mathbf{x} = \mathbf{b}$ of n linear equations in n unknowns, where A is a given $n \times n$ nonsingular matrix, $\mathbf{b}$ is a given n-vector, and $\mathbf{x}$ is an unknown n-vector.

ii Compute the eigenvalues and, possibly, the eigenvectors of a given $n \times n$ matrix A.

iii "Solve" an overdetermined system of linear equations $A\mathbf{x} = \mathbf{b}$, where A is a given $m \times n$ $(m > n)$ matrix, $\mathbf{b}$ is a given m-vector and $\mathbf{x}$ is an unknown n-vector.

Of these problems, the first two will be more familiar both in terms of having studied them in a linear algebra course and by encountering them in solving practical problems. Overdetermined systems may not be as familiar but they do arise often. The most notable occurrence, perhaps, is in doing a linear least-squares fit of a curve to some given data (see Section 2.3.1).

In dealing with each of the above problems, we first describe the basic algorithms currently in general use and then discuss aspects such as mathematical validity, numerical validity (effects of round-off errors), efficiency, and modifications that can take advantage of special features of a specific problem.

The description of each algorithm will be done in the context of a general format that is common to all algorithms in numerical linear algebra.

(2.1)

(a) Reduce or transform the given problem to an equivalent one which is more readily solved.

(b) Solve the reduced problem.

An *equivalent problem* is one which has the same solution as the original one. Within this general format, an algorithm can be described by first stating the form of the reduced problem and then defining the method for transforming a given problem to this form. In addition, a method for solving the reduced problem must be given although, in most cases, this is a simple, straightforward calculation. To illustrate the description of an algorithm using (2.1), we consider the problem of solving the system of linear equations

$$3x_1 - 5x_2 = 1$$

$$6x_1 - 7x_2 = 5$$

The familiar procedure for computing the solution is first to eliminate the variable x_1 from the second equation, and then backsolve. After the elimination, we have

$$3x_1 - 5x_2 = 1$$

$$3x_2 = 3$$

We know this system is equivalent to the original one because the operations involved in the elimination process do not alter the solution. The second system is said to be in *triangular* form and, clearly, it can be solved quite readily. We obtain $x_2 = 1$ and $x_1 = 2$. Hence, this method of solution, consists of

(a) Finding, by elimination of variables, an equivalent system which is in triangular form.

(b) Solving the triangular system.

This description is precisely in the format of (2.1).

We will now discuss, in turn, the three problems introduced earlier.

2.1 SYSTEMS OF n LINEAR EQUATIONS IN n UNKNOWNS

The problem is to determine the values of the unknowns $x_1, \ldots, x_n$ satisfying the system of n linear equations

(2.2)
$$
\begin{aligned}
a_{1,1}x_1 + a_{1,2}x_2 + \cdots + a_{1,n}x_n &= b_1 \\
a_{2,1}x_1 + a_{2,2}x_2 + \cdots + a_{2,n}x_n &= b_2 \\
\vdots \qquad\qquad \vdots \qquad\quad \vdots \\
a_{n,1}x_1 + x_{n,2}x_2 + \cdots + a_{n,n}x_n &= b_n
\end{aligned}
$$

where the coefficients $a_{i,j}$ and the numbers b_i on the right-hand side are given. In matrix-vector notation, this problem can be written as

(2.3) $A\mathbf{x} = \mathbf{b}$

where

$$
A = \begin{bmatrix} a_{1,1} & a_{1,2} & \ldots & a_{1,n} \\ a_{2,1} & a_{2,2} & \ldots & a_{2,n} \\ \vdots & \vdots & \ddots & \vdots \\ a_{n,1} & a_{n,2} & \ldots & a_{n,n} \end{bmatrix} \qquad \mathbf{x} = \begin{bmatrix} x_1 \\ x_2 \\ \vdots \\ x_n \end{bmatrix} \qquad \text{and} \qquad \mathbf{b} = \begin{bmatrix} b_1 \\ b_2 \\ \vdots \\ b_n \end{bmatrix}
$$

2.1.1. The Gauss Elimination Algorithm

We will describe the algorithm that is most often used for computing the solution of an $n \times n$ linear system in terms of the format of (2.1). The form of the reduced problem will be a linear system $U\mathbf{x} = \mathbf{d}$, where the coefficient matrix U is upper triangular. As we will see, the reduction process consists mainly of computing an LU *decomposition* or, alternatively, a *triangular factorization* of A, that is,

$A = LU$

where L is *unit* lower triangular (1's on the diagonal) and U is upper triangular. U will be the matrix of the reduced problem. In fact, the algorithm is nothing more than the well-known Gauss elimination and back substitution method. To see this, we first describe the algorithm in the traditional way and then show how it can be expressed in terms of matrix factorization and the solution of two triangular systems. We will describe the method with reference to the specific 4×4 example

$$5x_1 + 3x_2 - x_3 \qquad = 11$$
$$2x_1 \qquad + 4x_3 + x_4 = 1$$
$$-3x_1 + 3x_2 - 3x_3 + 5x_4 = -2$$
$$6x_2 - 2x_3 + 3x_4 = 9$$

or, in matrix-vector notation,

(2.4)
$$
\begin{bmatrix}
5 & 3 & -1 & 0 \\
2 & 0 & 4 & 1 \\
-3 & 3 & -3 & 5 \\
0 & 6 & -2 & 3
\end{bmatrix}
\begin{bmatrix}
x_1 \\ x_2 \\ x_3 \\ x_4
\end{bmatrix}
=
\begin{bmatrix}
11 \\ 1 \\ -2 \\ 9
\end{bmatrix}
$$

Formulation of the general algorithm for an arbitrary $n \times n$ system can easily be done using the ideas brought out in the example.

The first stage is to eliminate x_1 from:

Equation 2 by subtracting $2/5 = 0.4$ times Equation 1 from Equation 2.
Equation 3 by subtracting $-3/5 = -0.6$ times Equation 1 from Equation 3.
Equation 4 by subtracting $0/5 = 0.0$ times Equation 1 from Equation 4.

Since each of these operations does not alter the solution, the resulting system is equivalent to the original one. The numbers 0.4, −0.6, 0.0 are called *multipliers*. The divisor used to form each multiplier is called the *pivot*. In this case it is the (1, 1) element, which is 5. The resulting system is

(2.5)
$$
\begin{bmatrix}
5 & 3 & -1 & 0 \\
0 & -1.2 & 4.4 & 1.0 \\
0 & 4.8 & -3.6 & 5.0 \\
0 & 6.0 & -2.0 & 3.0
\end{bmatrix}
\begin{bmatrix}
x_1 \\ x_2 \\ x_3 \\ x_4
\end{bmatrix}
=
\begin{bmatrix}
11 \\ -3.4 \\ 4.6 \\ 9.0
\end{bmatrix}
$$

Next we can eliminate x_2 from the third and fourth equations in a similar manner. This time the pivot is the (2, 2) element, namely −1.2, and the multipliers are $-4.8/1.2 = -4.0$ and $-6.0/1.2 = -5.0$. However, the magnitude or absolute value of (at least one of) them is greater than 1.0 and, as explained in the next section, it is desirable to have multipliers that are ≤ 1.0 in magnitude in order to minimize the propagation of round-off errors. This is easily accomplished by interchanging the second and fourth equations so that the largest coefficient of x_2, excluding the first equation, is the one in the (new) second equation. We note that interchanging the order of equations does not affect the solution so, again, we obtain an equivalent system. In terms of the system (2.5), we simply scan the second column of the matrix from the diagonal down in order to find the element that is largest in magnitude. This is called *searching for the largest pivot*. The row containing this element is then interchanged with the second row. The same rows of the right-hand side vector are also interchanged.

$$(2.6) \quad \begin{bmatrix} 5 & 3 & -1 & 0 \\ 0 & 6.0 & -2.0 & 3.0 \\ 0 & 4.8 & -3.6 & 5.0 \\ 0 & -1.2 & 4.4 & 1.0 \end{bmatrix} \begin{bmatrix} x_1 \\ x_2 \\ x_3 \\ x_4 \end{bmatrix} = \begin{bmatrix} 11 \\ 9.0 \\ 4.6 \\ -3.4 \end{bmatrix}$$

Now we eliminate x_2 from:

Equation 3 by subtracting $4.8/6.0 = 0.8$ times Equation 2 from Equation 3
Equation 4 by subtracting $-1.2/6.0 = -0.2$ times Equation 2 from Equation 4

to obtain

$$(2.7) \quad \begin{bmatrix} 5 & 3 & -1 & 0 \\ 0 & 6.0 & -2.0 & 3.0 \\ 0 & 0 & -2.0 & 2.6 \\ 0 & 0 & 4.0 & 1.6 \end{bmatrix} \begin{bmatrix} x_1 \\ x_2 \\ x_3 \\ x_4 \end{bmatrix} = \begin{bmatrix} 11 \\ 9.0 \\ -2.6 \\ -1.6 \end{bmatrix}$$

Continuing, we see that the largest pivot for the third column is in the fourth row, so we interchange the third and fourth rows.

$$(2.8) \quad \begin{bmatrix} 5 & 3 & -1 & 0 \\ 0 & 6.0 & -2.0 & 3.0 \\ 0 & 0 & 4.0 & 1.6 \\ 0 & 0 & -2.0 & 2.6 \end{bmatrix} \begin{bmatrix} x_1 \\ x_2 \\ x_3 \\ x_4 \end{bmatrix} = \begin{bmatrix} 11 \\ 9.0 \\ -1.6 \\ -2.6 \end{bmatrix}$$

Finally, we eliminate x_3 from

Equation 4 by subtracting $-2.0/4.0 = -0.5$ times Equation 3 from Equation 4

which gives the upper triangular system

$$(2.9) \quad \begin{bmatrix} 5 & 3 & -1 & 0 \\ 0 & 6.0 & -2.0 & 3.0 \\ 0 & 0 & 4.0 & 1.6 \\ 0 & 0 & 0 & 3.4 \end{bmatrix} \begin{bmatrix} x_1 \\ x_2 \\ x_3 \\ x_4 \end{bmatrix} = \begin{bmatrix} 11 \\ 9.0 \\ -1.6 \\ -3.4 \end{bmatrix}$$

This system is equivalent to the original one (2.4).

The solution of (2.9) is easily determined. From the fourth equation, we have

$$x_4 = -1.0$$

Substituting this value into the third equation, we get

$$4.0x_3 + 1.6(-1.0) = -1.6 \quad \text{or} \quad x_3 = 0.0$$

Substituting the values of x_3 and x_4 into the second equation gives

$$6.0x_2 - 2.0(0.0) + 3.0(-1.0) = 9 \quad \text{or} \quad x_2 = 2.0$$

Finally, substituting into the first equation, we have

$$5x_1 + 3(2.0) - 1(0.0) + 0(-1.0) = 11 \quad \text{or} \quad x_1 = 1.0$$

Therefore, the vector $\mathbf{x} = [1.0, 2.0, 0.0, -1.0]^T$ is the solution of the original system (2.4).

The first part of the algorithm is called *(forward) elimination with partial pivoting*[1]. It consists of the computations leading to the system (2.9). The second part is known as *back substitution*. It should be clear how the algorithm fits into the format of (2.1). The elimination part corresponds to the reduction of the original problem to an equivalent system (2.9) while the back substitution corresponds to solving the reduced problem.

Now we show how the elimination part of the above algorithm can be expressed in terms of the computation of an LU decomposition of A. Actually, the equation $A = LU$ mentioned above is not correct because it does not include partial pivoting. The correct equation is

$$(2.10) \quad PA = LU$$

The matrix P is called a *permutation matrix*. It has exactly one 1 in each row and column and all other entries are 0. The effect of multiplying A on the left by such a matrix is to permute or interchange the rows of A. For example

$$(2.11) \quad PA = \begin{bmatrix} 1 & 0 & 0 & 0 \\ 0 & 0 & 0 & 1 \\ 0 & 1 & 0 & 0 \\ 0 & 0 & 1 & 0 \end{bmatrix} \begin{bmatrix} 5 & 3 & -1 & 0 \\ 2 & 0 & 4 & 1 \\ -3 & 3 & -3 & 5 \\ 0 & 6 & -2 & 3 \end{bmatrix} = \begin{bmatrix} 5 & 3 & -1 & 0 \\ 0 & 6 & -2 & 3 \\ 2 & 0 & 4 & 1 \\ -3 & 3 & -3 & 5 \end{bmatrix}$$

---

[1]It is possible to do *complete pivoting*. This involves column as well as row interchanges. One must search the entire subblock of the matrix below and to the right of the pivot position for the largest element and then interchange rows and columns to make this the pivot element. For instance, in the example we have been following, the initial pivot would be 6 and, putting it into the (1, 1) position would necessitate interchanging rows 1 and 4 and then columns 1 and 2. Compared to partial pivoting, there is considerably more work in complete pivoting since there are a lot more entries to be searched. This would be worthwhile if we could be assured of a correspondingly significant gain in accuracy. However, it has been found that, in most cases, there is not a sufficient improvement in accuracy so complete pivoting is not considered worthwhile.

This particular P turns out to be the one that incorporates the pivoting strategy that was used in the reduction (elimination) of the system from (2.4) to (2.9). If the equations of the original system (2.4) were reordered according to the right side of (2.11), then the elimination could be done without interchanges and the multipliers would all be ≤ 1 in magnitude.

Constructing P is very simple and it can be done during the elimination. We start with the identity matrix I and interchange its rows in correspondence with those of A as the elimination proceeds. For our example, we would have

$$
I = \begin{bmatrix} 1\ 0\ 0\ 0 \\ 0\ 1\ 0\ 0 \\ 0\ 0\ 1\ 0 \\ 0\ 0\ 0\ 1 \end{bmatrix} \xrightarrow{(1,\,1)} \begin{bmatrix} 1\ 0\ 0\ 0 \\ 0\ 1\ 0\ 0 \\ 0\ 0\ 1\ 0 \\ 0\ 0\ 0\ 1 \end{bmatrix}
$$

$$
\xrightarrow{(2,\,4)} \begin{bmatrix} 1\ 0\ 0\ 0 \\ 0\ 0\ 0\ 1 \\ 0\ 0\ 1\ 0 \\ 0\ 1\ 0\ 0 \end{bmatrix} \xrightarrow{(3,\,4)} \begin{bmatrix} 1\ 0\ 0\ 0 \\ 0\ 0\ 0\ 1 \\ 0\ 1\ 0\ 0 \\ 0\ 0\ 1\ 0 \end{bmatrix} = P
$$

(Note that each of these matrices, including the identity, is also a permutation matrix.) The ordered pair (i, k_i) indicates which rows are interchanged at the ith stage of the elimination, namely, rows i and k_i. In practice, it is not necessary to store the complete matrix P. The purpose of P is simply to record the pivoting strategy and this can easily be done by recording the successive ordered pairs (i, k_i). To do it, we set up a *pivot vector*, say NPIV, of length n (the number of equations). Then, at the ith stage of the elimination, we set $\text{NPIV}(i) = k_i$, which records the ordered pair (i, k_i). Actually, there are only $n - 1$ stages of the elimination procedure (there were $4 - 1 = 3$ stages in our example) so NPIV has an extra element, $\text{NPIV}(n)$. It is usual to utilize this element in the following way. Initialize $\text{NPIV}(n) = +1$ at the outset and then change its sign whenever an interchange of rows is made, that is, whenever $k_i \neq i$. We will see in a moment how the value $(+1$ or $-1)$ of this element can be used in computing $\det(A)$, the determinant of A, if this value is needed. For our example, NPIV would be formed as follows:

$$
\text{NPIV} = \begin{bmatrix} - \\ - \\ - \\ +1 \end{bmatrix} \xrightarrow{(1,\,1)} \begin{bmatrix} 1 \\ - \\ - \\ +1 \end{bmatrix} \xrightarrow{(2,\,4)} \begin{bmatrix} 1 \\ 4 \\ - \\ -1 \end{bmatrix} \xrightarrow{(3,\,4)} \begin{bmatrix} 1 \\ 4 \\ 4 \\ +1 \end{bmatrix}
$$

Note that only n storage locations are required for NPIV whereas n^2 are needed if P were stored completely. Since both contain the same information, it is much more efficient to use a pivot vector to record the pivoting strategy.

For our example, the matrices L and U in (2.10) turn out to be

$$
L = \begin{bmatrix} 1 & 0 & 0 & 0 \\ 0.0 & 1 & 0 & 0 \\ 0.4 & -0.2 & 1 & 0 \\ -0.6 & 0.8 & -0.5 & 1 \end{bmatrix} \qquad U = \begin{bmatrix} 5 & 3 & -1 & 0 \\ 0 & 6.0 & -2.0 & 3.0 \\ 0 & 0 & 4.0 & 1.6 \\ 0 & 0 & 0 & 3.4 \end{bmatrix}
$$

The subdiagonal elements of L are simply the multipliers used in the elimination process. The first column contains the multipliers from the first stage, the second column contains those from the second stage, etc. The order in which they appear down a column depends on the pivoting strategy and will be explained shortly [following (2.12)]. The matrix U is just the coefficient matrix of the reduced system (2.9). To verify that (2.10) holds, we have

$$
LU = \begin{bmatrix} 1 & 0 & 0 & 0 \\ 0.0 & 1 & 0 & 0 \\ 0.4 & -0.2 & 1 & 0 \\ -0.6 & 0.8 & -0.5 & 1 \end{bmatrix} \begin{bmatrix} 5 & 3 & -1 & 0 \\ 0 & 6.0 & -2.0 & 3.0 \\ 0 & 0 & 4.0 & 1.6 \\ 0 & 0 & 0 & 3.4 \end{bmatrix}
$$

$$
= \begin{bmatrix} 5 & 3 & -1 & 0 \\ 0 & 6 & -2 & 3 \\ 2 & 0 & 4 & 1 \\ -3 & 3 & -3 & 5 \end{bmatrix}
$$

which is the matrix PA in (2.11).

We digress a moment to show how the last entry of NPIV can be used in computing the value of $\det(A)$. From (2.10) and the well-known result that the determinant of the product of two matrices is the product of the individual determinants, we have

$$
\det(A) = \frac{1}{\det(P)} \cdot \det(L) \det(U)
$$

Now it is easy to show that $\det(P) = \pm 1$, where the positive sign is to be used if an even number of row interchanges is made during the elimination and the negative sign if an odd number is made. But this is precisely the information recorded in $NPIV(n)$. Therefore, $\det(P) = NPIV(n)$. In our example, $\det(P) = NPIV(4) = +1$. It is also easy to show (Exercise 1.3) that if T is either an upper or lower triangular matrix, then $\det(T)$ is just the product of the diagonal elements of T. Now, since L is unit lower triangular, this means that $\det(L) = 1$, and we have

$$\det(A) = \frac{1}{+1}(1)(5 \times 6.0 \times 4.0 \times 3.4) = 408.0$$

Therefore, all we have to do to compute $\det(A)$ is calculate the product of the diagonal elements of U and attach the correct sign, which is contained in NPIV(n).

Our discussion so far illustrates that, for the problem of solving $A\mathbf{x} = \mathbf{b}$, there exists a factorization of the form (2.10). In addition, it also indicates how the factorization can be determined. The latter point should be emphasized. This is that the method for computing P, L, and U is precisely the Gauss elimination with partial pivoting procedure originally described, that is, reducing the matrix in (2.4) to that of (2.9). Computing P (or NPIV) and L merely amounts to recording, respectively, the pivoting strategy and the multipliers. In order to illustrate how a computer subroutine carries out the procedure we must make some remarks on the efficient use of storage. First, we observe that only the subdiagonal elements of L need to be stored explicitly since the 1's on the diagonal and 0's above it can be understood. Similarly, we do not need to store the below-diagonal 0's of U. Hence L and U can be stored in the same array with U occupying the upper triangular part including the diagonal and L in the strictly lower triangular part. Second, there is a one-to-one correspondence between the formation of a multiplier and the creation of a zero below the diagonal of A. Since these zeros are actually the below-diagonal zeros of U, we do not need to store them. Instead, we can store each multiplier (element of L) in the location of its corresponding zero. Most computer subroutines will take advantage of these facts to do the elimination on A "in place." By this we mean that if A is stored in the array AMAT, the elimination procedure will successively overwrite AMAT at each stage so that, at the conclusion, it will contain both L and U. To illustrate, we show the evolvement of NPIV and AMAT for our example. For reading convenience, the elements of L are underlined.

$$(2.12) \quad \begin{bmatrix} - \\ - \\ - \\ +1 \end{bmatrix} \begin{bmatrix} 5 & 3 & -1 & 0 \\ 2 & 0 & 4 & 1 \\ -3 & 3 & -3 & 5 \\ 0 & 6 & 2 & 3 \end{bmatrix} \longrightarrow \begin{bmatrix} 1 \\ - \\ - \\ +1 \end{bmatrix} \begin{bmatrix} 5 & 3 & -1 & 0 \\ \underline{0.4} & -1.2 & 4.4 & 1.0 \\ \underline{-0.6} & 4.8 & -3.6 & 5.0 \\ \underline{0.0} & 6.0 & -2.0 & 3.0 \end{bmatrix}$$

$$\longrightarrow \begin{bmatrix} 1 \\ 4 \\ - \\ -1 \end{bmatrix} \begin{bmatrix} 5 & 3 & -1 & 0 \\ \underline{0.0} & 6.0 & -2.0 & 3.0 \\ \underline{-0.6} & \underline{0.8} & -2.0 & 2.6 \\ \underline{0.4} & \underline{-0.2} & 4.0 & 1.6 \end{bmatrix}$$

$$\longrightarrow \begin{bmatrix} 1 \\ 4 \\ 4 \\ +1 \end{bmatrix} \begin{bmatrix} 5 & 3 & -1 & 0 \\ \underline{0.0} & 6.0 & -2.0 & 3.0 \\ \underline{0.4} & \underline{-0.2} & 4.0 & 1.6 \\ \underline{-0.6} & \underline{0.8} & \underline{-0.5} & 3.4 \end{bmatrix}$$

The connection between the Gauss elimination with partial pivoting procedure originally described and the computation of P, L, and U for the triangular decomposition (2.10) can be seen by comparing the coefficient matrices in (2.4), (2.5), (2.7), and (2.9) with the respective stages of NPIV and AMAT in (2.12).

One or two remarks should be made at this point. First, in showing the correspondence between elimination and the LU factorization, we omitted the right-hand-side vector **b** whereas, in going from (2.4) to (2.9), the elimination was done on A and **b** simultaneously. This omission was intentional. It turns out to be advantageous to do the elimination on **b** separately. Second, since the elimination is done in place, the original matrix A is overwritten. If A will be needed at some future point in the overall calculations being done, then a copy of it should be made before beginning the elimination. Finally, we observe in (2.12) that when a row interchange is made, it is applied to the whole array AMAT. This means that those elements of L that have already been recorded are also interchanged. In this way, we can automatically determine the correct order in which the multipliers should appear in the columns of L.

In reality, a computer subroutine implementation of Gauss elimination does not quite follow the algorithm indicated by (2.12). The difference is that when a row interchange is made, it is not applied to the portion of AMAT currently containing elements of L. If, for example, rows i and k_i $(i \leq k_i)$ are to be interchanged, we only do it for columns i through n, that is,

$$\mathrm{AMAT}(i, j) \leftrightarrow \mathrm{AMAT}(k_i, j) \qquad j = i, i+1, \ldots, n$$

Hence, instead of the final form in (2.12), AMAT and NPIV will be

$$(2.13) \quad \begin{bmatrix} 1 \\ 4 \\ 4 \\ +1 \end{bmatrix} \begin{bmatrix} 5 & 3 & -1 & 0 \\ \underline{0.4} & 6.0 & -2.0 & 3.0 \\ \underline{-0.6} & \underline{0.8} & 4.0 & 1.6 \\ \underline{0.0} & \underline{-0.2} & \underline{-0.5} & 3.4 \end{bmatrix}$$

The interpretation of this representation in terms of matrix factorization is somewhat complicated, but a brief explanation will be given. A more detailed account can be found in [16]. The below-diagonal elements in, say, the second column of (2.13) are the multipliers, in order, from the second stage of the elimination. We form the unit lower triangular matrix

$$M_2 = \begin{bmatrix} 1 & 0 & 0 & 0 \\ 0 & 1 & 0 & 0 \\ 0 & 0.8 & 1 & 0 \\ 0 & -0.2 & 0 & 1 \end{bmatrix}$$

and similarly for M_1 and M_3. Now define P_2 to be the permutation matrix corresponding to the interchange $(2, 4)$, which was made at the second stage of the elimination, that is,

$$P_2 = \begin{bmatrix} 1 & 0 & 0 & 0 \\ 0 & 0 & 0 & 1 \\ 0 & 0 & 1 & 0 \\ 0 & 1 & 0 & 0 \end{bmatrix}$$

Similarly, we define P_1 and P_3. (In our example, $P_1 = I$ because no interchange was made at the start.) Then it can be shown (Exercise 1.4) that

$$P_1 P_2 P_3 = P$$

and

$$(2.14) \quad P_1 M_1 P_2 M_2 P_3 M_3 = P^{-1}L = P^T L$$

$$= \begin{bmatrix} 1 & 0 & 0 & 0 \\ 0.4 & -0.2 & 1 & 0 \\ -0.6 & 0.8 & -0.5 & 1 \\ 0.0 & 1 & 0 & 0 \end{bmatrix}$$

Now, the below-diagonal elements in (2.13) can be interpreted as representing the matrices M_1, M_2, and M_3—the first column corresponds to M_1, and so on. In addition, each P_i is represented by NPIV(i), $i = 1, 2, 3$. Therefore, given the array (2.13) and the pivot vector NPIV, it is possible to construct L from the relationship (2.14). While this explanation is a little involved, a computer implementation is relatively straightforward. Essentially, all we need is a mechanism for relating the location of a multiplier (element of L) in (2.13) to its position in (2.12). This can be done via the pivot vector NPIV [based on (2.14)]. Admittedly, this results in some overhead when accessing the elements of L but we have saved some work by not having to interchange them during the elimination. It has been found that, on average, the savings outweigh the extra cost, so the form (2.13) is preferred for implementation. On the other hand, it is much easier to discuss the algorithm on the basis of (2.12). Therefore, we will continue with it on the understanding that an implementation will use (2.13).

We now see how the LU factorization is used to solve the system (2.3). First, we premultiply both sides of the equation by P to get $PAx = Pb$. Then, using the factorization (2.10) of PA, we have $LUx = Pb$, which can be written as

(2.15) $Ld = Pb$

where the vector d is defined by

(2.16) $Ux = d$

Assuming that P, L, and U have been computed, there are two unknowns here—the vectors d and x. The latter is the one we want but, in order to compute it (as the solution of (2.16)), we need to know what d is. But d can be found by solving (2.15). Therefore, given P, L, and U, we can determine the solution x of the system $Ax = b$ by first solving (2.15) for d and then (2.16) for x. With this, we can restate the complete algorithm in the form

$$(2.17) \quad \begin{array}{l} \text{DCOMP} \\[4pt] \text{SOLVE} \end{array} \left\{ \begin{array}{ll} \textbf{i} & \text{Decompose } PA = LU, \\ \textbf{ii} & \text{Solve } Ld = Pb \text{ for } d, \\ \textbf{iii} & \text{Solve } Ux = d \text{ for } x \end{array} \right.$$

$$\left. \begin{array}{l} \\ \end{array} \right\} \text{elimination}$$

back substitution

The notations on the right indicate the correspondence with the elimination and back substitution parts of the algorithm as originally described. Those on the left indicate how it is implemented by computer subroutines. We will look at this shortly.

It probably is not immediately obvious as to why we say that steps (i) and (ii) in (2.17) correspond to the elimination process. We have already noted that step (i) is actually the elimination process, but applied only to the matrix A. Therefore, step (ii) should correspond to performing the elimination on the right-hand-side vector b. To see that it is, we write down the system

$$(2.18) \quad Ld = \begin{bmatrix} 1 & 0 & 0 & 0 \\ 0.1 & 1 & 0 & 0 \\ 0.4 & -0.2 & 1 & 0 \\ -0.6 & 0.8 & -0.5 & 1 \end{bmatrix} \begin{bmatrix} d_1 \\ d_2 \\ d_3 \\ d_4 \end{bmatrix} = \begin{bmatrix} 11 \\ 9 \\ 1 \\ -2 \end{bmatrix} = Pb$$

We remark that the right-hand side is obtained by taking b and applying the successive row interchanges that were recorded in NPIV. The system (2.18) is lower triangular and the solution can easily be computed as follows:

$$(2.19) \quad \begin{array}{lll} d_1 = 11 & & = 11 \\ d_2 = & 9 - \quad (0.0)(11) & = 9.0 \\ d_3 = & 1 - \quad (0.4)(11) - (-0.2)(9.0) & = -1.6 \\ d_4 = -2 - (-0.6)(11) - \quad (0.8)(9.0) - (-0.5)(-1.6) & = -3.4 \end{array}$$

Since this is precisely the set of computations carried out in the elimination on the right-hand side in (2.4) to (2.9), step (ii) does, in fact, correspond to doing the elimination on **b**. Finally, we note that the system $U\mathbf{x} = \mathbf{d}$ in step (iii) is exactly the reduced system (2.9), so step (iii) is the back substitution part of the algorithm.

It was mentioned previously that it is advantageous to do the elimination on **b** separately from that of A. In fact, it is usual to divide the whole procedure into two separate subroutines, say DCOMP and SOLVE, as indicated on the left in (2.17). The reason for doing this is because steps (ii) and (iii) are independent of A. In situations where there is more than one system, $A\mathbf{x} = \mathbf{b}_1$, $A\mathbf{x} = \mathbf{b}_2$, etc., each having the same coefficient matrix, we would only call DCOMP once to compute the LU factorization. Each individual system can then be solved by simply calling SOLVE. An important instance where this situation arises is in iterative improvement (Section 2.1.3). Another is in the computation of the eigenvectors of a matrix by inverse iteration (Section 2.2.3). The savings in using this idea can be quite substantial since the bulk of the work in solving a linear system consists of computing the LU factorization of A. To see this, we look at the operations count.

We assume that A is $n \times n$. During the elimination, we observe that each time an entry in A is changed, we must perform an operation of the form

$$a \leftarrow a - m \cdot b$$

For example, in (2.5), the (2, 3) element of the matrix is obtained as the result of the computation

$$4.0 - (0.4) \cdot (-1) = 4.4$$

Therefore, each change of an entry of A requires the execution of one flop (see Section 1.1.3). At each stage, the number of such changes is

$$(n - 1)^2 \text{ during the } \quad \text{1st} \quad \text{stage.}$$
$$(n - 2)^2 \text{ during the } \quad \text{2nd} \quad \text{stage.}$$
$$\vdots \qquad\qquad\qquad \vdots$$
$$1^2 \quad \text{during the } (n - 1)\text{th stage.}$$

We have not counted the zeros that are created below the diagonal since no computation is actually done for them. In addition, there are $(n - 1) + \cdots +$ $2 + 1 = n^2/2 - n/2$ multipliers to be formed, each of which requires 1D. We should also count the work necessary to search for the largest pivot at each stage. This will be a total of $(n - 1) + \cdots + 1 = n^2/2 - n/2$ comparisons of pairs of numbers. The execution of DCOMP therefore requires

$$\sum_{i=1}^{n-1} i^2 = \frac{n(n-1)(2n-1)}{6} = \frac{n^3}{3} - \frac{n^2}{2} + \frac{n}{6} = \frac{n^3}{3} + 0(n^2)$$

flops plus $(n^2/2 - n/2)D$'s and the same number of comparisons. Now, as n increases, the terms in n^2 and n become insignificant compared to the n^3 term, so it is usual to ignore the lower-order ones and say that DCOMP takes $n^3/3 + 0(n^2)$ flops. Turning to step (ii) of (2.17), it follows from (2.19) that

solving for d_1 requires no work at all.
solving for d_2 requires one flop.
solving for d_3 requires two flops.

$\cdot$ $\quad$ $\cdot$

$\cdot$ $\quad$ $\cdot$

$\cdot$ $\quad$ $\cdot$

solving for d_n requires $(n - 1)$ flops.

For step (iii), the number of operations is the same since it also consists of the solution of a triangular system. Actually, there are n additional divisions in step (iii) since the diagonal of U does not, in general, have 1's on it. However, as was the case with forming the multipliers, this number of operations turns out to be insignificant, so we ignore them in our count. Therefore, the execution of SOLVE requires

$$2 \sum_{i=1}^{n-1} i = 2 \cdot \frac{n(n-1)}{2} = n^2 - n = n^2 + 0(n)$$

flops.

To illustrate the difference in the amount of work done by DCOMP and by SOLVE, suppose $n = 50$. The DCOMP requires about 42,000 flops whereas SOLVE only requires about 2500. If, say, we had three such systems $A\mathbf{x}_k = \mathbf{b}_k$, $k = 1, 2, 3$, to be solved, we could compute their solutions by making one call to DCOMP and three calls to SOLVE. The total amount of work would be about 50,000 flops whereas, if the two parts of the algorithm were not separated, the cost would be about 135,000 flops. The difference is quite substantial and, of course, is even more pronounced for larger n. Therefore, by splitting the algorithm into the two parts, significant savings can be made in the case of more than one system with the same coefficient matrix A.

The parameter list for a decomposition subroutine is usually of the form

DCOMP(N,NDIM,NPIV,A,IND),

where

>N is the order n of the system.
>
>NDIM is the row dimension of the array A exactly as specified in the dimension statement of the calling program (see explanation below).
>
>NPIV is a vector, of length at least n, which, on return, will contain the pivot vector.
>
>A is a two-dimensional array, of size at least $n \times n$, containing, on entry, the matrix A and, on return, its LU factorization.
>
>IND is an indicator of numerical singularity.

Numerical singularity means that, in a relative sense, at least one of the pivots encountered during the elimination is very small. If the routine indicates, via IND, that A is numerically singular, it is not advisable to proceed with the back substitution because there is a strong possibility that an overflow condition will occur due to division by a relatively small number.

The parameter NDIM in the calling sequence is necessary for subroutines that are written in the Fortran language. We explain its purpose with the following example. Suppose a program begins with the declaration

DIMENSION AMAT(4,3),BVEC(6)

and that we want to solve a 2×2 linear system with coefficient matrix

$$A = \begin{bmatrix} -7 & 8 \\ 4 & 5 \end{bmatrix}$$

Fortran represents a two-dimensional array as a vector by columns. Therefore, the matrix A would be stored in AMAT in the following way:

$\underline{-7}$ $\underline{4}$ $\underline{}$ $\underline{}$ $\underline{8}$ $\underline{5}$ $\underline{}$ $\underline{}$ $\underline{}$ $\underline{}$ $\underline{}$ $\underline{}$

Col. 1 Col. 2 Col. 3

Clearly, in order to locate the elements of A in this representation, it is necessary to know how many rows were assigned to AMAT in the dimension statement. The parameter NDIM is the mechanism for passing this information to DCOMP. This is a standard device for (Fortran) subroutines that have to work with two-dimensional arrays. For our example, a call to DCOMP would take the form

> CALL DCOMP(N,4,NPIV,AMAT,IND)

or else

> NDIM = 4
> CALL DCOMP(N,NDIM,NPIV,AMAT,IND)

We remark that the argument NDIM is not needed at all with a programming language such as Algol, which does dynamic allocation of storage. With this feature, the space for storing a matrix A is not allocated until execution time so that the amount set aside need only be enough to store the particular matrix being processed at the time—four locations for our example. Consequently, the value of N is the only information required in order to access individual elements. The Fortran language does not have this feature. Space is allocated at compile time (before the actual size of A is known) and, as a consequence, the amount allocated must be sufficient to handle a matrix of the maximum size permitted by the dimension statement. The advantage of dynamic allocation is programming convenience, while the disadvantage is extra computational cost as a result of having to manage storage allocations during execution. Sometimes, the extra cost can be significant.

A further remark on the difference between Fortran and Algol is that the latter stores two-dimensional arrays by rows (instead of columns). Hence, if NDIM were necessary with Algol, it would have to specify the column dimension of AMAT—it is 3 in our example. A more important aspect of the difference in storage methods concerns efficiency of a program. To illustrate, we refer to the Gauss elimination procedure. The algorithm can be described as follows:

> FOR $k = 1$ TO $n - 1$ DO
> > search for largest pivot and, if necessary,
> > > interchange rows
> > FOR $i = k + 1$ TO n DO
> > > form the multiplier $m_{i,k}$
> > > FOR $j = k + 1$ TO n DO
> > > > $a_{i,j} \leftarrow a_{i,j} + m_{i,k} \cdot a_{k,j}$ (**)
> > > END
> > END
> END

The statement labeled (**) lies in the innermost part of a triple-nested loop structure and is executed about $n^3/3$ times. Therefore, any means of decreasing its execution time will significantly improve the overall efficiency of the algorithm. To this end, we look at the process of accessing elements $a_{i,j}$ of A. Due to differences in storage methods, the location of $a_{i,j}$ in the vector representation of AMAT is given by

$$\text{NDIM} \cdot (j-1) + i \qquad \text{in Fortran, and}$$
$$\text{NDIM} \cdot (i-1) + j \qquad \text{in Algol (with NDIM} = n)$$

Hence, in order to access an element of A, we must compute the correct subscript for AMAT. We emphasize that this kind of computation must be made every time a two-dimensional array is accessed. It is, of course, transparent to the user because the compiler will generate the appropriate code. Nevertheless, it is an overhead cost of which the user should be aware and make every effort to minimize. For our present algorithm, we note that the value of i is fixed within the innermost loop. Therefore, the Algol version can be made more efficient by only computing $\text{NDIM} \cdot (i-1)$ once for each execution of the loop—a saving of $n - k - 1$ integer multiplies each time. A so-called "optimizing" compiler will recognize this fact and automatically generate code accordingly. In effect, this saving is possible because our algorithm does the elimination across rows so that it accesses, in order, $a_{i,k+1}, a_{i,k+2}, \ldots, a_{i,n}$. Since Algol stores a matrix by rows, these elements are adjacent in AMAT and it is only necessary to compute the location of the first one in the sequence. In order to make the same kind of savings possible in a Fortran version of Gauss elimination, it is clear that we must reorganize the algorithm to make it "column oriented." This turns out to be quite easy. The alternate version is

```
FOR k = 1 TO n DO
        search for largest pivot and, if necessary,
                                        interchange rows
        FOR i = k + 1 TO n DO
            compute the multiplier m_{i,k}
        END
        FOR j = k + 1 TO n DO
            FOR i = k + 1 TO n DO
                a_{i,j} ← a_{i,j} + m_{i,k} · a_{k,j}
            END
        END
    END
```

An optimizing Fortran compiler would be able to achieve savings with this form of the algorithm (but an Algol compiler would not) because it accesses, in order, the elements $a_{k+1,j}, a_{k+2,j}, \ldots, a_{n,j}$ down a column that appear in sequence in AMAT. Hence, a Fortran version of DCOMP would be based on this form of the algorithm.

The subroutine for completing the solution of a linear system will be of the form

SOLVE(N,NDIM,NPIV,LU,B)

where

N, NDIM, NPIV are as before.

LU is a two-dimensional array, of size at least $n \times n$, containing the LU factorization of A.

B is a vector, of length at least n, containing, on entry, the right-hand side vector **b** and, on return, the solution vector **x**.

If our matrix A is stored in the array AMAT and the vector **b** is in BVEC, the program segment

CALL DCOMP(N,NDIM,NPIV,AMAT,IND)
IF (IND indicates singularity) THEN
(2.20)   stop
ELSE
    CALL SOLVE(N,NDIM,NPIV,AMAT,BVEC)

would compute the solution of $Ax = b$.

Many users have no need for the flexibility offered by the separation of the algorithm into two parts, so the necessity to make two subroutine calls is an inconvenience. Consequently, software packages also contain "black box" routines for solving linear systems. A typical calling sequence is

(2.21)   LINEQ(N,NDIM,AMAT,BVEC,IND)

Such routines consist, basically, of the program segment (2.20). Note that the pivoting strategy is transparent to the user.

In most subroutine packages, the argument B in the SOLVE routines is a two-dimensional array rather than a vector. This is in order to facilitate the simultaneous solution of, say, n_{sys} systems $Ax_k = b_k$, $1 \le k \le n_{sys}$, having the same coefficient matrix A. We can rewrite this set of systems in the form

$$AX = B$$

where X and B are $n \times n_{sys}$ matrices whose columns are, respectively, x_k, b_k, $1 \le k \le n_{sys}$. In this context, the Gauss elimination algorithm (2.17) is basically the same except that vectors are replaced by matrices. Hence, the algorithm for solving several systems simultaneously is a simple extension of (2.17). The calling sequence for routines with this feature would be of the form

SOLVE(N,NDIM,NSYS,NPIV,LU,B)

The only difference from the previous form is the addition of the argument

NSYS for specifying the number of systems to be solved. In the case of only one system (NSYS = 1), it is usually permissible to call the routine using a one-dimensional array BVEC for the argument B. In this way, a user is not inconvenienced by having to declare BVEC as a two-dimensional array. We note that the calling sequence for the LINEQ subroutine would be expanded similarly to include the argument NSYS.

2.1.2. Errors

The Gauss elimination algorithm that we have just described can easily be shown to be valid mathematically. That is, it can be proved that the solution of the reduced problem $Ux = d$ is identical to that of the original problem $Ax = b$ assuming that all computations are done using infinite precision. The proof simply involves establishing that the solution of $Ax = b$ is invariant under the types of operations[2] used to reduce the system to triangular form. Our aim in this section is to look at the numerical validity of the algorithm, that is, what happens when the computations are done using finite precision arithmetic. Let $\hat{x}$ denote the computed solution. Then we would like to be able to obtain some estimate as to how good a solution $\hat{x}$ is. This will involve defining what is meant by a "good" solution and then developing some practical measure of this property.

A natural method for assessing an approximate solution $\hat{x}$ would be to see how close it is to the true solution x. However, since we do not know the true solution, it is impossible to compare $\hat{x}$ with x directly. An alternative would be to see how well $\hat{x}$ satisfies the original equations by substituting it into the system and seeing what is left over. But this can be very misleading as the following example [15] illustrates:

$$\begin{bmatrix} 0.780 & 0.563 \\ 0.913 & 0.659 \end{bmatrix} \begin{bmatrix} x_1 \\ x_2 \end{bmatrix} = \begin{bmatrix} 0.217 \\ 0.254 \end{bmatrix}$$

Two possible solutions are

$$\hat{x}_1 = \begin{bmatrix} 0.999 \\ -1.001 \end{bmatrix} \quad \text{and} \quad \hat{x}_2 = \begin{bmatrix} 0.341 \\ -0.087 \end{bmatrix}$$

The correct solution is $x = [1, -1]^T$, so $\hat{x}_1$ is clearly better than $\hat{x}_2$. In fact, $\hat{x}_2$

---

[2] In the mathematical literature, these operations are called *elementary row operations.* Specifically, they are:

  i   Interchange two rows.
  ii   Multiply a row by a constant.
  iii   Add one row to another.

is ridiculously bad. But if we compute the *residual* vectors $r_1 = b - A\hat{x}_1$ and $r_2 = b - A\hat{x}_2$ by substituting $\hat{x}_1$ and $\hat{x}_2$, respectively, into the system, we get

$$r_1 = \begin{bmatrix} -0.001243 \\ -0.001572 \end{bmatrix} \quad \text{and} \quad r_2 = \begin{bmatrix} -0.000001 \\ 0 \end{bmatrix}$$

which leads to the incorrect conclusion that $\hat{x}_2$ is the better solution. Therefore, the residual vector r is not necessarily a good indicator of accuracy in $\hat{x}$. The reason why it is important to realize that this sort of situation can arise is that the Gauss elimination with partial pivoting algorithm (2.17) is designed to produce an approximate solution $\hat{x}$ for which the corresponding residual $r = b - A\hat{x}$ is small, that is, it will yield a solution like $\hat{x}_2$ rather than $\hat{x}_1$. But this is not to belittle the algorithm. The trouble, as we will see, lies in the problem itself. Admittedly, this example was made somewhat extreme in order to illustrate a point. In many (but not all) cases, a small residual will, in fact, imply that $\hat{x}$ is close to x but the difficulties still remain. How can we tell when the computed solution is not particularly good, and is there anything we can do to get a better one?

In discussing these problems, we will need to compare vectors with respect to their relative "sizes." Let $x = [x_1, \ldots, x_n]^T$ be an *n*-vector and define the *norm*

$$(2.22) \quad \|x\| = (x^T x)^{1/2} = (|x_1|^2 + |x_2|^2 + \cdots + |x_n|^2)^{1/2}$$

which is the well-known Euclidean length of x. Note that the absolute value signs are used so that the definition still applies if the entries of x are complex numbers. For example, if $x = [2, -1, 1 + i]^T$, then $\|x\| = (4 + 1 + 2)^{1/2} = \sqrt{7}$. The notion of a vector norm provides us with the desired means of comparing vectors in that we can say that x is "smaller" then y if $\|x\| < \|y\|$. For example, if $x = [2, 1]^T$ and $y = [-1, 3]^T$, then x is smaller than y since $\|x\| = \sqrt{5} < \sqrt{10} = \|y\|$.

Equation (2.22) is not the only way of defining the norm or "length" of a vector (although it is the only one we will use here). For instance, we could have defined $\|\cdot\|$ to be[3]

$$(2.23) \quad \begin{array}{l} \text{(a)} \quad \|x\|_1 = |x_1| + |x_2| + \cdots + |x_n|, \quad \text{or} \\[2mm] \text{(b)} \quad \|x\|_\infty = \max_{1 \le i \le n} |x_i|. \end{array}$$

---

[3]These are special cases of the so-called ℓ_p vector norm

$$\|x\|_p = (|x_1|^p + \cdots + |x_n|^p)^{1/p}$$

where $p \ge 1$ is an integer. The definition of $\|\cdot\|_\infty$ is the limiting case as $p \to \infty$. The norm defined in (2.22) is the special case $p = 2$.

In fact, any definition of $\|\cdot\|$ satisfying the following properties (which have been abstracted from the notion of length) qualifies as a vector norm and can be used to compare vectors:

(2.24)

   i $\|x\| \geq 0$, with equality if and only if $x \equiv 0$.

   ii $\|cx\| = |c| \cdot \|x\|$, where c is any constant.

   iii $\|x + y\| \leq \|x\| + \|y\|$ (triangle inequality).

It is easy to verify that each norm defined in (2.22) and (2.23) satisfies these conditions.

We also need to have the concept of a *matrix norm* $\|A\|$ in order to be able to compare matrices. This is defined in terms of the vector norm (2.22):

$$(2.25) \quad \|A\| = \sup_{x \neq 0} \frac{\|Ax\|}{\|x\|}$$

where "sup" means supremum or least upper bound. Again, there is a variety of ways of defining a matrix norm. As with vector norms, any definition of $\|A\|$ that satisfies the following properties is defined to be a matrix norm:

   i $\|A\| \geq 0$, with equality if and only if $A \equiv 0$.

   ii $\|cA\| = |c| \cdot \|A\|$, for any constant c.

   iii $\|A + B\| \leq \|A\| + \|B\|$.

   iv $\|A \cdot B\| \leq \|A\| \cdot \|B\|$.

The definition (2.25) of $\|A\|$ does not lend itself to easy computation. But fortunately, we will not actually have to compute matrix norms. It will suffice to have a feeling for the idea of the "length" or norm of a matrix and that it provides a means of comparing matrices. Before proceeding, we make note of a result which will be useful later.

$$(2.26) \quad \|Ax\| \leq \|A\| \cdot \|x\| \qquad \text{for any } x$$

This follows immediately from the definition (2.25) of $\|A\|$.

Let us return to our discussion of determining the accuracy in an approximate solution $\hat{x}$. We defined the error to be the amount by which $\hat{x}$ differs from x, the true solution. This can be expressed as the *error* vector

$$e = x - \hat{x}$$

Then to measure how good an approximation $\hat{x}$ is, we use the *relative error* $\|e\|/\|x\|$, that is, the size of the error vector relative to the size of the solution vector. This gives an indication of how many digits are correct in the components of $\hat{x}$. Since there is no way of computing the relative error explicitly, our problem is to estimate its size with reasonable accuracy.

In the preceding example, we saw that the residual vector **r** is not a reliable indicator of accuracy in $\hat{x}$. Nevertheless, **r** has two important virtues. The first is that it is very easy to compute. The second was alluded to in the discussion of the example, namely, that the Gauss elimination with partial pivoting algorithm (2.17) is designed to produce an $\hat{x}$ for which the *relative residual* $\|\mathbf{r}\|/\|\mathbf{b}\|$ is small[4]. Because of these features, it turns out that **r** can be a very useful tool in assessing the accuracy of $\hat{x}$ after all. But it must be used judiciously. In order to understand how and why, it is best to look at a geometric interpretation.

Consider the case of two equations in two unknowns.

$$L_1: \quad a_{1,1}x_1 + a_{1,2}x_2 = b_1$$

$$L_2: \quad a_{2,1}x_1 + a_{2,2}x_2 = b_2$$

Each equation represents a straight line and the solution $\mathbf{x} = [x_1, x_2]^T$ is their point of intersection. Now, if $\hat{x} = [\hat{x}_1, \hat{x}_2]^T$ is the computed solution, then the components of the residual $\mathbf{r} = [r_1, r_2]^T$ satisfy

$$r_1 = b_1 - (a_{1,1}\hat{x}_1 + a_{1,2}\hat{x}_2)$$

$$r_2 = b_2 - (a_{2,1}\hat{x}_1 + a_{2,2}\hat{x}_2)$$

The situation is pictured in Figure 2.1. The values $|r_1|$ and $|r_2|$ represent, respectively, the distances from $\hat{x}$ to the lines L_1 and L_2. Hence, $\|\mathbf{r}\| = (|r_1|^2 + |r_2|^2)^{1/2}$ is a measure of how close $\hat{x}$ is to the original lines whereas $\|\mathbf{e}\|$ is a measure of how close $\hat{x}$ is to the true solution **x**.

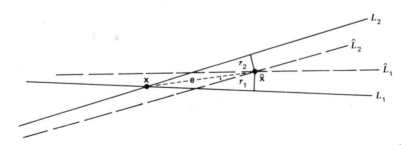

FIGURE 2.1

---

[4]The relative residual is

$$\frac{\|\mathbf{r}\|}{\|\mathbf{b}\|} = \frac{\|\mathbf{b} - A\hat{x}\|}{\|\mathbf{b}\|}$$

It can be viewed as a measure of the size of the residual vector relative to that of the problem itself.

Another way of interpreting $\hat{x}$ uses the fact that it is the point of intersection of the lines $\hat{L}_1$ and $\hat{L}_2$. Since we can view these lines as slight perturbations of the original lines L_1 and L_2, $\hat{x}$ represents the exact solution of a slightly perturbed or shifted problem. This perturbation is caused by round-off error incurred because the computations are done in finite precision. Hence, by doing everything we can to minimize the growth of round-off error as the computations proceed, we can minimize the resulting perturbation of the system. Partial pivoting is the way we accomplish this. To see why, we again look at the typical computation done during the elimination

$$a_{i,j} \leftarrow a_{i,j} - m_{i,k} a_{k,j}$$

The idea of partial pivoting is to ensure that each multiplier $m_{i,k}$ is no greater than 1 in magnitude and, in view of the discussions in Chapter 1, it is not hard to see how this in turn will ensure that the number of correct digits in the new value of $a_{i,j}$ is as large as possible. Geometrically, this means that the corresponding hyperplane (in n-space) represented by the kth equation is shifted as little as possible. We remark that there will be a further perturbation introduced by round-off error during the back substitution, but this will be relatively insignificant compared to that of the elimination. Referring again to Figure 2.1, it follows that, by minimizing the shift in the problem during the computations, the values of r_1 and r_2 will be kept small in magnitude so that $\|r\|$ is small.

To recapitulate, our goal is to obtain a computed solution $\hat{x}$ for which the relative error $\|e\|/\|x\|$ is small. However, we have no convenient way of computing e or estimating its norm $\|e\|$. On the other hand, the residual r is something we can determine explicitly. Moreover, we know that it is going to be small. But, as we have already seen, the residual r is an unreliable indicator of the size of the error e. The troublesome cases turn out to be when the lines are more nearly parallel as shown in Figure 2.2a. Here we

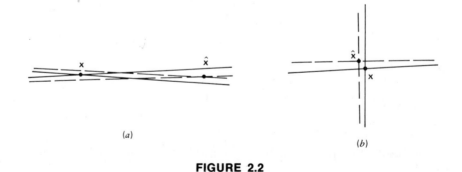

(a)

(b)

FIGURE 2.2

see that even a small shift from L_1 and L_2 can produce a large shift in $\hat{x}$ from x. At the other extreme is the case where L_1 and L_2 are *orthogonal* (at right angles) as in Figure 2.2b. In this situation, since $\|e\|$ and $\|r\|$ are approximately equal, a small residual will, in fact, guarantee a small error. Of course, we could encounter anything between these two extremes but the point is that the closer the lines are to being parallel, the less sure we are of having a small error e even though the residual r may be small.

A word or two about the above discussion is in order at this point. The idea of "looking backward" from the computed solution $\hat{x}$ to the problem for which it is the exact solution is a very important concept in numerical analysis. In Figure 2.1, we viewed $\hat{x}$ as the exact solution of a perturbed problem. It can be written as $(A + E)\hat{x} = b$, where the matrix E represents the perturbation in the system. We also saw that partial pivoting ensured that the amount of perturbation is minimal, that is, $\|E\|$ is small. Therefore, from a *backward error analysis* point of view, we will always do very well because we are guaranteed to obtain an $\hat{x}$ that is the exact solution of a problem that is very close to the original one.

Geometrically, we have seen that a small perturbation in the system ensured that r would be small. This can also be shown algebraically. We know that $\hat{x}$ satisfies each of the equations

$$r = b - A\hat{x}$$

$$0 = b - (A + E)\hat{x}$$

By subtracting, we get

$$r = E\hat{x}$$

Then, taking the norm of each side and applying the inequality (2.26), we have

$$\|r\| \leq \|E\| \cdot \|\hat{x}\|$$

Therefore, since a small perturbation in the system means that $\|E\|$ is small, we see that $\|r\|$ must also be small (relative to $\|\hat{x}\|$). This is why we say that the Gauss elimination with partial pivoting algorithm is designed to produce an $\hat{x}$ for which the corresponding residual r is small. The fact that such a small shift in the problem can produce a large shift in the solution, as in Figure 2.2a, is no fault of the algorithm. It is a difficulty with the problem itself. Such problems are called *ill conditioned*. On the other hand, systems like the one depicted in Figure 2.2b, where a small r does indeed guarantee a small e, are *well conditioned*.

The foregoing analysis was done only in the 2×2 case but the ideas introduced apply equally well for larger systems. Geometrically, the solution of an $n \times n$ linear system represents the point of intersection of the *n* hyperplanes defined by the equations. If two or more of the hyperplanes are nearly parallel, then a small shift in the problem could produce a large shift in the solution, that is, the system is ill conditioned.

The above discussion gives an explanation of the reasons *why* difficulties in solving a linear system can occur. But we are still faced with the more practical problem of recognizing *when* they are present in a problem. Usually, it is not obvious by inspection and drawing a picture is certainly not practical. (It is well nigh impossible if $n > 3$.) We therefore need some computational means for detecting ill conditioning. Another question we would like to resolve is, given that the system is ill conditioned and we obtain an $\hat{x}$ for which $\|e\|$ is not small, is there any way of correcting $\hat{x}$? The next section deals with these questions but first we need to express the above ideas algebraically.

A relationship between e and r is easily obtained as follows. We have

$$Ax = b$$

and

$$A\hat{x} = b - r$$

Subtracting gives $Ae = r$, or

$$e = A^{-1}r$$

Taking the norm of each side and applying the inequality (2.26), we have

$$\|e\| \le \|A^{-1}\| \cdot \|r\|$$

We also have

$$\|b\| \le \|A\| \cdot \|x\|$$

and, combining these, we obtain the inequality

$$(2.27) \quad \frac{\|e\|}{\|x\|} \le \text{cond}(A) \cdot \frac{\|r\|}{\|b\|}$$

where

$$(2.28) \quad \text{cond}(A) = \|A\| \cdot \|A^{-1}\|$$

is called the *condition number* of A. The inequality (2.27) provides us with a means for estimating the relative error $\|e\|/\|x\|$. The components of the bound are the relative residual and the condition number. The former is easily computed but the latter is not, so we have to estimate it. We will see how to do this in the next section.

As its name implies, the condition number is a measure of the "conditioning" of the matrix A. The range of values it can assume is given by

$$1 \leq \text{cond}(A) \leq +\infty$$

The lower bound follows from the fact that $AA^{-1} = I$ and, taking the norm of each side, we have

$$1 = \|I\| = \|AA^{-1}\| \leq \|A\|\|A^{-1}\| = \text{cond}(A)$$

The upper "bound" on $\text{cond}(A)$ can be explained by referring to the inequality (2.27). We have seen that the relative error $\|e\|/\|x\|$ can be arbitrarily large depending on the degree of parallelism in the system. On the other hand, the relative residual $\|r\|/\|b\|$ is always small. Therefore, if $\|e\|/\|x\|$ is large, the only way that (2.27) can be satisfied is for $\text{cond}(A)$ to be suitably large also. The more nearly parallel the system is, the larger $\text{cond}(A)$ must be (with no upper bound). Thus, the condition number provides an algebraic way of expressing the degree of ill conditioning in a system. If $\text{cond}(A)$ is near unity, the system is well conditioned and vice versa.

2.1.3. Iterative Improvement

Let $\hat{x}_s$ be an approximate solution to the system $Ax = b$. Then the *iterative improvement algorithm* for computing an improved solution $\hat{x}_{s+1}$ is as follows:

(2.29)

    i Compute the residual $r_s = b - A\hat{x}_s$ (using extended precision).
    ii Solve the system $Az_s = r_s$ (and obtain $\hat{z}_s$).
    iii Compute $\hat{x}_{s+1} = \hat{x}_s + \hat{z}_s$.

The process can be repeated until a specified stopping criterion is met (see below). Note that it is important that the residual vector be computed using extended precision arithmetic. This is in order to avoid bad cancellation in taking the difference $b = A\hat{x}_s$. We also remark that the system $Az_s = r_s$ in step (ii) has the same coefficient matrix A as the original system. Therefore, step (ii) can be done simply by calling a subroutine such as SOLVE.

    As an example, we consider the system

$$\begin{bmatrix} 1.23 & 4.56 & 9.87 \\ -9.61 & 6.02 & 11.1 \\ 7.31 & 2.89 & 5.04 \end{bmatrix} \begin{bmatrix} x_1 \\ x_2 \\ x_3 \end{bmatrix} = \begin{bmatrix} 4.12 \\ 5.34 \\ -3.56 \end{bmatrix}$$

whose solution, correct to three digits, is $x = [-0.449, -4.74, 2.66]^T$. Using three-digit arithmetic with one guard digit and chopping, the Gauss elimination algorithm (2.17) yields

$$L = \begin{bmatrix} 1 & 0 & 0 \\ -0.760 & 1 & 0 \\ -0.127 & 0.713 & 1 \end{bmatrix} \qquad U = \begin{bmatrix} -9.61 & 6.02 & 11.0 \\ 0 & 7.46 & 13.4 \\ 0 & 0 & 1.64 \end{bmatrix}$$

$$\text{NPIV} = \begin{bmatrix} 2 \\ 3 \\ +1 \end{bmatrix}$$

and $\hat{x}_1 = [-0.430, -4.78, 2.70]^T$. Then one iteration of the iterative improvement algorithm (2.29) gives us

$$r_1 = \begin{bmatrix} 4.12000 \\ 5.34000 \\ -3.56000 \end{bmatrix} - \begin{bmatrix} 1.23 & 4.56 & 9.87 \\ -9.61 & 6.02 & 11.1 \\ 7.31 & 2.89 & 5.04 \end{bmatrix} \begin{bmatrix} -0.430 \\ -4.78 \\ 2.70 \end{bmatrix}$$

$$= \begin{bmatrix} 4.12000 \\ 5.34000 \\ -3.56000 \end{bmatrix} - \begin{bmatrix} 4.32330 \\ 5.32670 \\ -3.34950 \end{bmatrix} = \begin{bmatrix} -0.203 \\ 0.0133 \\ -0.210 \end{bmatrix}$$

$$\hat{z}_1 = \begin{bmatrix} -0.0192 \\ 0.0383 \\ -0.0362 \end{bmatrix} \qquad \text{and} \qquad \hat{x}_2 = \begin{bmatrix} -0.449 \\ -4.74 \\ 2.66 \end{bmatrix}$$

which is the correct result. We remark that, if double precision is not used in the computation of r_1, we would get

$$r_1 = \begin{bmatrix} -0.220 \\ -0.0300 \\ -0.260 \end{bmatrix} \qquad z_1 = \begin{bmatrix} -0.207 \\ -0.0137 \\ -0.0134 \end{bmatrix} \qquad \text{and} \qquad x_2 = \begin{bmatrix} -0.637 \\ -4.79 \\ 2.68 \end{bmatrix}$$

We begin our discussion of the algorithm by establishing its mathematical validity. This is easily done. Assuming exact arithmetic, so that $\hat{z}_s = z_s$ in part (ii), we would have

$$\hat{x}_{s+1} = \hat{x}_s + z_s = \hat{x}_s + A^{-1}r_s = \hat{x}_s + A^{-1}(b - A\hat{x}_s) = A^{-1}b = x.$$

Hence, given *any* approximate solution $\hat{x}_s$, the iterative improvement algorithm (2.29) will produce the exact solution x. Therefore, the algorithm is valid mathematically. In practice, however, we do not do exact arithmetic and $\hat{x}_{s+1}$ will again be an an approximate solution. But is it a better solution, that is, is the iterative improvement algorithm valid numerically?

The answer to this question is a qualified yes. The qualification has to do with the conditioning of the problem and the number of digits being carried in the computation. We will try to explain.

Let us assume that the conditioning of the matrix A is such that the Gauss elimination algorithm (2.17) produces an approximate solution that has, say, at least two digits accuracy in each of its components. Now let $\hat{x}_1$ be any approximation for x [not necessarily the one produced by (2.17)]. By our assumption, the correction vector $\hat{z}_1$ will be accurate to at least two digits since it is obtained using (2.17). This means that the first two incorrect digits in $\hat{x}_1$ will be corrected. For example, if $\hat{x}_1$ is accurate to three digits, then $\hat{x}_2$ will be accurate to at least five digits. Continuing, the correction $\hat{z}_2$ will again have at least two digits accuracy, $\hat{x}_3$ will have at least seven digits accuracy, and so on. The process can be repeated until, say, the tth stage where $\hat{x}_t$ has the required accuracy, that is, $\|\hat{z}_t\|$ is sufficiently small.

The above analysis depends on the assumption that Gauss elimination will give a solution accurate to two digits. Of course, if A is better conditioned, more accuracy is achieved in the $\hat{z}_s$'s and convergence is faster. Similarly, it will be slower if A is not as well conditioned and, in the extreme when A is so badly conditioned that Gauss elimination gives no accuracy whatever, convergence will not take place at all. In the latter case, we say that the algorithm is numerically invalid. On the other hand, this difficulty can be overcome if we are prepared to use greater precision in the computations. The reasoning, of course, is that the round-off level will be much smaller, which implies that the perturbed system obtained after computing the LU decomposition will be closer to the original one. This, in turn, means that the approximate solution $\hat{z}_s$ of $A\hat{z}_s = r_s$ is closer to the exact correction vector z_s, that is, it is more accurate. In Figure 2.1, for example, if the perturbed lines $\hat{L}_1$ and $\hat{L}_2$ are closer, respectively, to L_1 and L_2, then $\hat{x}$ will be closer to x. Hence, we can always assure convergence (or numerical validity) of iterative improvement provided we use sufficiently high precision in the computations. The amount of precision required at any time depends on the conditioning of the problem at hand. But if we are only prepared to use a specified precision, then there will certainly be cases where iterative improvement will not converge. This is the meaning of the "qualified yes" to the question of numerical validity.

In practice, it is not apparent, at the outset, how much precision will be required to assure convergence. However, in the case of a subroutine library, the choice has been made by the designers of the computer and of the subroutines. By and large, routines, in "production" software packages such as LINPACK, IMSL, and NAG work to machine hardware precision[5]. This is generally sufficient to solve most problems that arise in practice. If it turns out that the problem being solved is too badly conditioned to be handled, then one should go back and try to reformulate the overall computation avoiding the need to solve such an ill-conditioned system. We will see an example of this in Section 2.3 on solving over-determined linear systems using the normal equations method.

From our discussion, it is apparent that iterative improvement can be very useful. For well-conditioned systems, it provides peace of mind in that it gives assurance that Gauss elimination has produced a good solution; for less well-conditioned problems, one or two iterations will give a better solution (and similar peace of mind); while for badly conditioned systems, it can inform us of the fact so that an appropriate remedy can be taken rather than proceed with the overall computations using an incorrect result. The usual test for convergence goes as follows. First, we compute the *relative correction*

$$\text{RELCOR} = \frac{\|\hat{\mathbf{z}}_s\|}{\|\hat{\mathbf{x}}_s\|}$$

This number gives an idea of how many digits in $\hat{\mathbf{x}}_s$ are correct. For example, if RELCOR $= 3.2E\text{-}3 = 0.0032$, we can assume that the elements of $\hat{\mathbf{x}}_s$ are accurate to about two digits since the first digit affected by $\hat{\mathbf{z}}_s$ is the third one. Hence, given a value TOL for the error tolerance, a stopping criterion for iterative improvement would be of the form

Condition	*Action*
RELCOR $<$ TOL	stop—convergence achieved
TOL $<$ RELCOR $<$ 1	continue iterations
1 $<$ RELCOR	stop—conditioning is excessive

In the latter case, we should stop because all of the digits in $\hat{\mathbf{x}}_s$ are being

---

[5]If full machine hardware precision is used, there will be a problem in calculating the residuals r_s since they must be computed in extended precision. However, many computer systems provide such a facility so that programming this part of the computation will present no real difficulty. For example, full machine precision on an IBM 3033 is double precision (i.e., 14 hexadecimal digits). The H-level Fortran compiler for this machine has a facility for quadruple precision arithmetic and one need only declare this precision for the appropriate variables. But it should be kept in mind that this capability has to be provided by system microprograms (for each of the arithmetic operations). Hence there is a considerable overhead cost in doing computations beyond hardware precision. But with regard to computing the residuals r_s, this is a relatively small part of the overall computation, so the extra overhead is relatively insignificant.

"corrected," which means that $\hat{\mathbf{x}}_s$ or $\hat{\mathbf{z}}_s$ (or both) have no accuracy at all[6]. The cause of the trouble is that A is so badly conditioned that Gauss elimination cannot give any accuracy within the precision being used. We say that A is *numerically singular* (with respect to this precision).

An estimate for cond(A) can be obtained from the results of the first iteration of (2.29) in the following way. From the inequality (2.27), we have

$$\left[\frac{\|\mathbf{r}_1\|}{\|\mathbf{b}\|}\right]^{-1} \cdot \frac{\|\mathbf{e}_1\|}{\|\mathbf{x}\|} \le \text{cond}(A)$$

We assume that $\|\mathbf{r}_1\|/\|\mathbf{b}\|$ is roughly at round-off level, that is, its size is about β^{-t}, where β is the base of the floating-point number system of the machine being used and t is the number of digits carried. Also, we use the approximation

$$\frac{\|\mathbf{e}_1\|}{\|\mathbf{x}\|} \doteq \frac{\|\hat{\mathbf{z}}_1\|}{\|\hat{\mathbf{x}}_1\|}$$

which is reasonable even if $\hat{\mathbf{x}}_1$ has only one or two digits accuracy. Therefore, with these approximations, we have the approximate lower bound

$$(2.30) \qquad \frac{\|\hat{\mathbf{z}}_1\|}{\|\hat{\mathbf{x}}_1\|} \cdot \beta^t \le \text{cond}(A)$$

In practice, this is almost always an underestimate and it is often a somewhat conservative one at that. Nevertheless, it does give some indication of the magnitude of cond(A) and this is really all that is needed. As a rough rule of thumb, if cond(A) $\doteq 10^p$, then the last p (decimal) digits in the solution $\hat{\mathbf{x}}_1$ may be in error.

Now we consider the efficiency of iterative improvement. We have talked about the virtues of it but what is the cost and is it worth it? It turns out to be relatively cheap. Let us look at the cost of each step in the algorithm (2.29). We have:

   i n^2 flops + overhead for extended precision.
   ii $n^2 + O(n)$ flops, assuming the LU decomposition of A is available.
  iii n A's.

The total work is about $2n^2$ flops, which is not much compared to the $n^3/3$

---

[6]It is possible that this situation can hold and yet RELCOR < 1. To distinguish it, we note that if improvement in $\mathbf{x}_s$ is actually made at each iteration, then RELCOR should decrease at a more or less constant rate. Hence we can assure that convergence is indeed taking place by monitoring the rate of decrease of RELCOR.

flops required to solve the system in the first place. Of course, this count depends on the fact that the LU decomposition does not have to be recomputed. We remark that, since both A and LU must be stored, n^2 additional storage locations are needed. But, since the cost of this is relatively insignificant, we ignore it. Hence, the cost of iterative improvement is relatively low if it is done properly. Here, then, is a case where peace of mind comes at bargain rates.

The parameter list for an iterative improvement subroutine is typically of the form

IMPRV(N,NDIM,NPIV,A,LU,B,X,CONDA,IER)

The routine will iterate until either machine accuracy in the solution is achieved or it has been determined that A is too ill-conditioned for convergence to occur. The parameter IER is used to indicate whichever situation holds. CONDA is used to return an estimate for the condition number. The (lower) bound (2.30) is generally used to compute it. As we saw, this also indicates the accuracy in the initial solution $\hat{x}_1$. Note that both A and its LU factorization are required by IMPRV. Consequently, before calling DCOMP, a copy of A must be made and similarly for **b** before calling SOLVE. Suppose A is stored in the array AMAT and **b** in BVEC. Then, to solve the linear system $Ax = \mathbf{b}$ with iterative improvement, the following sequence of steps should be followed

```
make a copy of A in LU
make a copy of b in X
CALL DCOMP(N,NDIM,NPIV,LU,IND)
IF (IND indicates singularity) THEN
   stop
ELSE
   CALL SOLVE(N,NDIM,NPIV,LU,X)
   CALL IMPRV(N,NDIM,NPIV,AMAT,LU,BVEC,X,CONDA,IER)
```

The final improved solution will be returned in X. We remark that "black box" subroutines such as LINEQ in (2.21) cannot be used with IMPRV because the pivoting strategy NPIV is not available from LINEQ.

We make a final remark concerning the implementation of algorithm (2.29). This is with respect to the computation of the residual vector in step (i). Suppose that one iteration of (2.29) has been done and it is decided that a second iteration is needed. The residual $\mathbf{r}_2$ is

$$\mathbf{r}_2 = \mathbf{b} - A\hat{x}_2 = \mathbf{b} - A(\hat{x}_1 + \hat{z}_1) = (\mathbf{b} - A\hat{x}_1) - A\hat{z}_1$$

$$= \mathbf{r}_1 - A\hat{z}_1$$

The latter representation tells us that r_2 can also be viewed as the residual error in the approximate correction vector $\hat{z}_1$. Mathematically, the two representations are equivalent but, numerically, they can be different. Assuming that $\hat{x}_2$ is a better solution than $\hat{x}_1$, it follows from the geometrical arguments in the previous section (see Figure 2.1) that the components of r_2 will be smaller than those of r_1. Hence, if we use $b - Ax_2$ to compute r_2, the cancellation will be worse than it was in computing r_1, and r_2 will have fewer correct digits. On the other hand, with $r_2 = r_1 - A\hat{z}_1$, we can expect the same number of correct digits as we got for r_1. If a further iteration is necessary, we should compute r_3 using $r_2 - A\hat{z}_2$ instead of $b - A\hat{x}_2$, and so on. Therefore, step (i) of algorithm (2.29) should be rewritten as

$$\mathbf{i}' \quad \text{compute } r_s = \begin{cases} b - A\hat{x}_1 & \text{if } s = 1 \\ r_{s-1} - A\hat{z}_{s-1} & \text{if } s > 1 \end{cases}$$

2.1.4. Special Properties

Sometimes the coefficient matrix A will have some particular property that can be exploited in order to make the Gauss elimination algorithm (2.17) more efficient. If this property occurs often enough in practice, it is worthwhile writing a special subroutine that takes advantage of it. In this section we discuss three such properties and indicate the advantages that can be gained from them.

The first property is symmetry, that is, $a_{i,j} = a_{j,i}$. Obviously, we can make some savings in storage by simply storing the upper (or lower) triangle of A. However, there is no facility for defining a triangular array in storage. (We would still need a rectangular array to store the upper triangle.) We therefore store the elements of the triangle as a vector by columns. For example

$$A = \begin{bmatrix} a_{1,1} & a_{1,2} & a_{1,3} \\ a_{1,2} & a_{2,2} & a_{2,3} \\ a_{1,3} & a_{2,3} & a_{3,3} \end{bmatrix} \rightarrow \begin{bmatrix} a_{1,1} \\ a_{1,2} \\ a_{2,2} \\ a_{1,3} \\ a_{2,3} \\ a_{3,3} \end{bmatrix} = \text{APAC}$$

Then

$$\text{APAC(IJ)} = a_{i,j} \quad \text{where } IJ = \frac{i + j(j-1)}{2} \quad 1 \le i \le j \quad 1 \le j \le n$$

This is known as the *packed form* for storing A.

Unfortunately, the symmetry property alone is not enough to save us anything. This is because the LU factorization process destroys symmetry so that we still need a full $n \times n$ array to store the LU decomposition. However if, in addition to being symmetry, A is positive definite[7], it can be shown [6, p. 164] that

> if A is real, symmetric, and positive definite, then there exists a real upper triangular matrix R such that

(2.31) $$A = R^T R$$

This is called the *Cholesky factorization* of A. Since R is upper triangular, R^T is lower triangular. Therefore (2.31) is simply another triangular decomposition of A. But the key point is that we can represent this particular decomposition by R alone, that is, in the same amount of space required to store A (in packed form). In other words, the Cholesky decomposition (2.31) preserves symmetry. As a simple example, we have

$$\begin{bmatrix} 4 & 2 \\ 2 & 5 \end{bmatrix} = \begin{bmatrix} 2 & 0 \\ 1 & 2 \end{bmatrix} \begin{bmatrix} 2 & 1 \\ 0 & 2 \end{bmatrix}$$

It turns out that, as with the LU decomposition, we can successively overwrite the entries of A in computing R so that we do not need any more storage than the $n(n + 1)/2$ vector APAC containing the upper triangle of A.

There is, of course, the problem of knowing, at the outset, whether or not a given real symmetric matrix is positive definite. It usually is not obvious by inspection. However, very often it is known to be true from the context of the overall problem being solved but we will not concern ourselves with this matter here.

We will not go into the details of how to compute the Cholesky decomposition (2.31). It turns out that savings in computation time over computing the LU decomposition can be made in two respects. First, it can be shown that it is unnecessary to do pivoting. This saves the time required to search for the largest pivot and also to do row interchanges. Second, the number of operations required is $n^3/6 + O(n^2)$—half that for Gauss elimination. However there are also n square roots to be computed in the Cholesky decomposition but we ignore them as being a

---

[7]An $n \times n$ real symmetric matrix A is *positive definite* if, for *any* vector $\mathbf{x} \neq \mathbf{0}$, it is true that $\mathbf{x}^T A \mathbf{x} > 0$. Alternatively, A is positive definite if all of its eigenvalues are positive. (Recall that the eigenvalues of a real symmetric matrix are always real, never complex. Therefore, it is meaningful to talk about all the eigenvalues being positive.)

relatively insignificant part of the computation. Therefore, the operations count to solve a symmetric positive definite system is:

i Compute the decomposition $A = R^T R$—$n^3/6$ flops.
ii Solve the system $R^T d = b$ —$n^2/2$ flops.
iii Solve the system $R x = d$ —$n^2/2$ flops.

Hence the cost is about half that of the general algorithm in the amount of work. In addition, we save on not having to do pivoting.

The second property has to do with the pattern of the nonzero elements of A. Specifically, we are interested in the case where they appear only in a band about the main diagonal. More formally, $A = (a_{i,j})$ is a *band* matrix whenever there exist integers $\underline{k}, \bar{k} \geq 0$ such that, for $1 \leq i, j \leq n$,

$$\text{if} \quad \text{either} \quad i - j > \underline{k} \quad \text{or} \quad j - i > \bar{k}, \quad \text{then} \quad a_{i,j} = 0$$

The number $k = \underline{k} + \bar{k} + 1$ is called the *band width* of A. An example of a 6×6 band matrix with $\underline{k} = 1$ and $\bar{k} = 2$ is

$$A = \begin{bmatrix} a_{1,1} & a_{1,2} & a_{1,3} & 0 & 0 & 0 \\ a_{2,1} & a_{2,2} & a_{2,3} & a_{2,4} & 0 & 0 \\ 0 & a_{3,2} & a_{3,3} & a_{3,4} & a_{3,5} & 0 \\ 0 & 0 & a_{4,3} & a_{4,4} & a_{4,5} & a_{4,6} \\ 0 & 0 & 0 & a_{5,4} & a_{5,5} & a_{5,6} \\ 0 & 0 & 0 & 0 & a_{6,5} & a_{6,6} \end{bmatrix} \rightarrow \begin{bmatrix} 0 & a_{1,1} & a_{1,2} & a_{1,3} \\ a_{2,1} & a_{2,2} & a_{2,3} & a_{2,4} \\ a_{3,2} & a_{3,3} & a_{3,4} & a_{3,5} \\ a_{4,3} & a_{4,4} & a_{4,5} & a_{4,6} \\ a_{5,4} & a_{5,5} & a_{5,6} & 0 \\ a_{6,5} & a_{6,6} & 0 & 0 \end{bmatrix} = \text{APAC}$$

The usual way of storing a band matrix in packed form is indicated by the array APAC. We use a rectangular array of size $k \times n$ and store each diagonal in the band as a column of this array. For this example, it is apparent that not much space has been saved but, in many applications, it is usual to have $k \ll n$ so that the savings in storage are very worthwhile (kn locations as opposed to n^2). But the real saving with band matrices comes in the operations count. In the elimination part of the algorithm, we can exploit the fact that there are already zeros below the band (below the $\underline{k}$th subdiagonal) so there is no point in going through the elimination procedure on these elements. Similar savings can also be made during the back substitution. An operations count for each part of the algorithm is

i Decompose $PA = LU$—$\leq (n - 1)\underline{k}(k - 1)$.
ii Solve $Ld = Pb$ —$\leq (n - 1)\underline{k}$.
iii Solve $U x = d$ —$\leq (n - 1)(k - 1)$.

The bounds represent the worst case in which pivoting may be necessary at each stage with the result that $\bar{k}$ can increase to $k-1$. To illustrate the savings one can achieve, suppose $n = 100$ and $\underline{k} = \bar{k} = 3$. Then $k = 7$ and something less than 2700 flops are required if we exploit the band structure whereas the full Gauss elimination algorithm would require over 330,000 flops! If, in addition, A is symmetric, positive definite then further savings can be made. Therefore, it can be exceedingly worthwhile to use a special band matrix routine—symmetric or not, as the case may be—when the structure is present in a problem.

The third property is sparseness. By this we mean that only a very small number ($\leq 5\%$) of the elements of A are nonzero. Large band matrices with very small band width are certainly sparse but we will exclude these from consideration and assume that the pattern of the nonzero entries is more or less random. This type of matrix occurs frequently in the numerical solution of partial differential equations using the so-called "finite element method." Since a sparse matrix has so few nonzero elements, there is an obvious potential for savings on computation costs and on storage. To store A, we can save a lot of space by storing only the nonzero entries. However, in the absence of any structure in the pattern of nonzero elements, we must also record the location of each element as well as its value. This is done by using rather sophisticated data structures such as doubly linked lists. But a disadvantage of such data structures compared to simple two-dimensional arrays is the overhead in managing them. However, we are willing to put up with some extra overhead in this respect as a small price for substantial savings in storage and computation costs. The crucial factor affecting the amount of the saving is the *fill-in*, that is, the number of nonzero elements in the LU factorization minus the number in A at the outset. The idea is that some of the entries that start out as zero become nonzero during the elimination and usually remain nonzero. Not only do we have to access these additional elements during the computation but there is also the problem of inserting them into the data structure at the time they arise. In the case of a doubly linked list, for example, we must record the value of the new element and also adjust the linkages (pointers) in order to record its location in the matrix. The latter operation takes some time. Therefore, one of the goals of a "sparse matrix algorithm" is to try to keep down the amount of fill-in as much as possible. This is accomplished through the pivoting strategy.

Up to now we have only considered one criterion for determining the pivoting strategy—to ensure that the multipliers are ≤ 1 in magnitude. This was in order to minimize the growth of round-off error. We will now use the criterion of trying to minimize the amount of fill-in. To illustrate the difference in fill-in, consider the following 6×6 example.

$$A = \begin{bmatrix} x & x & 0 & 0 & x & 0 \\ x & 0 & x & x & 0 & x \\ 0 & x & 0 & 0 & x & 0 \\ x & 0 & 0 & 0 & 0 & x \\ x & 0 & x & 0 & 0 & 0 \\ 0 & x & 0 & x & 0 & 0 \end{bmatrix} \quad \text{and} \quad PA = \begin{bmatrix} x & 0 & 0 & 0 & 0 & x \\ 0 & x & 0 & 0 & x & 0 \\ x & 0 & x & 0 & 0 & 0 \\ 0 & x & 0 & x & 0 & 0 \\ x & x & 0 & 0 & x & 0 \\ x & 0 & x & x & 0 & x \end{bmatrix}$$

$$NPIV = \begin{bmatrix} 4 \\ 3 \\ 5 \\ 6 \\ 6 \\ -1 \end{bmatrix}$$

The matrix PA is identical to A except that the rows have been interchanged using the pivoting strategy defined by NPIV. Note that x's have been used because we are only concerned with the locations of the nonzero entries and not with the actual values. If we do Gauss elimination (in place) with no pivoting on each of A and PA, the resulting LU arrays would have the following configurations, respectively, of nonzero entries

$$\begin{bmatrix} x & x & 0 & 0 & x & 0 \\ x & \emptyset & x & x & \emptyset & x \\ 0 & x & \emptyset & \emptyset & x & \emptyset \\ x & \emptyset & \emptyset & \emptyset & \emptyset & x \\ x & \emptyset & x & \emptyset & \emptyset & \emptyset \\ 0 & x & \emptyset & x & \emptyset & \emptyset \end{bmatrix} \quad \begin{bmatrix} x & 0 & 0 & 0 & 0 & x \\ 0 & x & 0 & 0 & x & 0 \\ x & 0 & x & 0 & 0 & \emptyset \\ 0 & x & 0 & x & \emptyset & 0 \\ x & x & 0 & 0 & x & \emptyset \\ x & 0 & x & x & \emptyset & x \end{bmatrix}$$

The fill-in is indicated by the "$\emptyset$" entries. It is 16 for A and only 4 for PA. The criterion we used for determining the pivoting stregy was to put the row with the most number of nonzero elements at the bottom and work up so that the (new) top row has the fewest number of nonzero elements. The reasoning is that, by eliminating with the sparser rows first, we are more likely to keep the amount of fill-in down. Unfortunately, this strategy does not always work out (see Exercise 1.18) so we are faced with the question as to what is a good stregy for minimizing the amount of fill-in. It turns out that a method for determining a pivoting strategy that is "optimal" in the sense that the fill-in is minimal is known. It is based on a result—the minimal degree algorithm—from the field of graph theory but it is beyond the scope of this book. In any event, it is not a practical method because it requires $0(n^3)$ operations so there would be no savings over a standard Gauss elimination method. Consequently, sparse matrix routines back off from trying to determine the optimal pivoting strategy and settle for some extra fill-in in exchange for a relatively quick determination of a pivoting strategy that can generally be expected to keep the fill-in down to a tolerable level.

We note that, since the criterion for determining the pivoting strategy is based entirely on the locations of the nonzero elements and not on their specific values, the strategy can be determined and applied at the outset. This is what a sparse subroutine will do. It is called a "preprocessing" stage. After this, the Gauss elimination algorithm is invoked. According to the above discussion, it should be done without pivoting so as not to negate the preprocessing effort to control fill-in. However, there is still a danger of too much round-off error being introduced if the pivots are allowed to get too large. Therefore it is usual for a sparse routine to monitor the sizes of the pivots and allow some row interchanges during the elimination in order to keep them under control. In this way, the routine tries to strike a reasonable balance between accuracy and cost.

A final word is to emphasize that, since sparse routines use complicated data structures (which substantially increases access time for elements of the matrix) and spend some time preprocessing the matrix, such routines are only advantageous for very large (sparse) systems. In this regard, such systems do not arise in a very wide variety of problems so a general purpose software package will not normally contain sparse routines. Instead, they can be found in specialized packages such as those for finite element analysis.

2.1.5. Subroutines

By and large, the linear-equation-solving algorithms that are found in subroutine packages are designed on the basis of the foregoing ideas with one possible exception. This is that iterative improvement may not have been included in the package. The LINPACK package is an example. The reasoning for this is as follows. Iterative improvement requires an extended precision capability in order to compute residuals. Therefore, assuming that full machine hardware precision is used for the Gauss elimination and back substitution, the use of extended precision will depend on the availability of it through system microprograms. But, since not all computer systems have such a facility, the designers of a package are faced with the problem of whether or not to provide a subroutine which depends on a system facility that is not always available. Due to this fact and its implication with respect to portability of programs from one system to another, the designers of LINPACK decided not to implement iterative improvement. However, in the LINPACK Guide [10, p. I4], it is indicated that if extended precision is available, an iterative improvement routine [implementing (2.29)] can easily be written and an example is given. On the other hand, both the IMSL and NAG packages do have iterative improvement subroutines. In the case of NAG they are built into "black box" routines that give "high accuracy" solutions.

For packages that do not provide iterative improvement, there is the problem of estimating the condition number of A in order to assess how good the approximate solution $\hat{x}$ is. This is usually done within the decomposition subroutines. Hence, a parameter list for such subroutines will be of the form

$$\text{DCOMP(N,NDIM,NPIV,A,CONDA)}$$

The argument CONDA is for returning the estimate of cond(A). It can be used to test for numerical singularity similar to the use if IND in (2.20). The method for estimating cond(A) is beyond the scope of this book. Briefly, it involves the solution of two linear systems having A as the coefficient matrix so that the extra cost will be about $2n^2$ flops—the same as one iteration of iterative improvement. Although this is insignificant compared to the $n^3/3$ flops required for the LU factorization, it still costs something and, on those occasions where one does not want an estimate for cond(A), a saving can be made by omitting it. Hence, it is usual to find decomposition routines in pairs—one that computes an estimate for cond(A) and one that does not. The user is expected to choose the more appropriate one for his or her particular application.[8]

Finally, we remark that the special subroutines for solving symmetric systems generally assume that the matrix A is stored in packed form. This can be an inconvenience and so, to facilitate the use of such subroutines, a software package will often provide utility subroutines for converting from one storage mode to another. A routine for converting a symmetric matrix from full to packed form would be of the form

$$\text{CONVFS(N,NDIM,A,APAC)}$$

where A is a two-dimensional array containing the matrix in its standard form and APAC is a vector of length at least $n(n + 1)/2$. On return from CONVFS, APAC will contain the original matrix in a form suitable for use by symmetric linear equation subroutines. The price one pays for this convenience is extra storage. However, one still gains the reduction in computation time for solving the system and, in any event, this is the more

---

[8]If, for instance, iterative improvement has been implemented by the user, then estimating cond(A) during the LU decomposition is redundant. Admittedly, this estimate is usually better but all we get is the estimate, there is no improvement in x.

significant saving to be gained by exploiting symmetry. Similarly, there are utility subroutines for converting band matrices to packed form.

2.2. EIGENVALUES AND EIGENVECTORS

We now turn to the problem of computing the eigenvalues and eigen-vectors of an $n \times n$ matrix A. The methods for doing this are reasonably easy to describe but subroutine implementations of the methods are exceedingly complex. This is because there is such a variety of special cases that a routine must be able to recognize and handle automatically— clustered eigenvalues and defective matrices[9] are examples. The methods for dealing with these special cases are beyond the level of this book. Therefore, we limit ourselves to describing the basic algorithms.

2.2.1. The QR Algorithm

The QR algorithm is a method for computing the eigenvalues of a matrix. As a means of motivating its description, we first discuss, in the context of the general format (2.1), the underlying idea of computational methods for eigenvalues.

The eigenvalues of an $n \times n$ matrix A are defined to be the roots of its characteristic polynomial $p(z) = \det(zI - A)$. For example, if

$$A = \begin{bmatrix} 3 & -6 \\ 1 & -4 \end{bmatrix} \quad \text{then} \quad zI - A = \begin{bmatrix} z-3 & 6 \\ -1 & z+4 \end{bmatrix}$$

and $p(z) = z^2 + z - 6$, so that the eigenvalues of A are $z = 2, -3$. Hence, the eigenvalues of a given matrix can be found by determining the charac-teristic polynomial $p(z)$ and then computing its roots. However, except in the case of 2×2 matrices, it is an exceedingly difficult job to determine $p(z)$ explicitly. To do it on a computer would require the use of a symbol manipulation system and this can be very expensive. In addition, once $p(z)$ has been determined, there is still the problem of finding its roots. But

---

[9]A matrix is *defective* if it does not have n linearly independent eigenvectors. Consider, for example, the matrices

$$A = \begin{bmatrix} 3 & 0 \\ 0 & 3 \end{bmatrix} \quad \text{and} \quad B = \begin{bmatrix} 1 & 1 \\ -4 & 5 \end{bmatrix}$$

Each has eigenvalues $\mu_1 = \mu_2 = 3$. A has two linearly independent eigenvectors $a_1 = [1, 0]^T$ and $a_2 = [0, 1]^T$. On the other hand, $b = [1, 2]^T$ is an eigenvector of B and all others are a constant multiple of it. Hence B is defective. This feature is equivalent to ill conditioning and can be troublesome in computing both the eigenvalues and eigenvectors.

there is a case where all this work is unnecessary. This is when A is *quasi upper triangular*.[10] For example, suppose we have the matrix

$$A = \begin{bmatrix} 2 & 5 & -1 & 3 & 0 & 0 \\ 0 & 1 & -1 & 6 & -3 & 9 \\ 0 & 1 & 1 & 2 & 4 & 0 \\ 0 & 0 & 0 & 4 & 1 & -3 \\ 0 & 0 & 0 & 6 & 3 & 1 \\ 0 & 0 & 0 & 0 & 0 & -8 \end{bmatrix}$$

If we partition it in the following way

$$A = \begin{bmatrix} 2 & 5 & -1 & 3 & 0 & 6 \\ 0 & 1 & -1 & 6 & -3 & 9 \\ 0 & 1 & 1 & 2 & 4 & 0 \\ 0 & 0 & 0 & 4 & 1 & -3 \\ 0 & 0 & 0 & 6 & 3 & 1 \\ 0 & 0 & 0 & 0 & 0 & -8 \end{bmatrix} = \begin{bmatrix} A_{1,1} & A_{1,2} & A_{1,3} & A_{1,4} \\ 0 & A_{2,2} & A_{2,3} & A_{2,4} \\ 0 & 0 & A_{3,3} & A_{3,4} \\ 0 & 0 & 0 & A_{4,4} \end{bmatrix}$$

then it is easy to compute the characteristic polynomial

$$p(z) = \det(zI - A_{1,1}) \det(zI - A_{2,2}) \det(zI - A_{3,3}) \det(zI - A_{4,4})$$
$$= (z - 2)(z^2 - 2z + 2)(z^2 - 7z + 6)(z + 8)$$

Moreover, since $p(z)$ is conveniently factored as the product of linear and quadratic terms, there is almost no work required to compute its roots. They are $z = 2$, $1 \pm i$, 1, 6, -8, where $i = \sqrt{-1}$. Similarly, the same kind of result holds for arbitrary $n \times n$ quasi-upper-triangular matrices. The simplicity of solving the eigenvalue problem in the quasi-triangular case makes this form a good candidate for the "reduced" problem in (2.1) and, indeed,

---

[10] An $n \times n$ matrix $A = (a_{i,j})$ is *upper triangular* if all of its below-diagonal elements are zero, that is,

$$a_{i,j} = 0 \qquad i > j$$

For a *quasi* upper triangular matrix, we relax this definition a little by permitting a few elements on the first subdiagonal to be nonzero also. The restriction is that we do not allow adjacent nonzero elements along this subdiagonal, that is,

if $a_{i,i-1} \neq 0$ then both $a_{i-1,i-2}$ and $a_{i+1,i} = 0$

In other words, A can have some 2×2 nonzero submatrices along its diagonal. The matrix above is an example.

Similar definitions can be made for *lower triangular* and *quasi lower triangular* matrices.

this is the form that is used in practice. The reduction process [step (a)] uses the concept of similarity transformations. An $n \times n$ matrix B is defined to be *similar* to A if there exists an $n \times n$ nonsingular matrix S such that

$$B = S^{-1}AS$$

A well-known result in linear algebra states that if A and B are similar, then their eigenvalues are identical. Hence, the basic idea of a computational algorithm for finding the eigenvalues of an $n \times n$ matrix A is to:

(a) Find a quasi upper triangular matrix B that is similar to A.
(b) Determine the eigenvalues of B.

As we will see, the process of reducing A to quasi-triangular form is quite involved. Therefore, since step (b) is essentially a trivial calculation, virtually all of the computational effort is expended on step (a).

Unfortunately, the reduction of a matrix to quasi-triangular form cannot be accomplished in a finite number of steps. We therefore settle for an algorithm that will produce a matrix B whose elements below the "quasi-diagonal" are sufficiently small. An iterative procedure is used whereby matrices $A_1(= A), A_2, A_3, \ldots$ are generated successively. Each is similar to its predecessor (so that the eigenvalues are the same). In addition, each is closer to a quasi-upper-triangular matrix in that the sum of squares of the elements below the quasi-diagonal is smaller than that of its predecessor. The QR algorithm, or some variant of it, is a procedure for accomplishing this. In order to describe it, we need to introduce some concepts.

We begin with a definition. An $n \times n$ matrix Q is *orthogonal* if $Q^T Q = I$, that is, $Q^T = Q^{-1}$. Note that Q^T is also orthogonal and, if Q_1, Q_2 are both orthogonal, then so are the products $Q_1 Q_2$ and $Q_2 Q_1$. The type of orthogonal matrices we shall be concerned with are based on the form

$$Q_B = \begin{bmatrix} \cos \theta & -\sin \theta \\ \sin \theta & \cos \theta \end{bmatrix}$$

where θ is an arbitrary real number[11]. We can construct an $n \times n$ orthogonal matrix $Q_{i,j}$ by taking the identity matrix and inserting Q_B in the ith

---

[11] In the language of linear transformations on vector spaces, Q_B corresponds to a transformation which simply rotates vectors in the plane through the angle θ.

and jth rows and columns. For example, if $n = 6$, $i = 5$, $j = 2$, we would have

$$Q_{5,2} = \begin{bmatrix} 1 & 0 & 0 & 0 & 0 & 0 \\ 0 & \cos\theta_{5,2} & 0 & 0 & -\sin\theta_{5,2} & 0 \\ 0 & 0 & 1 & 0 & 0 & 0 \\ 0 & 0 & 0 & 1 & 0 & 0 \\ 0 & \sin\theta_{5,2} & 0 & 0 & \cos\theta_{5,2} & 0 \\ 0 & 0 & 0 & 0 & 0 & 1 \end{bmatrix}$$

In six-dimensional space, $Q_{5,2}$ corresponds to the transformation that rotates vectors in the plane generated by the x_5- and x_2-axes through the angle $\theta_{5,2}$.

The QR algorithm is based on the *QR factorization* of a matrix:

> Given an $n \times n$ matrix A, there exists an orthogonal matrix Q and an upper triangular matrix R such that $A = QR$.

We remark that the upper triangular matrix R in this factorization of A is not the same as U in the LU factorization discussed in the previous section. The following example illustrates how Q and R can be determined. Computations are done using three-digit arithmetic. Let

$$(2.32) \quad A = \begin{bmatrix} 4 & 3 & 2 & 1 \\ 5 & 6 & -7 & 8 \\ 0 & -2 & 1 & 9 \\ 0 & 0 & 3 & -4 \end{bmatrix}$$

First we annihilate the (2, 1) element of A. To do this, we form a 4×4 orthogonal matrix $Q_{2,1}$ as indicated above, choosing $\theta_{2,1}$ so that the (2, 1) element of the product

$$Q_{2,1}^T A = \begin{bmatrix} \cos\theta_{2,1} & \sin\theta_{2,1} & 0 & 0 \\ -\sin\theta_{2,1} & \cos\theta_{2,1} & 0 & 0 \\ 0 & 0 & 1 & 0 \\ 0 & 0 & 0 & 1 \end{bmatrix} \begin{bmatrix} 4 & 3 & 2 & 1 \\ 5 & 6 & -7 & 8 \\ 0 & -2 & 1 & 9 \\ 0 & 0 & 3 & -4 \end{bmatrix}$$

is zero, that is,

$$-a_{1,1}\sin\theta_{2,1} + a_{2,1}\cos\theta_{2,1} = 0$$

From this, we have $\theta_{2,1} = \tan^{-1}(a_{2,1}/a_{1,1}) = \tan^{-1}(5/4)$ and

$$\sin\theta_{2,1} = \frac{a_{2,1}}{\sqrt{(a_{1,1}^2 + a_{2,2}^2)}} = \frac{5}{\sqrt{41}} \doteq 0.781$$

$$\cos \theta_{2,1} = \frac{a_{1,1}}{\sqrt{(a_{1,1}^2 + a_{2,1}^2)}} = \frac{4}{\sqrt{41}} \doteq 0.625$$

Then

$$Q_{2,1}^T A = \begin{bmatrix} 0.625 & 0.781 & 0 & 0 \\ -0.781 & 0.625 & 0 & 0 \\ 0 & 0 & 1 & 0 \\ 0 & 0 & 0 & 1 \end{bmatrix} \begin{bmatrix} 4 & 3 & 2 & 1 \\ 5 & 6 & -7 & 8 \\ 0 & -2 & 1 & 9 \\ 0 & 0 & 3 & -4 \end{bmatrix}$$

$$= \begin{bmatrix} 6.41 & 6.56 & -4.22 & 6.87 \\ 0 & 1.41 & -5.94 & 4.22 \\ 0 & -2 & 1 & 9 \\ 0 & 0 & 3 & -4 \end{bmatrix}$$

Next, we annihilate the $(3, 2)$ element by forming $Q_{3,2}$ and choosing $\theta_{3,2}$ so that the $(3, 2)$ element of $Q_{3,2}^T(Q_{2,1}^T A)$ is zero. We find that $\theta_{3,2} = \tan^{-1}(a_{3,2}/a_{2,2}) = \tan^{-1}(-2/1.41)$ so that $\sin \theta_{3,2} \doteq -0.816$ and $\cos \theta_{3,2} \doteq 0.576$. Then we have

$$Q_{3,2}^T(Q_{2,1}^T A) = \begin{bmatrix} 1 & 0 & 0 & 0 \\ 0 & 0.576 & -0.816 & 0 \\ 0 & 0.816 & 0.576 & 0 \\ 0 & 0 & 0 & 1 \end{bmatrix} \begin{bmatrix} 6.41 & 6.56 & -4.22 & 6.87 \\ 0 & 1.41 & -5.94 & 4.22 \\ 0 & -2 & 1 & 9 \\ 0 & 0 & 3 & -4 \end{bmatrix}$$

$$= \begin{bmatrix} 6.41 & 6.56 & -4.22 & 6.87 \\ 0 & 2.44 & -4.24 & -4.91 \\ 0 & 0 & -4.27 & 8.63 \\ 0 & 0 & 3 & -4 \end{bmatrix}$$

Note that the $(2, 1)$ element remains zero. This point is an important aspect of the process: those elements that were previously annihilated remain so. Finally, we form $Q_{4,3}$ with $\theta_{4,3} = \tan^{-1}(3/-4.27)$ and premultiply to get the upper triangular matrix R:

$$Q_{4,3}^T(Q_{3,2}^T Q_{2,1}^T A) = \begin{bmatrix} 1 & 0 & 0 & 0 \\ 0 & 1 & 0 & 0 \\ 0 & 0 & -0.818 & 0.575 \\ 0 & 0 & -0.575 & -0.818 \end{bmatrix}$$

$$\times \begin{bmatrix} 6.41 & 6.56 & -4.22 & 6.87 \\ 0 & 2.44 & -4.24 & -4.91 \\ 0 & 0 & -4.27 & 8.63 \\ 0 & 0 & 3 & -4 \end{bmatrix}$$

$$= \begin{bmatrix} 6.41 & 6.56 & -4.22 & 6.87 \\ 0 & 2.44 & -4.24 & -4.91 \\ 0 & 0 & 5.22 & -9.36 \\ 0 & 0 & 0 & -1.69 \end{bmatrix} = R$$

Now if we define the (orthogonal) matrix $Q = Q_{2,1}Q_{3,2}Q_{4,3}$, then $Q^T = Q_{4,3}^T Q_{3,2}^T Q_{2,1}^T$ and the last line can be rewritten as

$$Q^T A = R \qquad \text{or} \qquad A = QR$$

which is the factorization we sought. We emphasize that this is a factorization of A and not a similarity transformation. The eigenvalues of R (which are simply its diagonal elements) have no direct relationship whatever with those of A. We can, however, use this type of factorization to compute easily a matrix that is similar to A. This is the idea of the QR algorithm.

As stated above, the QR algorithm is an iterative process. We define $A_1 = A$. Then, given the matrix A_s from the sth iteration, we

(2.33)   i   Factor $A_s = Q_s R_s$.
        ii   Compute $A_{s+1} = R_s Q_s$.

The iterations are to continue until a convergence criterion is met. Note that the second step is simply a matter of reversing the order of multiplication of the factors computed in the first step. This is the QR *algorithm*. Each iteration of it involves a QR factorization of a matrix [step (i)] and then a matrix multiplication.

The mathematical validity of the algorithm is easily established. We must show that the eigenvalues of A are retained through each iteration. Noting that $R_s = Q_s^T A_s$, we have

(2.34) $A_{s+1} = R_s Q_s = Q_s^T A_s Q_s = Q_s^{-1} A_s Q_s$

Hence A_{s+1} can be viewed as being obtained from its predecessor A_s by a similarity transformation so it will have the same eigenvalues as A_s. The transformation (2.34) of A_s to A_{s+1} is generally referred to as the QR *transformation*. In the same way, A_s is similar to A_{s-1}, and so on. Therefore each A_{s+1} has the same eigenvalues as $A_1 = A$.

For numerical validity, we must consider the effects of computing in finite, rather than infinite, precision. Since the relationship (2.34) between A_{s+1} and A_s will not hold exactly, there will be a perturbation of the eigenvalues in each iteration of (2.33). We want this perturbation to be as small as possible and herein lies one of the virtues of the QR algorithm.

Each iteration is effectively an orthogonal transformation which, from a numerical analysis point of view is very stable, that is, the perturbation due to round-off are minimal. This is because, mathematically, orthogonal transformations are length and shape preserving[12]. Numerically, they will have almost the same property so round-off errors from one stage are less likely to be magnified in subsequent computations.

We have yet to consider the question of convergence of the successive iterates A_s to quasi upper triangular form. This is an important point since there is no use in doing all the computation if we cannot be guaranteed that we will ultimately arrive at the "simpler problem" of (2.1). The mathematical proof of convergence of the QR algorithm consists of showing that the sum of squares of the elements below the quasi-diagonal of A_{s+1} is less than that of A_s. In the case that all the entries of A are real, this result has been established (see [33] or [29]). However, for complex matrices, a rigorous proof is not yet known. Nevertheless, since wide experience with the method indicates that it does indeed converge in the complex case, subroutines have been written for it.

We remark that, for complex matrices, the reduction is to upper triangular form. The quasi upper triangular form is used for real matrices in order to avoid the need to do complex arithmetic. Suppose, for example, that A is real but some of its eigenvalues are complex. We know that there exists an S (not necessarily orthogonal) such that $S^{-1}AS = B$ is upper triangular. The diagonal of B consists of the eigenvalues of A so B must be a complex matrix and, consequently, S will be complex too. Therefore, in order to reduce A to upper triangular form by similarity transformations it is impossible to avoid the occurrence of complex numbers unless A has only real eigenvalues. On the other hand, the reduction to quasi upper triangular form can always be done in real arithmetic after which any complex eigenvalues can be found by applying the quadratic formula (using real arithmetic). Since the cost of complex arithmetic is at least twice that of real arithmetic, the savings from using the quasi upper triangular form for real matrices are significant.

---

[12]Let A be an $n \times n$ matrix, let O be an $n \times n$ orthogonal matrix and set $B = O^T A O$. A and B can be viewed as linear transformations on an n-dimensional vector space V_n. The *length-preserving* property means that

$$\|B\mathbf{x}\| = \|A\mathbf{x}\| \qquad \text{for any } \mathbf{x} \in V_n$$

where $\|\cdot\|$ is the ℓ_2 vector norm (2.22). This result follows from the fact that $\|O\|^2 = 1$ (see Exercise 2.3). From (2.25), we will therefore have $\|B\| = \|A\|$ (i.e., the two matrices have the same length). By *shape preserving*, we mean that if K is some geometrical shape in V_n, then in the image space, the new objects AK and BK will be similar in shape. This combined with the length-preserving property, means that AK and BK are congruent.

2.2.2. Subroutine Implementation

The QR algorithm turns out to be very efficient if the matrix A is in *upper Hessenberg form*, that is,

$$a_{i,j} = 0 \qquad \text{if } i \geq j + 2$$

In words, this means that all elements below the first subdiagonal are zero. The matrix (2.32) is upper Hessenberg. Of course, it is not often that this form arises in practice but we will discuss this point later. First we look at the reasons why the Hessenberg form makes the algorithm efficient.

Step (i) of each iteration (2.33) of the QR algorithm consists of the QR factorization of A_s. The procedure for doing this was illustrated in our example, that is, the successive premultiplication by suitably chosen orthogonal matrices in order to annihilate the below-diagonal elements of A_s. It follows from the example that premultiplying by, say, $Q_{i+1,i}^T$ only alters the elements in rows i and $i + 1$ of A. Each new element in each of these rows is the result of a computation of the form

$$a = b \cos \theta + c \sin \theta$$

which requires the execution of 1 flop and 1M. Now if A_s is upper Hessenberg, there are only $n - 1$ elements below the diagonal that need to be annihilated. Referring to the example again, we can see that the number of elements changed when premultiplying by

$$
\begin{array}{lll}
Q_{2,1}^T & \text{is} \quad n & + (n-1) \\
Q_{3,2}^T & \text{is} \ (n-1) + (n-2) \\
\quad \vdots & & \\
Q_{n,n-1}^T & \text{is} \quad 2 & + \quad 1
\end{array}
$$

The total is $n^2 - 1$. Noting that the computation of $\sin \theta_{i+1,i}$ and $\cos \theta_{i+1,i}$ at each stage requires the evaluation of a square root, we have the result that

> If A_s is upper Hessenberg, the operations count for step (i) of the QR algorithm is n^2 flops and M's plus $(n - 1)$ square roots.

By way of comparison, if A_s were full, there would be $n(n - 1)/2$ elements below the diagonal to annihilate and this would require about $n^3/3$ flops and M's plus $n(n - 1)/2$ square roots.

The second factor in the efficiency of the QR algorithm is the invariance of the upper Hessenberg form under the QR transformation (2.34), that is, if A_s is upper Hessenberg then so is A_{s+1}. Hence, if A_1 is upper Hessenberg in the first place, we are assured that this form is retained by each subsequent A_s. To illustrate this invariance, we again refer to the example. The orthogonal matrix Q is

$$Q = Q_{2,1}Q_{3,2}Q_{4,3} = \begin{bmatrix} 0.625 & -0.450 & 0.521 & 0.366 \\ 0.781 & 0.360 & -0.417 & -0.293 \\ 0 & -0.816 & -0.471 & -0.331 \\ 0 & 0 & 0.575 & -0.818 \end{bmatrix}$$

which is upper Hessenberg. (This will always be true when A is upper Hessenberg.) Then, from step (ii) of (2.33), $A_{s+1} = R_s Q_s$ is the product of an upper triangular matrix times an upper Hessenberg matrix and it is easy to show that the result will be upper Hessenberg. For our example,

$$RQ = \begin{bmatrix} 6.41 & 6.56 & -4.22 & 6.87 \\ 0 & 2.44 & -4.24 & -4.91 \\ 0 & 0 & 5.22 & -9.36 \\ 0 & 0 & 0 & -1.69 \end{bmatrix}$$

$$\times \begin{bmatrix} 0.625 & -0.450 & 0.521 & 0.366 \\ 0.781 & 0.360 & -0.417 & -0.293 \\ 0 & -0.816 & -0.471 & -0.331 \\ 0 & 0 & 0.575 & -0.818 \end{bmatrix}$$

$$= \begin{bmatrix} 9.13 & 2.92 & 6.54 & -3.80 \\ 1.91 & 4.34 & -1.84 & 4.70 \\ 0 & -4.26 & -7.84 & 5.93 \\ 0 & 0 & -0.972 & 1.38 \end{bmatrix}$$

In practice, the matrix Q is not formed at all. It turns out to be more efficient to multiply, successively, on the right of R by each $Q_{i+1,i}$ in the appropriate order. Since multiplication on the right by $Q_{i+1,i}$ will only affect the ith and $(i + 1)$th columns, we have, by an analysis similar to that above:

If A_s is upper Hessenberg, then the operations count for step (ii) of the QR algorithm is n^2 flops and M's

Therefore,

Assuming upper Hessenberg form, the operations count for each iteration of the QR algorithm is $2n^2$ flops and M's plus $(n - 1)$ square roots.

Now we consider the assumption that our matrix is in upper Hessenberg form at the outset. This is rarely true but it can be shown that,

Given an arbitrary real matrix A, there exists an orthogonal matrix O such that $A_1 = O^T A O$ is upper Hessenberg.

We will not describe the algorithm for computing A_1 except to say that the underlying idea is similar to the one for computing a QR factorization, that is, the successive annihilation of elements of A below the first subdiagonal. The difference is that when we multiply on the left by $Q_{i,j}^T$, we also have to multiply on the right by $Q_{i,j}$ in order to retain similarity. Actually, a more sophisticated technique— using what are known as Householder trans- formations—is employed whereby all elements down a column below the first subdiagonal can be eliminated simultaneously. The amount of work in reducing A to Hessenberg form A_1 in this manner turns out to be $5n^3/3 + O(n^2)$ flops. Again, since orthogonal transformations are used, the process is very stable.

From the above discussion it is evident that an eigenvalue subroutine based on the QR algorithm consists of three stages:

(2.35)
1. Reduce A to upper Hessenberg form A_1.
2. Apply the QR algorithm to A_1.
3. Compute the eigenvalues.

If we assume that m iterations of QR are required in step (2), the operations count is

1. $5n^3/3 + O(n^2)$ flops.
2. $2mn^2$ flops and M's plus $m(n-1)$ square roots.
3. A few square roots, perhaps.

Since it is usual to achieve convergence in at most n iterations, we generally say that QR requires about $4n^3$ flops plus n^2 square roots.

2.2.3. Special Properties

As in the case of linear equations, considerable savings in time and storage requirements can be made if A has some special form, so special subrou- tines that exploit these features have been written. Symmetry is one such property. (It is not necessary for A to be positive definite too.) The reduction to Hessenberg form $A_1 = O^T A O$ will preserve symmetry so A_1 will be tridiagonal—a band matrix with bandwidth 3. This structure will be preserved by the QR iteration (2.33). By using these facts, it turns out that each iteration of QR only requires about $8(n-1)$ flops and M's plus $(n-1)$ square roots. The reduction to tridiagonal form will required about $5n^3/6$ flops. We note that, due to the substantial savings from exploiting the tridiagonal structure for the QR iteration, the latter cost is the only significant factor in the total.

On the other hand, there is no advantage to be gained from sparsity unless there is a special structure such as bandedness. The reduction to Hessenberg form will usually produce an A_1 that is not sparse. However, if A is banded, A_1 will be also. If the bandwidth is small relative to the order n of the matrix, then it is worthwhile using a special subroutine which assumes a band structure. For general sparse matrices, research work is currently underway on the development of algorithms based on methods that retain the sparsity pattern of A.

2.2.4. Eigenvectors

The method generally used for determining eigenvectors is called *inverse iteration*. It is based on the so-called *power method*, which we describe briefly. Suppose B is an $n \times n$ matrix with eigenvalues β_k, $1 \le k \le n$, which are ordered as follows:

$$(2.36) \quad |\beta_1| > |\beta_2| \ge |\beta_3| \ge \cdots \ge |\beta_n|$$

that is, β_1 is a strictly *dominant* eigenvalue. Let $\mathbf{b}_k$, $1 \le k \le n$, be the corresponding "normalized" eigenvectors, that is,

$$B\mathbf{b}_k = \beta_k \mathbf{b}_k \qquad \text{with } \|\mathbf{b}_k\| = 1 \qquad 1 \le k \le n$$

Now, let $\mathbf{y}^{(0)} \ne \mathbf{0}$ be any initial vector and define $\mathbf{x}^{(0)} = \mathbf{y}^{(0)}/\|\mathbf{y}^{(0)}\|$. Then, the power method iteration is

$$(2.37) \quad \begin{aligned} \mathbf{y}^{(r)} &= B\mathbf{x}^{(r-1)} \\ \mathbf{x}^{(r)} &= \frac{1}{\|\mathbf{y}^{(r)}\|} \cdot \mathbf{y}^{(r)} \end{aligned} \qquad r = 1, 2, \ldots$$

It can be shown [6, p. 209] that, due to the dominance of β_1,

$$\lim_{r \to \infty} \mathbf{x}^{(r)} = \alpha \mathbf{b}_1$$

where α is a constant. The name "power method" comes from the fact that

$$\mathbf{x}^{(r)} = c_r B\mathbf{x}^{(r-1)} = c_r c_{r-1} B^2 \mathbf{x}^{(r-2)} = \cdots = cB^r \mathbf{x}^{(0)}$$

where $c_r = \|\mathbf{y}^{(r)}\|^{-1}$, and so on. In words, $\mathbf{x}^{(r)}$ can be viewed as being obtained directly from $\mathbf{x}^{(0)}$ by multiplication by a (normalizing) constant c and the rth power of B. The rate of convergence of $\mathbf{x}^{(r)}$ to $\mathbf{b}_1$ turns out to depend directly on the rate at which the ratio $(|\beta_2|/|\beta_1|)^r \to 0$ as r increases. Therefore, if $|\beta_2| \ll |\beta_1|$, that is, if β_1 is "very" dominant, convergence will be very fast.

Let us return to the problem of finding the eigenvectors of an $n \times n$

matrix A. We assume, for simplicity, that the eigenvalues μ_k, $1 \leq k \leq n$, are distinct and reasonably well separated. Let the (normalized) eigenvectors of A be $\mathbf{a}_k$, $1 \leq k \leq n$. Suppose we have obtained (by the QR algorithm) approximate values $\hat{\mu}_k$ for the eigenvalues. Choose one of them, say $\hat{\mu}_s$, and form the matrix $A - \hat{\mu}_s I$. Now consider the inverse matrix $B_s = (A - \hat{\mu}_s I)^{-1}$. We observe that

    i   The eigenvalues of B_s are $\beta_{s,k} = (\mu_k - \hat{\mu}_s)^{-1}$, $1 \leq k \leq n$.

    ii The eigenvectors of B_s are $\mathbf{b}_{s,k} = \mathbf{a}_k$, $1 \leq k \leq n$.

From (ii), we see that application of the power method to B_s will yield an eigenvector of A. The particular one that we get will be the one corresponding to the dominant eigenvalue of B_s. Now, from (i) and our assumption about the distribution of the μ_k's, it follows that the dominant eigenvalue of B_s is $\beta_{s,s} = (\mu_s - \hat{\mu}_s)^{-1}$. Hence, the iteration (2.37), applied to B_s, will yield the eigenvector $\mathbf{a}_s$ of A corresponding to μ_s. Finally, since B_s is the inverse of a matrix, the power method iteration (2.37) can be written in the form

$$(2.38) \quad \begin{aligned} &(A - \hat{\mu}_s I)\mathbf{y}^{(r)} = \mathbf{x}^{(r-1)} \\ &\mathbf{x}^{(r)} = \frac{1}{\|\mathbf{y}^{(r)}\|} \cdot \mathbf{y}^{(r)} \qquad r = 1, 2, \ldots \end{aligned}$$

and $\mathbf{x}^{(r)} \to \mathbf{a}_s$. This iteration must be done for each $s = 1, 2, \ldots, n$ in order to find all the eigenvectors of A.

Instead of each iteration consisting of a matrix-vector multiplication plus a normalization as in (2.37), we must solve a linear system of equations each time an iteration of (2.38) is performed. This seems bad but there are savings that more than compensate. First, notice that the coefficient matrix (for fixed s) is the same for each iteration. Therefore, we only need to do one LU factorization of B_s. But even this is too expensive—there are n such factorizations to compute, each of which requires $n^3/3$ flops for a total of $n^4/3$. We can do much better if we compute the eigenvectors of the upper Hessenberg form A_1 of A. Let $\mathbf{c}_s$ be an eigenvector of A_1 corresponding to μ_s, that is,

$$A_1 \mathbf{c}_s = \mu_s \mathbf{c}_s$$

But, since A_1 was obtained from A by the orthogonal transformation $A_1 = O^T A O$, we can rewrite the eigenvalue equation as

$$O^T A O \mathbf{c}_s = \mu_s \mathbf{c}_s \qquad \text{or} \qquad A(O\mathbf{c}_s) = \mu_s(O\mathbf{c}_s)$$

from which we conclude that the eigenvectors $\mathbf{a}_s$ of A are given by

$$(2.39) \quad \mathbf{a}_s = O\mathbf{c}_s \qquad 1 \leq s \leq n$$

Therefore, a more practical algorithm is as follows:

   i Compute the eigenvectors c_s of A_1 using (2.38) with A replaced by A_1.

   ii Compute the eigenvectors a_s of A using (2.39).

The advantage of using the Hessenberg form in (2.38) is that each LU factorization only requires $n^2/2$ flops for a total of $n^3/2$. The price we pay for this saving is the n matrix-vector multiplications (2.39): n^3 flops. Altogether, then, the cost is only $3n^3/2$ flops (compared to $n^4/3$). A big saving from using (2.38) is in the number of iterations required for convergence. Assuming that $\hat{\mu}_s$ is a good approximation for μ_s, the eigenvalue $\beta_{s,s} = (\mu_s - \hat{\mu}_s)^{-1}$ will be exceedingly dominant so that we will not need to do very many iterations. Typically, convergence is achieved in only one or two iterations. There is, of course, a potential danger with the method due to the fact that the matrix $A_1 - \hat{\mu}_s I$ is almost singular. But it has been shown (see [33]) that accuracy will not be affected if some care is taken in choosing the initial vector $y^{(0)}$. Fortunately, a method for choosing it can be automated so this aspect can be built into a subroutine.

   The operations count for computing each eigenvector is about:

   i $n^2/2$ flops to compute the LU factorization of $A_1 - \hat{\mu}_s I$.

   ii $m_s n^2$ flops, assuming m_s iterations of (2.38).

   iii n^2 flops.

Assuming that each $m_s \doteq 2$, the total count is about $7n^3/2$ flops. This is almost as much as the cost of finding the eigenvalues alone. It is for this reason that a software package will contain subroutines that find the eigenvalues only and separate ones for finding both the eigenvalues and eigenvectors. The latter should only be used when the eigenvectors are actually needed to solve a problem.

2.3. OVERDETERMINED LINEAR SYSTEMS

We now consider the problem of "solving" a system of linear equations $Ax = b$, where A is an $m \times n$ ($m \geq n$) matrix, b is a given m-vector and x is an n-vector of unknowns. To illustrate the ideas in this section, we will use the example

$$(2.40) \quad \begin{bmatrix} 1.0 & 0 & 0 \\ 1.0 & 0.6 & 0.565 \\ 1.0 & 1.2 & 0.932 \\ 1.0 & 1.8 & -0.751 \\ 1.0 & 2.4 & 0.675 \\ 1.0 & 3.0 & 0.141 \end{bmatrix} \begin{bmatrix} x_1 \\ x_2 \\ x_3 \end{bmatrix} = \begin{bmatrix} 5.00 \\ 6.66 \\ 7.53 \\ 7.10 \\ 5.30 \\ 2.56 \end{bmatrix}$$

Since there are more equations than unknowns, it is impossible, in general, to find a vector **x** that will exactly satisfy all of the equations. Our first concern, then, is to define what is meant by a "solution." After doing this, we will examine the problem of computing it.

2.3.1. Least-squares solution

We first define the residual vector

$$(2.41) \quad \mathbf{r}(\mathbf{x}) = \mathbf{b} - A\mathbf{x}$$

Then the solution of the overdetermined system $A\mathbf{x} = \mathbf{b}$ is defined to be the vector **x*** that minimizes the ℓ_2-norm (2.22) of the residual, that is,

$$(2.42) \quad \|\mathbf{r}(\mathbf{x}^*)\| = \min_{\mathbf{x}} \|\mathbf{r}(\mathbf{x})\| = \min_{\mathbf{x}} \left[\sum_{i=1}^{m} |r_i(\mathbf{x})|^2 \right]^{1/2}$$

x* is called the *least-squares solution* of the system. The term least squares comes from the fact that the norm of a vector is the square root of the sum of squares of its components.

We remark that the definition of **x*** in (2.42) depends on the particular vector norm being used. We happen to be using the Euclidean or ℓ_2-norm (2.22), which produces the least-squares solution, but there are other choices that are sometimes used in practice. If, for example, the underlying vector norm is the ℓ_∞- or "uniform" norm (2.23b)

$$\|\mathbf{r}\|_\infty = \max_{1 \le i \le m} |r_i|$$

then **x*** would be the so-called "minmax" solution satisfying

$$\|\mathbf{r}(\mathbf{x}^*)\|_\infty = \min_{\mathbf{x}} \max_{1 \le i \le m} |r_i(\mathbf{x})|$$

Another possibility is the ℓ_1-norm (2.23a)

$$\|\mathbf{r}\|_1 = \sum_{i=1}^{m} |r_i|$$

Each of these definitions leads to a different **x***. The choice of which particular norm to use in a problem depends on the type of solution desired and how much one is willing to pay for it. For instance, the **x*** from the uniform norm (2.23b) will give a residual **r(x*)** all of whose components are guaranteed to be (uniformly) small whereas the ones from the ℓ_1- and

ℓ_2-norms may have residuals in which a component or two is a good deal larger than the others[13].

The different choices [(2.22), (2.23a and b) for defining an x*] lead to different methods of computing it. As a general rule, least squares is the easiest (cheapest) one to compute so it is the one that is most commonly used. It is the only one that we discuss here. However, very good subroutines for the other two cases are widely available.

Returning to the least-squares solution, the following result characterizes x*:

> If A is a real $m \times n$ $(m \geq n)$ matrix and **b** a given m-vector, then the least squares solution **x*** of $A\mathbf{x} = \mathbf{b}$ satisfies the $n \times n$ linear system

$$(2.43) \qquad A^T A \mathbf{x}^* = A^T \mathbf{b}$$

The system (2.43) is called the *normal equations*. We remark that A^T cannot be canceled from each side because this would be the same as multiplying by $(A^T)^{-1}$, which is not defined since A is rectangular. It is instructive to see how this result is established. Let **x** be any n-vector. Then we want to show that $\|\mathbf{r}^*\| \leq \|\mathbf{r}\|$, where $\mathbf{r}^* = \mathbf{b} - A\mathbf{x}^*$ and $\mathbf{r} = \mathbf{b} - A\mathbf{x}$. First of all, we have

$$\mathbf{r} = \mathbf{b} - A\mathbf{x}$$
$$= \mathbf{b} - A\mathbf{x}^* + A\mathbf{x}^* - A\mathbf{x}$$
$$= \mathbf{r}^* + A(\mathbf{x}^* - \mathbf{x})$$

and, from (2.43),

$$A^T \mathbf{r}^* = A^T (\mathbf{b} - A\mathbf{x}^*) = 0$$

Therefore,

$$\|\mathbf{r}\|^2 = \mathbf{r}^T \mathbf{r}$$
$$= [\mathbf{r}^* + A(\mathbf{x}^* - \mathbf{x})]^T [\mathbf{r}^* + A(\mathbf{x}^* - \mathbf{x})]$$
$$= \|\mathbf{r}^*\|^2 + 2(\mathbf{x}^* - \mathbf{x})^T (A^T \mathbf{r}^*) + \|A(\mathbf{x}^* - \mathbf{x})\|^2$$
$$= \|\mathbf{r}^*\|^2 + \|A(\mathbf{x}^* - \mathbf{x})\|^2$$
$$\geq \|\mathbf{r}^*\|^2$$

---

[13]On the face of it, this seems to be a bad feature but very often it is a desirable one. For example, in the fitting of curves to data (see Section 3.2), there may be one or two bad data points as a result, perhaps, of inadvertent errors in the recording measurements. The ℓ_1- and ℓ_2-norm solutions will more or less ignore such spurious data items whereas the ℓ_∞-norm solution will not.

We remark that if A is of *full rank*, that is, $r(A) = n$, where $r(A)$ is the rank[14] of A, then x^* is unique. This is evident in the second last line of the proof because $A(x^* - x) = 0$ if and only if $(x^* - x) = 0$, that is, $x^* = x$. Moreover, if $r(A) = n$, then $A^T A$ is nonsingular (see Exercise 3.4) and the normal equations have a unique solution. On the other hand, if $r(A) < n$, then they will have an infinite number of solutions, each of which minimizes the residual.

2.3.2. Algorithms

We discuss three algorithms for computing the least squares solution x^*.

1. *Normal equations* (NE). This is a straightforward implementation of (2.43). We

    i From $A^T A$ and $A^T b$.
    ii Solve the system $A^T A x = A^T b$.

For our example, the normal equations are, to three digits,

$$\begin{bmatrix} 6.00 & 9.00 & 1.56 \\ 9.00 & 19.8 & 2.15 \\ 1.56 & 2.15 & 2.23 \end{bmatrix} \begin{bmatrix} x_1 \\ x_2 \\ x_3 \end{bmatrix} = \begin{bmatrix} 34.1 \\ 46.2 \\ 9.39 \end{bmatrix}$$

The solution is

$$x^* = \begin{bmatrix} 6.83 \\ -0.790 \\ 0.189 \end{bmatrix} \quad \text{with residual} \quad r^* = \begin{bmatrix} -1.83 \\ 0.200 \\ 1.48 \\ 1.84 \\ 0.241 \\ -1.92 \end{bmatrix}$$

As a measure of how well x^* satisfies the system, we use the *root mean square error*

$$(2.44) \quad \text{RMSE} = \left[\frac{1}{m} (r^T r) \right]^{1/2} \doteq 1.45$$

It can be interpreted as the "average" least-squares error in each equation. We remark that the value of RMSE in this example does not look

---

[14]The *rank* $r(A)$ of a matrix is the number of linearly independent columns (or, equivalently, rows) that it has.

particularly small but, according to the theory, any other x would have a larger value.

For this method to work, we must have $A^T A$ nonsingular or, equivalently, A must be of full rank. In most practical applications, this turns out to be the case anyway so it is not a serious restriction. On the other hand, the conditioning of $A^T A$ is very often a problem but we will discuss this point in Section 2.3.3.

Turning to the efficiency of the method, we first note that $A^T A$ is symmetric, positive definite. This follows from the fact that, for any n-vector $\mathbf{x} \neq \mathbf{0}$,

$$\mathbf{x}^T(A^T A)\mathbf{x} = (A\mathbf{x})^T(A\mathbf{x}) = \|A\mathbf{x}\|^2 > 0 \qquad \text{since } r(A) = n$$

Therefore, by exploiting this property, the operations count for the method is

   i $mn(n + 1)/2$ flops to form $A^T A$ and mn flops for $A^T \mathbf{b}$.
   ii $n^3/6$ flops to solve the normal equations.

The total is about $mn^2/2 + n^3/6$. In many applications, it is usual to have $m \gg n$ so we often say that the amount of work is about $mn^2/2$ flops—the work required to form the normal equations. The storage requirement is $mn + n^3/2$ locations.

2. *Modified Gram–Schmidt* (MGS). This algorithm is in the spirit of the general algorithm (2.1) because it consists of reducing the normal equations to a simpler form. It is based on the following mathematical result.

> Let A be a given $m \times n$ $(m \geq n)$ matrix with $r(A) = n$. Then there exists a unique $m \times n$ matrix Q with $Q^T Q = D$, an $n \times n$ diagonal matrix, and a unique $n \times n$ unit upper triangular matrix R such that

(2.45) $A = QR$

We remark that this is not the same QR factorization that we discussed in Section 2.2 on eigenvalues.

The reduction of the normal equations to a simpler form is done by substituting the factorization (2.45) into (2.43),

$$R^T Q^T QR\mathbf{x} = R^T Q^T \mathbf{b}$$

Now R^T is unit lower triangular so its inverse exists. Hence, upon multiplying both sides by $(R^T)^{-1}$ and using the fact that $Q^T Q = D$, we have

(2.46) $R\mathbf{x} = D^{-1} Q^T \mathbf{b}$

Since R is unit upper triangular, this system is quite easy to solve.

Therefore, the algorithm is:

   i Compute the decomposition $A = QR$.
  ii Compute the vector $D^{-1}Q^T\mathbf{b}$.
 iii Solve the triangular system (2.46).

For our example, the QR decomposition of A is

$$A = \begin{bmatrix} 1.0 & 0 & 0 \\ 1.0 & 0.6 & 0.565 \\ 1.0 & 1.2 & 0.932 \\ 1.0 & 1.8 & -0.751 \\ 1.0 & 2.4 & 0.675 \\ 1.0 & 3.0 & 0.141 \end{bmatrix}$$

$$= \begin{bmatrix} 1.0 & -1.5 & -0.307 \\ 1.0 & -0.9 & 0.277 \\ 1.0 & -0.3 & 0.662 \\ 1.0 & 0.3 & -1.00 \\ 1.0 & 0.9 & 0.442 \\ 1.0 & 1.5 & -0.0730 \end{bmatrix} \begin{bmatrix} 1.0 & 1.5 & 0.259 \\ 0 & 1.0 & -0.0317 \\ 0 & 0 & 1.0 \end{bmatrix} = QR$$

with $Q^T Q = D = \text{diag}(6.0, 6.3, 1.81)$. The solution $\mathbf{x}^*$ is, of course, the same as before.

We will not discuss the specifics of computing the matrices Q and R. The method consists, in effect, of orthogonalizing the columns of A. The classical method for doing this is the Gram–Schmidt (GS) orthogonalization process. However, numerically speaking, this method is not very satisfactory because it is very sensitive to ill-conditioning. (We discuss ill-conditioning in Section 2.3.3.) But there is a variant of the method, called the modified Gram–Schmidt (MGS) process, which does not suffer from this defect so it is the preferred method to use. Basically, the difference between the two methods is the order in which things are done—in GS, the elements of R are computed column by column whereas they are computed row by row in MGS. Mathematically, the two methods produce the same result but, numerically, they can be quite different.

The operations count for MGS turns out to be:

   i mn^2 flops to compute the QR decomposition.
  ii mn flops to form $D^{-1}Q^T\mathbf{b}$.
 iii $n^2/2$ flops to solve the triangular system.

The storage requirement is about the same as NE. Therefore, on the basis of efficiency, the NE method is superior. However, it turns out that MGS is less sensitive to ill-conditioning, an advantage that can well outweigh efficiency considerations. An explanation for this will be easier after we introduce the final method for finding $\mathbf{x}^*$.

One final remark about the MGS method is that, like the NE method, it assumes that A is of full rank. However, it is possible to drop this requirement by altering the algorithm a little. There are several possibilities, each of which finds a different $\mathbf{x}^*$ (from among the infinite number which exist in the rank deficient case). One is to find the "shortest" $\mathbf{x}^*$, that is, the one for which $\|\mathbf{x}^*\|$ is smallest. Another uses the idea that if, say, the kth column $\mathbf{a}_k$ of A is found to be dependent on the others, we simply set the corresponding component $\mathbf{x}_k^*$ of $\mathbf{x}^*$ to zero, which effectively removes this column from consideration.

   3. *Singular value decomposition* (SVD). This is also a method for reducing the normal equations to a simpler form in the spirit of (2.1). It is based on yet another factorization of A. The basic result is as follows.

> Let A be a given $m \times n$ $(m \geq n)$ matrix. Then there exists an $m \times m$ orthogonal matrix U, an $n \times n$ orthogonal matrix V, and an $m \times n$ matrix Σ such that

(2.47) $$A = U \Sigma V^T$$

> where

(2.48)
$$\Sigma = \begin{bmatrix} s_1 & 0 & \cdots & 0 \\ 0 & s_2 & & 0 \\ \vdots & & \ddots & \vdots \\ 0 & 0 & \cdots & s_n \\ 0 & 0 & \cdots & 0 \\ \vdots & \vdots & & \vdots \\ 0 & 0 & \cdots & 0 \end{bmatrix} = \begin{bmatrix} S \\ \hline 0 \end{bmatrix}$$

> with each $s_j \geq 0$.

The factorization (2.47) is called the *singular value decomposition* of A. The numbers $s_1, \ldots, s_n$ are the *singular values* of A. Now

(2.49) $A^T A = (U \Sigma V^T)^T (U \Sigma V^T) = VS^2 V^T$

where S is the $n \times n$ diagonal matrix defined in (2.48). Therefore, since V is orthogonal, $A^T A$ is similar to $S^2 = \mathrm{diag}(s_1^2, \ldots, s_n^2)$ and it follows that the singular values of A are the positive square roots of the (nonnegative) eigenvalues of $A^T A$.

Using the SVD factorization of A and noting (2.49), the normal equations can be written as

$$VS^2V^Tx = V \Sigma^T U^T b$$

Then the solution x^* is given by

(2.50) $$x^* = V \Sigma^\dagger U^T b = A^\dagger b$$

where $\Sigma^\dagger = S^{-2} \Sigma^T$ is the $n \times m$ matrix defined by

$$\Sigma^\dagger = \begin{bmatrix} s_1^{-1} & 0 & \cdots & 0 & 0 & \cdots & 0 \\ 0 & s_2^{-1} & & 0 & 0 & & 0 \\ \vdots & \vdots & \ddots & \vdots & \vdots & & \vdots \\ 0 & 0 & \cdots & s_n^{-1} & 0 & \cdots & 0 \end{bmatrix}$$

with the understanding that

$$s_j^{-1} = \begin{array}{ll} 1/s_j & \text{if } s_j \neq 0 \\ 0 & \text{if } s_j = 0 \end{array}$$

The matrix $A^\dagger = V \Sigma^\dagger U^T$ is called the *pseudo inverse* of A. As the name implies, it is an extension of the usual definition of an inverse for square matrices. Note, however, that $AA^\dagger \neq A^\dagger A$ since one is $m \times m$ while the other is $n \times n$.

For our example, the SVD of A is

$$\begin{bmatrix} -0.089 & 0.688 & 0.307 & * & * & * \\ -0.210 & 0.242 & 0.485 & * & * & * \\ -0.327 & -0.106 & 0.552 & * & * & * \\ -0.395 & 0.562 & -0.512 & * & * & * \\ -0.536 & -0.310 & 0.140 & * & * & * \\ -0.631 & -0.211 & -0.289 & * & * & * \end{bmatrix} \begin{bmatrix} 4.95 & 0 & 0 \\ 0 & 1.12 & 0 \\ 0 & 0 & 1.49 \\ 0 & 0 & 0 \\ 0 & 0 & 0 \\ 0 & 0 & 0 \end{bmatrix}$$

$$\times \begin{bmatrix} -0.442 & 0.771 & 0.458 \\ -0.890 & -0.310 & -0.335 \\ -0.117 & -0.556 & 0.823 \end{bmatrix}$$

Only the first n columns of U have been specified. The remaining columns are not necessary because they will be multiplied by zero in forming the product $U \Sigma$. An SVD subroutine will usually take advantage of this fact in order to save on storage—only an $m \times n$ array is required for U instead of an $m \times m$ one. This is significant if $m \gg n$.

The operations count for computing x^* using the singular value decomposition is

i Compute U, Σ, V—$2mn^2 + 4n^3$ flops.
ii Compute $x = V \Sigma^\dagger U^T b$—$mn^2$ flops.

In (i), the extra $4n^3$ flops is an estimate of the work required in the iterative phase of computing the SVD. (The method used is somewhat akin to the QR iteration for eigenvalues.) The total amount of work is $3mn^2$, which is much more than either NE or MGS. In addition, $2mn + n^2$ storage locations are needed and this again is much more than the other methods. However SVD has the advantages of stability and the fact that A does not have to be of full rank. [If $r(A) < n$, then at least one singular value is zero. But, since $\Sigma^\dagger$ is well defined, an x^* can still be found using (2.49)].

2.3.3. Comparison of Algorithms

The comparison of algorithms is done on the basis of efficiency and stability. For efficiency, we look at the operations counts and storage requirements. Assuming $m \gg n$, these are:

NE — $mn^2/2$ flops and $mn + n^2/2$ storage locations.
MGS— mn^2 flops and $mn + n^2/2$ storage locations.
SVD—$3mn^2$ flops and $2mn$ storage locations.

The NE method is clearly the most efficient. However, on the basis of stability, it turns out to be poor. We shall try to explain.

Stability (numerical validity) of a method is concerned with sensitivity to the fact that the calculations are done in a floating-point number system rather than the reals. To discuss this, we again need the concept of the "conditioning" of a problem. Actually, the definition of the condition number of a rectangular matrix is analogous to the one we defined for square matrices. It is

$$(2.51) \quad \text{cond}(A) = \|A\| \cdot \|A^\dagger\|$$

Both A and $A^\dagger$ are rectangular but their norms are still well defined by (2.25). We merely have to note that if x is an n-vector, then Ax is an m-vector. Their respective norms are well defined and, therefore, so is the quotient $\|Ax\|/\|x\|$, provided that $x \neq 0$.

From the singular value decomposition (2.47) of A and the fact that $\|U\| = \|V\| = 1$ (because they are orthogonal—see Exercise 2.4), we have

$$\|A\| = \|U \Sigma V^T\| \leq \|\Sigma\|$$

and

$$\|\Sigma\| = \|U^T A V\| \le \|A\|$$

Therefore $\|A\| = \|\Sigma\|$ and, similarly, $\|A^\dagger\| = \|\Sigma^\dagger\|$. But it is easily seen from (2.25) that

$$\|\Sigma\| = \max_{1 \le j \le n} s_j = s_{max}$$

(2.52)

$$\|\Sigma^\dagger\| = \max_{1 \le j \le n} s_j^{-1} = \frac{1}{\min_{\substack{s_j \\ s_j \ne 0}} s_j} = \frac{1}{s_{min}}$$

Therefore, from (2.51), we have

$$cond(A) = \frac{s_{max}}{s_{min}}$$

In words, the conditioning of a least-squares problem is given by the ratio of the largest to the smallest nonzero singular value of the coefficient matrix A.

Now in the NE method, we must solve the normal equations (2.43). Since $A^T A = V S^2 V^T$, it follows that the conditioning for this method is given by

$$cond(A^T A) = \|A^T A\| \cdot \|(A^T A)^{-1}\| = \left[\frac{s_{max}}{s_{min}}\right]^2$$

that is, it is the *square* of the condition number of A. Herein lies the disadvantage of the NE method: the normal equations can easily be very badly conditioned as a result of the squaring of the condition number of the original problem which may only be mildly bad. For example, if $cond(A) = 10^3$, then $cond(A^T A) = 10^6$. On the other hand, since neither the MGS nor SVD methods involve an operation like the formation of $A^T A$, the conditioning for these methods is just $cond(A)$.

To briefly summarize the comparison of the methods, we can say that

NE is the fastest but least dependable.
MGS is the next fastest and is dependable.
SVD is also dependable but is the slowest.

The NE method should only be used in those cases where the condition number of A is very low. In many applications, however, $cond(A)$ is not particularly small so, as a general rule, one should use MGS instead. The SVD algorithm, although it is the slowest, has the advantage of giving the user some insight into the problem through the singular values. Their comparative sizes can sometimes give an indication of the relative importance of different components of the solution. The SVD method can, therefore, be quite useful as an experimental tool.

EXERCISES

Section 2.1

1.1. Consider the matrices

i $\begin{bmatrix} 6.3 & 0.0 \\ -2.4 & 0.11 \end{bmatrix}$ ii $\begin{bmatrix} 3.82 & -1.56 & 0.135 \\ -4.02 & 1.08 & 9.11 \\ 3.59 & -5.67 & -6.61 \end{bmatrix}$

iii $\begin{bmatrix} 0.50 & 0.33 & 0.25 & 0.50 \\ 0.50 & 0.25 & 0.20 & 1.0 \\ 1.0 & 1.0 & 1.0 & 1.0 \\ 2.0 & 3.0 & 1.0 & 5.0 \end{bmatrix}$

iv $\begin{bmatrix} 8.67 & 2.15 & -4.11 & 3.88 & 0 & -5.51 \\ 6.29 & 0 & 2.71 & 5.16 & -4.04 & 9.12 \\ -4.15 & 3.57 & -1.15 & 0 & 2.89 & -6.69 \\ 9.87 & 1.16 & 4.33 & 0 & 5.11 & 4.87 \\ -3.46 & -2.87 & 0 & 2.47 & 9.86 & 2.14 \\ 4.65 & 1.88 & 8.44 & -6.35 & -4.75 & 8.24 \end{bmatrix}$

In each case, use a decomposition subroutine to:
   (a) Compute the matrices P, L, and U in the LU factorization and verify, by multiplication, that $PA = LU$.
   (b) Compute the determinant $\det(A)$.

1.2. For each of the matrices in Exercise 1.1, solve the linear system $Ax = b$, where:

   i $b = [4.8, -3.5]^T$
   ii $b = [-6.72, 10.1, -3.85]^T$
   iii $b = [13.0, 11.5, 40.0, 75.0]^T$
   iv $b = [5.81, -4.27, 7.72, 6.84, -1.19, 3.02]^T$

1.3. Let $A = (a_{i,j})$ be an $n \times n$ upper triangular matrix, that is, $a_{i,j} = 0$ if $i > j$. Show that $\det(A) = a_{1,1}a_{2,2} \ldots a_{n,n}$.

1.4. Verify (2.14) for the example illustrated.

1.5. According to the well-known Cramer's rule, the components of the solution of $Ax = b$ can be expressed as

$$x_i = \frac{\det(A_i)}{\det(A)} \qquad 1 \le i \le n$$

where $\det(A_i)$ is the determinant of the matrix formed by taking A and replacing its ith column by the right-hand side vector b. Show that the operations count for this method is $n^4/3 + 0(n^3)$ flops, making it much less efficient than Gauss elimination.

1.6. The Gauss–Jordan method is another well-known procedure for solving a linear system. It is the same as Gauss elimination with the modification that elimination is done *above* the diagonal as well as below. In other words, it reduces the problem $Ax = b$ to the equivalent one $Dx = q$, where D is a diagonal matrix. Thus, the reduced problem is especially easy to solve. But the overall algorithm is less efficient than Gauss elimination because the operations count is $n^3/2 + 0(n^2)$ flops. Verify this count.

1.7. The ith column of the inverse A^{-1} of an $n \times n$ matrix A can be determined as the solution of the linear system $Ax = e_i$, where e_i is the ith column of the $n \times n$ identity matrix.
   (a) Compute A^{-1} for each of the matrices in Exercise 1.1.
   (b) Another method for solving $Ax = b$ is first to compute the inverse A^{-1} and then the solution $x = A^{-1}b$. Show that the operations count for this algorithm is $4n^3/3 + 0(n^2)$ flops.

1.8. Show that Gauss elimination with complete pivoting is equivalent to finding two permutation matrices P and Q such that

$$PAQ = LU$$

where L is unit lower triangular and U is upper triangular. Using this factorization of A, what is the algorithm corresponding to (2.17) for solving $Ax = b$?

1.9. Let A be a given $n \times n$ matrix and consider the problem of solving the system $Bx = b$, where $B = A^2 + \beta A + \gamma I$, with β and γ arbitrary constants.
   (a) Sketch an algorithm for solving this problem. What is the operations count and storage requirement?
   (b) Suppose that β and γ are such that B is a perfect square, that is, $B = (A + \mu I)^2$. Show how this property can be exploited to produce a much more efficient algorithm.

(c) Solve the system $B\mathbf{x} = \mathbf{b}$, where $\beta = -10$, $\gamma = 25$, A is the matrix of Exercise 1.1(iii), and $\mathbf{b}$ is the vector of Exercise 1.2(iii).

1.10. Let $\mathbf{x} = [1, -3, 8]^T$ and $\mathbf{y} = [-9, -2, 1]^T$. Compute the norms $\|\mathbf{x}\|_p$ and $\|\mathbf{y}\|_p$ for each of $p = 1, 2, \infty$. How do the vectors compare in "length" with respect to each norm?

1.11. Let $D = \text{diag}(d_1, \ldots, d_n)$ be an $n \times n$ diagonal matrix with each diagonal entry $d_i \neq 0$.

(a) Show that $\|D\| = \max\limits_{1 \le i \le n} |d_i|$.

(b) Let $\|\cdot\|$ be the ℓ_2 vector norm (2.22). Show that $\|\cdot\|_D$ defined by

$$\|\mathbf{x}\|_D = \|D\mathbf{x}\|$$

satisfies the conditions (2.24) so that it is also a vector norm.

1.12. Show that $\|\mathbf{x} - \mathbf{y}\| \ge |\|\mathbf{x}\| - \|\mathbf{y}\||$. Similarly, show that $\|A - B\| \ge |\|A\| - \|B\||$.

1.13. Consider the $n \times n$ linear system $A\mathbf{x} = \mathbf{b}$, where the elements of A and $\mathbf{b}$ are given by

$$a_{i,j} = j^i \quad 1 \le i, j \le n \quad \text{and} \quad b_i = \sum_{j=1}^{n} (-1)^{j+1} a_{i,j} \quad 1 \le i \le n$$

The exact solution is $\mathbf{x} = [1, -1, \ldots, (-1)^{n+1}]^T$. For example, if $n = 3$, we have

$$A = \begin{bmatrix} 1 & 2 & 3 \\ 1 & 4 & 9 \\ 1 & 8 & 27 \end{bmatrix} \quad \mathbf{b} = \begin{bmatrix} 2 \\ 6 \\ 20 \end{bmatrix} \quad \text{and} \quad \mathbf{x} = \begin{bmatrix} 1 \\ -1 \\ 1 \end{bmatrix}$$

This is an instance where cond(A) increases very rapidly with increasing n, that is, A is more nearly singular as n increases.

(a) Generate the system in the case $n = 4$ and solve it using a DCOMP-SOLVE pair of subroutines. Compute both the relative error $\|\mathbf{e}\|/\|\mathbf{x}\|$ and the relative residual $\|\mathbf{r}\|/\|\mathbf{b}\|$. Repeat with $n = 5, 6, \ldots$ until the computed solution $\hat{\mathbf{x}}$ has no accurate digits. Verify that the relative residual always remains small.

(b) Is the value of det(A) a good indicator of ill conditioning? We know that A is badly conditioned if it is almost singular and that, mathematically, A is singular if and only if $\det(A) = 0$. Hence, the original question can be rephrased as follows. Is A badly conditioned if and only if det(A) is almost zero? Give an explanation for your answer. [To gain some insight, compute det(A) for each of the matrices in part (a). Also look at the individual diagonal entries of U in the LU factorization.]

(c) A curious thing about this example is that, provided sufficient precision is used to store the elements of A exactly, one can get a perfect solution by solving the system *without* doing partial pivoting. Explain why. [Hint: Solve the 4×4 system in part (a) by hand.]

1.14. Solve each of the systems in Exercise 1.1 and 1.2 to an accuracy of 6 significant (decimal) digits. In each case, obtain an estimate for cond(A).

1.15. Repeat Exercise 1.13(a) using iterative improvement. How large can n be before iterative improvement fails?

1.16. Consider the following algorithm for solving $Ax = b$:
  i   Compute the LU factorization of A.
  ii Choose an initial guess $x^{(0)}$ for x.
  iii Using iterative improvement, generate $x^{(1)}, x^{(2)}, \ldots$, until done

(a) Provide a suitable criterion for "until done."
(b) Try the algorithm on Exercises 1.1 and 1.2(iii) with $x^{(0)} = 0$.
(c) Is there any restriction on the choice of $x^{(0)}$?
(d) Compare the efficiency of this algorithm with the "normal" Gauss elimination, back substitution and iterative improvement procedure.

1.17. Let

$$
A = \begin{bmatrix}
2 & -1 & & & & \\
-1 & 2 & -1 & & & \\
& -1 & 2 & -1 & & \\
& & \ddots & \ddots & \ddots & \\
& & & & & -1 \\
& & & & -1 & 2
\end{bmatrix}
\quad \text{and} \quad
b = \begin{bmatrix} 1 \\ 1 \\ 1 \\ \vdots \\ 1 \end{bmatrix}
$$

be, respectively, $n \times n$ and $n \times 1$. For each of $n = 50, 75, 100$, solve the system $Ax = b$ using subroutines designed for each of the following cases:

    i General real matrices.
   ii Real symmetric positive definite matrices.
  iii Real symmetric positive definite band matrices.

Record the respective execution times. Do the comparative times agree with those predicted by the operations counts?

1.18. Suppose A has the following sparsity pattern

$$\begin{bmatrix} 0 & x & x & 0 & 0 & x \\ x & 0 & 0 & 0 & x & 0 \\ 0 & 0 & x & 0 & 0 & x \\ 0 & x & 0 & 0 & 0 & x \\ x & 0 & 0 & x & 0 & 0 \\ x & 0 & x & 0 & 0 & 0 \end{bmatrix}$$

  (a) Find a pivoting strategy based on the criterion of putting the sparser rows at the top. What is the fill-in?

  (b) Is your pivoting strategy in part (a) optimal? If so, explain why you think it is. If not, can you find an optimal strategy?

Section 2.2

2.1. Find the eigenvalues of each of the following matrices. In each case, be sure to select the most appropriate subroutine available.

  i
$$\begin{bmatrix} 3 & 8 & -6 \\ 0 & 3 & 9 \\ -4 & 5 & 3 \end{bmatrix}$$
  ii
$$\begin{bmatrix} 4 & 2+i & -3+5i \\ 6 & 9i & 0 \\ 7-i & -5 & 6+7i \end{bmatrix}$$

  iii
$$\begin{bmatrix} 4 & -1 & -1 & 0 \\ -1 & 4 & 0 & -1 \\ -1 & 0 & 4 & -1 \\ 0 & -1 & -1 & 4 \end{bmatrix}$$
  iv
$$\begin{bmatrix} 3 & 1+i & 6-5i \\ 1-i & 8 & 4 \\ 6+5i & 4 & 2 \end{bmatrix}$$

  v
$$\begin{bmatrix} 2 & -1 & 0 & 0 & 0 \\ -1 & 2 & -1 & 0 & 0 \\ 0 & -1 & 2 & -1 & 0 \\ 0 & 0 & -1 & 2 & -1 \\ 0 & 0 & 0 & -1 & 2 \end{bmatrix}$$

2.2. Let O be an $n \times n$ orthogonal matrix.

  (a) Show that, for any vector x, $\|Ox\| = \|x\|$, where $\|\cdot\|$ is the ℓ_2 vector norm (2.22).

(b) Using (2.25) and the result of part (a), show that $\|O\| = 1$, where $\|\cdot\|$ is the matrix norm (2.25) induced by the ℓ_2 vector norm.

(c) Let A be an $n \times n$ matrix and define $B = O^TAO$. Show that $\|A\| = \|B\|$.

2.3. Let A be an $n \times n$ real symmetric matrix. Then a well-known result in matrix theory says that there exists an $n \times n$ orthogonal matrix O such that $O^TAO = D$, where $D = \text{diag}(\mu_1, \ldots, \mu_n)$ is a diagonal matrix whose diagonal entries are the eigenvalues of A.

(a) Using this result and those of Exercises 1.11 and 2.2, show that $\|A\| = |\mu_{\max}|$, where $\mu_{\max}$ is the largest (in magnitude) eigenvalue of A. (This result does *not* hold for general real matrices. Why?)

(b) Show that, if A is also nonsingular, then $\text{cond}(A) = |\mu_{\max}/\mu_{\min}|$, where $\mu_{\min}$ is the eigenvalue of A that is closest to the origin.

(c) Use the result of part (b) to compute the condition number of the matrices (iii) and (v) in Exercise 2.1.

2.4. Let A and B be $n \times n$ matrices.

(a) Show that, if both are upper triangular, then so is the product AB.

(b) Show that, if A is upper Hessenberg and B is upper triangular, the product AB is upper Hessenberg. What about the product BA?

(c) If both are upper Hessenberg, what form does the product AB take?

2.5. Consider the following algorithm for solving an $n \times n$ system of equations $A\mathbf{x} = \mathbf{b}$:

    i Compute the QR factorization of A.
    ii Compute the vector $\mathbf{d} = Q^T\mathbf{b}$.
    iii Solve the system $R\mathbf{x} = \mathbf{d}$ for $\mathbf{x}$.

(a) Show that this algorithm is valid mathematically.

(b) What is the operations count? (Do not assume that A is upper Hessenberg.)

2.6. When the underlying vector norm, used in (2.25) to define a matrix norm $\|A\|$, is the ℓ_2-norm, it turns out that

$$\|A\| = \rho^{1/2}(A^TA)$$

where

$$\rho(B) = \max_{1 \le i \le n} |\mu_i(B)| \qquad \mu_i(B) \text{ an eigenvalue of } B$$

is the *spectral radius* of B. (In words, $\rho(B)$ is the radius of the smallest circle, centered at the origin, which contains the eigenvalues, or "spectrum" of B.) As an example,

$$\text{if } A = \begin{bmatrix} 1 & -2 \\ 3 & 4 \end{bmatrix} \quad \text{then} \quad A^T A = \begin{bmatrix} 10 & 10 \\ 10 & 20 \end{bmatrix}$$

The eigenvalues of $A^T A$ are $\mu_1 \doteq 26.18$ and $\mu_2 \doteq 3.82$, so $\|A\| \doteq \sqrt{26.18} \doteq 5.12$. Note that $A^T A$ is symmetric and that μ_1, μ_2 are both positive.

(a) Describe an algorithm for finding the ℓ_2-norm of a matrix. The algorithm should use existing subroutines including utility routines for finding the transpose of a matrix and doing matrix multiplication.

(b) How much work is required to compute $\|A\|$?

(c) Implement the algorithm of part (a) and use it to compute the norm of each matrix in Exercise 1.1.

2.7. The algorithm from Exercise 2.6 can be used to compute the condition number (2.28) of a matrix. How much work is required to compute cond(A) in this way? (Compare with the amount required to estimate it with iterative improvement.) Determine cond(A) for each of the matrices in Exercise 1.1. How do the results compare with the estimates obtained in Exercise 1.14?

2.8. Find the eigenvectors of each matrix in Exercise 2.1.

2.9. The power method (2.37) will determine the dominant eigenvalue β_1 of the matrix B as well as the eigenvector $\mathbf{b}_1$. The underlying result is that

$$\lim_{r \to \infty} \frac{(\mathbf{y}^{(r)})_i}{(\mathbf{x}^{(r-1)})_i} = \beta_1 \qquad 1 \le i \le n$$

where $(\mathbf{x})_i$ denotes the ith component of the vector $\mathbf{x}$.

(a) Prove this result assuming that $\mathbf{x}^{(r)} \to \alpha \mathbf{b}_1$.

(b) Outline an algorithm for finding β_1 and $\mathbf{b}_1$ by the power method. Under what condition(s) is it guaranteed to converge? Give an operations count for it. Are there any situations where the power method would be preferred to QR?

Section 2.3

3.1. Prove the relationships (2.52).

3.2. Consider the overdetermined linear systems

$$\mathbf{i} \quad \begin{bmatrix} 3 & 0 \\ -1 & 2 \\ 6 & 1 \\ 0 & 15 \\ 7 & 1 \end{bmatrix} \begin{bmatrix} x_1 \\ x_2 \end{bmatrix} = \begin{bmatrix} 5 \\ -2 \\ 0 \\ 1 \\ 3 \end{bmatrix}$$

ii $\begin{bmatrix} 0.4900 & 1.0 & 0.70 \\ 0.4624 & 1.0 & 0.68 \\ 0.4356 & 1.0 & 0.66 \\ 0.4761 & 1.0 & 0.79 \\ 0.5476 & 1.0 & 0.74 \\ 0.4900 & 1.0 & 0.70 \\ 0.3969 & 1.0 & 0.63 \\ 0.5184 & 1.0 & 0.72 \end{bmatrix} \begin{bmatrix} x_1 \\ x_2 \\ x_3 \end{bmatrix} = \begin{bmatrix} 1.61 \\ 1.64 \\ 1.40 \\ 1.54 \\ 2.10 \\ 1.64 \\ 1.26 \\ 1.72 \end{bmatrix}$

In each case, do the following.

(a) Compute the best least-squares solution x*. What is the value of the root mean square error RMSE defined by (2.44)?

(b) Find the value of cond(A).

3.3. Suppose A is an $n \times n$ matrix. Explain the differences between the QR factorization used in the QR algorithm (2.33) and that of (2.45) used in the MGS algorithm.

3.4. Let A be an $m \times n$ ($m \geq n$) matrix with rank $r(A) = n$. Show that $A^T A$ is nonsingular.

3.5. For the case where $m = 3$ and $n = 2$, the residual vector (2.41) is

$$\mathbf{r} = \mathbf{b} - A\mathbf{x} = \begin{bmatrix} b_1 - (a_{1,1}x_1 + a_{1,2}x_2) \\ b_2 - (a_{2,1}x_1 + a_{2,2}x_2) \\ b_3 - (a_{3,1}x_1 + a_{3,2}x_2) \end{bmatrix} = \mathbf{r}(x_1, x_2)$$

Let $S(x_1, x_2) = \mathbf{r}^T \mathbf{r}$. Now, from the result established in Section 2.3.1, we know that the best least-squares solution x* satisfies the normal equations (2.43). On the other hand, we could proceed to find x* as follows. S is a function of the two variables x_1, x_2. A well-known result states that a necessary condition for S to have a minimum at $\mathbf{x}^* = [x_1^*, x_2^*]^T$ is that x_1^* and x_2^* satisfy the system of equations

$$\frac{\delta S}{\delta x_j} = 0 \qquad j = 1, 2$$

Write out this system and show that it is exactly the normal equations.

3.6. In the description of each algorithm in Section 2.3.2, the case where $m = n$ is permitted. Therefore, a least-squares subroutine can be applied to solve an $n \times n$ system of equations.

(a) If $m = n$ and $r(A) = n$, the normal equations will reduce to the original system $A\mathbf{x} = \mathbf{b}$. Why?

(b) Verify that a least-squares routine will work for an $n \times n$ system by solving, say, Exercise 1.1 to 1.2(iii) in this way.

(c) Let

$$
A = \begin{bmatrix} -5 & -6 & 1 & 4 \\ -6 & 0 & 7 & 3 \\ 1 & 8 & 7 & -6 \\ 3 & 4 & -2 & 1 \end{bmatrix} \quad b_1 = \begin{bmatrix} -4 \\ 2 \\ -6 \\ 3 \end{bmatrix} \quad \text{and} \quad b_2 = \begin{bmatrix} 6 \\ 6 \\ -9 \\ 3 \end{bmatrix}
$$

Solve each of the systems $Ax = b_1$ and $Ax = b_2$ using a least squares subroutine. (The matrix A is singular so a subroutine that can handle rank deficiency should be used.) Compute the residual $r^* = b - Ax^*$ in each case and give an interpretation of the results.

(d) How well does a least-squares routine handle ill-conditioned systems? To answer this, try solving some of the systems of Exercise 1.14 and compare the results with those obtained using Gauss elimination with iterative improvement.

(e) Compare each of the least squares methods of this section with Gauss elimination on the basis of operations counts and stability or sensitivity to ill conditioning.

CHAPTER 3

INTERPOLATION AND APPROXIMATION

In this chapter, we deal with the problem of fitting a curve to a given set of data points $\{(x_i, f_i)\}_{i=1}^{m}$. Curve fitting plays an important role in the analysis and interpretation of such data. For example, the set of points may have come from observations or measurements taken during an experiment and the approximation (or fitted curve) can be used for predicting values at intermediate points or else in formulating a mathematical model to describe the process being studied. Alternatively, the data points could be viewed as points on the graph of a known function, say $y = e^x$, which is difficult to evaluate. In this case, an approximation that is accurate and easily evaluated could be useful as the basis for a subroutine for evaluating the function in question.

A general formulation of the type of problem we will consider is as follows:

(3.1)   Given a set of m data points $\{(x_i, f_i)\}_{i=1}^{m}$ in the plane and a prescribed set of function $\mathcal{G}$, find a function $g^* \in \mathcal{G}$ that best represents this data according to some predefined measure of "goodness of fit."

A familiar example is linear regression, that is, the least squares fit of a straight line to some data. The set $\mathcal{G}$ is all possible functions $g(x)$ of the form

$$g(x) = ax + b$$

that is, straight lines. The measure of goodness of fit is the least-squares function

$$S_2(a, b) = \sum_{i=1}^{m} [f_i - (ax_i + b)]^2$$

Then g^* corresponds to the values a^* and b^*, which minimize S_2. We discuss this example in more detail in Section 3.2. Thus, the class $\mathcal{G}$ can be interpreted as defining the form of the "mathematical model" that will be used to represent the data. The measure of goodness of fit is used to obtain the particular model within the class that gives the best interpretation of the data. We remark that, in general, there may be more than one $g^* \in \mathcal{G}$ that best fits the data, but this situation will not arise in the types of curve fitting we consider here, that is, g^* will be unique.

In the above formulation, we are free to choose both the class $\mathcal{G}$ of functions and the measure of goodness of fit. This provides us with a wide variety of possibilities. However, as a general rule, $\mathcal{G}$ should be restricted to types of functions that are easy to evaluate while the definition of the measure of fit should be such that g^* is not too difficult to compute. We discuss and compare some of the more common choices in practical use today. The aim is to show how to select the most appropriate type of approximation to use in a given situation. Comparisons of the different types will be based on the following three criteria:

   i   Cost of computing g^*.
   ii   Cost of evaluating g^*.
   iii   Accuracy.

Of the two costs, the second is usually the more important. This assumes, of course, that g^* will be used (evaluated) more than just a few times so that the single cost of determining it is relatively insignificant compared to the total cost of all the evaluations of it. Therefore, in our discussions, we will place more emphasis on the second and third criteria.

The organization of the chapter follows a standard format. In Section 3.1, we discuss interpolation and in Section 3.2, we consider approximation. The method of presentation is to consider various ways of defining the class $\mathcal{G}$ and the measure of goodness of fit in (3.1), as well as methods (subroutines) for computing and evaluating g^*.

3.1. INTERPOLATION

Interpolation is a well-known method of curve fitting. When we say that a function $g(x)$ "interpolates" a set of data points, we mean that its graph passes through each one of the points. In terms of the general formulation (3.1), this means that $g^*(x)$ must satisfy each of the equations

$$(3.2) \qquad g^*(x_i) = f_i \qquad 1 \le i \le m$$

that we call the *interpolation conditions*. This is the measure of goodness of fit, that is, the error must be zero at each data point. Note that nothing is said about intermediate points.

We consider two different classes $\mathcal{G}$ of interpolation functions—polynomials and piecewise polynomials. For convenience, it will be assumed that the x_i's are distinct, that is, $x_i \ne x_j$, if $i \ne j$.

3.1.1. Polynomial Interpolation

Let the class of functions $\mathscr{G}$ be the set $\mathscr{P}_n$ of all polynomials of degree $\leq n$, that is, $g(x) \in \mathscr{G} = \mathscr{P}_n$ has the form

$$(3.3) \quad g(x) = p_n(x) = a_0 x^n + a_1 x^{n-1} + \cdots + a_{n-1} x + a_n$$
$$= (\ldots((a_0 x + a_1) \cdot x + a_2) \cdot x + \cdots + a_{n-1}) \cdot x + a_n.$$

We will soon specify how large n must be. The latter form of $p_n(x)$ is called the *nested form*. It is preferable for computational purposes since it only takes n flops to evaluate whereas, for the other, more usual form, n flops plus n M's are needed.

Polynomials are the classical type of interpolating function found in the mathematical literature, mainly because they are easy to manipulate mathematically—add, multiply, differentiate, and integrate. However, as we will see, they have some serious shortcomings from the point of view of accuracy and efficiency. Nevertheless, it is important to understand some of the ideas and algorithms for polynomial interpolation so we will discuss them in detail.

First, let us determine the size of n (degree of polynomial) needed to ensure existence and uniqueness of g^*. We will do this both geometrically and algebraically. For the geometric derivation, we first consider the simple case of only three data points, that is, $m = 3$. It is clear from Figure 3.1 that a quadratic polynomial (the solid curve) can be made to interpolate the three data points. Moreover, there is only one such polynomial. Of course, we can also make a higher degree polynomial interpolate the same data but then we will lose uniqueness[1]. For instance, in Figure 3.1, the dotted curves illustrate two different cubics ($n = 3$) that interpolate the three points. Therefore, to guarantee existence and uniqueness of $g^* \in \mathscr{P}_n$, we need to choose $n \leq 3 - 1 = 2$. (The inequality allows for redundancy in the data,

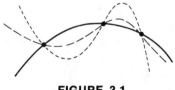

FIGURE 3.1

---

[1]Strictly speaking, there is no need to require uniqueness. *Any g^* that satisfies the interpolating conditions (3.2) should be acceptable. But we must also consider efficiency, that is, we want a g^* for which the computational cost is a minimum. For polynomials, this implies that the degree n must be as low as possible in which case g^* is unique. The converse is also true (i.e., uniqueness implies minimal degree). Hence, by requiring uniqueness, we get efficiency.

that is, the possibility that the data points lie on the same straight line.) This argument can easily be extended to include more data points. In essence, it asserts the well-known fact that there exists a unique polynomial of degree $\leq m - 1$, which passes through m given points. Therefore we should choose $n = m - 1$.

Now we look at an algebraic derivation of the same result. Again, we first consider the case $m = 3$. Suppose that we choose $n = 3 - 1 = 2$. Then $\mathcal{G}$ is the set $\mathcal{P}_2$ of all polynomials $p_2(x)$ of degree ≤ 2

$$p_2(x) = a_0 x^2 + a_1 x + a_2$$

and we want to determine a_0^*, a_1^*, a_2^*, which define p_2^*. Now the interpolating conditions (3.2) are

$$p_2(x_1) = a_0 x_1^2 + a_1 x_1 + a_2 = f_1$$

$$p_2(x_2) = a_0 x_2^2 + a_1 x_2 + a_2 = f_2$$

$$p_2(x_3) = a_0 x_3^2 + a_1 x_3 + a_2 = f_3$$

This is a system of linear equations in the unknowns a_0, a_1, a_2. In matrix-vector form it is $A\mathbf{a} = \mathbf{f}$, or

$$(3.4) \qquad \begin{bmatrix} x_1^2 & x_1 & 1 \\ x_2^2 & x_2 & 1 \\ x_3^2 & x_3 & 1 \end{bmatrix} \begin{bmatrix} a_0 \\ a_1 \\ a_3 \end{bmatrix} = \begin{bmatrix} f_1 \\ f_2 \\ f_3 \end{bmatrix}$$

Noting the one-to-one correspondence between vectors $\mathbf{a} = [a_0, a_1, a_2]^T$ and polynomials $p_2(x)$ of degree ≤ 2, it follows that there is a unique $p_2^* \in \mathcal{P}_2$ if and only if the linear system (3.4) has a unique solution. In turn, the latter condition will be true if and only if the coefficient matrix A is nonsingular. But we have

$$(3.5) \qquad \det A = (x_1 - x_2)(x_1 - x_3)(x_2 - x_3) = \prod_{\substack{i,j=1 \\ i<j}}^{m} (x_i - x_j)$$

so A is nonsingular ($\det A \neq 0$) if and only if $x_i \neq x_j$, $i \neq j$. Therefore, there is a unique interpolating polynomial $p_2^* \in \mathcal{P}_2$ if and only if the x_i's are distinct. Since we have assumed the latter condition to be true, the existence of p_2^* follows. With this analysis, it is clear why we must choose $n = 2$. If $n > 2$, the linear system corresponding to (3.4) is underdetermined—there are more unknowns than equations—and there is no unique solution, that is, p_n^* is not unique. On the other hand, if $n < 2$, the system is overdetermined and a solution will not exist at all unless the three data points lie on the same straight line. Now, for the general case of m data points, the argument is similar. We choose $n = m - 1$ and the interpolating conditions generate an $m \times m$ linear system $A\mathbf{a} = \mathbf{f}$ analogous to (3.4), where $\mathbf{a} =$

$[a_0, \ldots, a_{m-1}]^T$. The coefficient matrix A has a form similar to the matrix in (3.4), that is, the elements of each column are the x_i's, each raised to the same power. Specifically,

$$a_{i,j} = x_i^{m-j} \qquad 1 \le i, j \le m$$

This is called a Vandermonde matrix (see [6, p. 369]) and its determinant is given by the formula on the right side of (3.5). From this, it follows that A is nonsingular, that is, p_{m-1}^* exists and is unique, if and only if the x_i's are distinct. We will refer to this result later.

The determination of $p_{m-1}^*(x)$ is our next consideration. To illustrate the various methods of constructing it, we shall use the set of four data points

(3.6) $\{(-1, -7), (1, 7), (2, -4), (5, 35)\}$

An obvious way of determining p_{m-1}^* is to construct the $m \times m$ linear system as described above and then solve it. For the example data (3.6), we have

$$\begin{bmatrix} -1 & 1 & -1 & 1 \\ 1 & 1 & 1 & 1 \\ 8 & 4 & 2 & 1 \\ 125 & 25 & 5 & 1 \end{bmatrix} \begin{bmatrix} a_0 \\ a_1 \\ a_2 \\ a_3 \end{bmatrix} = \begin{bmatrix} -7 \\ 7 \\ -4 \\ 35 \end{bmatrix}$$

Solving the system gives $\mathbf{a}^* = [2, -10, 5, 10]^T$ whereupon the interpolating polynomial is

(3.7) $p_3^*(x) = 2x^3 - 10x^2 + 5x + 10$

This is not a very good method for several reasons. First, it requires $m^3/3$ flops, which, as we will see, is much more than is necessary. Second, the linear system is very often poorly conditioned—even for our small example, $\operatorname{cond}(A) \doteq 215$.

We now describe two other ways of computing $p_{m-1}^*(x)$. These are based on two different representations of it—the Lagrange and Newton forms. It turns out that, for computational purposes, the Lagrange form is less efficient. However, it is a useful form for deriving other mathematical results. In particular, we will use it in deriving the Gauss quadrature formulas in Section 5.1.2.

Lagrange Form of $p_{m-1}^*(x)$

We illustrate the derivation of p_{m-1}^* for the data (3.6). From this it will be clear how to extend the ideas to the general case. First, we define the polynomials

$$l_1(x) = \frac{(x-1)(x-2)(x-5)}{(-1-1)(-1-2)(-1-5)} = -\frac{1}{36}(x-1)(x-2)(x-5)$$

$$l_2(x) = \frac{(x+1)(x-2)(x-5)}{(1+1)(1-2)(1-5)} = \frac{1}{8}(x+1)(x-2)(x-5)$$

$$l_3(x) = \frac{(x+1)(x-1)(x-5)}{(2+1)(2-1)(2-5)} = -\frac{1}{9}(x+1)(x-1)(x-5)$$

$$l_4(x) = \frac{(x+1)(x-1)(x-2)}{(5+1)(5-1)(5-2)} = \frac{1}{72}(x+1)(x-1)(x-2)$$

Then the Lagrange form of p_3^* is

$$(3.8) \quad p_3^*(x) = f_1 l_1(x) + f_2 l_2(x) + f_3 l_3(x) + f_4 l_4(x) = \sum_{j=1}^{m} f_j l_j(x)$$

$$= (-7)l_1(x) + (7)l_2(x) + (-4)l_3(x) + (35)l_4(x)$$

$$(= 2x^3 - 10x^2 + 5x + 10)$$

In order to verify that this is, in fact, the interpolating polynomial we seek, we have to check that it has degree ≤ 3 and satisfies the interpolating conditions (3.2). To this end, we note two properties of the $l_j(x)$'s:

  i   Each $l_j(x)$ is a polynomial of degree 3.

  ii $l_j(x_i) = \begin{array}{l} 1, \quad \text{if } i = j. \\ 0, \quad \text{if } i \neq j. \end{array}$

From property (i), we see that p_3^* is a sum of polynomials, each of which has degree 3, so degree $p_3^* \leq 3$. Satisfaction of the interpolating conditions follows from property (ii). For example,

$$p_3^*(x_2) = (-7)l_1(x_2) + (7)l_2(x_2) + (-4)l_3(x_2) + (35)l_4(x_2)$$

$$= 0 + 7(1) + 0 + 0$$

$$= 7$$

We emphasize that, by the uniqueness of p_{m-1}^* established above, the polynomial (3.8) must be the same one that would be generated by the linear equations method. Therefore, (3.8) is simply a different representation—the Lagrange form—of the interpolation polynomial.

  The main disadvantage of the Lagrange form of p_{m-1}^* arises when one tries to add an extra point to the data. The new interpolating polynomial $p_m^*(x)$ cannot be obtained easily from $p_{m-1}^*(x)$. In our example, suppose we wish to add the point $(4, 20)$ to the data (3.6). In addition to having to determine a new Lagrange polynomial $l_5(x)$, the formulas for $l_1(x), \ldots, l_4(x)$ must also be changed. Another disadvantage of the Lagrange form is inefficiency. The representation (3.8) requires about m^2 flops to evaluate—there are m $l_j(x)$'s and each requires $m-1$ flops. But this is a little misleading because there is an alternative representation of the Lagrange form which is much cheaper to evaluate. Let

$$\psi_m(x) = \prod_{i=1}^{m} (x - x_i)$$

and

$$a_j = \prod_{i \neq j} (x_j - x_i) \qquad 1 \leq j \leq m$$

Then the Lagrange polynomials can be written in the form

$$l_j(x) = \frac{\psi_m(x)}{(x - x_j) \cdot a_j} \qquad 1 \leq j \leq m$$

and (3.8) becomes

$$p_{m-1}^*(x) = \psi_m(x) \cdot \sum_{j=1}^{m} \frac{f_j}{(x - x_j) \cdot a_j}$$

Using this representation, $p_{m-1}^*(x)$ only requires about $3m$ flops to evaluate. Note, however, that the difficulty in adding new data points remains.

Newton Form of $p_{m-1}^*(x)$

To construct this form of the interpolating polynomial p_{m-1}^*, we built it up successively from lower order interpolation polynomials. We illustrate the process by constructing p_3^* for the set of data points (3.6). The points are taken in reverse order because this is the most convenient in terms of algorithm design. Suppose we have determined

$$p_1^*(x) = 35 + 13(x - 5)$$

which interpolates the last two data points $(2, -4)$ and $(5, 35)$. To find p_2^*, which interpolates $(1, 7)$, $(2, -4)$, and $(5, 35)$, we write it in the form

$$p_2^* = p_1^* + h_2(x)$$
$$= 35 + 13(x - 5) + h_2(x)$$

and the problem is to determine what $h_2(x)$ must be. Now we know that $p_2^*(x)$ must be of degree ≤ 2, so deg $h_2(x) \leq 2$. Also, from the interpolation property for both p_1^* and p_2^*, we must have

$$-4 = p_2^*(2) = p_1^*(2) + h_2(2) = -4 + h_2(2) \Rightarrow h_2(2) = 0$$
$$35 = p_2^*(5) = p_1^*(5) + h_2(5) = 35 + h_2(5) \Rightarrow h_2(5) = 0$$

Hence, $h_2(x)$ must be of the form

$$h_2(x) = A_2(x - 5)(x - 2)$$

where A_2 is a constant to be determined. We define A_2 by requiring that p_2^* interpolate the new data point, that is, $p_2^*(1) = 7$. With this condition, we get $A_2 = 6$ and

$$p_2^*(x) = 35 + 13(x - 5) + 6(x - 5)(x - 2)$$
$$= 35 + (x - 5) \cdot [13 + 6(x - 2)].$$

Continuing in the same vein, we find that

$$p_3^*(x) = p_2^*(x) + h_3(x)$$
$$= p_2^*(x) + 2(x - 5)(x - 2)(x - 1)$$
$$= 35 + (x - 5) \cdot [13 + (x - 2) \cdot [6 + 2(x - 1)]]$$
(3.9) $$\qquad = A_4 + (x - x_4) \cdot [A_3 + (x - x_3) \cdot [A_2 + A_1(x - x_2)]]$$

By construction, this polynomial has degree 3 and it satisfies the interpolation conditions. Therefore, it must be the unique interpolating polynomial p_3^* in yet another form. This is the Newton form. Again, the nested version (3.9) is more efficient for evaluation.

The computation of the Newton form of p_{m-1}^* can be done very efficiently. First of all, we note from (3.9) that it can be characterized by the pair of m-vectors $(\mathbf{x}, \mathbf{A})$, where $\mathbf{x} = [x_1, \ldots, x_m]^T$ and $\mathbf{A} = [A_1, \ldots, A_m]^T$. Therefore, given the data points $\{(x_i, f_i)\}_{i=1}^m$, all we have to do is compute the A_j's. The most convenient way of doing this is to form a *divided difference table*. We illustrate such a table for our example.

i	x_i	$f[\ ]$	$f[\ ,\ ]$	$f[\ ,\ ]$	$f[\ ,\ ,\ ]$
1	-1	-7			
			$\frac{7-(-7)}{1-(-1)} = 7$		
2	1	7		$\frac{-11-7}{2-(-1)} = -6$	
			-11		$\frac{6-(-6)}{5-(-1)} = \underline{2}$
3	2	-4		$\underline{6}$	
			$\underline{13}$		
4	5	$\underline{35}$			

The computations that are shown in the table illustrate how to determine the entries. The column headed $f[\ ]$ consists of the y-coordinates of the data points. The elements in the column headed $f[\ ,\ ]$ are determined by the formula

$$f[x_i, x_{i+1}] = \frac{f[x_{i+1}] - f[x_i]}{x_{i+1} - x_i} \qquad \text{with } f[x_i] = f_i$$

These are called *first divided differences*. The next column is the *second divided differences*

$$f[x_i, x_{i+1}, x_{i+2}] = \frac{f[x_{i+1}, x_{i+2}] - f[x_i, x_{i+1}]}{x_{i+2} - x_i}$$

and so on. The important thing to note about the table is that the last entry in each column (underlined) is a coefficient A_j in (3.9). This, in fact, is true in general. Therefore, to find the Newton form of p_{m-1}^*, we only need to compute the divided difference table and retain the last entry in each column.

The amount of effort required to compute the Newton form of p_{m-1}^* can easily be determined. All of the work is in forming the divided difference table. Each entry requires $2A$'s plus $1D$ and there are $(m-1) + (m-2) + \cdots + 1 = m(m-1)/2$ entries. Hence, the work is substantially less than that for the linear equations method. Storage of the Newton form of p_{m-1}^* requires $2m$ locations—the x_i's and A_j's. It is worthwhile to point out that we do not need to provide storage for the entire difference table. We can start with a vector containing the f_i's and successively overwrite elements until it finally contains the A_j's. For our example, we would have

$$\begin{bmatrix} f_1 \\ f_2 \\ f_3 \\ f_4 \end{bmatrix} = \begin{bmatrix} -7 \\ 7 \\ -4 \\ \underline{35} \end{bmatrix} \rightarrow \begin{bmatrix} 7 \\ -11 \\ \underline{13} \\ \underline{35} \end{bmatrix} \rightarrow \begin{bmatrix} -6 \\ \underline{6} \\ \underline{13} \\ \underline{35} \end{bmatrix} \rightarrow \begin{bmatrix} \underline{2} \\ \underline{6} \\ \underline{13} \\ \underline{35} \end{bmatrix}$$

To illustrate how easy it is to add new data, suppose we want to add the point $(3, -27)$. All we have to do is insert the new point at the bottom of the table and compute the new divided differences. The equivalent changes in the f vector representation of the table would be

$$\begin{bmatrix} f_1 \\ f_2 \\ f_3 \\ f_4 \\ f_5 \end{bmatrix} = \begin{bmatrix} 2 \\ 6 \\ 13 \\ 35 \\ \underline{-27} \end{bmatrix} \rightarrow \begin{bmatrix} 2 \\ 6 \\ 13 \\ \underline{31} \\ \underline{-27} \end{bmatrix} \rightarrow \begin{bmatrix} 2 \\ 6 \\ \underline{18} \\ \underline{31} \\ \underline{-27} \end{bmatrix} \rightarrow \begin{bmatrix} 2 \\ \underline{6} \\ \underline{18} \\ \underline{31} \\ \underline{-27} \end{bmatrix} \rightarrow \begin{bmatrix} \underline{1} \\ \underline{6} \\ \underline{18} \\ \underline{31} \\ \underline{-27} \end{bmatrix}$$

The new interpolating polynomial will therefore be

$$p_4(x) = -27 + (x-3) \cdot [31 + (x-5) \cdot [18 + (x-2) \cdot [6 + 1 \cdot (x-1)]]].$$

To evaluate p_{m-1}^*, the nested version (3.9) of the Newton form requires $2(m-1)A$'s and $(m-1)M$'s. This is a little more than for the standard (nested) form (3.3) but we have the advantage of considerably less work to determine p_{m-1}^*. In addition, there is the fact that new data points can easily be added with the Newton form, that is, if a new point (x_{m+1}, f_{m+1}) is added, we can obtain the new polynomial p_m^* from p_{m-1}^* with very little work.

There is one more factor concerning polynomial interpolation that should be discussed. This is the question of error. The criterion for goodness of fit was defined to be the interpolating conditions (3.2). Since we can construct a p_{m-1}^* that satisfies these conditions exactly, there is no error at all except for the inevitable bit of round-off error. However, this does not take intermediate points into consideration, which is important if we plan to use p_{m-1}^* to predict values of f at intermediate points. Therefore, we define another measure of error. Suppose that the data points are values of a specific function $f(x)$. For convenience, we let $x_1 = a$ and $x_m = b$, and assume that each $x_j \in [a, b]$, $1 \le j \le m$. We define the new measure of error (in any function $g(x)$) to be

$$E(g) = \max_{a \le x \le b} |f(x) - g(x)|$$

Of course, this definition does not lend itself to easy computation. Nevertheless, it is a useful analytical tool for comparing different types of interpolating functions.

An expression for the error at intermediate points can be derived in the following way (see [5, p. 52]). Let $t \in [a, b]$ be any point different from $x_1, \ldots, x_m$. Then the Newton form of the polynomial $p_m^*(x)$ that interpolates $f(x)$ at the $m + 1$ points $x_1, \ldots, x_m, t$ is

$$p_m^*(x) = p_{m-1}^*(x) + f[x_1, \ldots, x_m, t] * \psi_m(x),$$

where $f[x_1, \ldots, x_m, t]$ is the mth divided difference with respect to the indicated points, and

$$\psi_m(x) = (x - x_1) \ldots (x - x_m) = \prod_{i=1}^{m} (x - x_i)$$

Evaluating $p_m^*(x)$ at $x = t$, we have

$$f(t) = p_m^*(t) = p_{m-1}^*(t) + f[x_1, \ldots, x_m, t] * \psi_m(t)$$

Since t is arbitrary, we can, for notational convenience, replace it by x, and we have

(3.10) $\quad f(x) - p_{m-1}^*(x) = f[x_1, \ldots, x_m, x] * \psi_m(x)$

where $x \ne x_i$, $1 \le i \le m$. An alternative expression for the error at intermediate points can be obtained from this by making use of the following result [5, p. 65], which shows the relationship between divided differences and derivatives.

> Suppose f is k times continuously differentiable on $[a, b]$ and let $x_1, \ldots, x_{k+1}$ be $k + 1$ points in $[a, b]$, distinct or not. Then there exists a point $\theta \in [a, b]$ such that

(3.11) $$f[x_1, \ldots, x_{k+1}] = \frac{f^{(k)}(\theta)}{k!}$$

Note that, if $k = 1$, this result is the well-known mean-value theorem for derivatives. Using this relationship, we can replace the divided difference in (3.10) and obtain

(3.10)′ $$f(x) - p_{m-1}^*(x) = \frac{f^{(m)}(\theta)}{m!} * \psi_m(x)$$

where $\theta \in [a, b]$ depends on x. From this, we obtain the bound

$$E(p_{m-1}^*) \leq \max_{a \leq x \leq b} \frac{|f^{(m)}(x)|}{m!} \cdot \max_{a \leq x \leq b} \left| \prod_{i=1}^{m} (x - x_i) \right|$$

Now, we are interested in what happens to $E(p_{m-1}^*)$ as m increases, that is, as more data points are added (within $[a, b]$). The reasoning here is that, by adding more data points, we make use of more information about f to derive the approximating function so we should expect to get better accuracy. In other words, $E(p_{m-1}^*)$ should decrease as m increases. Unfortunately, this does not always happen. Consider, for example, the function $f(x) = 1/(1 + x^2)$ on the interval $[-5, 5]$. Using equally spaced points and estimating $E(p_{m-1}^*)$ by computing the maximum error at 100 (equally spaced) points, we have

m	$E(p_{m-1}^*)$
2	6.5E-1
4	4.4E-1
8	1.0E 0
16	1.4E 1

Geometrically, the reason for such behavior is evident in Figure 3.2. By increasing m, the oscillations of the interpolating polynomial between data points will increase in amplitude. For an algebraic interpretation of this phenomenon, we look at our bound for $E(p_{m-1}^*)$. Despite the factorial term in the denominator, the first factor does not necessarily decrease with in-

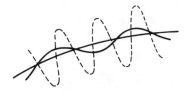

FIGURE 3.2

creasing m. The function $f(x) = \tan x$ on the interval $[0, \pi/4]$ is a case in point. Therefore, we have no guarantee that this term in the bound gets small as m increases. The same is true for the second factor. Its size and behavior as m increases depends on the locations of the x_i's. The optimum choice of points (which gives the smallest possible value for this term) is the so-called Tchebycheff points [5, p. 104] defined by

$$x_i = \frac{\{(b + a) - (b - a) \cdot \cos[\pi(2i - 1)/2m]\}}{2} \qquad 1 \le i \le m$$

For these particular x_i's, it can be shown that

$$\max_{a \le x \le b} \left| \prod_{i=1}^{m} (x - x_i) \right| \le 2 \left(\frac{b - a}{4} \right)^m$$

The behavior of this bound as m increases depends on the size of $(b - a)/4$. If it is small, then the bound goes to zero very rapidly. However, if it is greater than one, the bound will increase in size as m increases. For "non-Tchebycheff" points, the corresponding bound is larger but its behavior with increasing m still depends on the size of $[a, b]$. To summarize this discussion, we cannot guarantee an arbitrarily small bound for $E(p_{m-1}^*)$ by taking m sufficiently large. Therefore, we do not necessarily obtain a progressively better approximation of f by using polynomial interpolation of higher and higher degree. In fact, we usually get the opposite effect—as the degree of polynomial is increased beyond a certain value, the accuracy decreases. In practice then, one should use polynomials for interpolating only a relatively small number of data points. This, in fact, is the underlying idea used in the next section.

As a final point, we remark that it is possible to interpolate derivative values in addition to function values. The process is called *osculatory* interpolation. To illustrate, suppose we are given the data

$$\{(0, -6), (2, 12), (2, 41), (2, 92), (2, 162), (3, 135)\}$$

In this case, we have $x_2 = x_3 = x_4 = x_5 = 2$, which, of course, violates our initial assumption about having distinct x_i's. But suppose we view the corresponding values f_3, f_4, f_5 as the values of, respectively, the first, second, and third derivatives of f at x_2. To say that a function $g(x)$ interpolates such data, we mean that it passes through each of the points and, at the second one, its first three derivatives must assume the values specified. Hence, the interpolation conditions are

$$g(0) = -6 \qquad g(2) = 12 \qquad g(3) = 135$$
$$g'(2) = 41$$
$$g''(2) = 92$$
$$g'''(2) = 162$$

There are six conditions so, if we consider polynomial interpolation, we must choose $n = 6 - 1 = 5$. The linear system derived from the interpolating conditions is

$$\begin{bmatrix} 0 & 0 & 0 & 0 & 0 & 1 \\ 32 & 16 & 8 & 4 & 2 & 1 \\ 80 & 32 & 12 & 4 & 1 & 0 \\ 160 & 48 & 12 & 2 & 0 & 0 \\ 240 & 48 & 6 & 0 & 0 & 0 \\ 243 & 81 & 27 & 9 & 3 & 1 \end{bmatrix} \begin{bmatrix} a_0 \\ a_1 \\ a_2 \\ a_3 \\ a_4 \\ a_5 \end{bmatrix} = \begin{bmatrix} -6 \\ 12 \\ 41 \\ 92 \\ 162 \\ 135 \end{bmatrix}$$

Once again, the coefficient matrix is nonsingular if $x_1 \neq x_2 \neq x_3$, so p_5^* is unique. It is

$$p_5^*(x) = x^5 - 2x^4 + 3x^3 - 4x^2 + 5x - 6$$

For computational purposes, it is preferable to use the Newton form of $p_5^*(x)$. As before, its definition is

$$p_5^*(x) = A_6 + (x - x_6) * [A_5 + \cdots * [A_2 + (x - x_2) * A_1] \ldots]$$

where the coefficients are divided differences, that is,

$$A_j = f[x_j, \ldots, x_6] \qquad 1 \leq j \leq 6$$

which can be determined by constructing a difference table. However, the rules for forming the table must be modified because the x_i's are not all distinct and, as a consequence, some of the divided differences will have zero denominators. To describe the modification, we first assume that the data is ordered in such a way that

If $x_s = x_{s+k}$, $k \geq 0$, then $x_s = x_{s+1} = \cdots = x_{s+k}$, and $f(x_{s+j}) = f^{(j)}(x_s)$, $0 \leq j \leq k$.

Suppose that, in forming the rth column of the difference table, we find that $x_s = x_{s+r}$. Then, instead of forming the usual divided difference table, we simply set

$$f[x_s, \ldots, x_{s+r}] = \frac{f[x_{s+1}, \ldots, x_{s+r}]}{r}$$

This modification is motivated by the relationship between divided differences and the derivatives. If, in (3.11), $x_s = \cdots = x_{s+k}$, then the kth divided difference of f at x_s satisfies

$$(3.11)' \quad f[x_s, \ldots, x_{s+k}] = \frac{f^{(k)}(x_s)}{k!}$$

From the assumption on the ordering of the data, it is clear that our modification will produce these values. For our example data, the difference table is as follows.

i	x_i	$f[\ ]$	$f[\ ,\ ]$	$f[\ ,\ ,\ ]$	$f[\ ,\ ,\ ,\ ]$	$f[\ ,\ ,\ ,\ ,\ ]$	$f[\ ,\ ,\ ,\ ,\ ,\ ]$
1	0	-6					
			9				
2	2	12		16			
			41		15		
3	2	41		46		6	
			92		$\frac{81}{3} = 27$		1
4	2	92		$\frac{162}{2} = 81$		9	
			$\frac{162}{1} = 162$		$\frac{82-46}{3-2} = \underline{36}$		
5	2	162		$\frac{123-41}{3-2} = \underline{82}$			
			$\frac{135-12}{3-2} = \underline{123}$				
6	3	$\underline{135}$					

Hence, we see that the Newton form of $p_5^*(x)$ is

$$p_5^*(x) = 135 + (x - 3) * [123 + (x - 2)$$
$$* [82 + (x - 2) * [36 + (x - 2) * [9 + 1 * (x - 2)]]]]$$

We remark that the method of selecting the coefficients (A_j's) from the table must be altered in the case where derivative data is given for the last point, that is, when $x_{n-k} = \cdots = x_n$. The interpolating polynomial is derived in the same way, but the last k coefficients A_j, $k - n \leq j \leq n$, will be defined by (3.11)' and these are not the last elements in each column. To illustrate, suppose that the point $(3, 135)$ in our example data is placed at the beginning of the list. The resulting difference table, with the A_j's underlined, is

i	x_i	$f[\ ]$	$f[\ ,\ ]$	$\cdot$	$\cdot$	$\cdot$	$f[\ ,\ ,\ ,\ ,\ ]$
1	3	135					
2	0	-6	47	38			
3	2	$\underline{12}$	9	16	22	7	
4	2	41	$\underline{41}$	46	15		1
5	2	92	92	81	$\underline{27}$	$\underline{6}$	$\underline{1}$
6	2	162	162				

From this, we have

$$p_5^*(x) = 12 + (x - 2) * [41 + (x - 2) \\ * [46 + (x - 2) * [27 + (x - 2) * [6 + 1 * (x - 0)]]]]$$

Finally, we comment that, despite the apparent complexity in describing this modification, it can easily be incorporated into an interpolation algorithm. For details, see [5, p. 68].

3.1.2. Piecewise Polynomial Interpolation

We now look at the idea of using a continuous piecewise polynomial rather than a single polynomial to interpolate a set of data points. As the name implies, a *continuous piecewise polynomial* consists of segments of several different polynomials, joined together to form a continuous curve. In what follows, the continuity will be understood and we shall simply use the term "piecewise polynomial." The points at which the segments are joined are called *knots* or *joints*.

Piecewise polynomials have become a very popular form of function to use for curve fitting. As we will see, they have very desirable properties from the point of view of accuracy and computational efficiency. There is a wide variety of possible types of piecewise polynomial that one could choose for the class $\mathscr{G}$ in (3.1). We will discuss three of the more common choices. For convenience, we assume that the x_i's are distinct and ordered, that is, $x_1 < x_2 < \cdots < x_m$.

1. *Piecewise linear polynomials.* A piecewise linear polynomial $g_1(x)$ is the simplest form of piecewise polynomial. Each piece is a straight-line segment, that is, a polynomial of degree 1, and joining them gives a "sawtoothlike" curve as illustrated in Figure 3.3. Our problem, then, is to find a function $g_1^*(x)$ of this form that interpolates the data $\{(x_i, f_i)\}_{i=1}^m$. To do this, we consider the subintervals $I_i = [x_i, x_{i+1}]$, $1 \le i \le m - 1$, of $[x_1, x_m]$. (Recall that the x_i's are assumed to be ordered so there is no overlapping of subintervals.) Now each I_i contains two data points—(x_i, f_i) and (x_{i+1}, f_{i+1})— so we construct the line segment that interpolates them. Then, since these

FIGURE 3.3

points are at the ends of each subinterval, the resulting set of line segments will automatically join together, as shown in Figure 3.3, to form a continuous piecewise linear function that interpolates the data.

A more precise definition of $g_1^*(x)$ can be given as follows. First of all, let $\mathscr{S}_1(\mathbf{x})$ denote the class of functions that we are considering. It can be characterized as the set of all functions $g_1(x)$ of the form

$$(3.12) \quad g_1(x) = p_{1,i}(x) = c_{0,i}(x - x_i) + c_{1,i}$$

$$\text{if } x \in I_i = [x_i, x_{i+1}] \qquad 1 \le i \le m - 1$$

that is, the class of all piecewise linear polynomials with knots[2] at $\mathbf{x} = [x_1, x_2, \ldots, x_m]^T$. Then $g_1^*(x)$ is the function in $\mathscr{S}_1(\mathbf{x})$ that satisfies the interpolation conditions (3.2). For the example data (3.6), we have

$$(3.13) \quad g_1^*(x) = \begin{cases} 7(x + 1) - 7 & x \le 1 \\ -11(x - 1) + 7 & 1 \le x \le 2 \\ 13(x - 2) - 4 & 2 \le x \end{cases}$$

From this we see that, in general,

$$c_{0,i} = f[x_i, x_{i+1}] = \frac{f_{i+1} - f_i}{x_{i+1} - x_i} \quad \text{and} \quad c_{1,i} = f_i$$

Note that the definition of the first segment is extended from the subinterval $[-1, 1]$ to $(-\infty, 1]$ and similarly for the last segment. This is a common practice in order to define $g_1^*(x)$ on the whole real axis.

Turning to computational aspects, we can represent the piecewise linear function (3.12) by the pair $(\mathbf{x}, C)$, where $\mathbf{x}$ is an m-vector containing the knots x_i and C is a $2 \times (m - 1)$ matrix containing the coefficients $c_{k,i}$. The ith column of C contains the coefficients for the ith piece of $g_1(x)$. For example, the $g_1^*(x)$ of (3.13) can be represented as

$$\mathbf{x} = \begin{bmatrix} -1 \\ 1 \\ 2 \\ 5 \end{bmatrix} \qquad C = \begin{bmatrix} 7 & -11 & 13 \\ -7 & 7 & -4 \end{bmatrix}$$

To determine g_1^*, we have to compute the entries of C. The only work involved here is in the computation of the divided differences for the first row. There are $m - 1$ of them and each requires 2A's and 1D. Putting it

---

[2]Technically speaking, the endpoints x_1 and x_m are not knots, that is, they are not places where two pieces of $g_1(x)$ are joined. But, in (3.12), the knots are used to define the subintervals $[x_i, x_{i+1}]$ and, in this context, it is convenient to refer to x_1 and x_m as knots also.

another way, we only have to compute the first column of the divided difference table so, compared to the Newton form of p^*_{m-1}, computation of g^*_1 is much cheaper.

The evaluation of a piecewise linear polynomial is done in two stages. First, we must determine the correct piece of $g_1(x)$ to be evaluated and then, second, evaluate it. Suppose we want to compute the value of $g_1(x)$ at, say, $x = s$. To determine which piece of $g_1(x)$ to use, we must decide which subinterval I_i contains s. An efficient method for doing this is a binary search procedure. Let $d = [(m + 1)/2]$ be the greatest integer that is less than or equal to $(m + 1)/2$. (For example, if $m = 14$, then $d = 7$.) We can infer that either

$$s \in [x_1, x_d] \qquad \text{or} \qquad s \in [x_d, x_m]$$

depending on whether $s \le x_d$ or not. Whichever subinterval was found to contain s is again split into two, and so on until the correct subinterval I_i is found. The corresponding column of C is then selected for evaluation at $x = s$.

The cost of evaluating a piecewise linear polynomial $g_1(x)$ is measured by the number of comparisons[3] necessary to determine the correct subinterval I_i plus the work required to evaluate the piece $p_{1,i}(x)$. Since each stage of the binary search procedure reduces the set of possible subintervals by half, the number of comparisons required will be the smallest integer k such that $2^k \ge m$ or, equivalently[4], $k \ge \log_2 m$. The evaluation of $p_{1,i}(x)$ requires only 2A's and 1M. On the assumption that a comparison is equivalent to an add operation, the following table shows a comparison of evaluation costs of g^*_1 and the Newton form of the interpolating polynomial p^*_{m-1}:

	A	**M**
$g^*_1(x)$	$\log_2 m + 2$	1
$p^*_{m-1}(x)$	$2(m - 1)$	$(m - 1)$

---

[3] We assume that a comparison (to see which of two numbers a, b is the larger) is done by computing the difference $a - b$ and recording the sign of the result. Thus a comparison is roughly equivalent to an add operation.

[4] More precisely, $k = [1 + \log_2 m]$, where the square brackets denote the greatest integer function. The usual practice, however, is simply to write $k = \log_2 m$ with the understanding that we always round up to the next integer. For example, if $m = 12$, we take k to be 4. We adopt this convention in any subsequent discussions.

If, for example, $m = 12$, the cost for g_1^* is 6A's and 1M whereas, for p_{m-1}^* it is 22A's and 11M's. Hence, on the basis of computational efficiency, piecewise linear polynomials with m knots are superior to polynomials of deg $m - 1$. To confirm their overall superiority, we now analyze the error in piecewise linear interpolation.

A bound for the error $E(g_1^*)$ can be obtained by first looking at the error in each subinterval. Within I_i, we are interpolating two points with a polynomial. Consequently, a bound for the error in the ith piece of g_1^* is

$$E(p_{1,i}) \leq \frac{M_{2,i}}{2} \cdot \frac{\Delta_i^2}{4}$$

where $M_{2,i}$ is a bound on f'' in I_i and $\Delta_i = x_{i+1} - x_i$ is the length of I_i. From this it follows that

$$(3.14) \quad E(g_1^*) = \max_i E(p_{1,i}) \leq \frac{M_2 \Delta^2}{8}$$

where M_2 is a bound on f'' in the whole interval $[x_1, x_m]$ and $\Delta = \max_i \Delta_i$ is the maximum subinterval length. In order to make a comparison with polynomial interpolation, we will investigate the behavior of this bound as m increases, that is, as more data points are added. Now the only term in (3.14) that is affected by a change in m is Δ. Clearly, we can always ensure that Δ decreases with increasing m simply by making sure that the new data points are placed in the longer subintervals. Hence, as m increases, we can guarantee that the bound (3.14) for the error in piecewise linear interpolation goes to zero, that is, $g_1^*(x)$ can be made to approximate $f(x)$ as accurately as we like. Therefore, compared to the discussion of the bound for polynomial interpolation, it follows that piecewise linear functions have a much better ability to approximate f at intermediate points. In all (practical) respects, then, they are superior to polynomials.

Finally, we describe the definition of g_1^* in a more general way. The purpose is to provide a setting for extension to other types of piecewise polynomials. Any $g_1(x) \in \mathcal{S}_1(x)$, the class of piecewise linear polynomials with knots at $x_1, \ldots, x_m$, must satisfy the conditions

(3.15) **i** $g_1(x)$ is linear in each subinterval I_i, $1 \leq i \leq m - 1$.
          ii $g_1(x)$ is continuous in $[x_1, x_m]$.

From the first condition, we conclude that $g_1(x)$ must have the form (3.12). Therefore, since each $g_1(x)$ has $2(m - 1)$ parameters $c_{k,i}$, we need this many conditions to ensure the existence and uniqueness of $g_1^*(x)$. We derive them from the interpolating conditions (3.2) and continuity condition (3.15)(ii). Specifically, we have

			No. of Conditions
Interpolation at all knots	$g_1^*(x_i) = f_i$	$1 \le i \le m$	m
Continuity at interior knots	$p_{1,i-1}^*(x_i) = p_{1,i}^*(x_i)$	$2 \le i \le m - 1$	$m - 2$

The total is $2(m - 1)$, the required number. We will shortly be defining a specific form of piecewise polynomial called a "spline" function. Since the definition (3.15) is a special case of it, a piecewise linear polynomial is sometimes called a "linear spline."

2. *Piecewise cubic polynomials.* One possible criticism of piecewise linear polynomials is that they are not smooth enough, that is, they are not sufficiently differentiable. In fact, they are not differentiable at all at the knots x_i. In order to obtain more smoothness, we must go to higher-order piecewise polynomials. Piecewise quadratics $g_2(x)$ are the immediately obvious choice but, for reasons that we shall point out later, they are not used much in practice. The next choice, then, is cubics. In each subinterval I_i, a piecewise cubic polynomial $g_3(x)$ will have the form

$$(3.16) \quad g_3(x) = p_{3,i}(x)$$
$$= c_{0,i}(x - x_i)^3 + c_{1,i}(x - x_i)^2 + c_{2,i}(x - x_i) + c_{3,i}$$
$$\text{if } x_i \le x \le x_{i+1} \quad 1 \le i \le m - 1$$

There are $4(m - 1)$ parameters so we need to impose this many conditions in order to guarantee the existence and uniqueness of $g_3^*(x)$. There are several ways in which one can define a set of conditions. We discuss two of them here.

2. (a) *Piecewise cubic Hermite polynomials.* This form of piecewise cubic uses Hermite interpolation, that is, it interpolates first derivative values as well as function values. (It is a special case of osculatory interpolation discussed in the last section.) Suppose that we are given the data $\{(x_i, f_i, f_i')\}_{i=1}^m$. To construct $g_3^*(x)$, we proceed as we did in the piecewise linear case by considering each subinterval I_i separately. There are four conditions to interpolate in each I_i: (x_i, f_i), (x_i, f_i'), (x_{i+1}, f_{i+1}), (x_{i+1}, f_{i+1}'). Hence, each (cubic) piece $p_{3,i}^*(x)$ of $g_3^*(x)$ can be uniquely determined from these conditions. Since the conditions are imposed at the endpoints of each subinterval, the resulting set of cubic polynomial segments will automatic-

ally join together to form a continuous piecewise cubic function whose first derivative is also continuous.

In terms of the more general setting described above, we can verify the existence and uniqueness of $g_3^*(x)$. There are $4(m-1)$ conditions to be imposed and this is done as follows:

			No. of Conditions
Interpolation at all knots	$g_3^*(x_i) = f_i$	$1 \le i \le m$	m
	$g_3^{*'}(x_i) = f_i'$	$1 \le i \le m$	m
Continuity at interior knots	$p_{3,i-1}^*(x_i) = p_{3,i}^*(x_i)$	$2 \le i \le m-1$	$m-2$
	$p_{3,i-1}^{*'}(x_i) = p_{3,i}^{*'}(x_i)$	$2 \le i \le m-1$	$m-2$
			$4m-4$

We can represent a piecewise cubic by the pair $(\mathbf{x}, C)$, where, as before, $\mathbf{x}$ is the m-vector of knots x_i and C is the matrix of coefficients $c_{k,i}$ in (3.16). This time, however, C will have four rows, that is, it is $4 \times (m-1)$. Hence, the storage requirement for g_3^* is $5m - 4$ locations. The computation of g_3^* uses 8A's and 4M's per piece $p_{3,i}^*$ for a total of $8(m-1)$A's and $4(m-1)$M's. The cost of an evaluation is $k = \log_2 m$ comparisons (to find the correct I_i) plus 6A's and 3M's to evaluate the appropriate piece $p_{3,i}^*$ (in its nested form). Note that evaluation is only a little more work than for piecewise linear polynomials.

2. (b) *Cubic splines.* The major disadvantage of piecewise cubic Hermite interpolation is that the data must include derivative values as well as function values. A way of avoiding this difficulty is to use cubic splines as the form of interpolating function. To distinguish this type of function, we will use the notation $s_3(x)$. A *cubic spline* is a piecewise cubic polynomial $s_3(x)$ with the property that s_3, s_3', and s_3'' are all continuous. (Note the extra degree of smoothness compared to Hermite cubics.) The name "spline" derives from the same word employed by draftspeople for a flexible piece of metal used in drawing curves. Referring to Figure 3.4, we visualize the knots of $s_3(x)$ as fixed pins and thread the flexible strip through them as indicated. Then the resulting curve that is formed is approximated by a cubic spline. The determination of the interpolating cubic spline s_3^* is somewhat different from the previous cases because there are not enough interpolating conditions to completely determine all the coefficients. In-

FIGURE 3.4

stead, we have to use the continuity conditions directly. To explain, we first state the conditions which define $s_3^*(x)$. These are

Interpolation at all knots	$s_3^*(x_i) = f_i$	$1 \leq i \leq m$	m
Continuity at interior knots	$s_{3,\,i-1}^*(x_i) = s_{3,\,i}^*(x_i)$	$2 \leq i \leq m-1$	$m-2$
	$s_{3,\,i-1}^{*'}(x_i) = s_{3,\,i}^{*'}(x_i)$	$2 \leq i \leq m-1$	$m-2$
	$s_{3,\,i-1}^{*''}(x_i) = s_{3,\,i}^{*''}(x_i)$	$2 \leq i \leq m-1$	$m-2$
			$\overline{4m-6}$

However, since we need $4m-4$ conditions to guarantee existence and uniqueness of s_3^*, we are two short of the requirement. The usual practice for imposing the extra conditions is to ask that

$$(3.17) \quad s_3^{*'}(x_1) = f_1' \quad \text{and} \quad s_3^{*'}(x_m) = f_m'$$

that is, require that the derivative of s_3^* interpolate the derivative of f at the endpoints. If f_1' and f_m' are not known (which is usually the case), we can substitute divided differences for the derivative values and get the conditions

$$(3.17)' \quad s_3^{*'}(x_1) = \frac{f_2 - f_1}{x_2 - x_1} \quad \text{and} \quad s_3^{*'}(x_m) = \frac{f_m - f_{m-1}}{x_m - x_{m-1}}$$

If the derivative conditions are used, the resulting s_3^* is often called a spline with "clamped" boundary whereas, if the divided difference conditions are used, it is called a spline with "free" boundary. Motivation for these terms can be found in the analogy with the draftsperson's spline. For example, the clamped boundary is anlogous to clamping both ends of the (draftsperson's) spline at specified angles.

The computation of $s_3^*(x)$ can be done very efficiently. We give a brief derivation of the algorithm for doing it. Referring to the formula (3.16) for the ith piece $p_{3,\,i}(x)$, it follows from the interpolating condition at x_i that

$$(3.18) \quad c_{3,\,i} = f_i \quad 1 \leq i \leq m-1$$

For convenience, we denote

(3.19) $c_{2,i} = d_i$ $1 \le i \le m - 1$

We remark that d_i is the slope of s_3 at $x = x_i$ since, from (3.16), $p'_{3,i}(x_i) = c_{2,i} = d_i$. Now the continuity of s_3 and s'_3 at an interior knot $x = x_i$ gives

$$c_{0,i-1}\Delta_{i-1}^3 + c_{1,i-1}\Delta_{i-1}^2 + d_{i-1}\Delta_{i-1} + f_{i-1} = f_i$$

$$3c_{0,i-1}\Delta_{i-1}^2 + 2c_{1,i-1}\Delta_{i-1} + d_{i-1} \qquad = d_i$$

where $\Delta_{i-1} = x_i - x_{i-1}$. The unknowns in these (linear) equations are $c_{0,i-1}$, $c_{1,i-1}$, d_{i-1}, d_i. Solving for the first two in terms of the others, we get

(3.20)
$$c_{1,i} = \frac{f[x_i, x_{i+1}] - d_i}{\Delta_i} - c_{0,i}\Delta_i$$

$$\qquad\qquad 1 \le i \le m - 1$$

$$c_{0,i} = \frac{d_{i+1} + d_i - 2f[x_i, x_{i+1}]}{\Delta_i^2}$$

where $f[\,,\,]$ is a divided difference and, for notational convenience, we have increased the subscripts by one. Consequently, given the x_i's, f_i's and d_i's, we can determine all of the coefficients. Therefore, the problem is reduced to one of finding the d_i's. To this end, we use the continuity of s''_3 at the interior knots, that is,

$$6c_{0,i-1}\Delta_{i-1} + 2c_{1,i-1} = 2c_{1,i} \qquad 2 \le i \le m - 1$$

Upon substituting the expressions (3.20) for $c_{0,i-1}$, $c_{1,i-1}$, $c_{1,i}$ into these equations and doing some manipulation, we get the $m - 2$ relationships between the d_i's

(3.21) $\Delta_i d_{i-1} + 2(\Delta_{i-1} + \Delta_i)d_i + \Delta_{i-1}d_{i+1}$
$$= 3(\Delta_{i-1}f[x_i, x_{i+1}] + \Delta_i f[x_{i-1}, x_i]) \qquad 2 \le i \le m - 1$$

This is a system of $m - 2$ linear equations in the $m - 2$ unknowns $d_2, \ldots, d_{m-1}$. Note that d_1 appears on the left side of the first equation ($i = 2$). But, as we have already noted, this value represents the slope of s_3 at $x = x_1$. Consequently, d_1 is prescribed by either (3.17) or (3.17)'. Similarly, in the last equation of (3.21), we know the value of d_m, the (prescribed) slope of s_3 at $x = x_m$. Therefore, the d_i's can be determined by solving[5] the system (3.21). After this is done, computing the coefficients $c_{k,i}$ for s_3^* is a simple matter of substituting into (3.18), (3.19), and (3.20).

At this point, it is instructive to look at an example. We use the following data

$$\{(-1, -7), (1, 7), (2, -4), (3, -1), (5, 35), (6, 30)\}$$

---

[5]It can be shown [24, p. 76] that this system will have a unique solution, that is, the coefficient matrix is nonsingular if each $\Delta_i \ne 0$. Alternatively, a solution exists if the x_i's are distinct.

which is the data (3.6) with two points added. To set up the system (3.21), we first compute the Δ_i's and $f[\ ,\ ]$'s. These are

i	x_i	Δ_i	f_i	$f[x_i, x_{i+1}]$
1	-1		-7	
2	1	2	7	7
3	2	1	-4	-11
4	3	1	-1	3
5	5	2	35	18
6	6	1	30	-5

Using the conditions (3.17)′, we have

$$d_1 = f[x_1, x_2] = 7 \quad \text{and} \quad d_6 = f[x_5, x_6] = -5$$

Then the system (3.21) is

$$\begin{bmatrix} 6 & 2 & 0 & 0 \\ 1 & 4 & 1 & 0 \\ 0 & 2 & 6 & 1 \\ 0 & 0 & 1 & 6 \end{bmatrix} \begin{bmatrix} d_2 \\ d_3 \\ d_4 \\ d_5 \end{bmatrix} = \begin{bmatrix} -45-7 \\ -24 \\ 72 \\ 24+10 \end{bmatrix} = \begin{bmatrix} -52 \\ -24 \\ 72 \\ 34 \end{bmatrix}$$

We observe that the coefficient matrix has a band structure—it is tridiagonal—so the system can be solved very efficiently. In fact, it is clear from (3.21) that the tridiagonal structure will always be present. This is a very important feature because, by exploiting it, this part of the computation of s_3^* can be done very efficiently—$4(m-2)$ flops rather than $(m-2)^3/3$. The solution of the system, to three digits, is

$$\mathbf{d} = [-5.99, -8.03, 14.1, 3.31]^T$$

Finally, knowing the Δ_i's, f_i's, $f[\ ,\ ]$'s, and d_i's, we substitute into (3.18), (3.19), and (3.20) to get

$$C = \begin{bmatrix} -3.25 & 7.98 & 0.0960 & -4.64 & 8.31 \\ 6.49 & -13.0 & 10.9 & 11.2 & -16.6 \\ 7.0 & -5.99 & -8.03 & 14.1 & 3.31 \\ -7.0 & 7.0 & -4.0 & -1.0 & 35.0 \end{bmatrix}$$

whereupon

$$(3.22) \quad s_3^*(x) = \begin{cases} -3.25z_1^3 + 6.49z_1^2 + 7.00z_1 - 7.0 & \text{if } x \le 1 \\ 7.98z_2^3 - 13.0z_2^2 - 5.99z_2 + 7.0 & \text{if } 1 \le x \le 2 \\ 0.0960z_3^3 + 10.9z_3^2 - 8.03z_3 - 4.0 & \text{if } 2 \le x \le 3 \\ -4.64z_4^3 + 11.2z_4^2 + 14.1z_4 - 1.0 & \text{if } 3 \le x \le 5 \\ 8.31z_5^3 - 16.6z_5^2 + 3.31z_5 + 35.0 & \text{if } 5 \le x \end{cases}$$

where $z_i = x - x_i$, $1 \le i \le 5$.

With this example as a model, we can easily analyze the amount of work required to compute $s_3^*(x)$. The successive stages in the process and their approximate costs are:

		A	M
i	Compute Δ_i's and $f[\ ,\ ]$'s.	$2(m-1)$	$m-1$
ii	Set up the linear system (3.21).	$3(m-2)$	$2(m-2)$
iii	Solve the linear system (3.21).	$4(m-2)$	$4(m-2)$
iv	Compute the $c_{k,i}$'s.	$4(m-1)$	$2(m-1)$
		$13m$	$9m$

Note that the cost of step (iii) assumes that we take advantage of the tridiagonal structure of the linear system (3.21). The total cost is a little more than for the other types of interpolating functions we have considered. However, as we have already pointed out, the cost of determining s_3^* is not too important provided, of course, that it is not excessive, which is certainly the case here. In any event, the little extra work is well worth it. The interpolating cubic spline has good accuracy—the error bound is

$$E(s_3^*) \le \frac{M_4 \Delta^4}{384}$$

where M_4 is a bound on the fourth derivative $f^{(iv)}$ of f on $[x_1, x_m]$, and $\Delta = \max_i \Delta_i$. It is also quite smooth since it is twice differentiable. In addition, the cost of evaluating s_3^* is very cheap—$\log_2 m$ comparisons plus 6A's and 3M's.

In summary, piecewise polynomial interpolation has every computational advantage over polynomial interpolation. The choice between linear and cubic depends, basically, on the degree of smoothness desired. Cubic splines cost a little more to determine and to evaluate but are much more accurate and much smoother.

It is, of course, possible to use higher degree piecewise polynomials. Splines are the type considered most commonly. They are defined by imposing continuity conditions on derivatives of sufficiently high order. For example, quintic splines s_5^* would have $6(m-1)$ parameters $c_{k,i}$, defined by imposing the interpolating conditions at all knots and the continuity of $s_5(x)$ and its first four derivatives at interior knots. This specifies $6m-10$ conditions, leaving four degrees of freedom that can be used to define conditions at the endpoints as we did with cubic splines. We could go on to even higher-degree splines but it is rare that one would need so much smoothness. In this regard, cubic splines are usually quite adequate for most practical purposes. They certainly are the ones that are most commonly used.

Finally, we remark on why piecewise quadratics $q_2(x)$ were not considered. A piecewise quadratic has $3(m - 1)$ parameters to be defined. For quadratic splines, we would impose the interpolating conditions at all the knots and continuity of g_2 and g_2' at interior knots. Since this gives $3m - 4$ conditions, there is only one degree of freedom remaining. But if we use it to define some condition at an endpoint as we did with cubic splines, the resulting quadratic spline would have a certain lack of symmetry. In other words, there is no natural or convenient way of disposing of the extra degree of freedom.

3.2. APPROXIMATION

There are many curve-fitting problems where the use of interpolation as a criterion for goodness of fit is inappropriate. For example, in situations where m is large, the requirement that g^* pass through every data point will very often obscure some of the overall characteristics such as the general trend of the data. Another instance is when the data is subject to error, as is often the case when taking measurements or readings in an experiment. In this situation, it does not make sense to require that the approximating function g^* interpolate such data exactly. Instead, it is preferable for g^* to reflect the general behavior of the data as a function of x. In other words, it is usually better to find a g^* that approximates the data in some sense rather than one that reproduces it exactly. We will now consider ways of defining and computing such approximating functions. For convenience, we will assume that the x_i's are distinct and are contained in the interval $[a, b]$, that is, $a \leq x_i \leq b$, $1 \leq i \leq m$.

We will be looking at approximation using various types of functions—polynomials, piecewise polynomials, exponential functions, and so on. It turns out that all of these are special cases of a general theory of approximation using functions from what is called a "linear[6] function space." (The name may seem a bit overwhelming but the ideas involved are not particularly complicated.) The approach taken here will be to develop some of the concepts of the theory first (Section 3.2.1). This will provide a general framework from which we can easily describe and compare specific types of approximation (Section 3.2.2). In Section 3.2.3, we discuss the specific case of periodic functions.

---

[6]The term "linear" in this context does not mean that we are restricted to approximating by straight lines. Instead, it refers to the way of representing the different types of functions as linear combinations of functions from a specified set.

3.2.1. Linear Function Spaces

We recall that, in the general formulation (3.1) of the curve-fitting problem, we are free to choose both the class $\mathscr{G}$ of functions and the definition of goodness of fit. Let us look at the choice of $\mathscr{G}$ first.

In order to motivate some of the ideas involved, we will begin by considering, as the choice of $\mathscr{G}$, the set $\mathscr{P}_3$ of all polynomials of degree ≤ 3. We define the specific set $B = \{1, x, x^2, x^3\}$, each of which is an element of $\mathscr{P}_3$. Then it is clear that any $p_3(x) \in \mathscr{P}_3$ can be expressed as a *linear combination* of members of B, that is,

$$(3.23) \quad p_3(x) = c_1 \cdot 1 + c_2 x + c_3 x^2 + c_4 x^3$$

We can characterize any $p_3(x)$ by the pair $(\mathbf{c}, B)$, where $\mathbf{c} = [c_1, c_2, c_3, c_4]^T$ is the vector of coefficients in (3.23) and B is the "generating set" defined above. In other words, given the set B, every $p_3(x)$ has a unique representation given by its corresponding vector $\mathbf{c}$. We remark that it may seem redundant to have to include B in the characterization of $p_3(x)$. After all, it is easily understood that c_j is the coefficient of x^{j-1}, $1 \leq j \leq 4$. However, there are many other possible sets that will do the job of "generating" $\mathscr{P}_3$ and, for any given polynomial, the corresponding $\mathbf{c}$ that represents it will depend on the particular set B that is used. For example, consider the polynomial (3.7)

$$p_3(x) = 10 + 5x - 10x^2 + 2x^3$$

With respect to the set B above, this polynomial has the representation $\mathbf{c} = [10, 5, -10, 2]^T$. But two other possible generating sets (see Exercise 2.2) are

$$\{1, x, x^2 - 1/3, x^3 - 3x/5\}$$
(3.24) and
$$\{1_1(x), 1_2(x), 1_3(x), 1_4(x)\}$$

the Lagrange polynomials of (3.8). The representations of the polynomial (3.7) with respect to these sets are, respectively,

$$[2, -10, 31/5, 20]^T \quad \text{and} \quad [-7, 7, -4, 35]^T$$

The latter representation was given in (3.8). Therefore, in order to characterize p_3 precisely, we must specify both $\mathbf{c}$ and the set B used to generate the class $\mathscr{P}_3$. From this, it follows that the problem of finding a best approximation $p_3^* \in \mathscr{P}_3$ to some given data consists of two steps:

    i Define a generating set B for $\mathscr{P}_3$.

    ii Compute the vector $\mathbf{c}^*$ corresponding to p_3^* relative to B.

An obvious question is whether or not it makes any difference which set is chosen. For computing c^*, the answer is "not much." We will elaborate on this later. On the other hand, for evaluating p_3^*, it does make a difference. For instance, the representation (3.23) is clearly cheaper to evaluate than the corresponding representations with respect to either of the sets (3.24). Therefore, if p_3^* will be evaluated quite often in any subsequent computation, an appropriate choice of B could result in significant savings.

With this example in mind, we now formulate a general setting for the approximation problem. Let $B = \{\phi_1(x), \phi_2(x), \ldots, \phi_n(x)\}$ be a set of n specified functions. Then the class $\mathscr{G}$ of approximating functions will be defined to be the set of all functions $g(x)$ of the form

$$(3.25) \quad g(x) = c_1\phi_1(x) + c_2\phi_2(x) + \cdots + c_n\phi_n(x)$$

that is, $g(x)$ is a *linear combination* of functions $\phi_j(x)$ from the generating set B. Hence, the choice of the class $\mathscr{G}$ of approximating functions is effectively made by specifying the set $B = \{\phi_j(x)\}_{j=1}^n$. Any $g \in \mathscr{G}$ can be characterized by the pair (c, B), where $c = [c_1, \ldots, c_n]^T$ is the vector of coefficients relative to B. Therefore, given B, the problem of determining the best approximation g^* is equivalent to computing the corresponding vector c^*.

The example of the class $\mathscr{P}_3$ of cubic polynomials is clearly a special case of this formulation. Indeed, polynomials of any degree r can be described in this way by taking $n = r - 1$ and $\phi_j(x) = x^{j-1}$, $1 \le j \le n$. As another example, we let $n = 4$ and define $B = \{1, x, \sin(x), e^{-x}\}$. Then $\mathscr{G}$ is the class of all functions of the form

$$(3.26) \quad g(x) = c_1 + c_2x + c_3 \sin(x) + c_4e^{-x}$$

From this it is clear that polynomials are only one of many possible classes defined by (3.25). In fact, as we will see in the next section, even piecewise polynomials can be described in this form. Therefore, this theory can be used to describe a very wide range of types of approximating functions.

At this point, we need to introduce some terminology. The class $\mathscr{G}$ of functions $g(x)$ defined by (3.25) is called a *linear function space*. This name is meant to reflect the analogy with linear *vector* spaces for, if we substitute vectors x_j for the functions $\phi_j(x)$ in (3.25), we will have the usual definition of an element x of a vector space. This analogy is continued in the following definitions of other terms.

We will assume that the set $B = \{\phi_j\}$ is linearly independent. A formal definition of this term is:

> A set of functions $\{\phi_j(x)\}_{j=1}^n$ is *linearly independent* on $[a, b]$ if there exists at least one set of n distinct points $s_1, \ldots, s_n \in [a, b]$ such that the relationships

(3.27) $\qquad c_1\phi_1(s_k) + \cdots + c_n\phi_n(s_k) = 0 \qquad 1 \le k \le n$

imply that $c_1 = \cdots = c_n = 0$. Otherwise, the set is *linearly dependent*.

The analogy with the corresponding concepts in vector spaces is easier to see in the case of linear dependence. As a simple example, we consider the set $\{1, x, 3x - 2\}$. Quite clearly, $\phi_3 = -2\phi_1 + 3\phi_2$, so we have

$$2\phi_1(x) - 3\phi_2(x) + \phi_3(x) = 2(1) - 3(x) + (3x - 2) = 0 \qquad \text{for } any \ x$$

Therefore, it is impossible to find a set of distinct points s_1, s_2, s_3 satisfying the above definition and we conclude that this set of functions is linearly dependent (on $(-\infty, +\infty)$, the whole real line). On the other hand, any pair of functions—$\{1, x\}$, $\{1, 3x - 2\}$ or $\{x, 3x - 2\}$—from the set can be shown to be linearly independent. For instance, with the first pair, we can choose $s_1 = 0$, $s_2 = 1$ and the equations (3.27) are

$$s_1 = 0: \ c_1 \qquad = 0$$

$$s_2 = 1: \ c_1 + c_2 = 0$$

which are satisfied if and only if $c_1 = c_2 = 0$. Now, returning to the development of terminology, the set $B = \{\phi_j\}_{j=1}^n$ of linearly independent functions is called a *basis* for $\mathcal{G}$ and each member of it is called a *basis function*. We also say that the basis B *generates* $\mathcal{G}$. The *dimension* of $\mathcal{G}$ is $\dim(\mathcal{G}) = n$, the maximum number of linearly independent functions in it. Again, for the example of cubic polynomials, we have $\dim(\mathcal{P}_3) = 4$.

We now discuss the choice of the measure of goodness of fit. Again, we use a simple example in order to motivate the ideas involved. Consider the set of data given in the following table

(3.28)

i	x_i	f_i
1	0.1	1.97
2	0.2	3.81
3	0.3	5.40
4	0.5	7.85
5	0.7	9.51
6	1.0	11.1
7	1.4	12.3
8	2.0	13.3

which was generated from the function $y = 10\tan^{-1}x$. Suppose we want to approximate this data by a polynomial of degree ≤ 1, that is, a straight line. As a basis for the space $\mathscr{P}_1$, we will use $B = \{1, x\}$ so the form of approximating function is

$$g(x) = c_1 + c_2 x$$

Now, in order to define a measure of goodness of fit of $g(x)$ to the entire set of data, we need a measure of the error at each individual data point (x_i, f_i). To this end, we define the errors or *residuals*

$$\begin{align}
(3.29) \quad r_i(\mathbf{c}) &= f_i - g(x_i) \\
&= f_i - [c_1\phi_1(x_i) + c_2\phi_2(x_i)] \\
&= f_i - [c_1 + c_2 x_i] \qquad 1 \leq i \leq 8
\end{align}$$

Note the dependence of r_i on the vector $\mathbf{c} = [c_1, c_2]^T$ of coefficients of $g(x)$. Geometrically, as Figure 3.5 illustrates, each r_i is the vertical distance from (x_i, f_i) to the graph of $g(x)$. We remark that, theoretically, one could measure the errors in any one of a variety of directions. In particular, either the horizontal or perpendicular (to g) direction could be used. However, in terms of defining a good fit to the data, there is no particular reason to favor one method of measurement over another. Therefore, the choice is based on computational considerations and, in this respect, the vertical direction is by far the most convenient. We are now ready to define a measure of the goodness of fit to the data. There is a wide variety of possible measures that could be defined, but only three are ever used in practice:

$$S_1(\mathbf{c}) = |r_1| + |r_2| + \cdots + |r_8| = \sum_{i=1}^{m} |r_i|$$

$$(3.30) \quad S_2(\mathbf{c}) = [r_1^2 + r_2^2 + \cdots + r_8^2]^{1/2} = \left[\sum_{i=1}^{m} r_i^2\right]^{1/2}$$

$$S_\infty(\mathbf{c}) = \max\{|r_1|, |r_2|, \ldots, |r_8|\} = \max_{1 \leq i \leq m} |r_i|$$

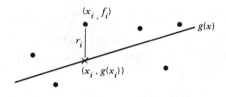

FIGURE 3.5

Of these, the second one is by far the most commonly used since it leads to a relatively straightforward algorithm for computing c^*. But, whichever measure $S_k(c)$ is chosen, we define the best approximation p_1^* to be the element of $\mathscr{P}_1$ corresponding to the vector c^* that minimizes $S_k(c)$. For example, if we use the measure $S_2(c)$, then c^* is the vector satisfying

$$(3.31) \quad S_2(c^*) = \min_c S_2(c) = \min_c \left[\sum_{i=1}^{m} [f_i - (c_1 + c_2 x_i)]^2 \right]^{1/2}$$

For obvious reasons, the corresponding p_1^* is called the *best least-squares fit* in $\mathscr{P}_1$ to the data. We discuss the existence and uniqueness of c^* below. We remark that c^* will be different for each measure. In other words, the best approximation depends on the method of measuring the goodness of fit.

It remains to specify a method for computing c^*. In order to do this, it is convenient to reformulate the above ideas in matrix-vector notation. For the example data, the relationships (3.29) defining the residuals form a system of eight linear equations in the two unknowns c_1, c_2. We can write them in the form

$$\begin{bmatrix} r_1 \\ r_2 \\ r_3 \\ r_4 \\ r_5 \\ r_6 \\ r_7 \\ r_8 \end{bmatrix} = \begin{bmatrix} 1.97 \\ 3.81 \\ 5.40 \\ 7.85 \\ 9.51 \\ 11.1 \\ 12.3 \\ 13.3 \end{bmatrix} - \begin{bmatrix} 1 & 0.1 \\ 1 & 0.2 \\ 1 & 0.3 \\ 1 & 0.5 \\ 1 & 0.7 \\ 1 & 1.0 \\ 1 & 1.4 \\ 1 & 2.0 \end{bmatrix} \begin{bmatrix} c_1 \\ c_2 \end{bmatrix}$$

or, simply,

$$(3.32) \quad r(c) = f - Ac$$

In other words, the equations (3.29) can be viewed as defining the residuals in the overdetermined system of linear equations $Ac = f$, where A and f are given above. With this formulation, each of the measures (3.30) can be expressed as a length or norm of the residual vector $r(c)$. Specifically, we have

$$S_1(c) = \|r(c)\|_1 \qquad S_2(c) = \|r(c)\|_2 \qquad S_\infty(c) = \|r(c)\|_\infty$$

where the respective vector norms are defined by (2.22) and (2.23). Again, taking S_2 as an example, the best approximation p_1^* corresponds to the vector c^* that satisfies

$$(3.33) \quad S_2(c^*) = \min_c \|r(c)\|_2$$

But now we observe that (3.32) and (3.33) are precisely the same as (2.41) and (2.42) in Section 2.3, which deals with the solution of overdetermined linear systems. Therefore, the problem of computing the best least-squares approximation c^* is exactly the same problem as that of computing the best least squares solution of the overdetermined linear system $Ac = f$. In Section 2.3, we have already discussed algorithms for solving the latter problem. Hence, all we have to do to compute c^* is set up the system $Ac = f$ and then call a least-squares subroutine for solving it. Doing this for our example data, we get $c^* = [3.68, 5.77]^T$, from which it follows that the best least-squares approximation in $\mathscr{P}_1$ relative to the basis $\{1, x\}$ is

(3.34) $\quad p_1^* = 3.68 + 5.77x$

Similarly, using either of the norms $\|\cdot\|_1$ and $\|\cdot\|_\infty$ as the measure of goodness of fit, one can define the best ℓ_1 or ℓ_∞ approximations to the data. However, as we pointed out in Section 2.3.1, the least-squares approximation is the easiest (cheapest) to compute so it is the one that is most commonly used. Therefore, as in Section 2.3, we restrict our discussion to least squares.

Starting with the set of data (3.28), the actual procedure for computing c^* is quite simple. First, we form the matrix A and vector f, and then call a subroutine for solving the overdetermined linear system $Ac = f$ in order to compute c^*. The formula for forming A is quite simple. Referring to the equations (3.29), it is evident that the jth column ($j = 1, 2$) of A should consist of values of the jth basis function $\phi_j(x)$ at each of the x_i's. Hence, recalling that $\phi_1(x) = 1$ and $\phi_2(x) = x$, we have

$$a_{i,1} = \phi_1(x_i) = 1 \quad \text{and} \quad a_{i,2} = \phi_2(x_i) = x_i \quad 1 \le i \le 8$$

We note that, if another basis set B is used, the matrix A will be different. For example, we illustrate three different sets B and their corresponding matrices A:

$$\{1, 3x - 2\} \qquad \{x, 3x - 2\} \qquad \{1, x, 3x - 2\}$$

$$
\begin{bmatrix}
1 & -1.7 \\
1 & -1.4 \\
1 & -1.1 \\
1 & -0.5 \\
1 & 0.1 \\
1 & 1.0 \\
1 & 2.2 \\
1 & 4.0
\end{bmatrix}
\qquad
\begin{bmatrix}
0.1 & -1.7 \\
0.2 & -1.4 \\
0.3 & -1.1 \\
0.5 & -0.5 \\
0.7 & 0.1 \\
1.0 & 1.0 \\
1.4 & 2.2 \\
2.0 & 4.0
\end{bmatrix}
\qquad
\begin{bmatrix}
1 & 0.1 & -1.7 \\
1 & 0.2 & -1.4 \\
1 & 0.3 & -1.1 \\
1 & 0.5 & -0.5 \\
1 & 0.7 & 0.1 \\
1 & 1.0 & 1.0 \\
1 & 1.4 & 2.2 \\
1 & 2.0 & 4.0
\end{bmatrix}
$$

The respective c^*'s are

$$[7.53, 1.92]^T \qquad [11.29, -1.84]^T \qquad [3.68, 5.77, 0.0]^T$$

The first two of these illustrate the uniqueness of p_1^*. For instance, with the first one, we have

$$p_1^*(x) = 7.53 + 1.92(3x - 2) = 3.68 + 5.76x$$

which is the same polynomial (3.34) that we originally obtained. (The discrepancies in the last digit are due to rounding of the c_j's to three digits.) The third example is also interesting. We have already seen that the set $B = \{1, x, 3x - 2\}$ is linearly dependent and this is reflected in the corresponding matrix A. It has rank $= 2$, that is, only two of its columns are linearly independent—col(3) $= -2 \cdot$ col(1) $+ 3 \cdot$ col(2). In effect, this means that there is an infinite number of least-squares solutions $\mathbf{c}^* = [c_1^*, c_2^*, c_3^*]^T$ corresponding to this (linearly dependent) set. Each of them will be equivalent to (3.34), that is,

$$c_1^* + c_2^*x + c_3^*(3x - 2) = 3.68 + 5.77x$$

The particular choice $\mathbf{c}^* = [3.68, 5.77, 0.0]^T$ amounts to ignoring the last function of the set B.

By now it should be clear how to proceed in the general case. Given the data $\{(x_i, f_i)\}_{i=1}^m$ and the set of n basis functions $B = \{\phi_j(x)\}_{j=1}^n$, we define the residuals

$$r_i(\mathbf{c}) = f_i - g(x_i)$$
$$= f_i - [c_1\phi_1(x_i) + \cdots + c_n\phi_n(x_i)] \qquad 1 \le i \le m$$

or, in matrix-vector notation,

$$\mathbf{r}(\mathbf{c}) = \mathbf{f} - A\mathbf{c}$$

where A is an $m \times n$ matrix and $\mathbf{f}$ is an m-vector defined by

$$(3.35) \qquad a_{i,j} = \phi_j(x_i) \qquad \text{and} \qquad (\mathbf{f})_i = f_i \qquad 1 \le i \le m \qquad 1 \le j \le n$$

Then the best least-squares approximation $g^*(x)$ relative to the basis B is characterized by the vector $\mathbf{c}^*$, which is the least-squares solution of the overdetermined linear system $A\mathbf{c} = \mathbf{f}$. The existence and uniqueness of $g^*(x)$ follow from the existence and uniqueness of $\mathbf{c}^*$ established in Section 2.3.

To summarize, the steps for finding a best linear least-squares approximation to some given data are as follows:

1. Select the (linear) class $\mathcal{G}$, that is, the form of the approximating functions to be used.

2.   i   Select a basis $\{\phi_j\}$ for $\mathcal{G}$.
     ii   Form A and $\mathbf{f}$ according to (3.35).
     iii   Call a subroutine to compute the least squares solution of the overdetermined system $A\mathbf{c} = \mathbf{f}$.

This breakdown is intended to illustrate how much of the work can be done automatically by a subroutine for performing curve fitting by least-squares approximation. Such a subroutine will be based on a specific choice $\mathscr{G}$ of approximating functions so a suitable basis can be assumed by the routine itself. Hence, once the data is provided, the job of forming A and $\mathbf{f}$ can be done by the subroutine. In addition, it can also do the subroutine call in step (2)(iii). Therefore, a least squares curve-fitting subroutine can perform all of step (2). This leaves the user to do step (1). In effect, it amounts to choosing an appropriate subroutine. This is the topic of the next section.

At this point, a few comments about the choice of basis are in order. We have already mentioned that the choice is important with respect to the evaluation of g^*. We now look at the effect on the computation of $\mathbf{c}^*$ (corresponding to g^*). The ideal basis is a set $\{\phi_j\}_{j=1}^n$, which is *orthogonal* with respect to the x_i's, that is,

$$(3.36) \quad \sum_{i=1}^m \phi_j(x_i)\phi_k(x_i) = \begin{array}{ll} d_j & \text{if } j = k \\ 0 & \text{otherwise} \end{array}$$

In terms of the matrix A, we see from (3.35) that this is really the inner product $\mathbf{a}_j^T \mathbf{a}_k$ of the jth column of A with the kth column. Hence, if the basis is orthogonal with respect to the x_i's, we will have $A^T A = D = \text{diag}(d_1, \ldots, d_n)$, a diagonal matrix. Then, as we saw in Section 2.3, the computation of $\mathbf{c}^*$ will be very easy because the normal equations $A^T A\mathbf{c} = A^T \mathbf{f}$ will be a diagonal system $D\mathbf{c} = A^T \mathbf{f}$. Now the job of finding an orthogonal basis at the outset is not easy but, in effect, it is done for us by the modified Gram–Schmidt (MGS) process (see Section 2.3.1). It computes the decomposition $A = QR$, where Q is an $m \times n$ matrix such that $Q^T Q$ is diagonal and R is an $n \times n$ upper triangular matrix. Consequently, the MGS algorithm can be viewed as a process of transforming to an orthogonal basis, solving the least-squares problem with respect to it, and then transforming back (via R) giving the solution in terms of the original basis B. Therefore, with respect to computing $\mathbf{c}^*$, it does not particularly matter which basis is selected.

Finally, we observe that, if $m = n$, the linear system $A\mathbf{c} = \mathbf{f}$ is square. Consequently, provided A is nonsingular, the system can be satisfied exactly [i.e., $\mathbf{r}(\mathbf{c}^*) = \mathbf{0}$]. In other words, $g^*(x)$ passes through each of the data points. But this is the definition of interpolation. Therefore, we can view interpolation as a special case of approximation.

3.2.2. Forms of Approximation

We are now ready to discuss some specific forms of functions for use in approximation. In the previous section, we saw that, no matter which class $\mathscr{G}$ is used, the problem of computing the best approximation $g^* \in \mathscr{G}$ is the same. Moreover, using the connection with overdetermined linear systems, we know how to compute g^* efficiently. The only stipulation is that $\mathscr{G}$ must be a linear space. Consequently, in order to describe the various forms of approximation, we only have to show how they fit into the mold of linear function spaces. In this regard, it is sufficient to demonstrate a basis B that generates a specific class $\mathscr{G}$ via (3.25). We will survey some different types of approximation first, defining a basis for each and stating the computational costs, and then compare their respective advantages and disadvantages.

In analyzing the computational costs, we consider the cost of determining g^* separately from the cost of evaluating it. With respect to the former, there are two components—the cost of forming A and $\mathbf{f}$, and that of solving the overdetermined linear system $A\mathbf{c} = \mathbf{f}$. Assuming that MGS is used for the second component, we already know from Section 2.3.2 that this requires mn^2 flops.

1. *Polynomials.* The examples in the previous section illustrate least-squares approximation using polynomials quite well and there is no need to elaborate here. With regard to the choice of basis for $\mathscr{P}_{n-1}$ (whose dimension is n), it is usual to use $B = \{1, x, \ldots, x^{n-1}\}$. This not only produces a form of p_{n-1}^* that can be evaluated efficiently but it also is a convenient form for manipulating mathematically. In particular, it is easy to differentiate and integrate. The computation costs are:

Determination of p_{n-1}^*

Form A	$m(n-2) \cdot M$
Solve $A\mathbf{c} = \mathbf{f}$ by MGS	mn^2 flops

Evaluation of p_{n-1}^*	$n - 1$ flops

Note that the first two columns of A require no work at all to determine them. The evaluation cost assumes that p_{n-1}^* is in the nested form (3.3).

2. *Exponentials.* The general form of this type of function is

$$g(x) = e^{p_{n-1}(x)} = e^{c_1 + c_2 x + \cdots + c_n x^{n-1}}$$

Now, this is not of the form (3.25) but we can easily make it so by taking the natural logarithm of each side to get

$$\ln g(x) = p_{n-1}(x) = c_1 + c_2 x + \cdots + c_n x^{n-1}$$

In effect, then, this form of approximation is equivalent to doing a polynomial fit to the modified data $\{(x_i, \ln(f_i))\}_{i=1}^m$, and it is sometimes called a "semilog" fit (with polynomials). The computation costs are the same as those for polynomials with the addition of some calls to the logarithm and exponential functions. Assuming that these cost about 10 flops each, the computational costs are:

Determination of g^*

Form A	$m(n-2)$ flops	
Form $\mathbf{f}$ (compute $\ln(f_i)$'s)	$10m$	flops
Solve $A\mathbf{c} = \mathbf{f}$ by MGS	mn^2	flops

Evaluation

Evaluate p^*_{n-1}	$n-1$	flops
Exponential evaluation	10	flops

We remark that it is rarely necessary to choose $n > 3$. Hence, the logarithm and exponential evaluations are significant factors in the respective costs.

2. *Trigonometric and other forms.* This category is intended to include various ad hoc forms of functions such as the example (3.26). Some other possible examples are

$$g(x) = c_1 + c_2 \sin(x) + c_3 \sin(2x) \qquad (x \in [-\pi, \pi])$$

$$g(x) = c_1 + c_2 x + c_3/x + c_4/x^2$$

$$g(x) = c_1 + e^{-x}(c_2 + c_3 x + c_4 x^2)$$

In each case, it is obvious how to define an appropriate basis B. The first of these examples is useful when the data displays periodic tendencies. In fact, this form is nothing more than a finite Fourier series with odd terms only (no cosines). We will discuss this particular type of approximation in Section 3.2.3. The functions x^{-k} in the second example are a good alternative for the exponential form $e^{-\alpha x}$ if $x > 0$, because they are much cheaper to evaluate

Analysis of the computational costs will depend on the particular form of $g(x)$ used and the cost of evaluating the corresponding basis functions. We omit the details.

4. *Piecewise polynomials.* In Section 3.1, we introduced the concept of piecewise polynomials and saw that, as interpolating functions, they have many advantages. It turns out that they are also a good form of function to use for approximation. But it is not at all obvious that they fit into the format of linear function spaces. For example, the cubic spline (3.22) is not in the form (3.25) of a linear combination of basis functions $\{\phi_j\}$. Consequently, in order to show that they do, in fact, fit into the theory, we must reformulate the way of representing a piecewise polynomial. We do this for linear and cubic splines. In both cases, we assume that there are n knots whose x-coordinates are denoted by t_j, $1 \le j \le n$. These will be fixed with $a = t_1 < t_2 < \cdots < t_n = b$. We let $\mathbf{t} = [t_1, \ldots, t_n]^T$ and use the notation $\mathcal{S}_1(\mathbf{t})$ and $\mathcal{S}_3(\mathbf{t})$, respectively, for the classes of linear and cubic splines with knots at these specified locations. In keeping with the notation of Section 3.1.2, we use $s_1(x)$ and $s_3(x)$ to denote, respectively, linear and cubic splines.

Linear Splines

In practice, linear splines are not used very often because cubics are much better. However, they provide a good vehicle for introducing the concept of least squares spline approximation. With each knot t_j, $1 \leq j \leq n$, we associate the function

$$(3.37) \quad \sigma_j(x) = \begin{cases} \dfrac{x - t_{j-1}}{t_j - t_{j-1}} & \text{if } x \in I_{j-1} = [t_{j-1}, t_j] \\[2mm] \dfrac{t_{j+1} - x}{t_{j+1} - t_j} & \text{if } x \in I_j = [t_j, t_{j+1}] \\[2mm] 0 & \text{otherwise} \end{cases}$$

In the cases $j = 1$ and n, it is understood that we omit the portion of the definition that involves x outside $[t_1, t_n] = [a, b]$. The graph of $\sigma_j(x)$ is illustrated in Figure 3.6. Due to their shape, such functions are often called "roof" functions. They form a basis for a function space of linear splines, that is, any continuous piecewise linear function $s_1(x)$ with knots of t_j, $1 \leq j \leq n$, has a representation in the form

$$(3.38) \quad s_1(x) = c_1\sigma_1(x) + c_2\sigma_2(x) + \cdots + c_n\sigma_n(x)$$

where the $\sigma_j(x)$'s are defined by (3.37). To see how this reconciles algebraically with the form (3.12) of a linear spline used in Section 3.1.2, we consider an example. Let $n = 4$ with knots located at $\mathbf{t} = [-1, 1, 2, 5]^T$, and define

$$(3.39) \quad s_1(x) = -7\sigma_1(x) + 7\sigma_2(x) - 4\sigma_3(x) + 35\sigma_4(x)$$

Now, suppose that $x = z \in I_2 = [t_2, t_3] = [1, 2]$. Then, from (3.37), we have $\sigma_1(z) = \sigma_4(z) = 0$, and

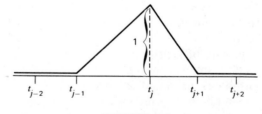

FIGURE 3.6

$$s_1(z) = 7\sigma_2(z) - 4\sigma_3(z)$$

$$= 7\left[\frac{2-z}{2-1}\right] - 4\left[\frac{z-1}{2-1}\right]$$

$$= -11z + 18$$

$$= -11(z-1) + 7$$

In the same way, we can obtain corresponding expressions for s_1 in either of the other subintervals I_1 and I_3 defined by the knots t_j. Consequently, the form (3.39) for $s_1(x)$ is equivalent to

$$s_1(x) = \begin{cases} -7\sigma_1 + 7\sigma_2 = & 7(x+1) - 7 & \text{if} & x \le 1 \\ 7\sigma_2 - 4\sigma_3 = -11(x-1) + 7 & \text{if} & 1 \le x \le 2 \\ -4\sigma_3 + 35\sigma_4 = & 13(x-2) - 4 & \text{if} & 2 \le x \end{cases}$$

which is precisely the piecewise linear polynomial (3.13). For the general case of a linear spline with n knots, we can show in the same way that the "basis" representation (3.38) is equivalent to the "piecewise" form (3.12). Therefore, the class $\mathcal{S}_1(\mathbf{t})$ of linear splines with knots at $\mathbf{t} = [t_1, \ldots, t_n]^T$ is a linear function space and the set $\{\sigma_j(x)\}_{j=1}^n$ of roof functions (3.37) forms a basis for it.

As usual, there is a variety of possible bases for $\mathcal{S}_1(\mathbf{t})$. However, the roof functions (3.37) are the most efficient for computational purposes because

Each $\sigma_j(x)$ is nonzero on the subinterval $[t_{j-1}, t_{j+1}]$ only,

that is, the $\sigma_j(x)$'s have (relatively) *small support* within $[a, b]$. Alternatively, we say that the set $\{\sigma_j\}$ is a *local* basis. In order to see how this property contributes to computational efficiency, we consider an example using the data (3.28). Suppose we choose $n = 4$ and put the knots at $\mathbf{t} = [0.0, 0.35, 0.8, 2.0]^T$. The graphs of the σ_j's are shown in Figure 3.7. The formulas for computing the entries of A are given by:

If $x \in [0.0, 0.35]$, $\begin{cases} (0.35 - x)/0.35 & = \sigma_1(x) \\ (x - 0.0)/0.35 \end{cases}$

$ = \sigma_2(x),$

If $x \in [0.35, 0.8]$, $\begin{cases} (0.8 - x)/0.45 \\ (x - 0.35)/0.45 \end{cases}$

$ = \sigma_3(x)$

If $x \in [0.8, 2.0]$, $\begin{cases} (2.0 - x)/1.2 \\ (x - 0.8)/1.2 \end{cases} = \sigma_4(x)$

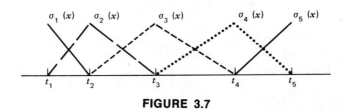

FIGURE 3.7

From these formulas, we can easily compute the entries of A, whereupon the overdetermined linear system is

$$(3.40) \quad \begin{bmatrix} 0.714 & 0.286 & 0 & 0 \\ 0.429 & 0.571 & 0 & 0 \\ 0.143 & 0.857 & 0 & 0 \\ 0 & 0.667 & 0.333 & 0 \\ 0 & 0.222 & 0.778 & 0 \\ 0 & 0 & 0.833 & 0.167 \\ 0 & 0 & 0.5 & 0.5 \\ 0 & 0 & 0.0 & 1.0 \end{bmatrix} \begin{bmatrix} c_1 \\ c_2 \\ c_3 \\ c_4 \end{bmatrix} = \begin{bmatrix} 1.97 \\ 3.81 \\ 5.40 \\ 7.85 \\ 9.51 \\ 11.1 \\ 12.3 \\ 13.3 \end{bmatrix}$$

Finally, on calling an MGS subroutine, we get $\mathbf{c}^*$.

The first, and most obvious, feature of this example is that the matrix A has a band structure—each row has only two nonzero entries (which are adjacent). As Figure 3.7 indicates, this is a direct consequence of the "local" property of the σ_j's. Therefore, in order to form A, we only need to perform $m \cdot (3A + 1D)$ operations. The second property to note about A is that, as a consequence of the band structure, the columns are "nearly" orthogonal. For instance, the first column is orthogonal to all but the second one, that is, $\mathbf{a}_1^T \mathbf{a}_3 = \mathbf{a}_1^T \mathbf{a}_4 = 0$. We remark that, in terms of the definition (3.36), this is equivalent to saying that the roof function $\sigma_1(x)$ is orthogonal to both $\sigma_3(x)$ and $\sigma_4(x)$. Now, recalling that the MGS process is essentially one of orthogonalizing the columns of A, it is evident that some computational effort can be saved by exploiting this "near-orthogonality" feature. In fact, it is possible to solve the system in about $2mn$ flops (instead of mn^2). Hence, a subroutine for doing a least-squares fit by linear splines would contain its own MGS algorithm, specially adapted to take advantage of the band structure.

For evaluating $s_1^*(x)$, the local property of the roof functions can again lead to savings because only two of them have to be evaluated at any one time. (Actually, we only need to evaluate $\sigma_j(x)$ because $\sigma_{j+1}(x) = 1 - \sigma_j(x)$, for $x \in I_j$.) Therefore, the work required is

$$\log_2 n \text{ comparisons} \quad \text{plus} \quad 3A + 3M$$

On the other hand, if $s_1^*(x)$ were expressed in the piecewise form (3.12), the work to evaluate it would be

$\log_2 n$ comparisons   plus $2A + 1M$

Since the cost of converting from the representation (3.38) to (3.12) is only $2n \cdot A$'s, it does not take many evaluations of s_1^* before savings from using the latter form are realized. Consequently, an algorithm for doing a least-squares fit by linear splines would compute $s_1^*(x)$ in the "basis" form (3.38) and convert to the "piecewise" form (3.12) for subsequent evaluation. Therefore the approximate computational costs will be:

Determination of $s_1^*(x)$

Form A	$m \cdot (3A + 1D)$
Solve $Ac = f$	$2mn$ flops
Convert to the form (3.12)	$2n \cdot A$

Evaluation of $s_1^*(x)$

Locate the correct $[t_k, t_{k+1}]$	$\log_2 n$ comparisons
Evaluate $p_{1,k}(x)$	$2A + 1M$

Finally, to facilitate the description of cubic splines, we introduce a more general approach. The idea is to begin by determining the dimension of $\mathscr{S}_1(\mathbf{t})$ in order to find out how many basis functions have to be found. Now, in the characterization (3.12) of a piecewise linear polynomial, there were $2(n-1)$ coefficients to be determined. Viewing these as $2(n-1)$ degrees of freedom, we use $n-2$ of them to ensure continuity at the interior knots. This leaves n degrees of freedom, that is, a linear spline $s_1(\mathbf{t})$ with n knots can be uniquely defined by specifying the remaining n coefficients. In other words, using the language of linear function spaces, we need exactly n basis functions in order to uniquely determine a linear spline in the form (3.38). Therefore, we conclude that the space $\mathscr{S}_1(\mathbf{t})$ of linear splines with n knots has dimension $\dim \mathscr{S}_1(\mathbf{t}) = n$ and this is the number of linearly independent functions we must find in order to define a basis.

Cubic Splines

First, we determine the dimensionality of a function space $\mathscr{S}_3(\mathbf{t})$ of cubic splines with n knots. From (3.16), a piecewise cubic polynomial has $4(n-1)$ coefficients or degrees of freedom. But the continuity requirements of a cubic spline—each of s_3, s_3' and s_3'' must be continuous at each interior knot—use $3(n-2)$ of them. Therefore, there are $4(n-1) - 3(n-2) = n + 2$ degrees of freedom remaining, that is, $\dim \mathscr{S}_3(\mathbf{t}) = n + 2$, and we must find $n + 2$ basis functions. We denote them by $\beta_j(x)$, $0 \le j \le n + 1$, so that any $s_3(x) \in \mathscr{S}_3(\mathbf{t})$ has a unique representation in the form

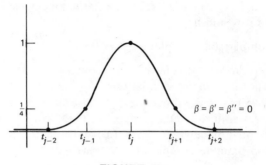

FIGURE 3.8

$$(3.41) \quad s_3(x) = c_0\beta_0(x) + c_1\beta_1(x) + \cdots + c_n\beta_n(x) + c_{n+1}\beta_{n+1}(x)$$

The most efficient basis for computational purposes is the so-called "B-splines" or bell-shaped splines illustrated in Figure 3.8. In the case where the knots t_j are equally spaced, each $\beta_j(x)$ is defined by

$$(3.42) \quad \beta_j(x) = \begin{cases} \gamma^3/4 & \gamma = (x - t_{j-2})/h & x \in I_{j-2} \\ (1 + 3\gamma + 3\gamma^2 - 3\gamma^3)/4 & \gamma = (x - t_{j-1})/h & x \in I_{j-1} \\ (1 + 3\gamma + 3\gamma^2 - 3\gamma^3)/4 & \gamma = (t_{j+1} - x)/h & x \in I_j \\ \gamma^3/4 & \gamma = (t_{j+2} - x)/h & x \in I_{j+1} \\ 0 & & \text{otherwise} \end{cases}$$

where $h = t_{j+1} - t_j$ is the (uniform) distance between knots and $I_j = [t_j, t_{j+1}]$. If the knots are unequally spaced, the expressions for $\beta_j(x)$ are quite complicated. However, the precise formulas are not important because, in practice, the equations for $\beta_j(x)$ can easily be computed by interpolating the values indicated in Figure 3.8 using the technique described in the previous section. By construction then, $\beta_j(x)$ is an element of $\mathscr{S}_3(\mathbf{t})$. Now, in the case of linear splines, we were able to associate a basis function $\sigma_j(x)$ with each knot t_j and then it was obvious that the set $\{\sigma_j\}$ was linearly independent. The subscripts used in (3.41) are intended to imply that we do the same here with the addition of two fictitious knots t_0, t_{n+1} to the left and right, respectively, of $[t_1, t_n]$. Noting that the support of each $\beta_j(x)$ is four subintervals—$[t_{j-2}, t_{j+2}]$—it is understood that, in the cases $j = 0, 1, 2, n - 1, n, n + 1$, we omit the portions lying outside $[t_1, t_n] = [a, b]$. With this one-to-one correspondence between a function $\beta_j(x)$ and a knot t_j, it is clear that the set $\{\beta_j(x)\}_{j=0}^{n+1}$ is linearly independent on $[a, b]$. Therefore, it must form a basis for $\mathscr{S}_3(\mathbf{t})$.

The computational aspects should be readily apparent by analogy with the case of linear splines. The matrix A will be $m \times (n + 2)$ and, because the support of each $\beta_j(x)$ is four subintervals, it will only have four nonzero entries per row. Therefore, it has a band structure that can be exploited in the MGS algorithm for determining $s_3^*(x)$. For evaluating $s_3^*(x)$, it is again more efficient to convert to the piecewise form (3.16). Hence the approximate computational costs will be:

Determination of s_3^*

Form A	$m \cdot (10A + 6M)$
Solve $Ac = f$	$4mn$ flops
Convert to the form (3.16)	$4n \cdot A$

Evaluation of s_3^*

Locate the correct $[t_k, t_{k+1}]$	$\log_2 n$ comparisons
Evaluate cubic piece	3 flops

This completes our survey of the various forms of approximating functions.

We now discuss some factors to be considered in choosing a particular form of approximation. One of these is accuracy. To measure the accuracy of an approximation g^*, we often use the *root mean square error*

$$(3.43) \quad \text{RMSE} = \left[\frac{1}{m} \sum_{i=1}^{m} |g^*(x_i) - f_i|^2 \right]^{1/2}$$

which is an indicator of the average deviation of $g^*(x)$ from each data point. By itself, however, accuracy at the data points is not a sufficient criterion on which to base a choice. To illustrate, consider the data $\{(x_i, f_i)\}$, where

$$x_i = -1 + (i - 1)h \qquad 1 \le i \le 50 \qquad \text{with } h = \tfrac{2}{49}$$

$$f_i = (1 + 25x_i^2)^{-1}$$

In Table 3.1, we show some results from using polynomials and cubic splines, with equally spaced knots, to approximate this data. The results give the RMSE computed with the 50 data points and also on a denser set of 200 equally spaced points, that is, the original 50 points plus some intermediate ones. For polynomials, we note the significant difference in the RMSE between the two sets of points indicating that the approximation of $f(x)$ at intermediate points is not very good. This is due to the oscillating behavior of polynomials. Cubic splines, on the other hand, are much smoother functions and, as the results indicate, they give a much better approximation at intermediate points. We recall a similar comparison in the case of interpolation and our conclusion is the same here, that a higher-order polynomial is an unsatisfactory form to use as an approximating function.

TABLE 3.1

Polynomials			Cubic Splines		
RMSE			RMSE		
Deg.	50 pts.	200 pts.	No. of knots	50 pts.	200 pts.
2	0.040	0.223	3	0.080	0.130
4	0.027	0.151	5	0.048	0.078
6	0.020	0.102	7	0.024	0.039
8	0.016	0.069			
10	0.012	0.046			

Another aspect we should consider is efficiency. Again, we have already discussed this with respect to interpolation and the same conclusion holds here, that is, cubic splines are more efficient. Therefore, on the basis of both accuracy and efficiency, cubic splines are a better choice than polynomials.

Now the above example is relatively simple but the conclusion that the cubic spline is a good form to use in approximation has been found to hold as a general rule. Consequently, software packages usually contain a subroutine for least squares approximation by cubic splines. Sometimes, in fact, this is the only (linear) least squares routine in the package. A typical calling sequence is of the form

$$\text{LSCSFK(N,M,X,F,XKNOT,C,MODE,RMSE,WK),}$$

where

N is the number n of knots (so there are $n + 2$ basis functions).

M is the number m of data points.

X, F are vectors, of length at least m, containing the data.

XKNOT is a vector, of length at least n, containing the x-coordinates of the knots.

C is a two-dimensional array, of size 4 by at least n, used to return the coefficients of $s_3^*(x)$.

MODE is a parameter for specifying what the subroutine is to do (see below).

RMSE is used to return the value of RMSE defined by (3.43).

WK is a work area of size at least $m \times n$ (containing, on return, the QR factorization of A.)

The parameter MODE is a device to facilitate the modification of the set of knots—add new ones or delete some—without having to repeat the entire calculation[7]. This feature allows the user to experiment with the number and placement of the knots at minimal expense.

With respect to experimenting with the location of the knots, it would be useful if a subroutine could automatically place them itself so that all the user has to do is specify the number n to be used. This can, in fact, be done and software packages usually contain a subroutine for "least squares approximation by cubic splines—variable knots." A typical calling sequence is

LSCSVK(N,M,X,F,XKNOT,C,RMSE,WK)

The only difference from the fixed knot case is that the parameter MODE is missing. Seemingly, this is a very useful type of subroutine but it has a major disadvantage—cost. It is substantially more expensive to use than a fixed-knot subroutine. In the latter case, s_3^* can be determined in a straightforward way by solving a linear system of equations. But when the locations of the knots must also be determined, the normal equations become nonlinear and this greatly increases the complexity of determining s_3^*. Now the extra expense of a variable-knot subroutine would be worthwhile if there is a sufficient benefit in return but this is seldom true. One can usually get satisfactory approximations by using a larger number of (fixed) knots and the cost is much less. The only possible increased cost in this procedure is in evaluation. There will be more intervals to be searched but if a binary search is used, this only amounts to one or possibly two extra comparisons. In this connection, we quote from [8, p. 272].

> It (variable knots) is warranted only when precise placement of some knots is essential for the quality of the approximation (e.g., when the data exhibit some discontinuity) and an approximation with as few parameters as possible is wanted. Otherwise, an approximation with two or three times as many well chosen knots is much cheaper to obtain and, usually, just as effective.

Finally, there is the problem of evaluating an approximating function $g^*(x)$ after it has been determined. A software package will provide

---

[7]This is made possible by retaining the QR factorization of A (in the array WK) between calls to LSCSFK. If a knot is deleted from the set, the corresponding column of Q is deleted and the remaining columns are still orthogonal. Therefore, provided the (old) QR factorization of A is available, the deletion of a knot amounts to nothing more than recomputing some of the entries of R, solving the (revised) triangular system $Rc = Q^T f$ and converting to the "piecewise" form (3.16). The process of adding a knot is the same except that a column is added to Q and it must be orthogonalized with respect to the old ones.

subroutines for this purpose. They are designed to use the representation of $g^*(x)$ produced by the generating routine. This is very convenient because the user does not have to be concerned about specific details of the representation of g^*. For example, suppose the routine LSCSFK is used to generate a cubic spline approximation $s_3^*(x)$. On return, its representation is contained in the variables N, XKNOT, and C. Therefore, an evaluation subroutine will have a calling sequence of the form

$$\text{S3VAL} = \text{CSEVAL(Z,N,XKNOT,C)}$$

where Z is the evaluation point and the remaining arguments are the same as for LSCSFK. The same routine can be used to evaluate a cubic spline generated by LSCSVK or an interpolation subroutine.

3.2.3. Periodic Functions

We now discuss the approximation of periodic functions, that is, those which satisfy the condition

$$f(x + \rho) = f(x) \qquad \text{for all } x$$

where ρ is a fixed number called the *period* of f. Periodic functions arise frequently in scientific applications. They are used, for example, to model physical phenomena such as sound and light, which can be described by wave theory. It is important, therefore, to be able to represent periodic functions efficiently and accurately.

The simplest types of periodic functions are the sine and cosine functions so we choose, as the form of approximation, the *trigonometric polynomial*

$$(3.44) \quad t_n(x) = \frac{a_0}{2} + \sum_{j=1}^{n} (a_j \cos jx + b_j \sin jx)$$

The coefficients a_j, b_j can be real or complex, depending on the type of function to be represented. We assume, for convenience, that the period of $f(x)$ is $\rho = 2\pi$, the same as $t_n(x)$. [If not, we can approximate the 2π-periodic function $g(x) = f(\rho x/(2\pi))$ by $t_n(x)$, after which the approximation for $f(x)$ will be $t_n(2\pi x/\rho)$.] Instead of (3.44), it is more usual to consider the equivalent complex form

$$(3.45) \quad t_n(x) = \sum_{j=-n}^{n} c_j e^{ijx} \qquad i = \sqrt{-1}$$

The connection between the two representations is via Euler's formula

$$(3.46) \quad e^{ix} = \cos x + i \sin x$$

We have

$$c_j e^{ijx} + c_{-j} e^{-ijx} = (c_j + c_{-j}) \cos jx + i(c_j - c_{-j}) \sin jx$$

Hence the representations (3.44) and (3.45) are equivalent with

(3.47) $\quad a_j = c_j + c_{-j} \qquad b_j = i(c_j - c_{-j}) \qquad j = 0, 1, \ldots, n$

or

(3.47)' $\quad c_j = \frac{1}{2}(a_j - ib_j) \qquad c_{-j} = \frac{1}{2}(a_j + ib_j) \qquad j = 0, 1, \ldots, n$

The trigonometric polynomial (3.45) is closely related to the well-known Fourier series. If $f(x)$ is piecewise continuous with period 2π, then it has a *Fourier series* representation (see [6, p. 409])

(3.48) $\quad f(x) = \sum_{j=-\infty}^{\infty} c_j e^{ijx}$

where the *Fourier coefficients* c_j are given by

(3.49) $\quad c_j = \frac{1}{2\pi} \int_0^{2\pi} f(x) e^{-ijx} \, dx \qquad \text{for all } j$

Hence, (3.45) can be interpreted as a truncated, or finite, Fourier series. In this context, there are two obvious questions that we would like to answer. First, how large does n have to be in order for $t_n(x)$ to be a good approximation for $f(x)$, that is, how fast does the Fourier series (3.48) converge? Second, how do we compute the coefficients c_j for $t_n(x)$?

With respect to the latter question, the obvious answer is to make use of (3.49). Clearly, we cannot use it directly because $f(x)$ is not known explicitly. However, a simple way of computing an approximation $\hat{c}_j$ for c_j is to replace $f(x)$ under the integral sign by an interpolating function that can be integrated easily. Specifically, we subdivide $[0, 2\pi]$ by the $N + 1$ equally spaced points $x_k = 2\pi k/N$, $k = 0, 1, \ldots, N$, and interpolate $f(x)$ at these points by a piecewise linear polynomial $g_1(x)$. Then, substituting into (3.49) and integrating, we get

(3.50) $\quad c_j \doteq \hat{c}_j = \frac{1}{2\pi} \int_0^{2\pi} g_1(x) e^{-ijx} \, dx = \frac{1}{N} \sum_{k=0}^{N-1} f(x_k) e^{-ijx_k}$

where we have used the periodicity assumption $f(2\pi) = f(0)$, that is, $f(x_N) = f(x_0)$. This approximation is, in fact, the well-known composite trapezoidal rule (see Section 5.1) for approximating an integral. It follows from the bound (3.14) for piecewise linear polynomial interpolation that each $\hat{c}_j$ can be made as accurate as we like provided N is taken sufficiently large. (For details, see the discussion in Chapter 5 on the accuracy of the composite trapezoidal rule.)

An alternative derivation of (3.50) uses some of the ideas developed earlier concerning interpolation by orthogonal functions. Suppose we interpolate $f(x)$ by the trigonometric polynomial (3.45) at the N data points $\{(x_k, f_k)\}_{k=0}^{N-1}$. Since there are $2n + 1$ coefficients c_j to be determined, we take $N = 2n + 1$. The x_k's are assumed to be equally spaced in $[0, 2\pi]$ so

$$(3.51) \quad x_k = \frac{2k\pi}{N} \qquad k = 0, 1, \ldots, N - 1$$

The interpolating conditions (3.2) are

$$(3.52) \quad \sum_{j=-n}^{n} c_j e^{i2jk\pi/N} = f_k \qquad k = 0, 1, \ldots, N - 1$$

or $A\mathbf{c} = \mathbf{f}$, where the entries of A are

$$a_{k,j} = e^{i2jk\pi/N}$$

For example, if $N = 3$ $(n = 1)$

$$A = \begin{bmatrix} 1 & 1 & 1 \\ e^{-i2\pi/3} & 1 & e^{i2\pi/3} \\ e^{-i4\pi/3} & 1 & e^{i4\pi/3} \end{bmatrix} = \begin{bmatrix} 1 & 1 & 1 \\ e^{-i2\pi/3} & 1 & e^{i2\pi/3} \\ e^{i2\pi/3} & 1 & e^{-i2\pi/3} \end{bmatrix}$$

Now, from the Euler formula (3.46), we see that A is a complex matrix. But it has an interesting property:

$$(3.53) \quad \frac{1}{N} A^*A = I$$

where A^* is the conjugate transpose[8] of A. With respect to the set $\{e^{ijx}\}_{j=-n}^{n}$ of functions, this is the complex analogue of the orthogonality property (3.36), that is,

$$(3.54) \quad \sum_{k=0}^{N-1} e^{i2\pi(r-s)k/N} = \begin{array}{ll} N & \text{if } r = s \\ 0 & \text{otherwise} \end{array}$$

For our 3×3 example, we have

$$A^* = \begin{bmatrix} 1 & e^{i2\pi/3} & e^{-i2\pi/3} \\ 1 & 1 & 1 \\ 1 & e^{-i2\pi/3} & e^{i2\pi/3} \end{bmatrix}$$

and it is easily seen that $A^*A = 3I$. From equation (3.53), it follows that

---

[8]The conjugate transpose A^* of a complex matrix is obtained by taking the complex conjugate $\bar{a}_{i,j}$ of each element $a_{i,j}$ of A and then the transpose, that is, $A^* = (\bar{A})^T$. If A is such that $A^*A = I$, we say it is *unitary*. This is the complex analogue of the orthogonality property for real matrices.

$A^{-1} = (1/N)A^*$. Hence, the solution of the linear system (3.52) is given by $\hat{\mathbf{c}} = (1/N)A^*\mathbf{f}$, or

$$(3.55) \quad \hat{c}_j = \frac{1}{N} \sum_{k=0}^{N-1} \bar{a}_{k,j} f_k = \frac{1}{N} \sum_{k=0}^{N-1} f_k e^{-i2jk\pi/N} \quad -n \le j \le n$$

which is precisely the formula (3.50) with $x_k = 2k\pi/N$. Hence, the approximate Fourier coefficients can also be obtained by interpolation of $f(x)$ at N equally spaced points x_k in $[0, 2\pi]$ using the set of orthogonal basis functions $\{e^{ijx_k}\}_{j=-n}^{n}$.

We stated that, by taking N sufficiently large, it is possible to make each $\hat{c}_j$ as accurate an approximation for c_j as we like. But there is another factor that must also be considered. This is an *aliasing effect*. From (3.49), we have, for any integer s,

$$c_{j+sN} = \frac{1}{2\pi} \int_0^{2\pi} f(x) e^{-i(j+sN)x} \, dx$$

Using (3.55), its approximation is

$$\hat{c}_{j+sN} = \frac{1}{N} \sum_{k=0}^{N-1} f_k e^{-i2(j+sN)k\pi/N}$$

$$= \frac{1}{N} \sum f_k e^{-i2jk\pi/N} e^{-i2sk\pi} = \frac{1}{N} \sum f_k e^{-i2jk\pi/N}$$

$$= \hat{c}_j$$

where we have made use of periodicity, that is, for any integer r,

$$e^{i2r\pi} = \cos 2r\pi + i \sin 2r\pi = 1$$

In words, this result says that the approximations for any of the Fourier coefficients c_{j+sN}, $s = 0, \pm 1, \ldots$, cannot be distinguished from each other, that is, they are "aliases" for one another. Now the whole purpose of performing a Fourier analysis on a set of data is to find out which frequencies are present in the data and in what strength, that is, which terms are present in (3.48) and how significant each one is. Hence, the aliasing effect is undesirable since it prevents us from distinguishing which particular frequency corresponds to each approximate coefficient $\hat{c}_j$. Aliasing results from periodicity and cannot be eliminated. However, we can minimize its effects by taking N sufficiently large. In this way, the aliasing coefficients will correspond to frequencies of sufficiently high order that they will be neglected anyway, with the result that each $\hat{c}_j$ corresponds to only one frequency (in which we have any interest).

The foregoing discussion explains why we must use a large number of data points in performing a finite, or discrete, Fourier analysis. Typically, N must be in the hundreds and, sometimes, in the thousands. But this introduces a new problem—cost. From the matrix-vector formulation $\hat{c} = (1/N)A^*f$, it follows that N^2 flops[9] are required to compute the $\hat{c}_j$'s. This in itself is not prohibitive but, in many applications, a large number of data sets must be analyzed with the result that the overall cost can be quite high. For example, if $N = 250$ and there are 100 sets of data to be analyzed, the work required is 6.25×10^6 flops. Fortunately, we can reduce this number significantly by using the so-called *Fast Fourier Transform* (FFT).

In order to explain the underlying principle of the FFT, we consider the case $N = 18 = 3 \times 6$. Let

$$w = e^{-i2\pi/18}$$

$$k = 3k_1 + k_0 \qquad \text{where } k_0 = 0, 1, 2, \qquad \text{and} \qquad k_1 = 0, 1, \ldots, 5$$

$$j = 6j_1 + j_0 \qquad \text{where } j_0 = 0, 1, \ldots, 5 \qquad \text{and} \qquad j_1 = 0, 1, 2$$

Then

$$\hat{c}_j = \frac{1}{18} \sum_{k=0}^{17} f_k w^{jk} = \frac{1}{18} \sum_{k=0}^{17} f_k w^{(6j_1+j_0)(3k_1+k_0)}$$

$$= \frac{1}{18} \sum_{k_0=0}^{2} w^{6j_1k_0+j_0k_0} \left(\sum_{k_1=0}^{5} f_{3k_1+k_0} w^{3k_1j_0} \right) \qquad (\text{since } w^{18j_1k_1} = 1)$$

$$= \frac{1}{3} \sum_{k_0=0}^{2} \hat{C}(j_0, k_0) w^{jk_0}$$

where

$$(3.56) \quad \hat{C}(j_0, k_0) = \frac{1}{6} \sum_{k_1=0}^{5} f_{3k_1+k_0} w^{3k_1j_0} \qquad 0 \le j_0 \le 5 \qquad 0 \le k_0 \le 2$$

Hence, given the $\hat{C}$'s, each $\hat{c}_j$ requires only three flops to evaluate. In turn, each $\hat{C}$ requires six flops. Consequently, the total work requirement is $18 \cdot (3 + 6) = 162$ flops instead of $(18)^2 = 324$. A further improvement can be made by noting that the formula (3.56) is of the same form as (3.55) with $N = 6 = 2 \times 3$ so that, in a similar fashion, each $\hat{C}$ requires only $2 + 3 = 5$ flops rather than 6. Therefore, using this procedure, the $\hat{c}_j$'s can be computed in $18 \cdot (3 + 3 + 2) = 144$ flops.

In the general case of N data points, we determine the prime factorization of N, that is,

$$N = p_1 p_2 \ldots p_r \qquad \text{where each } p_i \text{ is a prime.}$$

Then, by repeated use of the FFT idea just described, it follows that the $\hat{c}_j$'s can be computed in only $N \cdot (p_1 + p_2 + \cdots + p_r)$ flops instead of N^2.

---

[9]Even though the operations may be complex, we still use the term "flop" to mean a multiply-add combination.

Again, if $N = 250 = 2 \times 5^3$, the work requirement is $250 \cdot (2 + 5 + 5 + 5) = 4250$ flops (as opposed to 62,500) and 100 such computations only costs 4.25×10^5 flops. From this analysis, we conclude that the maximum savings occur for any number N that has a lot of prime factors. In this regard, the "optimum" choices are $N = 2^m$. For example, if $N = 256 = 2^8$, then the cost is $256 \cdot (16) = 4096$ flops, less than that for the case $N = 250$! On the other hand, $N = 241$ is a bad choice because its prime factorization is $241 = 13 \times 19$.

The calling sequence for an FFT subroutine is of the form

FFT(N,F,WK)

where

N is the number N of data points.
F is a vector, of length at least N, containing the data.
WK is a vector used as work area.

On return, F will contain the coefficients $\hat{c}_j$. The routine begins by factoring N into primes and then applies the FFT algorithm. The work area is needed both for factoring N and computing the coefficients. Since the choice $N = 2^m$ is favored by many users, a special routine for this case is also provided by most packages. The calling sequence will be of the form

FFT2(M,F,WK)

where M is the power of 2, that is, $N = 2^M$. In using this special routine, we save by not having to compute the prime factorization of N. In addition, it turns out that, instead of factoring N by 2's, the FFT process can be made more efficient by using a factorization into 4's. (If M is odd, we do one stage using a factor of 2.) For example, we would factor

$$N = 128 = 2^7 = 2 \times 4^3$$

and

$$N = 256 = 2^8 = 4^4$$

A routine like FFT2 would make use of such special procedures.

EXERCISES

Section 3.1

1.1. Consider the following tabulated function

x	1	3	4	5
$f(x)$	5	1	−1	0

(a) Find both the Lagrange and Newton forms of the polynomial $p_3^*(x)$ that interpolates the data.

(b) Find the coefficients c_j for the representation

$$p_3^*(x) = c_0 P_0(x) + c_1 P_1(x) + c_2 P_2(x) + c_3 P_3(x)$$

where $\{P_j(x)\}_{j=0}^3$ is the set of (Legendre) polynomials (3.24)(a).

(c) Add the point $(2, 4)$ to the data and compute both forms in part (a) of the new interpolating polynomial $p_4^*(x)$.

(d) Find the linear spline $s_1^*(x)$ that interpolates the original data and then with the new point $(2, 4)$. Is there much difficulty in modifying s_1^* to include the new point?

(e) Estimate the value of $f(3.5)$ using both forms of p_3^* from part (a) and also the linear spline that interpolates the original data.

1.2. Consider the function $f(x) = e^{-x^2/2}$ over the interval $[0, 2]$.

(a) Find the clamped cubic spline $s_3^*(x)$ that interpolates $f(x)$ at the points where $x = 0.0, 0.25, 0.5, 1.25, 2.0$.

(b) Estimate the accuracy of $s_3^*(x)$ by determining the maximum error at 101 equally spaced points in $[0, 2]$, that is, compute the value of

$$E_{max} = \max_{0 \le i \le 100} |f(x_i) - s_3^*(x_i)| \qquad x_i = \frac{i}{50}$$

How does this compare with the bound given in the text?

(c) Write down a representation for the derivative $ds_3^*(x)/dx$ as a piecewise (quadratic) polynomial and verify that it is continuous. How well does it approximate $f'(x)$? (Compute the maximum error as in (b).)

1.3. Verify that (3.22) is a cubic spline.

1.4. The following data has been collected from an experiment.

x	0	1	2	3	4	6	8	10	15	20
f	4.0	4.7	4.9	5.3	6.1	6.7	6.9	7.2	7.1	7.5

Interpolate the data with

    i A polynomial $p_9^*(x)$.
    ii A cubic spline $s_3^*(x)$.

Evaluate each of the interpolants at the set of points $x_i = i/5$, $0 \le i \le 100$, and plot the results. (Use a plotting subroutine.) Which interpolant gives the better representation of the trend in the data?

1.5. Given a set of data $D_0 = \{(x_i, f_i)\}_{i=1}^N$, it is desired to find an approximation for $f''(x)$. This is to be done by generating a new set of data $D_2 = \{(x_i, f''_i)\}_{i=1}^n$ and then interpolating it with a cubic spline. Two possible ways of generating the set D_2 are as follows.

i Interpolate D_0 with a cubic spline $s_3^*(x)$ and evaluate its second derivative at each x_i, that is, $f''_i = (d^2 s_3^*/dx^2)_{x=x_i}$. [In terms of the matrix representation C used for (3.22), $f''_i = 2C(2, I)$.]

ii Use a "spline-on-spline" technique (see [1, p. 43]). Interpolate the data D_0 as before but, this time, generate the data $D_1 = \{(x_i, f'_i)\}_{i=1}^n$, where $f'_i = (ds_3^*/dx)_{x=x_i}$. Now interpolate this set of data with another cubic spline $\hat{s}^*(x)$ and then generate D_2 by setting $f''_i = (d\hat{s}_3^*/dx)_{x=x_i}$.

Compare these two methods with the following data D_0:

x_i	f_i	x_i	f_i
0	0.0	6	-0.2794
1	0.8415	7	0.6570
2	0.9093	8	0.9894
3	0.1411	9	0.4121
4	-0.7568	10	-0.5440
5	-0.9589		

The data is derived from the function $f(x) = \sin(x)$ so it is easy to check the accuracy of the approximation for $f''(x)$.

1.6. The following data has been collected on the movement of an object during an experiment:

Time (sec)	t	0	1	2	5	10	15	20
Distance (cm)	$s(t)$	0	27	58	162	352	535	704
Velocity (cm/sec)	$v(t)$	25	29	32	37	38	35	32

(a) Use osculatory interpolation to find the polynomial $p_5^*(x)$ of deg 5 that interpolates the data $s(0)$, $s(2)$, $v(2)$, $s(10)$, $s(15)$, $v(15)$. [Use the fact that $v(t) = ds(t)/dt$.]

(b) Interpolate the complete set of data using a piecewise cubic Hermite polynomial.

(c) Interpolate the data for $s(t)$ using a clamped cubic spline.

(d) Repeat part (c) using a spline with free boundary.

(e) Use each of the above interpolants to estimate the distance traveled and velocity at time $t = 8$. (The correct values are $s(8) = 276$, $v(8) = 38$— see Exercise 1.10, Chapter 4.)

(f) Use each interpolant to estimate the acceleration $a(t)$ $(= dv(t)/dt)$ at time $t = 8$. Which of the interpolant(s) could not be used to estimate $a(10)$? Why?

Section 3.2

2.1. Find the best least squares fit to the data in Exercise 1.4 using

    i A polynomial of deg 1.
    ii A polynomial of deg 2.
    iii A function of the form $g(x) = c_1 + c_2 x + c_3/x$.

Which one gives the best fit?

2.2. Show that each of the sets defined in (3.24) generates the set $\mathcal{P}_3$ of all polynomials of degree ≤ 3.

2.3. Verify (3.53) in the case $N = 6$.

2.4. Show that $\beta_i(x)$ defined by (3.42) satisfies the definition of a cubic spline.

2.5. Consider the data in Exercise 1.4.

(a) Write down the overdetermined linear system $Ac = f$ for a least squares approximation by a straight line for each of the cases where the basis B is

    i $\{1, x\}$
    ii $\{10 - 3x, 5x + 1\}$

(b) Find c^* for each case in (a). Verify that they produce the same polynomial $p_1^*(x)$.

2.6. Consider the following data

x	$f(x)$	x	$f(x)$
0	0.72973	3.00	−0.45920
0.25	1.2952	3.25	−0.98761
0.50	0.90196	3.50	−1.2517
0.75	0.30183	3.75	−0.61894
1.00	0.040571	4.00	−0.13183
1.25	0.20050	4.25	−0.072410
1.50	0.36808	4.50	−0.31776
1.75	0.089530	4.75	−0.30720
2.00	−0.47661	5.00	0.14550
2.25	−0.83513	5.25	0.69583
2.50	−0.58981	5.50	0.78317
2.75	−0.31261	5.75	0.43508
		6.00	0.31600

(a) Find the best least-squares cubic spline approximation to the data with knots located at $t = [0.0, 1.0, 2.4, 4.5, 6.0]^T$. What is the RMSE?

(b) Estimate the value of $f(3.1)$.

(c) Compute a new spline approximation with the same set of knots except that the knot at 4.5 is moved to 4.1. Does this give a better approximation?

(d) Use a variable knot subroutine to compute the best least squares spline approximation with five knots. Compare the accuracy with that of the splines from parts (a) and (c).

2.7. Verify (3.54) for the case $N = 5$.

2.8. Consider the following functions defined on the indicated intervals:

    i $f(x) = x, 0 \le x < 2\pi$.

    ii $f(x) = \begin{matrix} 1, \ 0 \le x < \pi. \\ -1, \ \pi \le x < 2\pi. \end{matrix}$

    iii $f(x) = \sin x/2, 0 \le x < 4\pi$.

    iv $f(x) = \sin x/2, 0 \le x < 2\pi$.

    v $f(x) = \sin^{-1}[(\frac{1}{3}(\sin 5x + 2\cos x)], 0 \le x < 2\pi$.

In each case, generate the data $\{(x_k, f_k)\}_{k=0}^{N-1}$, where $x_k = \rho k/N$, with $\rho =$ period of f, and interpolate with a trigonometric polynomial using an FFT subroutine. Use $N = 64$.

CHAPTER 4

SOLUTION OF NONLINEAR EQUATIONS

We return to the problem of solving a system of n equations in n unknowns but this time we drop the assumption that each equation is linear in each of the unknowns. Such systems of equations are called *nonlinear* and can be written in the general form

(4.1) $\mathbf{f}(\mathbf{x}) = \mathbf{0}$

where $\mathbf{x} = [x_1, \ldots, x_n]^T$ is an n-vector and $\mathbf{f}$ is an n-vector whose ith component is the nonlinear function

(4.2) $f_i = f_i(\mathbf{x}) = f_i(x_1, \ldots, x_n)$ $1 \leq i \leq n$

For example,

(a) $\mathbf{f}(\mathbf{x}) = \begin{bmatrix} f_1(\mathbf{x}) \\ f_2(\mathbf{x}) \end{bmatrix} = \begin{bmatrix} 4x_1^2 + 9x_2^2 - 16x_1 - 54x_2 + 61 \\ x_1x_2 - 2x_1 - 1 \end{bmatrix} = \mathbf{0}$

(4.3)   or

(b) $\mathbf{f}(\mathbf{x}) = \begin{bmatrix} f_1(\mathbf{x}) \\ f_2(\mathbf{x}) \\ f_3(\mathbf{x}) \end{bmatrix} = \begin{bmatrix} x_2x_3^2 + x_3e^{x_2}\sin(x_1x_3) \\ x_1x_3^2 - e^{x_2}\cos(x_1x_3) \\ 2x_1x_2x_3 + x_1e^{x_2}\sin(x_1x_3) \end{bmatrix} = \mathbf{0}$

We begin by discussing the relatively simple case of a single equation in one unknown ($n = 1$) such as

(4.4)
(a) $f(x) = 9x^4 - 20x^2 + 16x + 4 = 0$
(b) $f(x) = e^x \sin(2x) - x = 0$

One reason for doing this is that many of the methods for solving single equations have natural extensions to systems and it is much easier to grasp the concepts involved by looking at the simpler case first. A second reason is that the problem of solving a single nonlinear equation arises very frequently in practical applications, making it worthwhile to implement special subroutines that take advantage of the simplifications when $n = 1$. Therefore, the solution of a single equation is not merely a (relatively) simple case of a more difficult problem. Instead, it is an important problem in its own right.

In section 4.2, we discuss single equations separately and then, in Section 4.3, we consider systems. But first we shall make a number of preliminary remarks about nonlinear equations (single equations and systems) and subroutines for solving them in order to introduce some of the ideas involved.

4.1 PRELIMINARIES

In Chapter 2, we considered the problem of solving a system of n linear equations in n unknowns. Dealing with this topic was a relatively simple matter. The solution of a linear system can be expressed in closed form in any one of a number of ways—Gauss elimination with back substitution, Cramer's rule, etc.—each of which defines an exact method (assuming infinite precision arithmetic is used) for the direct computation of the solution. Therefore, within the limitations of machine precision, there was no worry about being able to compute the solution. Instead, the main concern was to determine the most efficient way to compute it. By contrast, the situation for nonlinear equations is quite the reverse. In general, there is no way of expressing a solution in closed form so there are no exact or "direct" methods[1]. Instead, we have to use approximate methods. But the disadvantage of an approximate method is that it will sometimes fail. Therefore, the main concern when solving nonlinear equations is to ensure that a solution can, in fact, be computed. The efficiency with which it can be done, though still an important consideration, will necessarily be secondary.

Solutions
A *solution of root* of (4.1) is defined to be any vector r that satisfies each equation of the system. There is often more than one solution but the number varies from problem to problem. For example, the system (4.3)(a) has two (real) solutions:

$$\mathbf{r}_1 \doteq \begin{bmatrix} 0.37308 \\ 4.68036 \end{bmatrix} \quad \text{and} \quad \mathbf{r}_2 \doteq \begin{bmatrix} 4.75621 \\ 2.21025 \end{bmatrix}$$

---

[1]Occasionally, closed expressions for the solutions can be found. However, with only one notable exception, these expressions usually turn out to be so complex that they are impractical to use for computational purposes. The example (4.3)(a) is a case in point. The exceptional case is the quadratic equation

$$f(x) = ax^2 + bx + c = 0$$

The formulas for the solutions of a quadratic are well known. They are not complicated and can be evaluated easily. In fact, since this problem arises with some frequency, it is not unusual to find that a software package will contain a special subroutine for solving quadratics (directly).

On the other hand, if the second component of $f(x)$ were the function $f_2(x) = x_1x_2 - 3x_1 + 5$, the resulting system would have four solutions. If, instead, $f_2(x) = x_1x_2 + 3x_2 - 1$, there would be no (real) solution at all. There can even be an infinite number of solutions as is the case with the single equation (4.4)(b). For a given problem, the exact number of solutions is usually not known at the outset, nor is it easy to determine the number. Therefore, we usually have to proceed without knowing how many solutions there are to be found. While this is not a really serious complication, it can be somewhat annoying at times.

Methods of Solution

The methods used to compute solutions of nonlinear equations are of iterative type. Starting with an initial approximation x_0 for a solution r, an *iterative method* is a rule for computing, successively, a sequence of approximations $x_0, x_1, x_2, \ldots$. The aim is to choose an x_0 that generates a sequence that *converges to a solution* r, that is,

(4.5) $\quad \lim_{k \to \infty} \|x_k - r\| = 0$

A single application of an iterative rule (to obtain the next approximation in the sequence) is called an *iteration*. Sometimes this term is also used to refer to the entire sequence of approximations itself. In the following, both definitions are used freely. However, taken in context, there will be no difficulty in distinguishing which meaning is intended.

To illustrate the use of an iterative method, we will solve the single equation

$$f(x) = x^2 + 2x - 3 = 0$$

using the method defined by

(4.6) $\quad x_{k+1} = x_k + \dfrac{x_k^2 + 2x_k - 3}{x_k^2 - 5}$

By way of a slight digression, the derivation of this iterative rule is based on the following idea. Rewrite the equation $f(x) = 0$ in the form $x - g(x) = 0$. Then any root r of $f(x)$ is also a *fixed-point* of $g(x)$, that is,

(4.7) $\quad$ if $f(r) = 0 \quad$ then $\quad r = g(r)$

To find a fixed-point of $g(x)$, we can use the iterative method defined by

(4.8) $\quad x_{k+1} = g(x_k)$

and, in view of the relationship (4.7), this will also be a method for finding roots of $f(x)$. It is called, appropriately, *fixed-point iteration*. The rule (4.6) was derived from (4.8) by defining $g(x)$ to be of the form

TABLE 4.1

k	x_k	x_k	x_k	x_k
0	-5.0	0.0	1.5	5.0
1	-4.4000	0.6000	0.6818	6.6000
2	-3.8735	0.9103	0.9401	7.9942
3	-3.4480	0.9944	0.9974	9.2996
4	-3.1587	1.0000	1.0000	10.552
5	-3.0261	1.0000	1.0000	11.769
6	-3.0008			12.960
7	-3.0000			14.131
8	-3.0000			$\vdots$

$$g(x) = x + \frac{f(x)}{x^2 - 5}$$

Obviously, this is not the only iterative rule that can be derived in this way. We can define different forms for $g(x)$ to produce other rules. For instance, we might have

$$g(x) = \frac{3 - x^2}{2} \quad \text{or} \quad g(x) = x - \frac{x^2 + 2x - 3}{2(x + 1)} = x - \frac{f(x)}{f'(x)}$$

As a matter of interest, the latter form leads to the well-known Newton–Raphson method (Section 4.2.1).

Returning to our example, we have to choose an initial guess x_0. Unless we have some knowledge about the approximate location of the roots, our guess must be more or less arbitrary. Let us assume that we know nothing about the locations of the roots and see what happens with various choices for x_0. In Table 4.1, we show some results. With $x_0 = -5.0, 0.0$, and 1.5, the resulting iterations converge quite nicely. It is easy to check that the limiting values -3.0 and 1.0 are, in fact, roots of the equation in question. [Note that when a fixed point of $g(x)$ is found, it is still necessary to check that it is a root of $f(x)$, because the implication in (4.7) is only in one direction.] These are "good" initial guesses because their respective iterations tell us something about the roots of $f(x)$, namely, each one locates a root[2]. On the other hand, the initial guess $x_0 = 5.0$ is "bad". The iteration starting with it tells us nothing whatsoever about the roots of $f(x)$ (except

---

[2]Admittedly, there is some duplication of effort here in that both of the initial guesses 0.0 and 1.5 lead to the same root. However, the redundancy can easily be eliminated by using a process called *deflation* (Section 4.2.2).

that $5.0, 6.6, \ldots$ are not any of them). It is a complete waste of computational effort. Obviously, it would be nice to have some mechanism by which we can avoid choosing bad initial guesses in the first place, but this is easier said than done as we shall now see.

Guarantee of Convergence

We now explore the idea of trying to choose an initial guess that is guaranteed to be good. To this end, we look to the mathematical literature for results specifying conditions on x_0 that will guarantee convergence to a solution. Typically, such results run to the effect that convergence to a root r can be guaranteed if $x_0 \in N_\delta(r)$, where $N_\delta(r)$ is a *neighborhood* of r, satisfying conditions of the form

(4.9)

    i $r \in N_\delta(r)$.

    ii The iterative method maps $N_\delta(r)$ continuously into itself, that is, if $x_k \in N_\delta(r)$, then $x_{k+1} \in N_\delta(r)$ also.

    iii A "convergence" condition (which depends on the method being used).

δ is called the *diameter* of $N_\delta(r)$, that is,

    If $x, y \in N_\delta(r)$, then $\|x - y\| \le \delta$

We remark that the diameter is a useful measure for comparing iterative methods. A method for which δ is relatively large is said to be more "globally convergent." This is a nice property to have in a method since it decreases the likelihood of choosing a bad initial guess.

The first two conditions of (4.9) ensure that, when convergence occurs, it will be to a root of $f(x)$. The third condition ensures that convergence will, in fact, take place. Consider, for example, the fixed-point iteration (4.8) for single equations. It can be shown (see [5, p. 44]) that convergence to the root r is guaranteed for any $x_0 \in N_\delta(r) = [a, b]$ provided

(4.10)

    i $r \in [a, b]$.

    ii $g(x)$ is continuous on $[a, b]$ and, if $x \in [a, b]$, then $g(x) \in [a, b]$ also.

    iii $|g'(x)| < 1$, for all $x \in [a, b]$.

Applying this result to the specific iterative method (4.6), we find that:

    Convergence to $r = 1$ is guaranteed if $x_0 \in I_1 = [-1.69, 1.37]$.

    Convergence to $r = -3$ is guaranteed if $x_0 \in I_2 = (-\infty, -2.77]$.

If $x_0 \in I_1$ or I_2, then it is guaranteed to be a good initial guess. Note, however, that any $x_0 \not\in I_1$ or I_2 is not necessarily bad. For example, $x_0 = 1.5$ lies outside I_1 and I_2 and yet, from Table 4.1, we see that it is a good guess after all.

The disadvantage of results like (4.9) and (4.10) is that they are not very useful from a practical point of view. First, they presuppose knowledge about the location of **r** which, of course, is begging the question. Moreover, they are conservative, as the example with $x_0 = 1.5$ illustrates. Second, the computation of the diameter δ is usually so long and complicated that it is not worthwhile trying to do. For instance, in the example above, the determination of the intervals I_1 and I_2 required considerably more work than was needed to compute the whole of Table 4.1. From this we conclude that it is not practical to try to accept or reject an initial guess at the outset. Instead, it is better to choose an x_0, start an iteration with it, and continue until a decision can be made. Then choose another x_0 and so on until all the roots have been found. There is, of course, the possibility of continually choosing bad initial guesses but, in most practical situations, this will not happen if we exercise a little care and make use of any information that is available. Indeed, there are many situations where, in the context of the overall problem being solved at the time, the general vicinity of the roots is known or can easily be inferred and one can make "educated" initial guesses. It is always a good idea to take advantage of such information whenever possible.

Stopping Criteria

We now turn to some comments about subroutines. From the above discussion it is clear that a rootfinding algorithm will consist of more than just a straightforward implementation of an iterative rule for computing successive approximations. It must also be able to decide automatically whether an iteration has succeeded or failed. The usual procedure is to make a test after each iteration to see whether or not:

1. Convergence to a solution has taken place yet.
2. Or else the number of iterations performed so far has reached a specified maximum, say, ITMAX.

These tests are called the *stopping criteria*. Whenever the answer to either one is "yes," the iteration should be stopped and the appropriate result returned. In the case that (1) is satisfied, the result will be the value x_{k+1} of the most recent iterate computed. We will discuss the design of tests for convergence in the next paragraph. On the other hand, if (2) is satisfied (and (1) is not), the presumption is that the iteration will fail to converge and the result that is returned will indicate this. We remark that this may seem like a naïve and inefficient test for nonconvergence, that is, simply let the iteration run its course until $k = $ ITMAX iterations have been done and then, if (1) has still not been satisfied, surmise that it will never be so. On the other hand, if we were to include a specific test for divergence such as

$$\frac{|x_{k+1} - x_k|}{|x_k - x_{k-1}|} > 1$$

then we could recognize a bad iteration much earlier and avoid a lot of unnecessary work. Consider, for example, the iteration starting with $x_0 = 5.0$ in Table 4.1. With the above test, termination would occur after only two iterations. But the disadvantage of using such a test is that it will cause *premature termination* in those cases where an iteration seemingly diverges for a while before ultimately converging. To avoid this difficulty, we could try waiting until, say, $k = 5$ before applying the test. Alternatively, we could require that the test holds for, say five successive iterations before concluding that the sequence diverges. However, even these modifications can cause premature termination surprisingly often. It turns out that, on balance, (2) is a better strategy. This assumes, of course, that ITMAX is not excessively large.

Convergence Tests

Let us consider, for a moment, the form of the test (1) for detecting convergence to a solution. In essence, we want to determine the error in x_{k+1} and stop when it is sufficiently small, that is, when

$$(4.11) \quad \|e_{k+1}\| = \|x_{k+1} - r\| \le \text{XTOL} \cdot (1 + \|r\|)^3$$

where XTOL is some specified error tolerance. Now, since r is not known, we must look for an alternative test. One possibility is to approximate r by x_k in (4.11). The resulting test would be

$$(4.12) \quad \|\boldsymbol{\epsilon}_{k+1}\| = \|x_{k+1} - x_k\| \le \text{XTOL} \cdot (1 + \|x_k\|)$$

that is, stop if two successive iterates are sufficiently close to each other. There is, however, some danger in concluding that a sequence of numbers has converged just because two successive terms in it are close enough to each other. For instance, consider the example method (4.6) again. Suppose that, for some reason, we choose $x_0 = 2.23$ and use the test (4.12) with $\text{XTOL} = 5.0\text{E} - 3$. The results would be as follows.

---

[3]It is usual to think in terms of testing for the *relative* size of e_{k+1}, that is,

$$\|e_{k+1}\| = \|x_{k+1} - r\| \le \text{XTOL} \cdot \|r\|$$

However, if r is near 0, there can be a problem due to the possibility of either never being able to satisfy the inequality or underflow occurring in the evaluation of the right-hand side. In this case, it is better to test for the *absolute* size of e_{k+1}, that is,

$$\|e_{k+1}\| = \|x_{k+1} - r\| \le \text{XTOL}$$

The test (4.11) is intended to combine both of these into one, that is, depending on the size of $\|r\|$, we effectively get one or the other.

k	x_k	$|x_{k+1} - x_k|$	XTOL*$(1 + |x_k|)$	
			XTOL $= 5.0E - 3$	$1.0E - 3$
0	2.23	237.3	0.016	0.003
1	-235.1	1.0	1.18	0.236
2	-234.1	1.0	1.17	0.235
3	-233.1			

After three iterations, the test for convergence is satisfied but the result $x_3 = -233.1$ is incorrect. Hence we have another case of premature termination. (If allowed to continue, the iteration would converge, albeit slowly, to the root $r = -3.0$.) We can easily avoid this difficulty by using a smaller value for XTOL, but choosing it too small can have the opposite effect, that is, termination may not occur soon enough and this downgrades the efficiency. Hence, in choosing XTOL, one has to strike a balance between reliability and efficiency, which is not easy to do because we cannot predict how an iteration will behave.

Another possible test for convergence is one that uses the residual $\rho_{k+1} = f(x_{k+1})$, that is, stop when

$$(4.13) \quad \|\rho_{k+1}\| = \|f(x_{k+1})\| \leq \text{FTOL}$$

But, once again, we have the problem of choosing the tolerance in order to strike a balance between reliability and efficiency. We have to make FTOL reasonably small in order to prevent early termination. But choosing it too small can delay termination unnecessarily. In Figure 4.1, we illustrate the difficulties for the case of a single equation. The function $f(x)$ in Figure 4.1a is quite flat[4] near the root r so ρ_{k+1} is small in which case (4.13) causes termination unless FTOL is very small. But the error $e_{k+1} = x_{k+1} - r$ is not small so termination at this stage is premature. On the other hand, if FTOL is too small, termination may not occur soon enough as we see in Figure 4.1b.

While neither of the above tests is very satisfactory by itself, it turns out that they complement each other in the sense that if one of them fails (to detect convergence) the other will succeed. Let us see why this is true. For

---

[4]This is an example of *ill conditioning* in the root **r**. Any small shift in **f(x)**, say $f(x) + \epsilon$, causes a large shift in **r**. In Figure 4.1a, such a shift moves the graph of $f(x)$ in a vertical direction and, since f is almost horizontal in this region, r will shift substantially. We emphasize that it is the root **r** that is ill conditioned and not **f**. **f** can quite easily have other roots that are well behaved. A discussion of the effects of ill conditioning is given in Section 4.2.3. Finally, note the similarity between this concept and the corresponding one for linear equations.

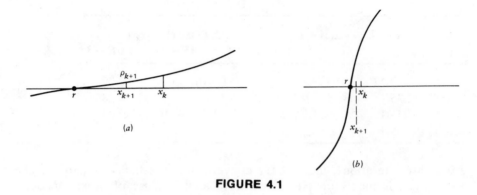

FIGURE 4.1

convenience, we shall refer to (4.12) as the "X-test" and (4.13) as the "F-test." Again referring to Figure 4.1b, the F-test may fail to detect convergence if FTOL is too small. However, the X-test will succeed, even if XTOL is relatively small. Similarly, the F-test will usually succeed where the X-test fails. Therefore, it is usual for a subroutine to use both tests and terminate the iteration when

(4.14)   *Either* the X-test or the F-test is satisfied.

By choosing XTOL and FTOL reasonably small, we can minimize the risk of premature termination on either test and, at the same time, be confident that there is no delay in detecting convergence. The documentation for a subroutine will usually suggest appropriate values for XTOL and FTOL.

We remark that there is still the possibility of early termination using the test (4.14). Hence, there is the question of testing for this occurrence. As a general rule, a subroutine will not perform such a test explicitly. This is because XTOL and FTOL can be chosen sufficiently small so that only somewhat contrived or pathological problems can cause difficulties. The routine would certainly not have trouble with most problems that arise in practical applications provided, of course, that XTOL and FTOL are suitably chosen. Therefore, a user need not be concerned about testing for early termination unless he or she has reason to suspect that the problem is somewhat pathological. If a test is considered necessary, then early termination on the X-test can easily be detected by checking the size of $f(x_{k+1})$. To see if the F-test was at fault, one should look at the size of $\epsilon_{k+1} = x_{k+1} - x_k$. In case this information is not available on return from a subroutine, an alternative is to test for ill conditioning (of the root r) by perturbing the system a little and, after re-solving, seeing how much the roots have shifted. Since the latter test can be expensive, we emphasize that, unless there is reason to suspect difficulties with a problem, there is no great need to build such tests into a program.

Calling Sequence

The general format of an algorithm for solving nonlinear equations is:

1. Choose an initial guess x_0.
2. FOR $k = 0, 1, 2, \ldots$ UNTIL stopping criteria satisfied,
   └ compute x_{k+1}.
3. RETURN with the result.

From the foregoing discussion, we see that it is virtually impossible to automate such an algorithm to the point where it can choose its own initial guess and stopping criteria. These must be left for the user to specify. Hence, a typical calling sequence for a root-finding subroutine called, say ROOT, is of the form

> CALL ROOT(F,XO,XTOL,FTOL,ITMAX,IND)

where

> F is the name of a (user-supplied) subprogram for evaluating the function $f(x)$.
> XO is the initial guess.
> XTOL, FTOL, ITMAX define the stopping criteria.
> IND indicates (on return) which test caused termination.

On return, XO will contain the value of x_{k+1}, and ITMAX will be set equal to k, the number of iterations performed. In addition, many subroutines will also return the values of $\|x_{k+1} - x_k\|$ and $\|f(x_{k+1})\|$ in XTOL and FTOL, respectively. Combined with the value of IND, this is plenty of information in case we want to check the reliability of the results. We remark that ROOT will only find one root and then exit. If several roots of a function are desired, the routine must be called repeatedly with different initial guesses. It would be more convenient if the subroutine itself had this capability so that all the user would have to do is specify the number of roots desired. This, in fact, can be done. We discuss the details in Section 4.2.2.

Comparison of Methods

In Section 4.2.1, we describe and compare various iterative methods. The bases for comparison will be (1) guarantee of convergence and (2) efficiency. We have already mentioned the former. The diameter δ of the neighbourhood $N_\delta(r)$ satisfying (4.9) provides a good means for defining a measure of this property but, as we have seen, it is difficult to use in practice. For any given method, it is well nigh impossible to determine a general expression for δ, let alone trying to compare such expressions for different methods. Instead, we rely on inferences gathered from experience and/or analysis of a method. Based on this, it is usual to make statements to the effect that, as a general rule, one method is more globally convergent than another one. In other words, for most problems, the δ for one method appears to be greater than the δ for the other one. In the following we make such statements without trying to justify them mathematically since they are based on experience rather than rigorous analysis.

By efficiency, we mean the total amount of computation required to calculate a good approximation for r (disregarding any unsuccessful iterations). This is determined from the amount of computation per iteration times the number of iterations required. The former is usually measured by counting the number of times (per iteration) that we must evaluate $f(x)$ since this is usually the predominant factor in computing x_{k+1}. As to the number of iterations required, this is strongly dependent on the behaviour of the function $f(x)$ in question and also on the closeness of x_0 to r. But we would prefer to use an indicator that is more or less independent of these factors. To this end, one can usually perform some analysis on a method and establish an asymptotic relationship, between successive errors of the following form: if x_k is sufficiently close to r, then

(4.15) $\qquad \|e_{k+1}\| \doteq C\|e_k\|^p \qquad$ as k increases

where $C = C_M(f)$ depends on both the particular method M under consideration and the function $f(x)$. The number p, on the other hand, depends only on the method and this is what we want. We call p the *rate of convergence*. It is used to compare the number of iterations required. To illustrate its significance, suppose that $\|e_0\| = 0.1$ and $C = 1$. The following table shows the effect of different rates of convergence.

k	$p = 1.62$	$p = 2.0$
0	$1.0E-1$	$1.0E-1$
1	$2.4E-2$	$1.0E-2$
2	$2.4E-3$	$1.0E-4$
3	$5.6E-5$	$1.0E-8$
4	$1.3E-7$	

From this, we might conclude that a method with a higher rate of convergence is better because fewer iterations will be required. But this can be misleading. We are actually interested in how much computation is required to find a root. Suppose, for example, that the $p = 1.62$ method requires one function evaluation per iteration while the $p = 2$ method requires two. Then the total number of function evaluations needed by each method to achieve an accuracy of $1.0E\text{-}6$ is 4 and 6, respectively, so the slower method is better after all. Therefore, to measure efficiency, it is important to consider both factors—rate of convergence and amount of work per iteration.

We make one further remark on comparison of methods. Almost invariably it turns out that, if a method is superior with respect to guarantee of convergence, it will usually be relatively slow, and conversely. Therefore, in choosing a method, one must decide which property is the more important at the time. If, for example, we have no idea about the locations of the roots, then we will prefer a method which is slower but less likely to diverge.

We are now ready to examine some specific methods and algorithms.

4.2. SINGLE EQUATIONS

In this section, we consider the problem of solving a single nonlinear equation $f(x) = 0$ in one unknown. A software package will usually contain several subroutines for solving this problem and we discuss various aspects of some typical ones. Our aim is to provide a basis for choosing the most appropriate routine for a particular problem at hand. In order to assess a subroutine properly, one should know something about the rootfinding method(s) on which it is based. Therefore, we first discuss, in Section 4.2.1, some commonly used methods. Then, in Section 4.2.2, we look at the subroutines themselves. In Section 4.2.3, we consider special routines for the case where $f(x)$ is a polynomial.

4.2.1. Methods

We first survey and compare some methods, and then discuss their incorporation into subroutines. The derivation of each method is done from a geometric point of view since this provides a good basis on which to discuss the method's advantages and disadvantages. Algebraic details have been kept to a minimum. For simplicity, we assume that $f(x)$ is continuous and real valued. By the latter, we mean that if x is a real number then $f(x)$ is also real. Note, however, that f can still have complex roots.

1. Bisection
Suppose that we have an interval $[a_k, b_k]$ over which $f(x)$ changes sign an odd number of times, that is, $\operatorname{sgn} f(a_k) \neq \operatorname{sgn} f(b_k)$. Then, by continuity, $[a_k, b_k]$ contains at least one root of $f(x)$. $[a_k, b_k]$ is called a *bracket*. An iteration of the bisection method consists of two steps. First, we compute the point

(4.16) $\quad c_k = \dfrac{a_k + b_k}{2} = a_k + \dfrac{1}{2} \cdot (b_k - a_k)$

which bisects $[a_k, b_k]$. The second form is the preferable one to use[5]. We then determine a new interval $[a_{k+1}, b_{k+1}]$ according to the rule

(4.17) $\quad [a_{k+1}, b_{k+1}] = \begin{cases} [a_k, c_k] & \text{if } \operatorname{sgn} f(a_k) \neq \operatorname{sgn} f(c_k) \\ [c_k, b_k] & \text{otherwise} \end{cases}$

Again, by continuity, $[a_{k+1}, b_{k+1}]$ contains at least one root so it is a bracket also. Continuing, we compute the midpoint c_{k+1} and decide which subinterval will be the new bracket, and so on. The process is illustrated in Figure 4.2. Of course, if some c_k is such that $f(c_k) = 0$, then it is a root and we are finished. Otherwise, the iteration continues until one of the stopping criteria is met. Hence, given an initial bracket $[a_0, b_0]$, the method computes a sequence of nested brackets $[a_0, b_0] \subset [a_1, b_1] \subset \dots$, each of which is smaller by half than its predecessor. At the kth stage, we use the midpoint c_k as an approximate value for the root so the method can also be viewed as generating the sequence of approximations $c_0, c_1, \dots$.

The main virtue of bisection is guarantee of convergence. Given an initial bracket $[a_0, b_0]$, the method is absolutely guaranteed to find a root because, by halving the length at each stage, we can always make the bracket as small as we like (subject, of course, to the limitations of

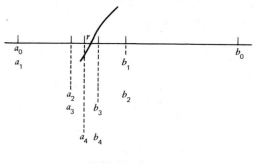

FIGURE 4.2

<hr>

[5]We recall from the example in Chapter 1 that the second form should only be used when $\operatorname{sgn}(a_k) = \operatorname{sgn}(b_k)$. Otherwise, we should use the first form. However, in the present context, it is not necessary to make a choice because, unless the root in question is zero, the iteration will eventually reach a stage beyond which the signs always agree. Prior to this, there is no need to be concerned about minimizing round-off error because it is insignificant compared to the total error in the current approximation for the root. For these reasons, the second form of (4.16) is preferred.

machine precision) from which it follows that $c_k \to r$. We even get precise bounds for the root—$a_n \le r \le b_n$, where n is the number of iterations performed.

A major disadvantage of the bisection method is inefficiency. The rate of convergence in (4.15) is only $p = 1$. (This follows from the fact that $|e_{k+1}| \doteq |e_k|/2$.) To illustrate how bad this is, suppose $\text{XTOL} = 1.0E - 6 \doteq 2^{-20}$. Then the number of iterations required to achieve this accuracy will be the smallest integer n satisfying

$$(b_0 - a_0) \le 2^{n-20} \cdot (1 + |c_0|)$$

For example, if $[a_0, b_0] = [0.0, 1.0]$, then $n = 20$. Since the method requires one function evaluation per iteration plus two to begin, a total of 22 evaluations will be needed. As we will see, this is quite excessive.

There are some other aspects of the bisection method that should be noted before we go on to other methods. First of all, finding an initial bracket $[a_0, b_0]$ in order to get started can sometimes be troublesome. For instance, difficulties can arise in the case of "clustered" roots. Suppose, for example, that $f(x)$ has two roots that are close together, say $r_1 = 1.10$ and $r_2 = 1.15$. Then, to find either one, we will need a bracket having an endpoint lying between them and this may not be a very easy thing to do without any prior knowledge about their locations. This leads us to the second point—the method cannot locate roots that are of even multiplicity. For example, consider the function

$$f(x) = x^4 + 2x^3 - 2x^2 - 6x + 5 = (x - 1)^2(x^2 + 4x + 5)$$

which has a root of multiplicity $m = 2$ at the point $x = 1$. This situation can be viewed as an extreme example of clustering. The two roots at $x = 1$ are so tightly clustered that it is impossible to separate them. Geometrically, as Figure 4.3 illustrates, the graph of $f(x)$ touches, but does not cross the x-axis at $x = 1$ so there is no sign change in f. Therefore, even if this root does lie in an initial bracket $[a_0, b_0]$, the method will never converge to it at

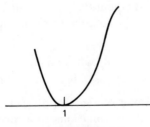

FIGURE 4.3

all. Similarly, the method will fail to find any root r whose multiplicity is even since f will not change sign at r. As a final point, we note that the bisection method will not locate complex roots either. Again, this is because $f(x)$ does not change sign at a complex root. We remark that the foregoing comments apply to any "bracketing method," that is, any method that uses the idea of computing a sequence of nested brackets. We shall be discussing two others methods of this type—regula falsi and Brent—and it will be understood that these comments apply to them as well.

2. Regula Falsi

The regula falsi method is a modification of bisection. The formula (4.16) used to compute c_k in the bisection method can be written in the more general form

$$(4.18) \quad c_k = a_k + w_k \cdot (b_k - a_k)$$

where w_k is a *weight* satisfying $0 < w_k < 1$ so that $a_k < c_k < b_k$. For bisection we had each $w_k = \frac{1}{2}$ but now we use a different definition:

$$(4.19) \quad w_k = \frac{f(a_k)}{f(a_k) - f(b_k)}$$

The motivation for this choice is as follows. First of all, we again assume that $[a_k, b_k]$ is a bracket, that is, $\operatorname{sgn} f(a_k) \neq \operatorname{sgn} f(b_k)$. Then it follows from (4.19) that

$$0 < w_k \le \frac{1}{2} \quad \text{if } |f(a_k)| \le |f(b_k)|$$

and

$$\frac{1}{2} < w_k < 1 \quad \text{if } |f(a_k)| > |f(b_k)|$$

Now, in Figure 4.3, we observe that $|f(a_k)| < |f(b_k)|$ from which we conclude that r is probably closer to a_k than it is to b_k. Hence, instead of the midpoint of $[a_k, b_k]$, a more appropriate choice for c_k would be some point closer to where r is more likely to be. Quite clearly, this is precisely what the weight (4.19) will do. By choosing c_k in this way, we hopefully can achieve convergence in significantly fewer iterations than bisection. Therefore, the definition of the regula falsi method is, given a bracket $[a_k, b_k]$,

    i Compute c_k using (4.18) with weight (4.19).
    ii Define a new bracket $[a_{k+1}, b_{k+1}]$ according to (4.17).

The process continues until one of the stopping criteria is met. The points $c_0, c_1, c_2, \ldots$ are successive approximations to a root r of $f(x)$.

A geometric derivation of regula falsi will explain how the form (4.19)

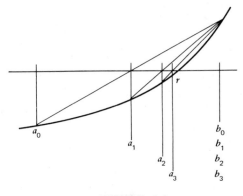

FIGURE 4.4

for the weight w_k was derived. Consider, as illustrated in Figure 4.4, the straight line through the two points $(a_k, f(a_k))$ and $(b_k, f(b_k))$ on the graph of $f(x)$. The line is called the *secant* line to f at these points. Its equation is

$$y - f(a_k) = \frac{f(a_k) - f(b_k)}{a_k - b_k} \cdot (x - a_k)$$

Then it is easily verified that the x-intercept of this line has coordinates $(c_k, 0)$, where c_k is given by (4.18) with w_k defined by (4.19). In other words, regula falsi uses the x-intercept of this secant line as an estimate for the location of r. We remark that the method can also be described in the language of the previous chapter, that is, we approximate $f(x)$ in the neighbourhood of r by a simpler function and then take c_k to be the root of it. For the regula falsi method, the approximating function is the straight line that interpolates $f(x)$ at $(a_k, f(a_k))$ and $(b_k, f(b_k))$. We will see this idea again in the description of other methods.

The motivation for considering regula falsi was to improve on the efficiency of bisection. The amount of work per iteration is the same—one function evaluation—so any improvement must come from the rate of convergence. Let us consider the example

(4.20) $f(x) = x^3 - 6x^2 - 2x + 12 = (x^2 - 2)(x - 6)$

In Table 4.2, we show the results of two iterations using regula falsi. The initial intervals were $I_1 = [0, 4]$ and $I_2 = [-4, 0]$, each of which contains one root of $f(x)$. The a's and b's beside the c_k columns indicate which endpoint is replaced by c_k. (The final brackets are given at the end of each column.) The convergence test was (4.14) with XTOL = FTOL = $1.0E - 3$. In both cases, termination was on the X-test. For comparison, we note that the

TABLE 4.2

k	c_k	$f(c_k)$	c_k	$f(c_k)$
	[0.0, 4.0]		[−4.0, 0.0]	
1	1.200 a	$2.688E\ 0$	−0.3158 b	$1.200E\quad 1$
2	1.445 b	$-4.010E-1$	−0.6067 b	$1.078E\quad 1$
3	1.413 a	$1.574E-2$	−0.8493 b	$8.758E\quad 0$
4	1.414 a	$2.770E-3$	−1.035 b	$6.534E\quad 0$
·	[1.414, 1.445]		−1.167 b	$4.573E\quad 0$
·			·	
·			·	
14			−1.411 b	$6.728E-2$
15			−1.412 b	$4.637E-2$
			[−4.0, −1.412]	

bisection method would require 11 iterations starting with the same initial brackets. Hence, in the case of I_1, regula falsi gives a very significant improvement in efficiency. On the other hand, with I_2, it is worse than bisection. On closer inspection, we observe that the left endpoint remained the same throughout the iteration whereas, with I_1, both left and right endpoints were changed at one stage or another. Geometrically, the reason for this can be seen in Figure 4.4. If the graph of $f(x)$ does not change concavity over $[a_k, b_k]$, that is, f has no point of inflection within the bracket, then c_k will consistently lie on one side of r. When this happens, the rate of convergence of the method is $p = 1$, the same as bisection[6]. Hence, any improvement in efficiency is entirely dependent on the particular equation $f(x) = 0$ being solved at the time[7]. Unfortunately, there is no practical way of telling, beforehand, whether there will be any improvement or not.

We make one further remark about Table 4.2. We have already noted that, in the iteration with I_1, both endpoints of the bracket were changed.

---

[6]For a proof of this result, see [6, p. 230].

[7]Whenever two methods have the same rate of convergence, the difference in the number of iterations required for each method will lie in the value of C in the relationship (4.15). For bisection, we have $C_B \doteq \frac{1}{2}$ while, for regula falsi, it is shown in the above reference that if e_k is sufficiently small,

$$C = C_{RF} \doteq |f''(\theta)/2f'(\theta')| \qquad \text{where } a_k < \theta, \theta' < b_k$$

Hence, if f is such that $C_{RF} < \frac{1}{2}$, then regula falsi will be faster, and conversely. But the comparison depends entirely on $f(x)$.

The reason is that, since there is an inflection point at $x = 2$, the c_k's will not necessarily all lie on one side of the root $r = \sqrt{2}$. However, when $k = 3$, the bracket no longer includes this point and f is concave upward throughout $[a_3, b_3]$. Up to this stage, the speed of convergence is quite good but, for any subsequent iterations, it will deteriorate to $p = 1$. This would have been evident in Table 4.2 if we had carried, say, eight digits and continued the iteration beyond $k = 4$.

From the foregoing discussion, one would conclude that, at least in the vicinity of a root, regula falsi is not a particularly good method. However, it is possible to make the method more viable by introducing a modification. The idea is to somehow prevent the c_k's from falling on only one side of r. One modification that is sometimes used is to keep a record, after each iteration, of which endpoint was replaced by c_k in (4.17). If, say, a_k is replaced twice in a row then we presume that f is concave upward so we replace $f(b_k)$ by $f(b_k)/2$ in the computation (4.18) of c_k. As Figure 4.5 illustrates, the aim is to try to make c_k fall to the right of r. If it does not work, we repeat on the next iteration and so on until we succeed. Using this modification, the iteration with I_2 in Table 4.2 would become the following.

k	a_k	$f(a_k)$		b_k	$f(b_k)$	
0	-4.0	$-1.400E$	2	0.0	$1.200E$	1
1	—	—		-0.3158	$1.200E$	1
2	—	$-7.000E$	1	-0.6067	$1.078E$	1
3	—	$-3.500E$	1	-1.060	$6.187E$	0
4	-1.502	$-1.921E$	0	—	—	
5	—	—		-1.397	$3.579E-1$	
6	—	$-9.605E-1$		-1.413	$2.543E-2$	
7	-1.432	$-3.762E-1$		—	—	
8	-1.421	$-1.428E-1$		—	$1.272E-2$	
9	-1.417	$-5.851E-2$		—	$6.358E-2$	
10	-1.415	$-1.650E-2$		—	$3.179E-2$	

We see that the modification does, in fact, give faster convergence. However, near the root, it evidently can still be quite slow.

3. Secant

The secant method is similar to the regula falsi method in that it also uses a secant line to approximate $f(x)$ in the neighbourhood of a root. The difference between the two methods is that the secant method does not use

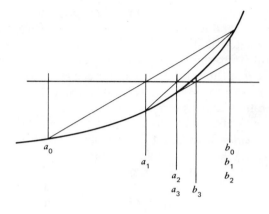

FIGURE 4.5

the idea of brackets. Since the method is based on secant lines, we need two points on the graph of $f(x)$, say (x_{k-1}, f_{k-1}) and (x_k, f_k), where f_s denotes the value of $f(x_s)$. The equation of the line through these points is

$$y - f_k = \frac{f_k - f_{k-1}}{x_k - x_{k-1}} \cdot (x - x_k)$$

and the x-intercept will be $(x_{k+1}, 0)$, where

$$(4.21) \quad x_{k+1} = x_k - \frac{f_k}{f_k - f_{k-1}} \cdot (x_k - x_{k-1})$$

Hence, given two initial guesses x_0, x_1, the secant method computes a sequence $x_0, x_1, x_2, \ldots$ using the rule (4.21).

The secant method is much easier to get started than the previous methods. All we need is two points x_0, x_1 and they do not have to form a bracket. On the other hand, the convergence properties of the method are erratic and unpredictable. Aside from the fact that it can diverge altogether, it will very often wander about for a while before ultimately converging. It may even converge to a root that is some distance away despite the fact that the initial guesses x_0, x_1 were close to some other root. To illustrate, we apply the method to the equation (4.20). In Table 4.3, we show some results. None of the iterations shown in the table converges directly to a root. Moreover, the third one has skipped over the root at $\sqrt{2}$. The source of this erratic behavior is quite easy to pinpoint. From (4.21), it is clear that there will be a large change between x_k and x_{k+1} if the weight $w_k = f_k/(f_k - f_{k+1})$ is large and this, in turn, will be true if $|f_k - f_{k+1}|$ is small. Therefore, if we are unfortunate enough to choose x_0, x_1 such that $|f_1 - f_0|$ is

TABLE 4.3

k	x_k	f_k		x_k	f_k		x_k	f_k	
0	0.0	$1.20E$	1	-0.1	$1.21E$	1	-0.25	$1.21E$	1
1	0.1	$1.71E$	1	0.0	$1.20E$	1	0.25	$1.11E$	1
2	4.6332	$-2.66E$	1	8.6331	$1.91E$	2	6.0047	$1.60E-1$	
3	1.4879	$-9.65E-1$		-0.57882	$1.10E$	1	6.0886	$3.11E$	0
4	1.3695	$5.76E-1$		-1.1393	$5.01E$	0	6.0001	$3.40E-3$	
5	1.4138	$5.36E-3$		-1.6120	$-4.56E$	0	6.0000	0.0	
6	1.4142	$1.76E-4$		-1.3869	$5.65E-1$				
7				-1.4117	$5.26E-2$				
8				-1.4143	$-1.81E-3$				
9				-1.4142	$1.69E-4$				

small, we could experience erratic behavior such as that in Table 4.3. Geometrically, the difficulties arise whenever the slope of the secant line is close to zero. As we see in Figure 4.6, this will certainly happen if x_{k-1} and x_k lie in a region where $f(x)$ has a relatively small slope. We conclude, therefore, that direct convergence to a root r can only be guaranteed if $x_0, x_1 \in [a, b]$ satisfy conditions of the form:

(4.22)
    i $r \in [a, b]$.
    ii   If $x_{k-1}, x_k \in [a, b]$, then so is x_{k+1}.
    iii $|f'(x)| \geq C$ for all $x \in [a, b]$, where $C > 0$ is sufficiently large.

Again, we emphasize that the method will not necessarily diverge if $x_0, x_1 \notin [a, b]$. It simply means that we cannot predict what will happen.

Let us now look at the efficiency of the secant method. Again, the amount of work per iteration is the same as before—one function evaluation—so any improvement in efficiency over the previous methods must be in the rate of convergence. It can be shown [6, p. 229] that, when $x_{k-1}, x_k \in [a, b]$ defined by (4.22), the rate of convergence is $p = 1.62$, which

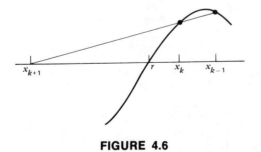

FIGURE 4.6

is much faster than either regula falsi or bisection. The emphasis, however, is on "when." If $x_0, x_1 \notin [a, b]$, we may still get convergence but, as we have seen, the iterations may diverge for a while at first and the overall efficiency will not be so good. In summary, the secant method is quite good provided x_0, x_1 are close enough to r. We remark that this conclusion might suggest a combination, or "hybrid", method whereby we start with, say, bisection and then switch to the secant method when it is "safe" to do so. This, in fact, is part of the idea behind Brent's method, which will be discussed shortly.

4. Newton–Raphson

The Newton–Raphson method is also based on the idea of approximating $f(x)$ locally by a straight line but this time it is a tangent line. Let x_k be an approximation for a root r. Then the equation of the tangent line to $f(x)$ at (x_k, f_k) is given by

$$y - f_k = f_k' \cdot (x - x_k)$$

and the x-intercept is $(x_{k+1}, 0)$, where

$$(4.23) \quad x_{k+1} = x_k - \frac{f_k}{f_k'}$$

The process is illustrated in Figure 4.7. Hence, the Newton–Raphson method starts with an initial guess x_0 and computes the sequence $x_0, x_1, x_2, \ldots$ according to the rule (4.23).

Before discussing the method, it is interesting to note its connection with the secant method. The derivative f_k' in (4.23) can be approximated by the divided difference

$$f_k' \doteq \frac{f_k - f_{k-1}}{x_k - x_{k-1}}$$

Substituting this into (4.23) and doing some manipulation, we get the

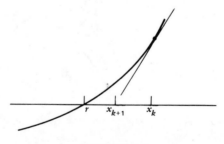

FIGURE 4.7

formula (4.21) for the secant method. Hence, we can view the secant method as an approximation to the Newton–Raphson method. In this respect, the secant method is a natural alternative to the Newton–Raphson method whenever it is inconvenient to provide an explicit representation for $f'(x)$. Such might be the case when the functional form of $f(x)$ is very complicated, or when $f(x)$ is only given in tabular form as, perhaps, data from an experiment.

From the geometry of the method, it is clear that, like the secant method, the Newton–Raphson method can be erratic in regions where $f(x)$ has a small slope so we can only guarantee direct convergence to a root r if x_0 is sufficiently close to r. Actually, it is possible to establish a convergence result that is more precise than (4.22) is for the secant method. This arises from the fact that (4.23) can be expressed as a fixed-point iteration (4.8) with

$$g(x) = x - \frac{f(x)}{f'(x)}$$

Therefore, convergence is guaranteed for any $x_0 \in [a, b]$ satisfying (4.10) with condition (iii) written as

$$|g'(x)| = \left| \frac{f(x)f''(x)}{(f'(x))^2} \right| < 1 \qquad \text{for all } x \in [a, b]$$

Note that this agrees with our geometric intuition, that is, if $|f'(x)|$ is too small, we cannot guarantee convergence. Hence, like the secant method, the Newton–Raphson method is only dependable when we are sufficiently close to r.

A significant disadvantage of the method was mentioned above. This is the requirement for an explicit representation of the derivative $f'(x)$. In many instances, this is a great inconvenience. Moreover, since $f'(x)$ is usually a more complicated function than $f(x)$, it is more costly to evaluate. It turns out (see below) that the method offers very little in return for the extra work and inconvenience involved so it is not usually implemented in a software package. We remark, however, that if $f(x)$ is a polynomial, this disadvantage vanishes and the method does have some practical value. We discuss this in Section 4.2.3.

The main advantage of the Newton–Raphson method is the rate of convergence. It is *quadratic* (i.e., $p = 2$). However, each iteration requires two function evaluations—$f(x)$ and $f'(x)$—so, as we have already seen, it is not necessarily more efficient than secant. To illustrate, we again consider the example (4.20). The following table shows two comparative iterations (with XTOL = FTOL = 5.0E − 4). Even though the Newton–Raphson method converged in only three iterations, it nevertheless required more

k	Secant x_k	f_k	Newton–Raphson x_k	f_k
0	0.5	9.63E 0	0.5	9.63E 0
1	1.0	5.00E 0	1.8276	$-5.59E$ 0
2	1.5405	$-1.66E$ 0	1.4257	$-1.49E-1$
3	1.4055	1.13$E-1$	1.4142	1.76$E-4$
4	1.4141	1.47$E-3$		
5	1.4142	1.76$E-4$		

work—eight function evaluations compared to six for secant. In the vicinity of a root, the method gives very rapid improvement in accuracy due to the quadratic rate of convergence. For example, the improvement from x_2 to x_3 in the above iteration is three significant digits. But we observe that the secant method is just as efficient in the same vicinity. Now this is only an isolated example but the results are typical. As a general rule, we can say that the efficiency of the two methods is about the same in the vicinity of a root. Hence, the quadratic convergence of the Newton–Raphson method is, in effect, countered by the extra cost of evaluating $f'(x)$. This, combined with the inconvenience of having to use $f'(x)$, makes it an unsatisfactory method for practical purposes.

We remark that the statement concerning the quadratic convergence of the method has to be qualified by the condition that the root r is simple [i.e., $f'(r) \neq 0$]. Actually, on the face of it, one may wonder why the method works at all for multiple roots since $f'(x_k)$ will be small when x_k is close to such a root and this may cause overflow problems in computing the "correction term" f_k/f_k'. To see why this is of no concern, suppose that r is a triple root of $f(x)$. Then we can write $f(x) = (x - r)^3 q(x)$, where $q(r) \neq 0$. Now, if some $x_k = r$, then $f'(x_k) = 0$. But $f(x_k) = 0$ also and the iteration would be stopped on the (correct) conclusion that a root has been found. Therefore, there is no danger of division by 0 in (4.23). If, on the other hand, x_k is close to r, say $x_k - r = \epsilon$, then (4.23) would take the form

$$(4.24) \quad x_{k+1} = x_k - \frac{\epsilon^3 q(x_k)}{3\epsilon^2 q(x_k) + \epsilon^3 q'(x_k)} = x_k - \frac{\epsilon}{3} + O(\epsilon^2)$$

Therefore, even though the denominator $f'(x_k)$ is small near a multiple root, the numerator is even smaller—by a factor of ϵ—and the division is no problem. This analysis also helps explain why the rate of convergence is slower for a multiple root. In the case of a simple root [i.e., $f(x) = (x - r)q(x)$], with $q(r) \neq 0$, the equivalent of (4.24) is

$$x_{k+1} = x_k - \frac{\epsilon q(x_k)}{q(x_k) + \epsilon q'(x_k)} = x_k - \epsilon + O(\epsilon^2)$$

Neglecting the higher-order terms in ϵ, we see that the improvement in x_k is by the amount ϵ whereas, in (4.24), it is only $\epsilon/3$.

One further point about the Newton–Raphson method is that, although we have only talked in terms of finding real roots, it can also be used to find complex roots. One simply has to start with a complex initial guess in order to get the iterations off the real axis—if x_k is real then so are f_k, f'_k and, from (4.23), it follows that x_{k+1} is also real.

5. Müller

We have looked at different ways of approximating $f(x)$ in the vicinity of a root by a straight line. We now move to approximation by a quadratic. Müller's method is based on interpolation of $f(x)$ locally by a quadratic curve, that is, a parabola. Since it takes three points to define a quadratic uniquely, we assume that we have three approximate values x_{k-2}, x_{k-1}, x_k for r along with their respective coordinate values f_{k-2}, f_{k-1}, f_k. Now there are two possible forms for the quadratic:

$$y = ax^2 + bx + c \qquad \text{and} \qquad ay^2 + by + c = x$$

The former is the equation of a parabola that opens up (or down) while the latter opens to the right (or left). Müller's method uses the first form because it turns out to be better with respect to guarantee of convergence. (The second form is called the "inverse" form. It is used in Brent's method which will be discussed next.) But, as we see in Figure 4.8, a dilemma arises with this form of the quadratic, that is, it has two roots and we must pick only one of them as the next approximation x_{k+1}. The choice is resolved in the following way. In the computation of the roots of the quadratic, there is an expression of the form $u \pm \sqrt{v}$. We simply choose the sign of the square root to agree with that of u. Note that the choice is desirable from a numerical point of view since it avoids loss of significance

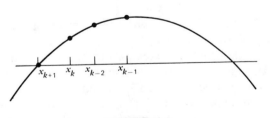

FIGURE 4.8

due to cancellation. Since the algebra of the method is quite messy, we omit the details. A good reference is [5, p. 74]. Suffice it to say that, given three initial guesses x_0, x_1, x_2, the method generates a sequence $x_0, x_1, x_2, x_3, \ldots$ of approximations. At each stage, the new approximation is derived from the three most recent ones by quadratic interpolation.

Müller's method is the best yet with respect to guarantee of convergence. It is essentially global in the sense that, for almost all problems, it will converge to a root starting with almost any set of initial guesses x_0, x_1, x_2. Any problem where it fails to converge will usually be somewhat contrived or pathological and not likely to arise in practical applications. As a result, a subroutine implementation of the method will very often require only one initial guess. The other two will be generated by the subroutine itself since their precise locations are not critical. For example, if we let $x_0 = \sigma$, then the routine might set $x_1 = 0.9\sigma$ and $x_2 = 1.1\sigma$.

An additional feature of the method results from the fact that the interpolating quadratic can have complex roots, that is, its graph may not cross the real axis. Therefore, Müller's method has the capability of finding complex roots even if the initial guesses are real. However, in a way, this can be a disadvantage because the method has to be implemented using complex arithmetic in order to handle the possibility of complex x_k's. For the same reason, the user-supplied function subprogram for evaluating $f(x)$ must also be programmed in complex arithmetic. Since arithmetic operations for complex numbers take at least twice the time as those for real numbers, this penalizes the efficiency somewhat in the case of finding real roots. On the other hand, it can be considered a relatively small price to pay for the near-global convergence of the method. We discuss this point further in Section 4.2.2.

The rate of convergence of Müller's method is $p \doteq 1.84$ which is almost as fast as the Newton–Raphson method. It is true that only one function evaluation per iteration (plus three to begin) is required but this is essentially negated by the fact that we must use complex arithmetic. We also note that each iteration of Müller has to perform a square root but this is usually insignificant compared to an evaluation of f.

6. Brent

In discussing the secant method, mention was made of the idea of devising a "hybrid" method from two or more separate methods. The aim is to produce an algorithm that possesses all the good features and, hopefully, none of the bad ones of each individual method. Brent's algorithm [17, p. 161] is an example of such a hybrid. It combines the bisection, secant, and inverse quadratic interpolation methods. The latter one, as its name implies, is based on interpolating $f(x)$ locally using the inverse form

$ay^2 + by + c = x$ of the quadratic. In contrast to the form used by Müller's method, the inverse form has only one root (at $x = c$) and it is always real (if c is real). An iteration with the inverse method is less work than Müller's method because it uses real arithmetic and no square root has to be taken. Moreover, the rate of convergence is the same, that is, $p \doteq 1.84$. On the other hand, it does not have anything approaching the global convergence properties of Müller. Therefore, it is not a particularly good method by itself.

Brent's algorithm is an attempt to gain the advantages of inverse quadratic interpolation and compensate for the lack of global convergence by combining it with secant, which has better global convergence properties but is slower, and bisection, which has guaranteed convergence but is even slower. The specific details of the algorithm will not be given here. Briefly, the idea is to use inverse quadratic interpolation primarily, reverting to secant and, ultimately, bisection when, and only when, it is necessary to do so in order to achieve convergence. The result is a fast, efficient method with guaranteed convergence. The following table shows the results of applying the method to solve the example problem (4.20).

k	c_k	f_k	c_k	f_k
	[0.0, 4.0]		[−4.0, 0.0]	
1	1.200	2.69E 0	−0.3158	1.20E 1
2	1.516	−1.34E 0	−0.9723	7.35E 0
3	1.411	4.17E − 2	−1.340	1.50E 0
4	1.414	2.77E − 2	−1.420	−1.22E − 1
5			−1.414	4.48E − 3

Compared to the results using regula falsi, these are much better. Finally, we remark that Brent's method uses bracketing and the previous comments with regard to roots of even multiplicity and to finding an initial bracket apply.

4.2.2. Subroutines

There are normally two types of rootfinding subroutines contained in software packages. One is the general-purpose type, designed to find roots under almost any circumstances—for example, both real and complex roots, and bad initial guesses. The other type is special purpose where advantage is taken of knowledge about the type and location of the roots in order to find them very efficiently. From the discussion in the previous section, Müller's method is clearly an ideal method to use in the former type, while Brent's method is a good example of a special-purpose method. We briefly discuss their implementations.

A general-purpose subroutine should provide as much flexibility as possible in the ways it can be used. Among other things, this means that it should be capable of finding a specified number of roots of $f(x)$ with a single call to it. Suppose a user wants to determine, say, s roots $r_1, \ldots, r_s$ of $f(x)$. Now it is easy to design an algorithm that will do s sets of iterations of a method but, as we saw in Table 4.1, there is a danger of two or more of the iterations converging to the same root. To avoid this possibility, we use a process called *deflation* whereby, once a root is located, it is removed as a possible root for future iterations to find. The idea is as follows. Suppose we have found a root r_1. Then we "deflate" $f(x)$ by dividing by the factor $(x - r_1)$, that is, we define the new function

$$f_1(x) = \frac{f(x)}{(x - r_1)}$$

Proceeding, we apply the root-finding method to $f_1(x)$ and find a root r_2 which, clearly, is also a root of $f(x)$. Deflating by the factor $(x - r_2)$, we obtain the new function

$$f_2(x) = \frac{f_1(x)}{(x - r_2)} = \frac{f(x)}{(x - r_1)(x - r_2)}$$

and so on. We note that, since r_1 is not a root[8] of $f_1(x), f_2(x), \ldots, f_{s-1}(x)$, there is no possibility of it being found more than once and similarly for $r_2, r_3, \ldots, r_s$.

We remark that an implementation of this process usually employs a modification in that each iteration is split into two parts. For example, to determine the root r_m, the algorithm begins by trying to locate it as a root of $f_{m-1}(x)$. Then, when the iteration has converged sufficiently, it switches to $f(x)$. The presumption here is that, when the iteration is close enough to r_m, the change to working with $f(x)$ can be done with no danger of the iteration being attracted to another root (that may have been found already). In effect, then, the purpose of working with the deflated function $f_{m-1}(x)$ is simply to provide a good initial guess for an iteration with $f(x)$. The reason for using this modified procedure is for numerical stability. In evaluating the deflated function $f_m(x)$ at, say, $x = x_k$, we are effectively scaling the value $f(x_k)$ by the factor $[(x - r_1) \ldots (x - r_m)]^{-1}$ and this can sometimes

---

[8]In order for this statement to be true, r_1 must be a simple root of $f(x)$. To account for a root of multiplicity $m > 1$, we permit repetitions in the list of roots of $f(x)$. For example, if r_1 has multiplicity $m = 3$, then we will say that $r_1 = r_2 = r_3$ so that each one is found only once.

produce misleading results. Suppose, for example, that three roots of $f(x)$ are $r_1 = 1$, $r_2 = 2$, $r_3 = 100$ and, having found the first two, we define

$$f_2(x) = \frac{f(x)}{(x - 1)(x - 2)}$$

If, in the iteration for r_3, we arrive at the point where $x_k = 102$ and $f(102) = 0.02$, then

$$f_2(102) = \frac{0.02}{(102 - 1)(102 - 2)} \doteq 1.9E - 6$$

Hence, if FTOL $= 5.0E - 6$, termination of the iteration would occur on the F-test with a result that is only accurate to two digits. If, on the other hand, the iteration is switched to $f(x)$ before this stage is reached, the difficulty will not occur. But there is still the question of determining when to switch. If it is done too soon, the iteration may be drawn to another root. This problem is resolved by the designer of the subroutine so it need not be of concern to the user. However, we remark that, as m increases, the scaling effect from deflation gets progressively worse and it is increasingly difficult to determine an appropriate point to make the switch. Therefore, the possibility of failure to converge increases as the number of roots removed by deflation increases. The conditioning of the problem (see Section 4.2.3) is a significant factor in the rate of increase.

The calling sequence for a general-purpose subroutine (based on Müller's method) will be of the form

    RTMLR(F,XO,NK,NN,XTOL,FTOL,ITMAX,ITER,IND)

where

>   F is a complex function subprogram for evaluating $f(x)$.
>   XO is a complex vector of length $\geq$ NK + NN.
>   NK specifies the number of known roots of $f(x)$ (stored in XO(1), ..., XO(NK)).
>   NN specifies the number of new roots to be found.
>   XTOL, FTOL, ITMAX define the stopping criteria.
>   ITER is an NN-vector used to return the number of iterations required for each (new) root.
>   IND is used to indicate whether or not failure to converge occurred for any of the NN iterations.

This calling sequence provides a good deal of flexibility for the user. If, for example, we initially want to compute two roots of $f(x)$, we can do it by calling the routine with NK = 0 and NN = 2. Then, if we subsequently want to find three more roots, we can reenter the routine with NK = 2 and

NN = 3. The subroutine will assume that the known roots (as computed from the original call) are contained in XO(1) and XO(2), and immediately remove them from consideration by means of deflation. Initial guesses for the new roots are to be contained in the next three components of XO. In this regard, since Müller's method has near-global convergence properties, it is possible to make the specification of initial guesses for the routine optional. In this case, another parameter—say, NG—specifying the number of roots for which initial guesses are supplied, must be added to the calling sequence.

We emphasize that, in order to use a subroutine like RTMLR, the subprogram F for evaluating $f(x)$ must be complex. But in situations where the user only wants to locate real roots, this feature is both inconvenient and inefficient. Now in the previous section, we said that this is a small price to pay for the advantage of near-global convergence. Nevertheless, since such situations arise with some frequency, it would be desirable to have a special subroutine which eliminates the need for complex arithmetic. There is, however, a difficulty in that we want the routine to retain the near-global convergence feature. This means that we need a root-finding method that has this property and, at the same time, is limited to the real line. Such a method is not known. Therefore, we consider an alternative, namely, modifying Müller's method by restricting it to the real line. One such modification is as follows. Recall that each approximate root x_k generated by Müller's method is defined to be a root of an interpolating quadratic. Suppose that the roots of it are $u_k \pm \sqrt{v_k}$, where u_k, v_k are real. Then, since x_k is complex if and only if $v_k < 0$, we modify the definition of x_k to read

$$x_k = \begin{cases} u_k \pm \sqrt{v_k} & \text{if } v_k > 0 \\ u_k & \text{if } v_k \leq 0 \end{cases}$$

This clearly eliminates the need for complex arithmetic. With respect to guarantee of convergence, we would not expect this modified method to be as good as Müller's method. However, it turns out to be reasonably good. Moreover, it can even be enhanced with one or two additional modifications. Therefore, given the savings from using real arithmetic, a subroutine that is based on this modification of Müller's method can be very useful. An example of such a routine is ZREAL1 and IMSL package.

A subroutine based on Brent's method will be more or less a straightforward implementation of the method as outlined in the previous section. There is no need to include deflation since there is no danger of an iteration going outside the current bracket. A typical calling sequence is

RTBRT(F,A,B,RT,XTOL,FTOL,ITMAX,IND)

where

> F is a real function subprogram for evaluating $f(x)$.
>
> A, B are the endpoints of the initial bracket on entry, and those of the final bracket on return.
>
> RT is used to return the approximate root.
>
> XTOL, FTOL, ITMAX, IND are the same as for RTMLR.

4.2.3. The Special Case of Polynomials

Let us now assume that the function $f(x)$ is the polynomial

$$(4.25) \quad p(x) = a_0 x^n + a_1 x^{n-1} + \cdots + a_{n-1} x + a_n$$
$$= (\ldots ((a_0 x + a_1) \cdot x + a_2) \cdot x + \cdots + a_{n-1}) \cdot x + a_n$$

where the coefficients a_k are real numbers. The second form, called the *nested form*, is computationally more efficient, as we saw in Section 3.1.1. Polynomial equations arise very often in practice, and special subroutines for solving them are generally included in software packages. These routines exploit the special features of polynomials, some of which we now discuss.

First of all, a polynomial $p(x)$ can be uniquely represented in a computer by the pair (n, A), where n is a positive integer specifying the degree of the polynomial and A is an $(n + 1)$-vector containing the coefficients a_i, $0 \le i \le n$, in order. To find the value of $p(x)$ at, say $x = s$, we form numbers b_k as follows:

$$
\begin{aligned}
& b_0 = a_0 \\
(4.26) \quad & \text{FOR } k = 1, 2, \ldots, n \\
& \quad \lfloor \; b_k = s \cdot b_{k-1} + a_k
\end{aligned}
$$

Then $b_n = p(s)$. The justification for this procedure is quite simple. We have $b_1 = s \cdot a_0 + a_1$, that is, b_1 is the value, at $x = s$, of the term within the innermost set of brackets of the nested form of (4.25). Similarly, b_2 will be the value of the term within the next set of brackets, and so on. For example, we consider the polynomial (4.20)

$$p(x) = x^3 - 6x^2 - 2x + 12$$
$$= ((x - 6) \cdot x - 2) \cdot x + 12$$

To find the value $p(2)$, we have

$$b_0 = a_0 \qquad\qquad\qquad = \quad 1$$
$$b_1 = 2b_0 + a_1 = \quad 2(1) + (-6) = \quad -4$$
$$b_2 = 2b_1 + a_2 = \quad 2(-4) + (-2) = -10$$
$$b_3 = 2b_2 + a_3 = 2(-10) + \quad 12 \quad = \quad -8 = p(2)$$

Actually, this is nothing more than the familiar process of synthetic division [6, p. 16]. Since the procedure is the same for all polynomials, it can be incorporated directly into a subroutine and the user does not have to supply a function subprogram for evaluating $p(x)$. All one has to do is define the polynomial by specifying n and A. Hence, the calling sequence for a polynomial rootfinder will be of the form

CALL ROOT(N,A,XO,XTOL,FTOL,ITMAX,IND)

We remark that this feature is more in the way of providing user convenience. It does not necessarily increase the efficiency of the algorithm.

The next feature does contribute to efficiency (as well as user convenience). Any polynomial rootfinding subroutine that uses a method such as Newton–Raphson will require values of the derivative $p'(x)$. Suppose we want the value of p' at $x = s$, the same point used in (4.26). This can be done very efficiently by using the numbers b_k. We can write $p(x)$ in the form

(4.27) $\quad p(x) = (x - s) \cdot q(x) + b_n$

where

(4.28) $\quad q(x) = b_0 x^{n-1} + b_1 x^{n-2} + \cdots + b_{n-2} x + b_{n-1}$

is a polynomial of degree $(n - 1)$ whose coefficients are given by (4.26). This result follows easily by noting that, from (4.26),

$$a_0 = b_0 \qquad \text{and} \qquad a_k = b_k - s \cdot b_{k-1} \qquad k = 1, \ldots, n$$

and then substituting into the first form of (4.25). Now, by differentiating (4.27), we get

$$p'(x) = q(x) + (x - s) \cdot q'(x)$$

and it follows that $p'(s) = q(s)$. In other words, to find the value of the derivative $p'(x)$ at $x = s$, all we have to do is evaluate the polynomial $q(x)$ at $x = s$. This can be done at the same time as we find $p(s)$ by expanding the program segment (4.26) to the following:

$$b_0 = a_0$$

$$c_0 = b_0$$

(4.29) FOR $k = 1, 2, \ldots, n-1$

$$b_k = s \cdot b_{k-1} + a_k$$

$$c_k = s \cdot c_{k-1} + b_k$$

$$b_n = s \cdot b_{n-1} + a_n$$

Then $b_n = p(s)$ and $c_{n-1} = p'(s)$. For our example, we have

$$b_0 = \qquad\qquad 1 \qquad c_0 = \qquad\qquad\qquad 1$$

$$b_1 = \quad 2(1) + (-6) = \ -4 \qquad c_1 = \ 2(1) + \ (-4) = \ -2$$

$$b_2 = \ 2(-4) + (-2) = -10 \qquad c_2 = 2(-2) + (-10) = -14$$

$$b_3 = 2(-10) + \ \ 12 \ = \ -8$$

Therefore $p(2) = -8$ and $p'(2) = -14$. The amount of work required is n flops for $p(s)$ and $(n-1)$ for $p'(s)$. By comparison, if we represent $p'(x)$ in the usual way

$$p'(x) = na_0x^{n-1} + (n-1)a_1x^{n-2} + \cdots + 2a_{n-2}x + a_{n-1}$$

$$= [\ldots [na_0x + (n-1)a_1]x + \cdots + 2a_{n-2}]x + a_{n-1}$$

then, even in the nested version, an extra $n-1$ multiplications are required to evaluate it. Again, since the program segment (4.29) is the same for any polynomial, it can be incorporated directly into a subroutine, making it transparent to the user.

Quite clearly, the above ideas can be extended to evaluation of higher order derivatives and this opens up the possibility of considering methods which use them. We discuss one such method which is often used.

Laguerre's Method

Suppose that the roots r_i of $p(x)$ are real and ordered such that

$$r_1 \le r_2 \le \cdots \le r_n$$

with strict inequality at least once, that is, they are not all equal. Let x_k be an approximation to a root and suppose that $x_k \in I_i$, where

$$I_i = [r_i, r_{i+1}] \qquad 0 \le i \le n \qquad \text{with } r_0 = -\infty \qquad r_{n+1} = +\infty$$

Then the idea of Laguerre's method is to construct a parabola having the following property:

> Both of its roots are in I_i and at least one of them is closer to a root—r_i or r_{i+1}—of $p(x)$ than x_k is.

Now in general, it is impossible to construct a quadratic having this property without prior knowledge about the locations of the roots. However, in the case of polynomials with real roots, it turns out to be possible. There are an infinite number of such quadratics but the method, in essence, considers only a one-parameter family of them. It chooses, from this family, the one that has a root that is as close as possible to a root of $p(x)$. The actual derivation of the method is very involved and is not given here—a good reference is [24, p. 380]. However, the resulting iteration is quite easy to state. It is

$$(4.30) \qquad x_{k+1} = x_k - \frac{np_k}{p'_k \pm \sqrt{H(x_k)}}$$

where

$$p_k = p(x_k), \qquad p'_k = p'(x_k)$$

and

$$H(x) = (n-1)[(n-1)(p'(x))^2 - np(x)p''(x)]$$

The sign of the square root is chosen to agree with that of p'_k. Not only does this choice avoid loss of significance through cancellation, it also makes $|x_{k+1} - x_k|$ as small as possible. Now the derivation of (4.30) relies on the assumption that all the roots of $p(x)$ are real. But there is nothing to prevent us from applying the method to any polynomial. In fact, we note that, if $H(x_k) < 0$, then x_{k+1} will be complex. Therefore, the method has the potential for finding complex roots and, in fact, it will do so. Moreover, like Müller's method, an iteration can start on the real axis and move into the complex plane on its own. One could, of course, consider dropping all restrictions on using (4.30) and try applying the method to solve general nonlinear equations. However, apart from convergence considerations, it is usually very inconvenient having to provide subprograms to evaluate each of f, f', and f''.

Under the assumption that $p(x)$ has real roots only, Laguerre's method is *globally convergent*, that is, it will converge to a root for *any* choice of initial guess. Moreover, it will locate a nearby root, that is, if $x_0 \in I_i$, then the method is guaranteed to converge to either r_i or r_{i+1}. (If $i = 0$ or n, then convergence is to r_1 or r_n, respectively.) By contrast, we have seen that the Newton–Raphson method will not necessarily converge to a root which is nearby. The results in Table 4.4 illustrate this comparison. Again, this discussion assumes that $p(x)$ has only real roots. If $p(x)$ has complex roots, Laguerre's method is no longer globally convergent. However, empirical evidence indicates that nonconvergence is exceptional. Therefore, subroutine implementations of the method do not usually restrict application to the case of real roots only.

TABLE 4.4

k	Müller x_k	Müller x_k	Newton–Raphson x_k	Newton–Raphson x_k	Laguerre x_k	Laguerre x_k
0	0.0	0.5	0.0	0.5	0.0	0.5
1	1.2581	1.3647	6.000	1.8276	1.1369	1.3426
2	1.3926	1.4109		1.4257	1.4124	1.4142
3	1.4139	1.4142		1.4142	1.4142	
4	1.4142					
No. flops	21	18	10	20	18	18
No. sq. rt.	4	3			3	3

Turning to efficiency considerations, Laguerre's method is cubically convergent ($p = 3$) for simple roots, which is exceedingly fast. For multiple roots, the rate deteriorates but it is still better than the other methods we have considered. On the negative side, it requires three function evaluations per iteration—p, p', and p''. Actually, since we are dealing only with polynomials, the precise number of operations can be determined. Assuming that the suggested method of polynomial evaluation is used, the comparative amounts of work per iteration are:

> Müller: n $= n$ flops + 1 square root.
> Newton–Raphson: $n + (n - 1)$ $= 2n - 1$ flops.
> Laguerre: $n + (n - 1) + (n - 2)$
> $= 3n - 3$ flops + 1 square root.

By combining these results with the respective rates of convergence, it appears that, from an efficiency point of view, Laguerre's method is at least competitive. Table 4.4 illustrates this. The example used is the polynomial (4.20), which has roots $r_1 = -\sqrt{2}$, $r_2 = \sqrt{2}$, and $r_3 = 6.0$. Note that both initial guesses 0.0 and 0.5 are in $[r_1, r_2]$. However, both of the Newton–Raphson iterations go outside this interval. Moreover, the iteration with $x_0 = 0.0$ converges to r_3. (The fact that it gets there in only one iteration is purely fortuitous.) In summary, Laguerre's method is very good. Its main advantage is global convergence which, incidentally, is not offset by relatively poor efficiency. It is only our lack of understanding of its behavior in the case of complex roots that has prevented it from gaining more widespread use.

Returning to our discussion of special features, the nature of the roots of a polynomial equation can also be exploited in designing a subroutine. For one thing, we know that, counting multiplicities, a polynomial of degree n has exactly n roots so there is never any question about when to stop looking for more roots. More important is the fact that, since $p(x)$ has real coefficients a_i, complex roots occur in conjugate pairs. That is, if $r = s + it$ is a root, then so is its complex conjugate $\bar{r} = s - it$. Hence, whenever a complex root is found, we automatically have another one without doing any extra work—two for the price of one, so to speak—which helps to compensate for the need to do complex arithmetic. We return to this point shortly.

The process of deflation is particularly efficient with polynomials. In fact, it need not involve any additional work at all. Suppose that r is a root of $p(x)$. Then we want to find the deflated polynomial $p(x)/(x - r)$. With $s = r$ in (4.27), we have

$$\frac{p(x)}{x - r} = q(x) + \frac{b_n}{x - r}$$

But, since r is a root, it follows that $b_n = p(r) = 0$. Therefore, by using (4.26) or (4.29) for evaluating $p(x)$ at $s = r$, we also obtain the coefficients b_i of the deflated polynomial. A subroutine can take advantage of this fact in the following way. Each iteration will compute the value of $p(x_{k+1})$ for use in the F-test for convergence. We simply save the b_i's from the evaluation process. If the iteration has converged, then $x_{k+1} \doteq r$ and we automatically have the (approximate) coefficients for the deflated polynomial. If the iteration continues, then we overwrite the current b_i's with the next set of them, and so on. Therefore, deflation can be done for the small cost of an additional $n - 1$ memory locations and storing data (b_i's) in them.

A further point concerns the need to do complex arithmetic. Suppose that r is a complex root. Then the deflated polynomial $q(x) = p(x)/(x - r)$ will have complex coefficients. However, since we know that $(x - \bar{r})$ is also a factor of $p(x)$, we really want to determine the polynomial

$$t(x) = \frac{p(x)}{(x - r)(x - \bar{r})} = \frac{p(x)}{x^2 - \alpha x + \beta^2}$$

where $\alpha = 2 \operatorname{Re}(r)$ and $\beta = |r|^2$. It follows that $t(x)$ will have real coefficients since the quadratic in the denominator is real. The deflated polynomial is

$$t(x) = c_0 x^{n-2} + c_1 x^{n-3} + \cdots + c_{n-3} x + c_{n-2}$$

where

$$c_0 = a_0$$

$$c_1 = a_1 + \alpha c_0$$

$$c_k = a_k + \alpha c_{k-1} - \beta c_{k-2} \qquad 2 \le k \le n - 2$$

We remark that these formulas can be derived from (4.29) with s replaced by $\bar{s}$ in line 5, that is,

$$c_k = \bar{s} \cdot c_{k-1} + b_k$$

Therefore, deflation can be done without having to use complex arithmetic. Now this does not mean that complex arithmetic can be avoided altogether. If an iteration converges to a complex root, then it is inevitable that complex arithmetic must be done from some stage on. However, by retaining real coefficients, we can revert back to real arithmetic to find the next root (at least until such time as the iteration for it moves into the complex plane). Therefore, the efficiency of an algorithm can be enhanced by having two implementations of the iterative rule—one in real arithmetic and one in complex. The latter is used only when necessary.

Finally, in view of the above comments, we should reexamine the calling sequence for a polynomial root-finding subroutine. Since we know that $p(x)$ has n roots, we can request that a subroutine find $n_r \le n$ of them. Moreover, the roots could be complex. Therefore, a typical calling sequence is of the form

CALL RTPOLY(N,A,NR,XREAL,XIMAG,XTOL,FTOL,ITMAX,IND)

where

> NR specifies the number of roots to be found.
> XREAL, XIMAG are NR-vectors, On entry, they will contain the initial guesses and, on return, they will contain the real and imaginary parts of the roots. Note that, if the routine uses Müller or Laguerre, then we need only specify XREAL on entry.

The other arguments are as before.

Finally, we discuss the concept of ill conditioning as it applies to nonlinear equations. For simplicity, we restrict the discussion to polynomials. A polynomial is *ill conditioned* if small changes in its coefficients produce large shifts in its roots. An example is the polynomial (1.6) discussed in Chapter 1. We saw that a very small perturbation in just one coefficient produced very large changes in some of the roots. However, not all of the roots were badly affected. In fact, any shift induced in the first few of them by the perturbation was too small to be noticeable within five digits. Due to such differences in behavior, it is usual to talk about the conditioning of individual roots rather than the polynomial itself. Suppose r_j is a simple root of the polynomial (4.25). Then its condition number cond(r_j) is defined to be

$$(4.31) \quad \text{cond}(r_j) = \frac{\sum_{i=1}^{n} |(2i + 1)a_{n-i}r_j^i|}{|r_j p'(r_j)|}$$

We observe that this number will be large whenever $p'(r_j)$ is small, that is, whenever $p(x)$ has a cluster of roots very close to r_j. Hence, the conditioning of a root depends on its separation from the others. But the roots of the polynomial (1.6) are $1, 2, \ldots, 20$, which would seem to be nicely separated whereas we know the larger ones are badly conditioned. For instance, the root $r_{14} = 14$ has condition number $\text{cond}(r_{14}) \doteq 1.35 \times 10^{15}$. On the other hand, the polynomial

$$(4.32) \quad p(x) = (x - 2^{-1})(x - 2^{-2}) \ldots (x - 2^{-20})$$

has roots that are seemingly not well separated and yet it can be shown [6, p. 246] that all the condition numbers are bounded by 3.83×10^3. However, instead of looking at the absolute separation of the roots, we should be considering the *relative separation*. This is not an easy concept to define algebraically but, for our two examples, a suitable definition might be

$$s = \prod_{i=1}^{19} \frac{|r_{i+1} - r_i|}{|r_i|}$$

A small value for s would indicate poor relative separation. For the polynomials (1.6) and (4.32), we have, respectively, $s \doteq 8.2 \times 10^{-18}$ and $s = 1$. Hence, although the roots of (4.32) are close in absolute terms, they are relatively well separated, and conversely for the polynomial (1.6).

4.3. NONLINEAR SYSTEMS

Let us now consider the general problem of solving the system (4.1) of n nonlinear equations in n unknowns. This is a much more complicated problem than single equations due to the higher dimensionality—for a single equation we have to deal with a one-dimensional curve whereas, for a system, it is an n-dimensional hypersurface. In fact, much of the material on the topic is beyond the level of this book. Nevertheless, the problem of solving a nonlinear system is one that arises with increasing frequency in applications so it is becoming more important to have at least an intuitive understanding of some of the main ideas involved in solving such problems. The brief introduction to the topic given here is intended to accomplish this end. More detailed (and more mathematical) treatments can be found in [9] or [5, Chapter 5].

4.3.1. Methods

In the case of single equations, it was convenient to derive and discuss methods in the context of their geometric interpretations. For systems, this approach is not so convenient. Instead, it is better to view a method as an n-dimensional analogue of the algebraic formula for a method for single equations. This is the approach we take here.

To begin, it is relatively easy to contemplate an extension of the bracketing idea to n dimensions. However, the resulting methods turn out to be very impractical from an efficiency point of view so we will not discuss them at all.

Newton's Method

Perhaps the best known method for solving a nonlinear system is Newton's method. It is an extension of the Newton–Raphson method. We can rewrite (4.23) in the form

$$(4.33) \quad x_{k+1} = x_k - (f_k')^{-1} \cdot f_k$$

and it follows that, in order to extend the method to higher dimensions, we need an analogue of the derivative $f'(x)$. To this end, we note that the derivative of $f(x)$ at $x = x_k$ is a number f_k' that satisfies the condition

$$\left| \frac{f_k - f_p}{x_k - x_p} - f_k' \right| \to 0 \quad \text{as} \quad x_p \to x_k$$

where $f_p = f(x_p)$. Alternatively, we can write this in the form

$$(4.34) \quad |(f_k - f_p) - f_k' \cdot (x_k - x_p)| \to 0 \quad \text{as} \quad x_p \to x_k$$

Then the analogue of f_k' in n dimensions is an $n \times n$ matrix J_k, which satisfies the condition

$$(4.35) \quad \|(\mathbf{f}_k - \mathbf{f}_p) - J_k(\mathbf{x}_k - \mathbf{x}_p)\| \to 0 \quad \text{as} \quad \mathbf{x}_p \to \mathbf{x}_k$$

where $\mathbf{f}_p = \mathbf{f}(\mathbf{x}_p)$. Moreover, this condition must be satisfied by J_k independent of the direction or path that $\mathbf{x}_p$ takes in approaching $\mathbf{x}_k$. It turns out that we can determine J_k by evaluating the *Jacobian* matrix $J(\mathbf{x})$ whose entries are the partial derivatives

$$(J)_{i,j} = \frac{\partial f_i(\mathbf{x})}{\partial x_j} \quad 1 \le i, j \le n$$

Then $J_k = J(\mathbf{x}_k)$ satisfies (4.35). In other words, $J(\mathbf{x})$ corresponds to $f'(x)$ in the sense that each is a formula for determining the value of the "derivative" at a specific "point." As an example, suppose

$$\mathbf{f}(\mathbf{x}) = \begin{bmatrix} 4x_1^2 + 9x_2^2 - 16x_1 - 54x_2 + 61 \\ x_1 x_2 - 2x_1 - 1 \end{bmatrix} \quad \text{and} \quad \mathbf{x}_k = \begin{bmatrix} 3 \\ -1 \end{bmatrix}$$

Then

$$J(\mathbf{x}) = \begin{bmatrix} 8x_1 - 16 & 18x_2 - 54 \\ x_2 - 2 & x_1 \end{bmatrix} \quad \text{and} \quad J_k = \begin{bmatrix} 8 & -72 \\ -3 & 3 \end{bmatrix}$$

With this definition, we have, as the analogue of (4.33),

(4.36) $\quad \mathbf{x}_{k+1} = \mathbf{x}_k - (J_k)^{-1}\mathbf{f}_k$

where $\mathbf{f}_k = \mathbf{f}(\mathbf{x}_k)$ and $J_k = J(\mathbf{x}_k)$. This defines Newton's method for nonlinear systems. Actually, for computational purposes, an iteration of the method can be considered to consist of the following steps:

(4.37)
   i Compute $\mathbf{f}_k$ and J_k.
   ii Solve the linear system $J_k\mathbf{h}_k = \mathbf{f}_k$ for $\mathbf{h}_k$.
   iii Compute $\mathbf{x}_{k+1} = \mathbf{x}_k - \mathbf{h}_k$.

The convergence properties of Newton's method are similar to those of the Newton–Raphson method. We saw that the latter method behaves erratically in regions where $|f'(x)|$ is small. The corresponding property in n dimensions is near-singularity of the Jacobian matrix $J(\mathbf{x})$. Newton's method will behave erratically if $\mathbf{x}_k$ lands in a region where $J(\mathbf{x})$ is nearly singular. This is a far more significant disadvantage than it was for single equations because, as we shall see, the cost of each iteration is quite high. Therefore, we want to avoid, as much as possible, any erratic behavior of an iteration. But, in order to ensure direct convergence, a particular problem may require a very good initial guess $\mathbf{x}_0$ and this can also be a difficulty. Consequently, as with the Newton–Raphson method, Newton's method is not a good method for general use.

A major disadvantage of Newton's method is efficiency. Like the Newton–Raphson method, the rate of convergence is quadratic whenever $\mathbf{x}_k$ is "sufficiently close" to $\mathbf{r}$ but, once again, this is very often outweighed by the amount of work required to perform each iteration. Let us see how much is involved. In step (i) of (4.37), we must evaluate $\mathbf{f}(\mathbf{x})$, and $J(\mathbf{x})$, each component of which is a "scalar function" $g(\mathbf{x}) = g(x_1, \ldots, x_n)$. Since $\mathbf{f}$ has n components and J has n^2, there is a total of $n^2 + n = n(n + 1)$ scalar functions to be evaluated. (We assume that the cost of evaluating each is the same.) Looking at it another way, J has n times as many components as $\mathbf{f}$ so the cost for an evaluation of J is roughly equivalent to n evaluations of $\mathbf{f}$. Therefore, the cost for each step of (4.37) is:

   i $n + 1$ evaluations of $\mathbf{f}$,
            (or $n(n + 1)$ scalar function evaluations).
   ii $n^3/3 + O(n^2)$ flops.
   iii n additions.

The total is the cost for each iteration of the method. We remark that this result also gives the cost per iteration for the Newton–Raphson method ($n = 1$). The following table shows some comparative costs (in number of flops). We have assumed that each scalar function evaluation uses 10 flops so that an evaluation of f requires $10n$ flops.

n	10	25	50
Step (i)	1,100	6,500	25,500
Step (ii)	400	5,500	44,500
Total	1,500	12,000	70,000

The costs for step (iii) were not included because they are insignificant. From these results, we conclude that, if n is not large, Jacobian evaluations contribute most to the cost. However, as n increases, the cost of solving the linear system in step (ii) accounts for an increasing proportion of the total. In any event, the total cost of an iteration is quite substantial and, overall, Newton's method is relatively inefficient. We remark that, subsequently, we will be looking at variations of Newton's method that are aimed at decreasing the cost of an iteration. It is evident from the above results that we will have to effect a decrease for both steps (i) and (ii) in order to achieve a significant reduction in cost.

Another aspect of Newton's method that should be mentioned is the fact that it requires an explicit formula for evaluating the Jacobian. Hence, any subroutine that uses the method will require that the user supply a subprogram for evaluating the n^2 components of $J(x)$. Quite obviously, this can be a formidable task. Therefore, this feature is an important disadvantage of the method.

We should not be entirely negative about Newton's method. There are times when f has some special property which can be exploited to make the method very efficient. One such property is a sparse Jacobian. This will occur if each component f_i of f is dependent on only a very small number of the unknowns x_j. For example, suppose $n = 50$ and, say, the seventh component of $f(x)$ is

$$f_7(x_1, \ldots, x_{50}) = x_4^3 - x_4 x_{38}$$

Then the only nonzero components in the seventh row of J are

$$(J)_{7,4} = 3x_4^2 - x_{38} \quad \text{and} \quad (J)_{7,38} = -x_4$$

If each of the other components of f also depends on only two or three of the x_j's, then J will have relatively few nonzero entries (i.e., it will be sparse). In this event, the amount of work to evaluate J is equivalent to only 2 or 3 evaluations of $\mathbf{f}$ rather than 50, which is a significant saving. Moreover, it would be relatively easy to write a subprogram to evaluate $J(\mathbf{x})$. In addition, we can use sparse matrix methods to solve the linear system in step (ii) and greatly reduce the amount of work in this part of the method. In this respect, a significant saving can be made by noting that each J_k has the same sparsity pattern so that the preprocessing stage of a sparse matrix algorithm only has to be used once. Problems with sparse Jacobians do not arise sufficiently often to justify inclusion of a separate subroutine in a general purpose software package such as IMSL or NAG. Such subroutines do exist but they usually reside in special purpose packages that do not normally have wide distribution. One particular type of application where nonlinear systems with sparse Jacobians arise is in chemical reaction problems. Any software package that is designed to handle such problems will usually contain a special subroutine that exploits sparsity of J.

Quasi-Newton Methods

This is the name of a whole class of methods based on the idea of approximating the Jacobian J in order to avoid the computational effort required to evaluate it. In the case of a single equation, the secant method fills this role for the Newton–Raphson method since it is based on approximating the derivative $f'(x)$. Hence, a quasi-Newton method can be regarded as an n-dimensional analogue of the secant method.

In what follows, we use B_k to denote an approximation for $J_k = J(\mathbf{x}_k)$. Then a quasi-Newton method is characterized by its particular definition of B_k. Each iteration of such a method will consist of the following steps:

(4.38)

    i Compute $\mathbf{f}_k$ and B_k.
    ii Solve the linear system $B_k \mathbf{s}_k = \mathbf{f}_k$ for $\mathbf{s}_k$.
    iii Compute $\mathbf{x}_{k+1} = \mathbf{x}_k - \mathbf{s}_k$.

As a general rule, quasi-Newton methods have convergence properties analogous to those of the secant method. They behave erratically in regions where $J(\mathbf{x})$ is nearly singular and the rate of convergence is superlinear (i.e., $1 < p < 2$). Having said this, we will limit our presentation to describing some methods and discussing the efficiency of them.

Perhaps the most obvious way of defining B_k is to use a finite difference approximation for each component of J_k, that is,

$$(B_k)_{i,j} = \frac{f_i(\mathbf{x}_k) - f_i(\mathbf{x}_{k-1})}{(\mathbf{x}_k)_j - (\mathbf{x}_{k-1})_j} \doteq \left(\frac{\partial f_i(\mathbf{x})}{\partial \mathbf{x}_j} \right)_{\mathbf{x}=\mathbf{x}_k}$$

The resulting method is often called the *finite difference Newton* method. It is easy to see that B_k can be determined at a cost of n^2D's plus $2nA$'s. Hence, the total cost of one iteration is approximately:

i   One evaluation of f plus n^2D's.
      (or n scalar function evaluations plus n^2D's).
ii $n^3/3 + O(n^2)$ flops.
iii Insignificant.

The following table illustrates some costs (in number of flops). Again, we assume the cost of a scalar function evaluation is 10 flops.

n	10	25	50
Step (i)	150	500	1,800
Step (ii)	400	5,500	44,500
Total	550	6,000	46,300

Comparing these results with the corresponding ones for Newton, we see that there is a sizable reduction in cost. However, all the savings come from not having to evaluate $J(\mathbf{x})$. There is no reduction in the cost of step (ii). Indeed, we see that this is now the predominant factor in the total cost of an iteration. One technique for trying to reduce this cost is to hold B_k fixed for a given number of iterations. Then the LU decomposition part of step (ii) in (4.38) need only be called when B_k is changed. Each subsequent iteration (until B_k is changed again) would only require $2n^2$ flops. This idea is useful when the Jacobian does not change very rapidly but it is difficult trying to decide how long to hold B_k fixed.

We consider one other quasi-Newton method, namely, *Broyden's method*. For single equations, an approximation b_k for f'_k can be defined by setting $x_p = x_{k-1}$ in (4.34) and equating to zero. This gives

$$b_k \cdot (x_k - x_{k-1}) = f_k - f_{k-1}$$

that is,

$$f'_k \doteq b_k = \frac{f_k - f_{k-1}}{x_k - x_{k-1}}$$

the familiar finite difference approximation that defines the secant method. For systems, we can derive an analogous condition for B_k from (4.35), that is,

(4.39) $B_k(\mathbf{x}_k - \mathbf{x}_{k-1}) = \mathbf{f}_k - \mathbf{f}_{k-1}$

But now we observe that B_k is not uniquely defined. It has n^2 components whereas (4.39) only specifies n conditions for them. Therefore we have $n^2 - n = n(n - 1)$ degrees of freedom. By contrast we note that, when $n = 1$, b_k is uniquely defined. In this context, we see why there is a whole class of methods that can be considered as extensions of the secant method to n dimensions.

In order to complete the definition of B_k, we need to use the idea of direction. A more precise interpretation of (4.39) is that it is a condition for B_k to approximate J_k in the direction of the vector $s_k = x_k - x_{k-1}$. Now recall that J_k must satisfy (4.35) independent of the direction of $z = x_k - x_p$. Therefore, we must also prescribe how B_k is to approximate J_k in directions other than s_k. Broyden's method is characterized by its definition of B_k in these other directions. In essence, it says that if z is any direction which is orthogonal (perpendicular) to s_k (i.e., $z^T s_k = 0$), then it does not matter how well we approximate J_k in this direction. Therefore we might as well complete the definition of B_k with an eye to ease of computation. Specifically, we let B_k be the same as B_{k-1} in any direction orthogonal to s_k, that is,

(4.40) $B_k z = B_{k-1} z$ for any z such that $z^T s_k = 0$

To see that this specifies the remaining $n(n - 1)$ conditions for B_k, we observe that z lies in an $(n - 1)$-dimensional hyperplane that is orthogonal to s_k (see Figure 4.9). Suppose $\{z_1, \ldots, z_{n-1}\}$ is a set of n-vectors that generates this hyperplane. Then (4.40) will hold if and only if it holds for each z_i, that is,

$$B_k z_i = B_{k-1} z_i \qquad 1 \le i \le n - 1$$

Each of these equations specifies n conditions on B_k for a total of $n(n - 1)$. Therefore (4.39) and (4.40) define B_k uniquely.

To summarize so far, Broyden's method uses conditions (4.39) and (4.40)

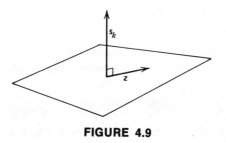

FIGURE 4.9

to define B_k. It turns out that B_k can easily be determined by using the formula

$$(4.41) \quad B_k = B_{k-1} + \frac{1}{s_k^T s_k} (v_k - B_{k-1} s_k) s_k^T,$$

where $y_k = f_k - f_{k-1}$ and $s_k = x_k - x_{k-1}$. For example, suppose

$$B_{k-1} = \begin{bmatrix} 1 & 8 & 7 \\ 9 & 2 & 4 \\ 6 & 5 & 3 \end{bmatrix} \qquad y_k = \begin{bmatrix} 2 \\ -1 \\ 1 \end{bmatrix} \qquad s_k = \begin{bmatrix} 1 \\ 0 \\ -1 \end{bmatrix}$$

Then

$$B_k = \begin{bmatrix} 1 & 8 & 7 \\ 9 & 2 & 4 \\ 6 & 5 & 3 \end{bmatrix} + \tfrac{1}{2} \left(\begin{bmatrix} 2 \\ -1 \\ 1 \end{bmatrix} - \begin{bmatrix} 1 & 8 & 7 \\ 9 & 2 & 4 \\ 6 & 5 & 3 \end{bmatrix} \begin{bmatrix} 1 \\ 0 \\ -1 \end{bmatrix} \right) [1, 0, -1]$$

$$= \begin{bmatrix} 1 & 8 & 7 \\ 9 & 2 & 4 \\ 6 & 5 & 3 \end{bmatrix} + \begin{bmatrix} 4 & 0 & -4 \\ -3 & 0 & 3 \\ -1 & 0 & 1 \end{bmatrix} = \begin{bmatrix} 5 & 8 & 3 \\ 6 & 2 & 7 \\ 5 & 5 & 4 \end{bmatrix}$$

The "correction" term on the right in (4.41) is often called an *update* (of B_{k-1}). In the example, we note that it is singular. In fact, it has rank 1 since the second and third columns are simply multiples of the first. This can easily be shown to be true in general. Hence, (4.41) is an example of a *rank-one update* method.

To start an iteration with Broyden's method, we need both x_0 and B_0. Then $x_1 = x_0 - B_0^{-1} f_0$, and so on. The question is how do we choose B_0? Now B_0 only influences B_1 through the condition (4.40). But this condition is aimed at computational convenience, that is, it does not affect the way in which B_1 approximates J_1 (in the direction of $s_1 = x_1 - x_0$). Therefore, we can also choose B_0 for computational convenience. The only condition is that it should be nonsingular. In particular, it should be well conditioned. In this regard, it is usual to choose $B_0 = I$. But the important point is that the choice of B_0 is not critical to the rate of convergence. Hence, a subroutine can define B_0 itself and a user need not worry about it.

The amount of work to compute B_k is about $2n^2$ flops. On the surface, it appears that we are still faced with the $n^3/3$ flops for step (ii) of (4.38), but this is not so. It turns out that B_k^{-1} can be determined explicitly if B_{k-1}^{-1} is known. That is, given B_{k-1}^{-1}, we can update it to B_k^{-1}. The formula is of the same form as (4.41) so the work requirement is about $2n^2$ flops. If B_k^{-1} is known, step (ii) only requires n^2 flops. Therefore, a table of comparative costs corresponding to the previous tables is

n	10	25	50
Step (i)	300	1,875	7,500
Step (ii)	100	625	2,500
Total	400	2,500	10,000

One can therefore do several iterations of this method in the same time it takes to do one Newton iteration.

The calling sequence for a subroutine for solving nonlinear systems is essentially the same as for single equations. It will be of the form

$$RTSYS(N,F,XO,XTOL,FTOL,ITMAX,WK,IND)$$

where

> N specifies the number n of equations in the system
> F is a subroutine for evaluating $f(x)$.
> XO is an n-vector used to apply the initial guess and to return the solution.
> XTOL, FTOL, ITMAX define the stopping criteria.
> WK is a workspace.
> IND is used to indicate which stopping criterion caused termination.

The maximum of ℓ_∞-norm is usually employed for both the X- and F-tests. That is, the X-test (4.12) would be

$$\max_{1\le i\le n} (\mathbf{x}_{k+1} - \mathbf{x}_k)_i \le XTOL \cdot (1 + \max_{1\le i\le n} (\mathbf{x}_k)_i)$$

and similarly for the F-test (4.13). In other words, the tests are applied componentwise to the respective vectors.

EXERCISES

Section 4.1

1.1. Consider the function

$$f(x) = \begin{cases} ln(x + 1) - x \csc x & \text{if } x \ne 0 \\ -1, & \text{if } x = 0 \end{cases}$$

Define

$$g(x) = \sin(x) \ln(x + 1)$$

Show that any root of $f(x)$ is also a fixed point of $g(x)$ but that the converse is not true. (Hint: Try an iteration (4.8) with $x_0 = 1.0$.)

1.2. In Table 4.1, the iteration using $x_0 = 5.0$ does not converge and yet $|g'(5.0)| < 1$, that is, condition (iii) of (4.10) is satisfied. Which condition is not satisfied?

1.3. Discuss the suitability of the following as a stopping criterion for an X-test:

$$|x_{k+1} - x_k| \le 4 \cdot \text{EPS} \cdot |x_k| + \text{XTOL}$$

where EPS is machine epsilon.

1.4. In order to locate the root of $f(x) = e^{-x} - \cos x$ which is near $\pi/2$, we could use a fixed-point iteration (4.8) with $x_0 = \pi/2$, where $g(x)$ is one of the following:

   i $g(x) = \cos^{-1}(e^{-x})$.
   ii $g(x) = -\ln(\cos x)$.
   iii $g(x) = x - \dfrac{e^{-x} - \cos x}{1 - e^{-\pi/2}}$.

  (a) In each case, verify that any root of $f(x)$ is a fixed-point of $g(x)$.
  (b) Using the conditions (4.10), determine which of the three iterative methods will converge for $x_0 = \pi/2$. Verify the answers.

1.5. Consider the function

$$f(x) = (x - 1)e^{-nx} + x^n$$

It is easy to see that, for any n, $f(x)$ has a root in the interval [0, 1]. Find this root, to five significant figures, for each of $n = \pm 1, \pm 5, \pm 10, \pm 12$. In each case, state the values of XTOL and FTOL that were used. Note that, as $n > 0$ increases, the graph of $f(x)$ in [0, 1] gets increasingly closer to the x-axis similar to the illustration in Figure 4.1a. Correspondingly, as $n < 0$ decreases, the graph of $f(x)$ is like Figure 4.1b. Therefore, care must be taken in specifying XTOL and FTOL in order to get the requested accuracy.

1.6. Consider a fixed-point iteration for nonlinear systems,

$$\mathbf{x}_{k+1} = \mathbf{g}(\mathbf{x}_k)$$

Formulate convergence conditions corresponding to (4.10).

Section 4.2

2.1.   Find the real roots, to five significant figures, of each of the following functions:

   i $f(x) = \tan x - \sin 2x + \pi$.
   ii $f(x) = 3^{-x} - \ln x$.
   iii $f(x) = \cos x - xe^x$.
   iv $f(x) = \ln|x^2 - 5x + 8| - e^x \sin 2x$.
         (There are an infinite number of real roots. Find the five that are nearest zero.)
   v $f(x) = x^5 - 2x^4 + 3x^3 - 4x^2 + 5x - 6$.

2.2.   Consider the function

$$f(x) = (x^2 + 1) \sin x - e^{\sqrt{|x|}}(x - 1)(x^2 - 5).$$

(a) Find the smallest positive root of $f(x)$.
(b) Does $f(x)$ have any complex roots?

2.3.   Consider the function $f(x) = x \cdot \sec x - \cot x$.
   (a) It is easy to verify that $f(\pi/4) < 0$ and $f(3\pi/4) > 0$. However, the interval $[\pi/4, 3\pi/4]$ is not a bracket. Why? How does a rootfinding subroutine that uses brackets behave with this interval as an initial guess?
   (b) Find the four real roots of $f(x)$ that are closest to the origin.

2.4.   Consider the polynomial

$$p(x) = x^5 - 3.01x^4 + 31x^3 + 387.31x^2 + 1366.94x + 1571.22$$

and the matrix

$$C = \begin{bmatrix} 0 & 0 & 0 & 0 & -1571.22 \\ 1 & 0 & 0 & 0 & -1366.94 \\ 0 & 1 & 0 & 0 & -387.31 \\ 0 & 0 & 1 & 0 & -31.0 \\ 0 & 0 & 0 & 1 & 3.01 \end{bmatrix}$$

   (a) Show that the characteristic polynomial of C is $p(x)$, that is, $p(x) = \det(xI - C)$. C is called the *companion matrix* of $p(x)$.
   (b) Given an arbitrary polynomial (4.25), show how to form its companion matrix.
   (c) The connection between a polynomial and its companion matrix suggests another algorithm for finding the roots of a polynomial, that is,

   i   Form the companion matrix C.
   ii Find the eigenvalues of C.

Find the roots of the polynomial $p(x)$ above in this way.

(d) Compare the companion matrix method with Laguerre's method on the basis of efficiency and reliability. Does C have a special form that can be exploited to enhance efficiency? To assess reliability, try each method on an ill-conditioned polynomial such as in Exercise 2.5.

2.5. Experiment with root-finding subroutines to see how well they perform on ill-conditioned problems by finding the roots of

$$p_n(x) = \prod_{i=1}^{n} (x - i) = (x - 1)(x - 2) \ldots (x - n)$$

for $n = 5, 6, \ldots$ [Note that $n = 20$ gives the polynomial (1.6).] For general-purpose root-finding subroutines, the subprogram F *for evaluating* p_n can use the factored form above. However, a special-purpose subroutine designed for polynomials will require the coefficients a_i in (4.25). These can be generated from the roots r_j, $1 \le j \le n$, in the following way. Two vectors A(I) and R(J) of length $\ge n + 1$ are required. At the outset, it is assumed that

A(1) = 1.0,
A(I) = 0.0, $1 \le I \le N + 1$,
R(J) = r_j, $1 \le J \le N$,
R(N + 1) = 1.0.

Given this initialization, a program segment for computing the a_i's is

```
    NP1 = N + 1
    DO 1 J = 1,N
        NP1MJ = NP1 - J
        DO 2 K = 1,NP1MJ
            A(K + 1) = A(K + 1) - R(K)*A(K)
            R(K) = R(K + 1)
2       CONTINUE
1 CONTINUE
```

The array A will contain the a_i's with A(I + 1) = a_i, $0 \le i \le n$. Note that the array R containing the roots is overwritten.

2.6. Verify that the polynomial (4.32) is not badly conditioned by repeating the experiment of Exercise 1.5 with the polynomials

$$p_n(x) = \prod_{i=1}^{n} (x - 2^{-i})$$

for $n = 5, 6, \ldots$, and comparing the results of the two experiments.

2.7. A root-finding subroutine can be used to find the eigenvalues of a matrix by finding the roots of its characteristic polynomial. Let A be an $n \times n$ matrix and denote its characteristic polynomial by

$$\phi(x) = \det(xI - A)$$

There is no need to obtain an explicit representation for $\phi(x)$ in order to evaluate it. Instead, to obtain the value of ϕ at $x = x_k$, we can form the matrix $x_k I - A$ and then compute its determinant. (An efficient method for computing determinants was discussed in Section 2.1.1.)

(a) Use this idea to find the eigenvalues of each of the matrices of Exercise 2.1 in Chapter 2.

(b) Comment on the efficiency and reliability of this procedure.

2.8. We stated that the Newton–Raphson method has a quadratic rate of convergence only in the case of simple roots. That is, if r is a root of multiplicity $m > 1$, the method converges at a rate $p < 2$. However, the quadratic rate can be restored by modifying the definition (4.23) of the method to

$$x_{k+1} = x_k - m \cdot \frac{f_k}{f_k'}$$

(a) Explain why this modification gives quadratic convergence when r has multiplicity m. (Hint: see the discussion of equation (4.24).) Is this a practical idea? Why?

(b) Verify that the modification works by applying both the unmodified and modified Newton–Raphson methods to find a root of

$$p(x) = x^6 - 6x^5 + 10x^4 - 32x + 32$$

which has a root of multiplicity $m = 4$. In each case, use $x_0 = 4.0$ as the initial guess.

2.9. Find, to five significant figures, values of x and y satisfying the equations

$$x = \sinh y$$
$$2y = \cosh x$$

2.10. The data for the distance $s(t)$ given in Exercise 1.6, Chapter III was derived from the expression

$$s(t) = 25t - 64e^{(12-t)/8}\left(\frac{t}{8} + 1\right) + 64e^{1.5}$$

At what times $t > 0$ does $s(t) = 276$ and 1000?

2.11. For turbulent flow of fluid in a smooth pipe, the following relationship exists between the friction factor c_f and the Reynold's number R:

$$\sqrt{\frac{1}{c_f}} = -0.4 + 1.74 \cdot \ln (R\sqrt{c_f})$$

Compute c_f, to four significant digits, for each of $R = 10$, 10^2 and 10^4.

Section 4.3

3.1. Find all the roots of each of the following systems:

i $\quad \mathbf{f(x)} = \begin{bmatrix} x_1^2 + 4x_1 + 4x_2 - 25 \\ x_2^2 + 4x_1 - 4x_2 - 9 \end{bmatrix}$

ii $\quad \mathbf{f(x)} = \begin{bmatrix} x_1^2 + 31x_2^2 - 64x_2 - 32 \\ 2x_1x_2 - 2x_2^2 + 32 \end{bmatrix}$

iii $\quad \mathbf{f(x)} = \begin{bmatrix} 8x_1^2 + 2x_1x_2 + 12x_1 - 2x_2 + 4 \\ 2x_2^2 + 2x_1x_2 - 4x_1 + 10x_2 + 12 \end{bmatrix}$

3.2. Consider the system given in (4.3)(*b*). Find the solution which is closest to the origin.

3.3. Verify that the definition of B_k in (4.41) satisfies both (4.39) and (4.40).

3.4. Let $f(z)$ be a complex function of the complex variable $z = x + iy$. We can write $f = u + iv$, where $u = u(x, y)$, $v = v(x, y)$ are real functions of the real variables x, y. Consequently, the (complex) equation $f(z) = 0$ is equivalent to the (real) system of two equations

$$u(x, y) = Re(f) = 0$$
$$v(x, y) = Im(f) = 0$$

One can therefore find the roots of f either by using a routine like RTMLR or by forming the equivalent system of equations and using an appropriate subroutine to solve it. Use both methods to find the roots of

i $\quad f(z) = z^3 + (1 - 2i)z^2 + 2z - (4 + 5i)$.
ii $\quad f(z) = 1 - 3^{z^2}$.

3.5. [4, p. 319] Find two solutions of the nonlinear system

$$\frac{1}{2} \sin (x_1x_2) - \frac{x_2}{4\pi} - \frac{x_1}{2} = 0$$

$$\left(1 - \frac{1}{4\pi}\right)(e^{2x_1} - e) + \frac{ex_2}{\pi} - 2ex_1 = 0$$

3.6.   [4, p. 321] In the study of a chemical equilibrium problem, the following system of equations arises.

$$\frac{1}{2}x_1 + x_2 + \frac{1}{2}x_3 - \frac{x_6}{x_7} = 0$$

$$x_3 + x_4 + 2x_5 - \frac{2}{x_7} = 0$$

$$x_1 + x_2 + x_5 - \frac{1}{x_7} = 0$$

$$-28{,}837x_1 - 139{,}009x_2 - 78{,}213x_3 + 18{,}927x_4 + 8427x_5$$
$$+ \frac{13{,}492}{x_7} - 10{,}690\frac{x_6}{x_7} = 0$$

$$x_1 + x_2 + x_3 + x_4 + x_5 = 1$$

$$400x_1x_4^3 - 178{,}370x_3x_5 = 0$$

$$x_1x_3 - 2.6058x_2x_4 = 0$$

Find a solution of this system.

CHAPTER 5

QUADRATURE

The topic of quadrature is concerned with the problem of obtaining an approximation for the value of the definite integral

$$(5.1) \quad I(f; a, b) = \int_a^b f(x)\, dx$$

From the calculus, one learns that the value of the integral is given by $I(f; a, b) = F(b) - F(a)$, where $F(x) = \int f(x)\, dx$ is the antiderivative of $f(x)$. For instance, if $f(x) = \cos x$, then the antiderivative is $F(x) = \sin x + C$, where C is an arbitrary constant of integration. Hence, the problem is one of finding an expression for $F(x)$, and then evaluating it at the limits of integration. There are, of course, a variety of rules for finding $F(x)$ but none of them applies universally, that is, each one applies only for certain specific forms of the integrand $f(x)$. Consequently, integration is essentially a process of recognizing the form of $f(x)$ and then using the appropriate rule to find $F(x)$. Now, from the point of view of designing a general-purpose subroutine to approximate $I(f; a, b)$, this approach is clearly an unsatisfactory one to use. For one thing, it would require the use of a symbol manipulation system which can be expensive. Also, since each integration rule is specialized, one would, in effect, have to implement a complete table of integrals in order to be able to handle a wide variety of the forms of the integrand $f(x)$. But even if this were done, there are still a good many integrals, which commonly arise in practice, that cannot be handled in this way because no integration rule for finding $F(x)$ exists. Two examples are the beta and gamma functions

$$B(m, n) = \int_0^1 x^m (1 - x^2)^n\, dx \qquad \Gamma(m) = \int_0^\infty e^{-x} x^{m-1}\, dx$$

respectively, which cannot be integrated exactly (by any known method) unless m and n are positive integers.

An alternative approach to approximating the value of $I(f; a, b)$ is to use an n-point *quadrature rule* or *formula*

$$(5.2) \quad Q_n(f) = a_1 f(x_1) + a_2 f(x_2) + \cdots + a_n f(x_n) = \sum_{i=1}^n a_i f_i$$

199

where $f_i = f(x_i)$, that is, a linear combination of values of the integrand $f(x)$ taken at the *quadrature points* x_i, $1 \le i \le n$. In terms of designing a subroutine, this is a much more viable approach. In the first place, (5.2) is very easy to implement on a computer. Moreover, since quadrature rules are generally not restricted to specific forms of the integrand $f(x)$, they are better suited for general-purpose subroutines. For these reasons, then, quadrature is the approach taken to computing an approximation for the value of $I(f; a, b)$.

While we will be discussing various different quadrature rules, our main interest is in subroutines—their design and use. To make things easy for the user, a subroutine to evaluate a definite integral normally only needs to be supplied with a subprogram to evaluate the integrand $f(x)$, the limits of integration a and b, plus an error tolerance TOL. That is, the calling sequence would be of the form

$$\text{QUAD} = \text{INTGL(F,A,B,TOL)}$$

The subroutine will attempt to compute, as efficiently as possible, a value for $I(f; a, b)$ that is accurate to within the specified tolerance. The design of such a subroutine is by no means easy. One must decide on the quadrature rule(s) to be used but this is a comparatively minor consideration. The difficult part is building, around the rule(s), an overall algorithm that achieves the goals of efficiency and reliability. By reliability, we mean that the approximate value of $I(f; a, b)$ returned by the routine is guaranteed to have the accuracy requested by the user. As we will see, these two goals are virtually impossible to meet simultaneously and there will be the familiar tradeoff between speed and reliability.

In the next section, we survey some quadrature rules that are often used as bases for subroutines. Then, in Section 5.2, we look at some of the ideas involved in designing an algorithm for such subroutines.

5.1. QUADRATURE RULES

The mathematical literature abounds with a great variety of quadrature rules that one might use. Rather than selecting a few for detailed discussion, we will try to give an overview of how formulas can be derived. In this general context, the comparison between various rules will be relatively easy. There are two classes of rules—Newton–Cotes and Gauss—that we will consider, but first we must develop some ideas about quadrature rules in general.

The derivation of rules of the form (5.2) can be viewed in a very simple way, namely, that we replace the integrand $f(x)$ by the polynomial $p_{n-1}(x)$ of degree $n - 1$, which interpolates $f(x)$ at the n quadrature points

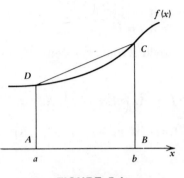

FIGURE 5.1

$x_1, \ldots, x_n$ and then integrate $p_{n-1}(x)$ exactly. In other words, $I(f; a, b) \doteq Q_n(f) = I(p_{n-1}; a, b)$. As an example, let $n = 2$ and set $x_1 = a$, $x_2 = b$, the endpoints of the interval of integration. Then the interpolating polynomial (in Newton form) through (x_1, f_1) and (x_2, f_2) is the straight line

$$p_1(x) = f_2 + f[x_1, x_2] \cdot (x - x_2) = f_2 + \frac{f_1 - f_2}{x_1 - x_2} \cdot (x - x_2)$$

and

$$(5.3) \quad I(f; a, b) \doteq I(p_1; a, b) = \int_{x_1}^{x_2} p_1(x)\, dx = \frac{h}{2} \cdot (f_1 + f_2) = T(f)$$

where $h = (b - a)$. This, of course, is the well-known *trapezoidal rule*, so-called because, as we see in Figure 5.1, it computes the area of the trapezoid $ABCD$, which approximates the area represented by $I(f; a, b)$—the region bounded by the graph of $f(x)$, the x-axis and the lines $x = a$, $x = b$. Since we will refer to this rule quite often, it has been denoted by $T(f)$.

From (5.2), it follows that a quadrature rule can be characterized by specifying the number of terms n in it, along with the coefficients a_i and the quadrature points x_i. In point of fact, though, the a_i's depend on the location of the x_i's so it is only necessary to specify the latter. This dependence is not altogether clear in the above derivation of the trapezoidal rule but it would have been so if we had written the interpolating polynomial $p_{n-1}(x)$ in its Lagrange form (3.8). Briefly, given the points $x_1, \ldots, x_n$, we define the polynomials

$$l_i(x) = \frac{(x - x_1) \ldots (x - x_{i-1})(x - x_{i+1}) \ldots (x - x_n)}{(x_i - x_1) \ldots (x_i - x_{i-1})(x_i - x_{i+1}) \ldots (x_i - x_n)} \quad 1 \le i \le n$$

which are of degree $(n - 1)$ and have the property that

$$(5.4) \qquad l_i(x_j) = \delta_{i,j} = \begin{array}{ll} 0 & \text{if } i \neq j \\ 1 & \text{if } i = j \end{array}$$

where $\delta_{i,j}$ is the well-known Kronecker delta. Then the Lagrange form of $p_{n-1}(x)$ is

$$p_{n-1}(x) = l_1(x) \cdot f_1 + l_2(x) \cdot f_2 + \cdots + l_n(x) \cdot f_n = \sum_{i=1}^{n} l_i(x) \cdot f_i$$

Upon integrating this form of $p_{n-1}(x)$ over $[a, b]$, we see by comparison with (5.2) that

$$(5.5) \qquad a_i = \int_a^b l_i(x)\, dx \qquad 1 \leq i \leq n$$

Hence, each a_i is directly dependent on the locations of all of the x_i's. For example, with the trapezoidal rule, the Lagrange form of $p_1(x)$ is

$$p_1(x) = \frac{(x - x_2)}{(x_1 - x_2)} \cdot f_1 + \frac{(x - x_1)}{(x_2 - x_1)} \cdot f_2$$

from which we obtain

$$a_1 = \int_{x_1}^{x_2} \frac{(x - x_2)}{(x_1 - x_2)}\, dx = \frac{h}{2} \qquad \text{and} \qquad a_2 = \int_{x_1}^{x_2} \frac{(x - x_1)}{(x_2 - x_1)}\, dx = \frac{h}{2}$$

Therefore, a quadrature rule is completely characterized by specifying the locations of the quadrature points x_i, $1 \leq i \leq n$. Consequently, to define a class of rules, all we have to do is describe the means of deciding how to place the x_i's. As a final point, we emphasize the distinction between specifying a quadrature rule and representing it for efficient use in a computer. Although the a_i's depend on the x_i's, it is better to store them explicitly rather than implement (5.5) in order to compute them each time the rule is used. Therefore, the rule (5.2) will be represented by the triple $(n, \mathbf{x}, \mathbf{a})$, where $\mathbf{x} = [x_1, \ldots, x_n]^T$ and $\mathbf{a} = [a_1, \ldots, a_n]^T$, even though it is sufficient to specify n and $\mathbf{x}$ only.

5.1.1. Newton–Cotes Rules

For this class of rules, the quadrature points are defined by

$$x_i = a + (i - 1)h \qquad 1 \leq i \leq n \qquad \text{where } h = \frac{b - a}{n - 1}$$

That is, the points are *equally spaced* throughout the interval $[a, b]$ with

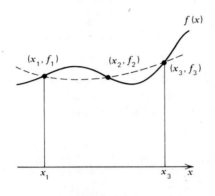

FIGURE 5.2

$x_1 = a$ and $x_n = b$. Note that we must have $n \geq 2$. The simplest case, $n = 2$, gives the trapezoidal rule (5.3). Another well-known quadrature formula in this class is Simpson's rule, which is obtained by choosing $n = 3$. The quadrature points are $x_1 = a$, $x_2 = (a + b)/2$, $x_3 = b$ and the rule is

$$(5.6) \quad I(f; a, b) \doteq S(f) = \frac{h}{3}(f_1 + 4f_2 + f_3) \quad \text{where } h = \frac{b - a}{2}$$

It gives the area bounded by the quadratic that interpolates at (x_1, f_1), (x_2, f_2), (x_3, f_3) as shown in Figure 5.2.

We now turn our attention to analyzing the *quadrature error*

$$E_n(f) = I(f; a, b) - Q_n(f)$$

An expression for $E_n(f)$ is easily obtained by using the connection with interpolation. Using the expression (3.10) for the error in polynomial interpolation, we have

$$E_n(f) = I(f; a, b) - Q_n(f) = I(f; a, b) - I(p_{n-1}; a, b)$$
$$= I(f - p_{n-1}; a, b)$$

$$(5.7) \qquad = \int_a^b f[x_1, \ldots, x_n, x] \cdot \psi_n(x)\, dx$$

where $f[x_1, \ldots, x_n, x]$ is an nth divided difference, and

$$(5.8) \quad \psi_n(x) = (x - x_1)(x - x_2) \ldots (x - x_n) = \prod_{i=1}^{n}(x - x_i)$$

is a polynomial of degree n whose roots are the quadrature points x_i. Now, by the mean-value theorem for integrals, if $f(x)$ is n times continuously differentiable and $\psi_n(x)$ is of one sign on (a, b), we can write

$$(5.9) \quad E_n(f) = \frac{f^{(n)}(\theta)}{n!} \int_a^b \psi_n(x)\, dx \quad \text{for some } \theta \in (a, b)$$

But it is clear from (5.8) that $\psi_n(x)$ is of one sign on (a, b) only for the case $n = 2$ so it appears that this line of analysis will go nowhere. However, it can be shown [24, p. 119] that (5.9) does, in fact, hold whenever n is even. If n is odd, it turns out that

$$(5.10) \quad E_n(f) = \frac{f^{(n+1)}(\theta)}{(n + 1)!} \int_a^b x\psi_n(x)\, dx \quad \text{for some } \theta \in (a, b)$$

From these results, it is possible to obtain bounds for $|E_n(f)|$ and use them to compare different formulas. However, it is more instructive to pursue an intuitive approach as we shall now do.

As a measure of the "size" of $E_n(f)$ for a given quadrature rule, we look at the size of the class of functions $\mathscr{C}$ for which the rule is exact, that is, $E_n(f) \equiv 0$ for all $f \in \mathscr{C}$. Since this depends heavily on what type of functions one is willing to allow in $\mathscr{C}$, we simplify matters by restricting ourselves to polynomials. We define $\mathscr{C}$ to be $\mathscr{P}_m$, the set of all polynomials of degree $\leq m$ and quadrature rules will be compared by looking at the maximum degree m of polynomial for which each rule is exact. For example, the trapezoidal rule has $m = 1$, that is, it will be exact if $f(x)$ is a straight line.

We digress for a moment to remark that this approach to measuring the error seems to imply that we will get more accuracy by taking n larger, that is, by using a formula based on a higher-order interpolation polynomial. On the other hand, this flies in the face of the comments in Section 3.1.1. about the accuracy of interpolation using higher-order polynomials. Specifically, as n increases, the accuracy at intermediate points deteriorates due to oscillations in $p_{n-1}(x)$. However, integration is a "smoothing" operation because, as indicated in Figure 5.3, errors due to oscillations in p_{n-1} tend to

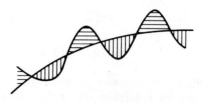

FIGURE 5.3

cancel each other with the result that accuracy will indeed improve with increasing n. It is easy, however, to construct integrands $f(x)$ where the positive and negative errors do not cancel so nicely. This usually happens when $f(x)$ fluctuates quite rapidly at an inopportune time—behavior that is very "unpolynomial" in nature. By and large, therefore, one should only use higher-order formulas when f is reasonably smooth.

An alternative to using higher-order formulas is to interpolate f with a piecewise polynomial $s_k(x)$ and integrate it exactly. This is equivalent to subdividing $[a, b]$ by the points (knots) $a = x_1 < x_2 < \cdots < x_N = b$ and applying an n-point rule in each subinterval $[x_j, x_{j+1}]$, $1 \le j \le n - 1$. Such rules are called *composite rules*. For example, the rule corresponding to piecewise linear interpolation is the composite trapezoidal formula. Assuming equally spaced points $x_j = a + (j - 1) \cdot h$, with $h = (b - a)/(N - 1)$, it is

$$(5.11) \quad T_N(f) = \frac{h}{2}(f_1 + f_2) + \frac{h}{2}(f_2 + f_3) + \cdots + \frac{h}{2}(f_{N-1} + f_N)$$

$$= h \cdot \left(\frac{1}{2}f_1 + f_2 + f_3 + \cdots + f_{N-1} + \frac{1}{2}f_N\right)$$

Note that the second version is more efficient because it avoids double function evaluations. (This type of saving can be made with any composite Newton–Cotes rule.) Again, carrying over the comparison of polynomial versus piecewise polynomial interpolation, it generally turns out to be better to use a composite rule based on a low-order formula (small n) and many subdivisions (large N) in order to get a more accurate approximation to $I(f; a, b)$.

We now return to the analysis of the error $E_n(f)$. Given a quadrature rule $Q_n(f)$, we want to determine the maximum degree m of polynomial for which it is exact. Now it is obvious, from the interpolation aspect, that if $f(x)$ is any polynomial of degree $\le n - 1$, an n-point formula will integrate it exactly so we have $m \ge n - 1$. Geometric intuition might suggest that m cannot be greater than $n - 1$ but sometimes it can. To see why, we use the fact that if $f(x)$ is a polynomial of degree k, then

$$\frac{d^s f}{dx^s} = \begin{cases} \text{a polynomial of deg } k - s & \text{if } s < k \\ K, \text{ a constant} & \text{if } s = k \\ 0 & \text{if } s > k \end{cases}$$

Therefore, it follows from (5.9) and (5.10) that

$$E_n(f) \equiv 0 \begin{cases} \text{if } n \text{ is even and degree } f \le n - 1 \\ \text{if } n \text{ is odd and degree } f \le n \end{cases}$$

From this we conclude that an n-point Newton–Cotes rule will be exact for all polynomials of degree $\le m$, where

$$m = \begin{cases} n-1 & \text{if } n \text{ is even} \\ n & \text{if } n \text{ is odd} \end{cases}$$

In effect, then, we get a bonus whenever an odd number of quadrature points is used. For example, if three points are used, the corresponding formula—Simpson's rule—will integrate any polynomial of degree ≤ 3 exactly, and the four-point formula cannot do any better. By way of verification that Simpson's rule (5.6) will integrate cubics exactly, we consider the integral

$$(5.12) \quad I(f; 0, 2) = \int_0^2 (2x^3 - 3x^2 + 5x - 6)\, dx = -2$$

Then $h = (2-0)/(3-1) = 1$ and

$$S(f) = \tfrac{1}{3}(-6) + \tfrac{4}{3}(-2) + \tfrac{1}{3}(8) = -2$$

which is the exact answer.

5.1.2. Gauss Rules

We first illustrate the ideas used in the placing of the Gauss quadrature points by deriving a simple two-point rule. It is convenient to assume that the interval of integration $[a, b]$ is $[-1, 1]$. This is no real restriction since the simple change of variables

$$(5.13) \quad x = a + \frac{b-a}{2}(t+1) \qquad -1 \leq t \leq 1$$

maps $[a, b]$ onto $[-1, 1]$ and we have

$$I(f; a, b) = \int_a^b f(x)\, dx = \frac{b-a}{2} \int_{-1}^1 g(t)\, dt = \frac{b-a}{2} I(g; -1, 1)$$

where $g(t) = f([a + (b-a)(t+1)/2])$. Therefore, there is no loss of generality in dealing with the integral $I(g; -1, 1)$.

Consider the set $\{P_0(t), P_1(t), P_2(t)\}$ of polynomials defined by

$$P_0(t) = 1 \qquad P_1(t) = t \qquad P_2(t) = \tfrac{1}{2}(3t^2 - 1)$$

On the interval $[-1, 1]$, these polynomials have an interesting property, that is, for $1 \leq r, s \leq n$,

$$(5.14) \quad \int_{-1}^1 P_r(t)P_s(t)\, dt = \begin{cases} K_{r,s} \text{ a constant} & \text{if } r = s \\ 0, & \text{if } r \neq s \end{cases}$$

This is called an *orthogonality* property. (It is the continuous analogue of the definition (3.36) of orthogonality with respect to a discrete or finite set of points.) In addition, if $h(t)$ is any polynomial of degree ≤ 1, it has a unique representation in the form

(5.15) $\quad h(t) = c_0 P_0(t) + c_1 P_1(t)$

That is, the set $\{P_0, P_1\}$ forms an (orthogonal) *basis* for the linear function space $\mathcal{P}_1$ of all polynomials of degree ≤ 1. Finally, we note that the roots $t = \pm 1/\sqrt{3}$ of $P_2(t)$ are in $[-1, 1]$.

Now we are ready to derive the Gauss two-point formula for approximating $I(g; -1, 1)$. Suppose that $g(x)$ is any polynomial of degree ≤ 3. We will show that it is possible to select the quadrature points t_1, t_2 so that $E_2(g) \equiv 0$. (Recall that the Newton–Cotes two-point formula—trapezoidal rule—is only exact for polynomials of degree ≤ 1.) We know that the divided difference $g[t_1, t_2, t]$ will be a polynomial of degree $\leq 3 - 2 = 1$ so, using (5.15), the expression (5.7) for the quadrature error $E_2(g)$ can be written in the form

$$E_2(g) = \frac{1}{2} \int_{-1}^{1} [c_0 P_0(t) + c_1 P_1(t)] \psi_2(t) \, dt$$

Now, if it could be arranged to have $\psi_2(t) = K_2 P_2(t)$, where K_2 is any constant, then by the orthogonality property (5.14), we would have

$$E_2(g) = c_0 K_2 \int_{-1}^{1} P_0(t) P_2(t) \, dt + c_1 K_2 \int_{-1}^{1} P_1(t) P_2(t) \, dt = 0$$

But this is easy to accomplish. Noting the form (5.8) of $\psi_2(t)$, we simply factor $P_2(t)$ and define

$$\psi_2(t) = (t - t_1)(t - t_2) = \tfrac{2}{3} P_2(t)$$

From this argument, it follows that the quadrature points t_1, t_2 should be the roots of $P_2(t)$, namely,

$$t_1 = -\frac{1}{\sqrt{3}} \quad \text{and} \quad t_2 = \frac{1}{\sqrt{3}}$$

Then, using (5.5), the coefficients will be

$$a_1 = 1 \quad \text{and} \quad a_2 = 1$$

whereupon

$$I(g; -1, 1) = 1 \cdot g(t_1) + 1 \cdot g(t_2) + E_2(g)$$

where $E_2(g) \equiv 0$ if $g(t)$ is any polynomial of degree ≤ 3. For the more general integral $I(f; a, b)$, we use the transformation (5.13) to get

(5.16)　$I(f; a, b) \doteq \dfrac{b-a}{2} [f(x_1) + f(x_2)] + E_2(f)$

where

$$x_1 = a + \frac{b-a}{2}(t_1 + 1) \qquad x_2 = a + \frac{b-a}{2}(t_2 + 1)$$

and $E_2(f) \equiv 0$ if $f(x)$ is any polynomial of degree ≤ 3. The quadrature points x_1, x_2 are the images in $[a, b]$ of the "Gauss points" t_1, t_2 under the transformation (5.13). To illustrate the exactness of the formula for degree 3 polynomials, we apply the rule to the example (5.12). In this case, since $a = 0$ and $b = 2$, the transformation (5.13) is $x = t + 1$. Then

$$f(x_1) = f(t_1 + 1) = 2(t_1 + 1)^3 - 3(t_1 + 1)^2 + 5(t_1 + 1) - 6$$

$$= -1 - \left(\frac{17}{3\sqrt{3}}\right)$$

and similarly for $f(x_2)$. Hence,

$$I(f; 0, 2) = \frac{2-0}{2} \cdot \left[\left(-1 - \frac{17}{3\sqrt{3}}\right) + \left(-1 + \frac{17}{3\sqrt{3}}\right)\right] = -2$$

which is the exact answer. Note that it is more efficient to compute $x_1 = t_1 + 1$ and evaluate $f(x_1)$ rather than work out the expansion $g(t) = 2t^3 + 3t^2 + 5t - 2$ and evaluate it at $t = t_1$.

A comparison of the Gauss rule (5.16) with Simpson's rule (5.6) is useful at this point. On the basis of our measure of error, the two are equal since they are both exact for polynomials of degree ≤ 3. But, on the basis of computational effort, the Gauss rule comes out ahead because it only requires two evaluations of $f(x)$ whereas Simpson requires three. Hence, the Gauss rule is more efficient. We remark, however, that the corresponding composite rules turn out to be comparable. If $[a, b]$ is subdivided by $a = x_1 < \cdots < x_N = b$, then the composite two-point Gauss rule will require $2(N-1)$ function evaluations while composite Simpson will need $2(N-1) + 1$. The latter figure results from savings on combining function evaluations at the endpoints of each subinterval. No such savings can be made with the Gauss rule because it does not use the endpoints.

In Figure 5.4, we illustrate why the two-point Gauss rule (5.16) is more accurate than the two-point Newton–Cotes or trapezoidal rule (5.3). The curve $f(x)$ is a quadratic and we see that, by interpolating at the Gauss points x_1, x_2, the area under the resulting line is the exact result due to cancelation of the errors. On the other hand, with the trapezoidal rule (broken line in Figure 5.4), there is no canceling effect.

The theory for deriving Gauss rules in general is a relatively simple

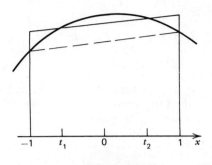

FIGURE 5.4

extension of the above ideas. Instead of (5.1), we now suppose that our integral is of the slightly more general form

$$(5.17) \quad I(f; a, b) = \int_a^b w(x)f(x)\, dx$$

where $w(x)$ is a *weight function* that is restricted to being of one sign ($+$ or $-$) on $[a, b]$. Up to now, we have had $w(x) \equiv 1$ but, as we shall see, the extra generality can be very useful. The underlying idea of Gauss quadrature is to make use of orthogonal polynomials. Suppose that we can find a set of polynomials $\{P_k(x)\}_{k=0}^n$ such that

$$(5.18)$$

$$\textbf{i} \quad \deg P_k(x) = k \qquad\qquad 0 \le k \le n$$

$$\textbf{ii} \quad \int_a^b w(x)P_r(x)P_s(x)\, dx = K_{r,s}\delta_{r,s} \qquad 0 \le r, s \le n$$

where $\delta_{r,s}$ is the Kronecker delta defined by (5.4) and the $K_{r,s}$'s are constants. The set $\{P_k(x)\}$ is said to be *orthogonal* on $[a, b,]$ *with respect to the weight function* $w(x)$. There are many examples of orthogonal polynomials in the mathematical literature and we will enumerate a few of them shortly but first we show how to use (5.18) to generate quadrature rules.

We suppose that $f(x)$ is a polynomial of $\deg \le 2n - 1$. Then its nth divided difference $f[x_1, \ldots, x_n, x]$ is a polynomial of degree $\le (2n - 1) - n = n - 1$. Now, by property (5.18)(i), the set $\{P_k\}_{k=0}^{n-1}$ is linearly independent on $[a, b]$. Therefore, it forms a basis for $\mathscr{P}_{n-1}$, the set of all polynomials of degree $\le n - 1$, and we can write

$$f[x_1, \ldots, x_n, x] = c_0 P_0(x) + c_1 P_1(x) + \cdots + c_{n-1} P_{n-1}(x).$$

so that the expression (5.7) for the quadrature error will be

$$E_n(f) = \int_a^b w(x)[c_0 P_0(x) + \cdots + c_{n-1}P_{n-1}(x)]\psi_n(x)\, dx$$

Finally, using the orthogonality property (5.18)(ii), it follows that $E_n(f)$ can be made identically equal to zero if we choose the quadrature points $x_1, \ldots, x_n$ to be the roots of $P_n(x)$, that is,

$$\psi_n(x) = (x - x_1)(x - x_2)\ldots(x - x_n) = K_n P_n(x)$$

It can be shown [22, p. 203] that the roots are real and lie in $[a, b]$. Next, with the quadrature points defined, we determine the coefficients a_i. For the integral (5.17), the formula corresponding to (5.5) is

$$(5.19) \quad a_i = \frac{1}{P_n'(x_i)} \int_a^b \frac{w(x)P_n(x)}{(x - x_i)}\, dx$$

It turns out (see [22, p. 333]) that the coefficients are always positive, which is good from a round-off error point of view.

To summarize, the steps in deriving a Gauss n-point rule to approximate the integral (5.17) are as follows:

(5.20)

    i   Define a set $\{P_k(x)\}_{k=0}^n$ of polynomials on $[a, b]$ that are orthogonal with respect to $w(x)$.

    ii   Find the zeros $x_1, \ldots, x_n$ of $P_n(x)$.

    iii   Determine the coefficients a_i using (5.18).

From this we obtain

$$(5.21) \quad \int_a^b w(x)f(x)\, dx = \sum_{i=1}^n a_i f(x_i) + E_n(f)$$

with $E_n(f) \equiv 0$ if $f(x)$ is a polynomial of degree $\leq 2n - 1$. Note that the weight function does *not* appear explicitly in the quadrature formula itself. Instead, it is contained implicitly in each of the coefficients a_i.

It remains to illustrate some of the rules that can be generated using various types of orthogonal polynomials. We do this by simply listing them in Table 5.1. Details concerning the polynomials cited can be found in most books on engineering mathematics or on numerical analysis. For a particular type of rule, the derivation of the x_i's and a_i's can be done as indicated in (5.20), but it is easier to simply consult a book that tabulates them (such as [30]).

TABLE 5.1

Name	$[a, b]$	$w(x)$	$P_k(x)$
1. Legendre	$[-1, 1]$	1	$\dfrac{1}{2^k k!}\left[\dfrac{d^k}{dx^k}(x^2 - 1)^k\right]$
2. Tchebychev, first kind	$[-1, 1]$	$\dfrac{1}{\sqrt{1 - x^2}}$	$\cos(k \cdot \cos^{-1} x)$
3. Laguerre	$[0, +\infty]$	e^{-x}	$e^x\left[\dfrac{d^k}{dx^k}(e^{-x}x^k)\right]$
4. Hermite	$[-\infty, +\infty]$	e^{-x^2}	$(-1)^k e^{x^2}\left[\dfrac{d^k}{dx^k}(e^{-x^2})\right]$

For Gauss–Laguerre quadrature, the interval of integration is $[0, -\infty]$, which can be very useful. The points and coefficients for a two-point rule are, to five digits,

$$x_1 = 0.58579 \qquad a_1 = 0.85355$$
$$\text{and}$$
$$x_2 = 3.4142 \qquad a_2 = 0.14645$$

The theory says that this rule is exact for all $f \in \mathcal{P}_3$. Indeed, we have

$$\int_0^\infty e^{-x}x^3 \, dx = a_1 x_1^3 + a_2 x_2^3 = 6.0001$$

which is correct except for a small amount of error due to the fact that the x_i's and a_i's are not exact. Incidentally, this type of quadrature rule gives a nice method for evaluating the Gamma function. The above example is $\Gamma(4) = 3!$.

We remark that each set of polynomials listed in Table 5.1 is orthogonal on a specific interval $[a, b]$. If the interval over which the integral is defined is different, then a transformation like (5.13) will have to be performed. For example, the interval $[5, +\infty]$ is mapped onto $[0, +\infty]$ by the transformation $x = t + 5$ and then

$$\int\limits_{5}^{\infty} e^{-x} \sin x \, dx = \int\limits_{0}^{\infty} e^{-(t+5)} \sin(t+5) \, dt$$

$$= e^{-5} \int\limits_{0}^{\infty} e^{-t} \sin(t+5) \, dt$$

$$\doteq e^{-5}[a_1 \sin(t_1+5) + \cdots + a_n \sin(t_n+5)]$$

where $t_1, \ldots, t_n$ are the zeros of the Laguerre polynomial of degree n.

One further remark concerns the case where the integrand $f(x)$ has a singularity. For example, consider the integrals

$$\int\limits_{0}^{1} x^{-1/2} \, dx \quad \text{and} \quad \int\limits_{0}^{1} x^{-1} \, dx$$

In both cases, the singularity is at the endpoint $x = 0$ so any Newton–Cotes rule will have problems. On the other hand, Gauss–Legendre rules will not encounter this difficulty since they do not need to evaluate the integrand at an endpoint. Now this is all right for the first example but it is totally misleading for the second one because this integral does not even exist! These are examples of improper integrals, which are discussed in Section 5.3.

5.2. QUADRATURE ALGORITHMS

We now consider the problem of taking a quadrature rule or combination of rules and devising an algorithm suitable for implementation as a quadrature subroutine. The basic idea of any such algorithm is to subdivide $[a, b]$ into $N - 1$ subintervals $[x_i, x_{i+1}]$, where $x_{i+1} = x_i + h_i$, $1 \le i \le N - 1$, with $x_1 = a$ and $x_N = b$, and then apply a composite quadrature formula. Note that the subdivision is not necessarily uniform. For example, the composite trapezoidal rule, with unequal subdivisions, is

$$(5.22) \quad T_N(f) = \frac{h_1}{2}(f_1 + f_2) + \frac{h_2}{2}(f_2 + f_3) + \cdots + \frac{h_{N-1}}{2}(f_{N-1} + f_N)$$

$$= \frac{h_1}{2} f_1 + \left(\frac{h_1 + h_2}{2}\right) f_2 + \cdots + \left(\frac{h_{N-2} + h_{N-1}}{2}\right) f_{N-1} + \frac{h_{N-1}}{2} f_N$$

$$= \sum_{i=1}^{N-1} \frac{h_{i-1} + h_i}{2} \cdot f_i \qquad \text{with } h_0 = h_N = 0$$

Now, given the step sizes h_i, the task of evaluating a composite formula such as (5.22) is straightforward so there is no difficulty with this aspect.

On the other hand, choosing an appropriate set of h_i's is a more intricate process. As we will see, the choice of step sizes directly affects the reliability and efficiency of a subroutine so it is important that the "step-size choosing algirithm" should strike an acceptable balance between the two measures of performance. We will consider two methods for choosing step sizes—Romberg integration and adaptive quadrature—and discuss their merits and implementation in subroutines. Both methods are based on the idea of starting with a subdivision of $[a, b]$ and successively refining it until the composite quadrature formula being used produces the required accuracy. The methods are distinguished by the way in which they do the subdivision refinement.

Before considering the methods in detail, we briefly discuss the accuracy of a composite formula. Again, using the composite trapezoidal rule as an example, we have

$$I(f; a, b) = T_N(f) + E_N(f)$$

where $E_N(f)$ is the composite quadrature error. Now, assuming that $f(x)$ is twice continuously differentiable on $[a, b]$, it follows from (5.9), that a bound for the quadrature error in each subinterval $[x_i, x_{i+1}]$ is

$$|E(f; x_i, x_{i+1})| \le \frac{h_i^3 |f''(\theta_i)|}{12} \qquad \text{for some } x_i < \theta_i < x_{i+1}$$

Summing these individual bounds and using the continuity of f'' on $[a, b]$, we get the bound

$$(5.23) \quad |E_N(f)| \le h_{\max}^2 \frac{(b-a)M_2}{12}$$

where $h_{\max} = \max_i h_i$ and $M_2 = \max_{[a, b]} |f''(x)|$. For composite rules based on other quadrature formulas—Simpson's rule, two-point Gauss–Legendre, etc.—the corresponding error bounds have the same form, that is, $|E| \le Kh_{\max}^p$, where $K > 0$ is a constant that is independent of the step sizes h_i, and p is a positive integer. Therefore, it is clear that the accuracy of a composite rule can be controlled through the choice of $h_{\max}$. For example, with the composite trapezoidal rule, it follows from (5.23) that any $h_{\max}$ satisfying the inequality

$$h_{\max}^2 \le \frac{12}{(b-a)M_2} \cdot \text{TOL}$$

will ensure that $|E_N(f)| \le \text{TOL}$. But this is not a very satisfactory procedure for choosing step sizes. In the first place, it requires knowledge of a bound M_2 on $|f''|$, which can be very inconvenient. Moreover, the bound (5.23) is often quite pessimistic with the result that $h_{\max}$ is unnecessarily small. This makes the algorithm inefficient because some needless evaluations of the integrand

$f(x)$ will have to be done. We remark that this illustrates the tradeoff between reliability and efficiency in choosing the h_i's. We will encounter it again in discussing other algorithms.

5.2.1. Romberg Integration

We assume an initial subdivision of $[a, b]$ into $N - 1$ equal subintervals $[x_i, x_{i+1}]$, where $x_i = a + (i - 1)h$, $1 \le i \le N$, with $h = (b - a)/(N - 1)$. (The size of N is not particularly important as long as it is ≥ 2.) First, we describe a simple algorithm, based on successive halving of the step-size h, for computing an approximate value for $I(f; a, b)$ to within a prescribed accuracy. We begin by computing the composite trapezoidal rule approximation $T_N(f)$ on the given subdivision. Next, we halve the step size and compute the approximation $T_{2N}(f)$—composite trapezoidal rule with $2N$ equally spaced points. If the two values agree to the required number of digits, we assume that we have sufficient accuracy[1] and take T_{2N} as our approximation for $I(f; a, b)$. If they do not agree, we halve the step size again, compute T_{4N} and compare with T_{2N}, and so on until sufficient agreement between successive approximations has been attained.

We digress for a moment to make some general comments. The above procedure follows the pattern mentioned previously, namely, it is based on successive refinement of an original subdivision of $[a, b]$ until convergence is achieved. The basic ingredients of the method, which are typical also of most quadrature algorithms, are as follows:

1. A method for refining the subdivision.
2. A composite quadrature rule for computing approximate values $Q(f)$ for $I(f; a, b)$.
3. A means of estimating the error in $Q(f)$.
4. A stopping criterion.

The algorithm is iterative in that it computes successive approximations for the value of $I(f; a, b)$. Hence, in analogy with iterative algorithms for solving nonlinear equations, we see that the stopping criterion is a critical factor affecting reliability and efficiency. We remark that this is still in line with the previous comment to the effect that the choice of step sizes h_i is the critical factor in the performance of an algorithm. This is because we can also view our algorithm as a method of determining an appropriate step

---

[1] The difference $T_N - T_{2N}$ is really an estimate for the error in T_N. This idea is a common device in numerical algorithms. It is often referred to as the *one-step, two half-step* method for estimating the error.

size. In effect, it tells us that a suitable one is $h = (b - a)/\{2^k(N - 1)\}$, where k is the number of times the subdivision is halved. The particular value of k is, of course, determined by the stopping criterion.

One disadvantage of the above algorithm is that the rate of convergence is too slow. As a remedy, we can use an extrapolation procedure due to Romberg [26]. The underlying mathematical result on which it is based is as follows:

If $f(x)$ has $2s + 2$ continuous derivatives on $[a, b]$, then

$$(5.24) \qquad I(f; a, b) = T_N + C_1 h^2 + C_2 h^4 + \cdots + C_s h^{2s} + O(h^{2s+2})$$

where $C_1, \ldots, C_s$ are independent of the step size h and T_N is the composite trapezoidal rule approximation with uniform step size [that is, the rule (5.11)].

To see how this kind of result can be used, suppose that we have computed T_N and T_{2N} using step sizes h and $h/2$, respectively. Using the expansion (5.24) with $s = 1$, we have

$$I(f; a, b) = T_N + C_1 h^2 + O(h^4)$$

and

$$I(f; a, b) = T_{2N} + C_1 \left(\frac{h}{2}\right)^2 + O(h^4)$$

The h^2 term can be eliminated by multiplying the second equation by 4 and subtracting the first one from it. We get

$$I(f; a, b) = T_{2N, 1} + C_{2, 1} h^4 + O(h^6)$$

where

$$(5.25) \qquad T_{2N, 1} = T_{2N, 0} + \frac{T_{2N, 0} - T_{N, 0}}{2^2 - 1}$$

the notation $T_{N, 0}$ for T_N having been adopted for reasons of consistency. What we have done here is show how to take the two values $T_{N, 0}$ and $T_{2N, 0}$ that have h^2 errors and extrapolate on the basis of (5.24) to form a new approximation $T_{2N, 1}$ whose error expansion has leading term of order h^4. (In fact, it can be shown that $T_{2N, 1}$ is actually the composite Simpson's rule S_N on the original subdivision.) Continuing, we again halve the step size, compute $T_{4N, 0}$, and extrapolate using this value and $T_{2N, 0}$ to obtain $T_{4N, 1}$. But it turns out that, with $s = 2$ in (5.24), we can also extrapolate from $T_{2N, 1}$ and $T_{4N, 1}$ to obtain a value $T_{4N, 2}$ whose error expansion begins with h^6 and so on. In this way we form a triangular array, called the *Romberg table*:

h^2	h^4	h^6	$\cdots$	h^{2k+1}
$T(0,0)$				
$T(1,0)$	$T(1,1)$			
$T(2,0)$	$T(2,1)$	$T(2,2)$		
.	.	.	.	
.	.	.	.	.
.	.	.	.	.
$T(k,0)$	$T(k,1)$	$T(k,2)$	$\cdots$	$T(k,k)$
.	.	.	.	. .
.	.	.	. .	. . .

(5.26)

where

$$(5.27) \quad T(k, m) = T_{2^k N, m} = T(k, m-1) + \frac{T(k, m-1) - T(k-1, m-1)}{2^{2m} - 1}$$

$$m = 1, 2, \ldots, k$$
$$k = 1, 2, \ldots$$

The process continues until a stopping criterion is met. As an example, we consider the integral

$$I(f; 0, 3) = \int_0^3 x^2 \cos x \, dx \doteq -4.952$$

Using $N = 3$, the first six rows of the Romberg table are

k \ m	0	1	2	3	4	5
0	−5.579					
1	−5.104	−5.495				
2	−4.990	−4.952	−4.952			
3	−4.962	−4.952	−4.952	−4.952		
4	−4.952	−4.952	−4.952	−4.952	−4.952	
5	−4.952	−4.952	−4.952	−4.952	−4.952	−4.952

(5.28)

From the description, it follows that the entries in the table should be computed row by row. A new row is begun by halving the current step size and calculating a new trapezoidal rule approximation. Then the rest of the entries in the row are determined using (5.27). Note that it is only necessary to store the latest row of the table at any one time since this is all that is needed to compute the entries in the next row.

The calculation of the entries in the first column of the Romberg table is equivalent to the simple algorithm described at the beginning of this section since it consists of successive trapezoidal rule approximations by interval halving. The remaining columns are the extrapolated values obtained by using (5.27). Noting that an evaluation of (5.27) requires very little computational effort—$2A + 1M + 1D$, assuming that 4^{m-1} is calculated by $4 \cdot 4^{m-2}$—we see that there is virtually no additional work in computing the Romberg table compared to the previous algorithm. Therefore, a saving can be made if convergence is achieved at some stage in the table before it occurs down the first column. For instance, in the example (5.28), convergence is achieved along the third row ($k = 2$) whereas it does not occur down the first column until the sixth row ($k = 5$). Hence, the Romberg method will save a considerable amount of work by not having to compute $T(3, 0)$, $T(4, 0)$, and $T(5, 0)$.

We now consider the question of a stopping criterion. Looking at the example (5.28), we see that convergence can occur along rows, down columns and down diagonals. It turns out to be more convenient to check along rows since this is the way we calculate and store the table. In any event, we expect faster convergence along rows because the error terms in this direction should behave like h^2, h^4, $h^6, \ldots$, whereas down, say, the first column they are like $h^2, h^2/4, h^2/16, \ldots$. Assuming that $h < 1/2$, the former sequence tends to zero much faster. Therefore, in addition to being convenient, it makes sense on theoretical grounds to check for convergence along rows. We define the row difference

$$d_r(k, m) = T(k, m) - T(k, m - 1)$$

Then a possible stopping criterion would be when a relative row difference becomes small enough, that is,

(5.29) $\quad |d_r(k, m)| \leq \text{TOL} \cdot |T(k, m)| \qquad$ for some $m \leq k$

where TOL is a specified error tolerance. We will refer to this as a test for *row convergence*. Another possible criterion would be to wait until we have row convergence in two successive rows, that is,

(5.30) $\quad |d_r(k - 1, m)| \leq \text{TOL} \cdot |T(k - 1, m)|$

$$\text{and} \qquad |d_r(k, m)| \leq \text{TOL} \cdot |T(k, m)|$$

At first glance, this may appear to embody a certain amount of overkill but we would like to guard against the possibility of the stopping criterion being fooled. For example, consider the integral

$$\int_0^2 (0.5 + x \sin \pi x) \, dx \doteq 0.3634$$

With $N = 2$, the first four rows of the Romberg table are

k \ m	0	1	2	3
0	1.000			
1	1.000	1.000		
2	0.5000	0.3333	0.2889	
3	0.3964	0.3619	0.3638	0.3650

Using (5.28) with TOL $= 1.0E - 4$, the Romberg process would have been terminated after computing only two rows and the answer (1.000) returned would be incorrect. On the other hand, using (5.30) with the same tolerance, six rows would be computed and a correct result produced. Of course, it is easy to see how to fool (5.30). We need only concoct an integrand for which both $d_r(k - 1, m)$ and $d_r(k, m)$ are zero at an early stage. An example is $f(x) = 0.5 + x \sin 2\pi x$ over $[0, 2]$. But this anomaly can be prevented by using a test based on row convergence in three successive rows, and so on. Of course the reliability increases in that the counter-examples become more pathological. On the other hand, the efficiency deteriorates because extra rows must be computed in order to ensure convergence and, for many problems, this is not necessary. Here, then, is where one must strike a balance between reliability and efficiency. It has been found that, for most integrals that arise in practice, the two-row convergence check (5.30) is adequate and this is the criterion commonly used in subroutines.

Implicit in the preceding discussion is the assumption that the error expansion (5.24) holds, that is, it contains only even powers of h. To illustrate what can happen when this condition is violated, we consider the simple example

$$(5.31) \quad I(f; 0, 1) = \int_0^1 \sqrt{x} \, dx = \tfrac{2}{3}$$

In this case, $f'(x)$ is not continuously differentiable on $[0, 1]$, which violates the conditions for the expansion (5.24) to hold. The first eight rows of the Romberg table (with $N = 2$) are shown in the following table. Computations along each row were terminated when convergence was detected.

k \ m	0	1	2	3
0	0.5000			
1	0.6036	0.6381		
2	0.6433	0.6565	0.6577	
3	0.6581	0.6630	0.6634	0.6634
4	0.6636	0.6654	0.6656	0.6656
5	0.6656	0.6663	0.6664	0.6664
6	0.6663	0.6665	0.6665	
7	0.6667	0.6668		
8	0.6667	0.6667		

Using the stopping criterion (5.30) with $\text{TOL} = 5.0E - 4$, the algorithm would terminate at $k = 4$ and return the answer 0.6656 which, of course, does not have the requested accuracy. Hence, whenever the condition (5.24) is violated, we cannot rely on the Romberg integration algorithm to give accurate results. The difficulty lies in the fact that the formula (5.27) for extrapolation is derived from (5.24) so the extrapolation process is not valid. Therefore, we need to devise a means of detecting when this situation is present and dealing with it.

We define a column difference

$$d_c(k, m) = T(k, m) - T(k - 1, m)$$

Now, assuming that (5.24) holds, it follows that the extrapolation (5.27) will yield values $T(k, m)$ such that

$$I(f; a, b) - T(k, m) = C_{m+1} \left(\frac{h}{2^k}\right)^{2(m+1)} + O(h^{2(m+2)})$$

Hence

$$d_c(k, m - 1) = C_m \left(\frac{h}{2^k}\right)^{2m} - C_m \left(\frac{h}{2^{k-1}}\right)^{2m} + O(h^{2(m+1)})$$
$$= C_m h^{2m}(1 - 4^m) \cdot 4^{-km} + O(h^{2(m+1)})$$

and

$$d_c(k - 1, m - 1) = C_m h^{2m}(1 - 4^m) \cdot 4^{-(k-1)m} + O(h^{2(m+1)})$$

Therefore

(5.32) $\quad \dfrac{d_c(k-1, m-1)}{d_c(k, m-1)} \rightarrow \dfrac{4^{-(k-1)m}}{4^{-km}} = 4^m \qquad$ as k increases

Consequently, before computing $T(k, m)$, we should first check that the ratio (5.32) of column differences approximates 4^m. In this respect, it is sufficient to have agreement to one digit so a typical test will be of the form

(5.33) $\quad \left| \left| \dfrac{d_c(k-1, m-1)}{d_c(k, m-1)} \right| - 4^m \right| \leq 0.1 \cdot 4^m$

If the test fails, we should stop computing elements in the current row and begin a new one. A Romberg algorithm that includes a test like (5.33) is said to do *cautious extrapolation* [12]. For the examples (5.28) and (5.31), the respective ratios in the first column are

(5.34)   4.17   2.61
           4.07   2.68
                   2.69
                   2.75
                   2.86

(Only two ratios are shown for (5.28) because the stopping criterion (5.30) terminates the algorithm after computation of four rows.) Hence, with $m = 1$ in (5.33), we see that extrapolation to the second column in the example (5.28) using the formula (5.27) is valid whereas, in (5.31), it is not. In the latter case, a cautious algorithm will only compute the first column of the table and convergence (to the correct answer) will be detected at $k = 8$. This raises a further point—that the stopping criterion based on the row convergence test (5.30) is no longer adequate. We must also check for *column convergence*. A suitable test is

(5.35) $\quad |d_c(k-1, m)| \leq \text{TOL } T(k-1, m)$

$$\text{and} \qquad |d_c(k, m)| \leq \text{TOL} \cdot T(k, m)$$

Again, the double check is intended to obtain a reasonable tradeoff between reliability and efficiency.

In summary, a cautious Romberg integration algorithm will employ a test of the form (5.33) to check for the validity of each extrapolation. The stopping criterion will consist of (5.30) and, whenever necessary, (5.35). Termination will occur if either one is satisfied. As the example (5.31) illustrates, the "cautiousness" aspect greatly increases the reliability of Romberg integration. Since the additional cost of performing the tests (5.33) and (5.35) is negligible, we gain the extra reliability with almost no additional cost.

Finally, we discuss the efficiency of the Romberg process. As already indicated, we measure cost by counting the number of function calls (evaluations of f) required. Now the number of function calls to compute a trapezoidal rule approximation $T(s, 0)$ is $2^s N + 1$ and, for $T(s + 1, 0)$, it is $2^{s+1} N + 1$. But there is a good deal of duplication of effort here. First, since the step size is halved at each stage, the points used for $T(s + 1, 0)$ are precisely those for $T(s, 0)$ plus the midpoints of each subinterval. Therefore, we should be able to use the function evaluations already made in the computation of $T(s, 0)$. Secondly, we note that the coefficients in the formula for $T(s + 1, 0)$ are simply one-half those for $T(s, 0)$. Consequently, instead of implementing (5.11) to compute $T(s + 1, 0)$, it is more efficient to use the formula

$$(5.36) \quad T(s + 1, 0) = \tfrac{1}{2} T(s, 0) + h_{s+1} \sum_{i=1}^{2^s N} f[a + (2i - 1)h_{s+1}]$$

where $h_{s+1} = h_s/2 = (b - a)/[2^{s+1}(N - 1)]$. Note that the value of $T(s, 0)$ is the only piece of information needed from the previous level. Therefore, even though we are making use of previously calculated values of $f(x)$, we do not have to retain them in storage. Given $T(s, 0)$, the cost of computing $T(s + 1, 0)$ by (5.36) is $2^s N$ function evaluations. Therefore, the total cost of computing the first $k + 1$ rows of the Romberg table is

$$(N + 1) + N + 2N + 2^2 N + \cdots + 2^{k-1} N = 2^k N + 1$$

the same as for computing $T(k, 0)$ alone.

5.2.2. Adaptive Quadrature

The Romberg method, as described, is a good way of automatically choosing an appropriate step size h. But it is not necessarily the most efficient way of computing the value of $I(f)$. This is because it uses a uniform subdivision of $[a, b]$ at any stage. Consider, for example, the situation in Figure 5.5. Within the region marked I, the graph of the integrand $f(x)$ does not fluctuate very much so h would not have to be very small in order to obtain good accuracy. On the other hand, it is clear that a

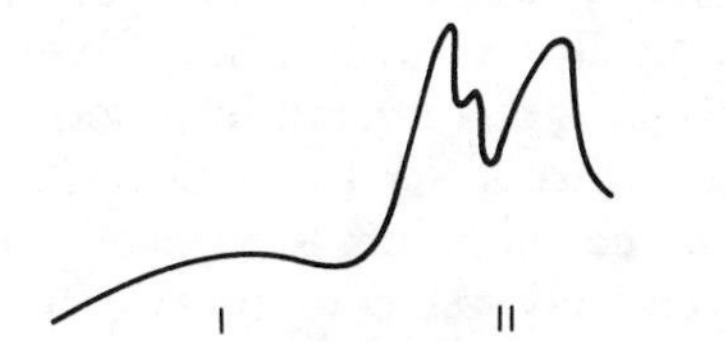

FIGURE 5.5

much smaller h would be necessary in the region marked II. The trouble with an algorithm based on a method such as Romberg extrapolation, which refines the subdivision uniformly, is that the smaller h for region II must be used over the whole interval $[a, b]$ so a lot of unnecessary function evaluations are made in region I. Therefore, it would be useful to have an algorithm which is based on a nonuniform step size and automatically "adapts" by choosing step sizes according to the behavior of $f(x)$. Algorithms which do this are called, appropriately enough, *adaptive quadrature algorithms*.

The idea of adaptive quadrature is as follows. Subdivide $[a, b]$ by $a = x_1 < \cdots < x_N = b$ and choose a basic (not composite) quadrature formula to be used in each subinterval. Take the first subinterval $[x_1, x_2]$ and apply the quadrature formula on it. Now before moving on to the next subinterval to the right, we want to decide if we have achieved sufficient accuracy on the present one. In order to make this decision, we need an error estimate and, again, we use the "one-step, two half-steps" idea. We divide $[x_1, x_2]$ in half by $x_{1.5} = x_1 + (x_2 - x_1)/2$ and apply the basic quadrature formula on each half. If the sum of the values over the two half-intervals agrees sufficiently with that over the whole subinterval, we accept this value and move on. If not, we repeat the process on the subinterval $[x_1, x_{1.5}]$, with $[x_{1.5}, x_2]$ becoming the "next subinterval to the right," and so on. The process of subdivision continues until either a subinterval is "accepted" or its width is too small to permit further refinement within machine precision. In the latter case, this is usually a sign of trouble such as a singularity in the integrand. Each time the value on a subinterval is accepted, it is added to a running total which ultimately becomes the approximate value for $I(f)$. In effect, then, this type of algorithm is a composite rule using variable step sizes h_i, which are determined dynamically rather than being preassigned.

Some remarks about the design and implementation of an adaptive algorithm should be made. First, an adaptive algorithm can be fooled into premature acceptance of a subinterval in much the same manner that Romberg integration can be fooled. A possible remedy might be to use a "one-step, two half-steps, four quarter-steps" acceptance criterion in the same spirit as requiring two-row convergence for Romberg. But, again, even this is not foolproof. In any event, it doubles the amount of work required which, for most integrals arising in practice, is not necessary. A better way of detecting problems is to look at the number of function evaluations used or else the minimum step size used. If they seem unusually low or high, respectively, the computation should be repeated using a finer subdivision of $[a, b]$ at the start.

With respect to implementation of an adaptive algorithm, we need a method for keeping track of which subinterval is "next to the right." The usual mechanism employed is a stack that operates on a last-in, first-out (LIFO) basis. There is some overhead cost in managing the stack but this is a small price to pay for the potential savings to be gained from the adaptive feature. Actually, the most elegant way to implement an adaptive quadrature algorithm is to write a recursive subroutine—one that can call itself. When a subinterval is halved, the routine can call itself twice in order to integrate over each half, and so on. This is not to say that recursion is more efficient than using a stack. It simply makes the implementation easier to understand. However, recursiveness is not available in Fortran which is the programming language used in most scientific computations, so there is, in effect, no choice. The stack structure is generally used.

An interesting idea that is sometimes used in adaptive algorithms is "banking." When a subinterval is accepted, the error estimate may be significantly below the tolerance permitted for it. The difference can then be saved against a rainy day. That is, if some subinterval along the line presents problems, then, rather than doing more subdividing in order to meet the required tolerance on it, we simply accept the interval and deduct the excess error from the savings in the bank. This is a good idea but devising a satisfactory banking strategy is not particularly easy. There are many decisions that must be made. For instance, should overdrafts be allowed, that is, should we tolerate some excess error at the outset in the hope that there will be savings to be made later on? If so, what overdraft limit shall be set? What is the maximum size of withdrawal to be permitted at any one time? Satisfactory answers to questions like these can only be found after extensive testing of various strategies over a wide range of problems.

5.2.3. Adaptive Romberg Integration

As the title of this section implies, it is possible to combine the Romberg integration method and adaptivity in one algorithm. Basically, the idea is to begin the integration using Romberg with $N = 2$, that is, no subdivision of $[a, b]$. If convergence does not occur within, say, k_{max} rows of the table, we superimpose an adaptive procedure in the following way. The interval $[a, b]$ is halved and the Romberg method is applied on the left half until either convergence occurs or else k_{max} rows have been computed. In the latter case, we halve the subinterval and apply Romberg on the left part, and so on. When convergence of Romberg occurs on a subinterval, we "accept" it, move on to the next subinterval to the right and continue. The rationale for such an algorithm lies in the fact that Romberg integration involves less overhead than an adaptive algorithm. Hence, for the same number of function calls, Romberg is cheaper. Now the two methods will use the same number of function calls in any region where $f(x)$ is sufficiently regular, that is, has no bad fluctuations. Since the degree of regularity is indicated by the rate of convergence in the Romberg table, it follows that the adaptive Romberg algorithm just described is a means of delineating the subregions where Romberg integration (with a uniform stepsize) can be applied effectively.

The best-known implementation of an adaptive Romberg algorithm is a subroutine called CADRE—Cautious ADaptive Romberg Extrapolation. It has proven to be a reliable, efficient routine and is widely available. (It is included in the IMSL package. In fact, it is the only general-purpose subroutine for one-dimensional integration contained in that package.) As the name of the routine implies, it uses cautious extrapolation. An additional feature is that it attempts to determine the error expansion automatically and modifies the extrapolation formula accordingly. To illustrate, we saw in the table for (5.31) that the extrapolation formula (5.27) is not valid when $f(x) = \sqrt{x}$. This is because the error expansion is not in powers of h^2 as in (5.24). Instead, it is

$$(5.37) \quad I(f; a, b) = T_N + C_1 h^{3/2} + O(h^2)$$

Therefore, instead of (5.25), the correct extrapolation formula to use is

$$(5.38) \quad T_{2N, 1} = T_{2N, 0} + \frac{T_{2N, 0} - T_{N, 0}}{2^{3/2} - 1}$$

Using this formula for our example, the element $T(1, 1)$ of the Romberg table will be 0.6603, which is much better than 0.6036. Now, comparing (5.25) and (5.38), the only difference is in the power of 2 used in the denominator of the correction term. Moreover, the appropriate power to be used is the same as the power of h in the first term of the error expansion. Therefore, given the latter, we can modify the Romberg extrapolation formula (5.27) suitably and make the algorithm effective for a wider class of integrals. The only difficulty with this idea is that the powers of h in the error expansion are not usually known. However, they can be estimated by taking the ratio of successive column differences as in (5.32). Indeed, we see from (5.34) that these ratios approach $2^{2/3} \doteq 2.83$ for the example $f(x) = \sqrt{x}$. This is the kind of procedure used by CADRE in order to make the correct extrapolation automatically.

5.3. IMPROPER INTEGRALS

An improper integral is one where either the integrand has a singularity within the range of integration $[a, b]$, or one (or both) of the limits of integration is infinite. The two integrals at the end of Section 5.1.2 are examples of a singular integrand. If the singularity is at $x = c$, then such integrals are well defined if

$$(5.39) \quad \lim_{\epsilon \to 0} \left[\int_a^{c-\epsilon} f(x)\, dx + \int_{c+\epsilon}^b f(x)\, dx \right] \text{ exists}$$

In this case $f(x)$ is said to have a "removable" singularity at c. For example, the integral $\int_0^1 x^{-1/2}\, dx$ has a removable singularity at $x = 0$. The value of the integral is 2. On the other hand, the integral $\int_0^1 x^{-1}\, dx$ is not defined because the limit (5.39) does not exist. The problem, then, is to recognize when such an integral is defined and to approximate its value. It would be nice if some standard procedure for doing this was known but, unfortunately, this is not the case. Consequently, quadrature subroutines are not designed to handle improper integrals of this type. Instead, the user must devise an individual means of dealing with them. We list some suggestions that can be useful. In each case, the idea is to rearrange things in order to make use of quadrature routines for proper integrals.

1. Remove the singularity by subtracting it out. We illustrate this idea with the following example taken from [7]

$$(5.40) \quad \int_0^1 \frac{dx}{x^{1/2} + x^{1/3}}\, dx = \int_0^1 \left(\frac{1}{x^{1/3}} - \frac{1}{x^{1/6}} \right) dx + \int_0^1 \frac{dx}{1 + x^{1/6}}$$

The first integral on the right side has a singular integrand but we can easily perform the integration analytically—the value is 0.3. The second integral can be evaluated using a quadrature subroutine. To see why the singularity has been "subtracted out," we have

$$\frac{1}{x^{1/2} + x^{1/3}} = \frac{1}{x^{1/3}(1 + x^{1/6})} = \frac{1}{1 + x^{1/6}} - \frac{x^{1/2} - 1}{x^{1/3}}$$

2. Modify the definition of the integrand. As an example where this can be applied, we consider the integral

$$\int_0^2 \frac{\sin x}{x}\, dx$$

Noting that $(\sin x)/x \to 1$ as $x \to 0$, we redefine the integrand as

$$f(x) = \begin{cases} \dfrac{\sin x}{x} & \text{if } x \neq 0 \\ 1 & \text{if } x = 0 \end{cases}$$

This gives an integrand that is well defined everywhere in $[0, 2]$ and no difficulty will arise in evaluating it.

3. Use a Gauss–Legendre method. In each of the above examples, the difficulty with the original form of the problem is that the integrand has a singularity at an endpoint of the interval of integration. Therefore, algorithms such as CADRE (which are based on a Newton–Cotes type of formula) will run into difficulty. We have already noted that Gauss–Legendre formulas do not use the endpoints as quadrature points. Consequently we could consider rewriting an integral like (5.40) as

$$\int_0^1 f(x)\,dx = \int_0^d f(x)\,dx + \int_d^1 f(x)\,dx$$

for some d near 0—say, $d = 0.1$. The first integral on the right side can be evaluated by an n-point Gauss–Legendre formula (with n chosen sufficiently large to achieve the required accuracy). The second integral can be evaluated by a standard routine. We remark that, in order to use this idea, it is desirable to have a Gauss–Legendre subroutine available.

4. Ignore the singularity. Consider the integral

$$\int_1^4 \frac{dx}{(x - \pi)^{1/3}}$$

The integrand has a removable singularity at $x = \pi$. If we use a Romberg algorithm to approximate the integral, the integrand will not have to be evaluated at this point because it will not be a quadrature point.

We now consider improper integrals where the limits of integration are infinite, that is,

$$\int_0^\infty f(x)\,dx \qquad \text{or} \qquad \int_{-\infty}^\infty f(x)\,dx$$

Such integrals are defined if

$$\lim_{R \to \infty} \int_0^R f(x)\,dx$$

exists, and similarly when both limits are infinite. We list two suggestions for dealing with this type of problem.

1. Use a Gauss-type formula. In Section 5.1.2, we discussed such formulas in some detail. If $f(x)$ can be written in the form $w(x)g(x)$, where $g(x)$ has polynomial-like behavior, this is a very useful method to use. A

particular advantage is that it avoids evaluations of the exponential function. For example, suppose we have the integral

$$\int_0^\infty e^{-x} \sin x \, dx$$

If we use Gauss–Laguerre quadrature, the function evaluations will only be for $g(x) = \sin x$.

2. Make the range of integration finite. We write the integral as

$$(5.41) \quad I = \int_0^\infty f(x) \, dx = \int_0^R f(x) \, dx + \int_R^\infty f(x) \, dx$$

where R is such that

$$\left| \int_R^\infty f(x) \, dx \right| < \text{TOL}$$

In effect, the value of I is found (to within an accuracy of TOL) by evaluating the integral over the finite interval $[0, R]$. Now a suitable value for R is not known but we can determine one in the following way. Choose a set of numbers $0 < R_1 < R_2 < \cdots$. Then evaluate, successively, the integrals

$$\int_0^{R_1} f(x) \, dx, \int_{R_1}^{R_2} f(x) \, dx, \ldots, \int_{R_{k-1}}^{R_k} f(x) \, dx, \ldots$$

and keep a running total of their values. The process continues until the value of the integral over, say, $[R_{n-1}, R_n]$ does not make a significant contribution to the total. At this point we conclude that the integral over $[R_n, \infty]$ is also insignificant so no further change in the total will be made. In other words, we take R_n as a good value for R in (5.41). The "running total" will be the value of the integral. We remark that nonconvergence of this process can be used as an indicator that the integral is not defined.

EXERCISES

Section 5.1

1.1. Find the coefficients for the quadrature rule

$$I(f; -1, 1) \doteq a_1 f(-\tfrac{1}{2}) + a_2 f(\tfrac{1}{2})$$

What is the maximum degree of polynomial for which it is exact?

1.2. Use the formula (5.5) to derive the coefficients for Simpson's rule (5.6). (Hint: Let $c = (a + b)/2$. Then the formula for, say, a_1 will be

$$a_1 = \int_{c-h}^{c+h} \frac{(x - c)(x - (c + h))}{(-h)(-2h)} \, dx$$

1.3. The so-called Lobatto type of Gauss quadrature formulas fixes two of the quadrature points at the endpoints, that is,

$$I(f; a, b) = a_1 f(a) + a_2 f(x_2) + \cdots + a_{n-1} f(x_{n-1}) + a_n f(b)$$

The locations of $x_2, \ldots, x_{n-1}$ are determined in the usual way by requiring the rule to be exact for as high degree a polynomial as possible.

(a) What is the maximum degree of polynomial that can be integrated exactly by an n-point formula of this type?

(b) Assume that $[a, b] = [-1, 1]$. Find the three- and four-point Lobatto formulas for this interval.

(c) Write down the composite four-point Lobatto rule for approximating $I(f; a, b)$. (Be sure the formula has no duplicate function evaluations.) Compare the accuracy and efficiency of this rule with the composite trapezoidal, Simpson, and two-point Gauss–Legendre rules.

1.4. In Table 5.1, the formula for generating Tchebychev polynomials $T_n(x)$ is given.

(a) Determine $T_0(x), \ldots, T_5(x)$.

(b) The roots of each $T_n(x)$ are real and contained in $[-1, 1]$. Prove this result. Verify it for the particular case of $T_5(x)$ by finding its roots (using a root-finding subroutine).

(c) Prove the orthogonality property (5.18)(b). Verify it for the case $n = 5$, $r = 2$, $s = 5$. What are the values of the constants $K_{r, s}$?

(d) Find the three-point Gauss–Tchebychev formula and use it to approximate each of the following integrals:

i $\displaystyle\int_{-1}^{1} \frac{dx}{\sqrt{1 - x^2}}$

ii $\displaystyle\int_{0}^{1} \frac{dx}{\sqrt{1 - x^2}}$

iii $\displaystyle\int_{0}^{1} \frac{\cos x}{\sqrt{1 - x^2}} \, dx$

1.5. Consider the Hermite polynomials $H_n(x)$ defined in Table 5.1.

(a) Determine $H_0(x), \ldots, H_5(x)$.

(b) The roots of each $H_n(x)$ are real. Verify this for $H_5(x)$.

(c) Verify the orthogonality property (5.18)(b) in the case $r = 2$, $s = 3$.

(d) Find the three-point Gauss–Hermite quadrature formula and use it to approximate each of the following integrals:

i $\quad \displaystyle\int_{-\infty}^{\infty} e^{-x^2/2} \, dx$

ii $\quad \displaystyle\int_{-\infty}^{\infty} x^2 e^{-x^2} \, dx$

iii $\quad \displaystyle\int_{-\infty}^{\infty} \cos x e^{-x^2/2} \, dx$

1.6. Consider the quadrature formula given by

$$I(g; -1, 1) = \int_{-1}^{1} g(t) \, dt \doteq \tfrac{11}{6} g(0) + \tfrac{1}{12}[g(2) + g(-2)]$$

(a) Show that this formula integrates polynomials of degree ≤ 3 exactly.

(b) Derive the corresponding formula for the general integral

$$I(f; a, b) = \int_{a}^{b} f(x) \, dx$$

(c) Show that the corresponding composite rule is

$$I(f; a, b) \doteq \frac{h}{24}[(f_{-1} + f_0) + 26(f_1 + f_2) + 30(f_3 + \cdots + f_{N-2})$$
$$+ 26(f_{N-1} + f_N) + (f_{N+1} + f_{N+2})]$$

where $f_i = f(x_i)$, with $x_i = a + ih$, $-1 \le i \le N + 2$, and $h = (b - a)/(N - 1)$.

(d) What restrictions must one place on the integrand $f(x)$ in order to apply this formula? (Hint: Try applying it to the integral $\int_0^1 (1 - x^2)^{1/2} \, dx$.)

(e) Compare the accuracy and efficiency of this composite rule with the composite Simpson and two-point Gauss–Legendre rules.

Section 5.2

2.1. Find values, correct to five significant digits, for each of the following integrals:

i $\displaystyle\int_{-1}^{2} \sin 5x \, dx$

ii $\displaystyle\int_{0}^{2} e^{\cos x} \, dx$

iii $\displaystyle\int_{0}^{1} e^x \cos\left(\frac{3\pi x}{2}\right) dx$

iv $\displaystyle\int_{0}^{2} \sqrt{1 - 0.25 \sin^2 t} \, dt$

v $\displaystyle\int_{0}^{1} x^{x^2} \, dx$

vi $\displaystyle\int_{0}^{\pi/2} \frac{\sin x}{1 + x^2} \, dx$

2.2. In order to investigate the performance of a quadrature subroutine, it is usual to apply it to a set of test problems that exhibit a variety of difficulties. The following integrals are examples of such test problems. Each of them illustrates a particular difficulty that can be made arbitrarily bad by varying a parameter. Use these examples to experiment with a quadrature subroutine. Collect statistics on accuracy and efficiency (number of function calls). The examples are taken from [12].

(a) Integrand with a peak that is much narrower than its height:

$$\int_{0}^{1} \frac{1}{\sigma^2 + (x - \beta)^2} \, dx = \frac{1}{2}\left[\tan^{-1}\left(\frac{1 - \beta}{\sigma}\right) + \tan^{-1}\left(\frac{\beta}{\sigma}\right)\right]$$

where $\sigma = 2^{-k}$. The peak is located at β and its width and height are determined by k. Try $k = 1, 2, \ldots, 8$. Choose a value of β so that it will be a quadrature point and then a value which will not be one.

(b) Highly oscillatory integrand:

$$\int_{0}^{1} x^k \sin m\pi x \, dx$$

Try $k = 0, 1, 2, 3$ and $m = 5, 10, 15, 20, 25$.

(c) Integrand with jump discontinuities:

$$\int_0^1 \lfloor mx \rfloor x^{k-1} \, dx$$

where $\lfloor mx \rfloor$ is the integral part of mx. For example, $\lfloor 15.83 \rfloor = 15$. Try the same values of k and m as in (b).

(d) Integrand with a (removable) singularity in the interval of integration

$$\int_0^1 \frac{dx}{(x - \beta)^\sigma} .$$

Try $\sigma = 0.5, 0.6, 0.75$. Choose β as in (a).

2.3. Compute the value, to five significant figures, of the integral

$$I = \int_0^1 y(x) \, dx$$

where $y(x)$ is defined implicitly by the relation

$$x^2 + x = ye^y$$

2.4. Derive the formula (5.38) assuming the expansion (5.37).

2.5. In an experiment to study a certain quadrature formula, the rule is used to evaluate an integral for which the exact result is known (from which the error can be determined precisely). The results were

Step size h	2^{-4}	2^{-5}	2^{-6}	2^{-7}
Error E	$3.50E - 6$	$5.35E - 7$	$7.56E - 8$	$1.00E - 8$

What appears to be the order of the formula? (A rule is of order p if $E = Ch^p + O(h^{p+1})$, where C is a constant.) Using this estimated value of p, devise an appropriate extrapolation formula for Romberg integration. What appears to be the order of the extrapolated formula?

2.6. Recompute the second column of the table for (5.31) using the formula (5.38). Determine the appropriate formula for extrapolating to the third column and then compute it also.

2.7. The integral

$$E(x) = \int_0^x \sqrt{1 - k^2 \sin^2 t} \, dt \qquad 0 < k < 1$$

is called an "elliptic integral of the second kind" (see [21, p. 179]). It arises in computing the arc length of an ellipse. Find, to five significant figures, the values of $x \in [0, \pi/2]$ for which $E(x) = 1.5$ when $k = 0.25, 0.5, 0.9, 0.95,$ and 0.99. Note: Efficiency can be greatly enhanced by making use of the fact that

$$E(x_1 + x_2) = E(x_1) + \int_{x_1}^{x_1 + x_2} \sqrt{1 - k^2 \sin^2 t}\, dt$$

CHAPTER 6

ORDINARY DIFFERENTIAL EQUATIONS

An *ordinary differential equation* is an equation involving derivatives of an unknown function of one independent variable. A solution of such an equation consists of an analytic expression for the function in question. Some example equations, along with their solutions, are:

	Equation	Solution
i	$y'(x) = 2x$	$y(x) = x^2 + c$
ii	$y'(x) = 2y$	$y(x) = ce^{2x}$
iii	$y'(x) = \dfrac{x}{y}$	$y(x) = \sqrt{x^2 + c}$
iv	$y''(x) = -y$	$y(x) = c_1 \cos x + c_2 \sin x$
v	$y''(x) = 5y' - 6y$	$y(x) = c_1 e^{3x} + c_2 e^{2x}$

The c's in each solution are arbitrary constants (of integration), that is, the given formulas are solutions of the corresponding equations no matter what values are assigned to the constants.

As a mathematical form, the ordinary differential equation is a very important tool. It is used in the modeling of a wide variety of physical phenomena—chemical reactions, satellite orbits, vibrating or oscillating systems, electrical networks, and so on. In many cases, the independent variable represents time so that the differential equation describes changes, with respect to time, in the system being modeled. The solution of the equation will be a representation of the state of the system at any point in time and one can use it to study the behavior of the system. Consequently, the problem of finding the solution of a differential equation plays a significant role in scientific research. In this chapter, we discuss various means for solving this problem. We begin with some general remarks concerning the form of a problem and methods of solution.

6.1. MATHEMATICAL PRELIMINARIES

Each of the solutions in the above examples is a *general* solution, that is, any solution of the corresponding equation will necessarily be of the form indicated. In examples (i) to (iii), there is one arbitrary constant c. Hence, in these cases, the general solution can be viewed as a one-parameter family of *particular* solutions. Each member of the family corresponds to a specific value of c. However, in most applications, we only want one particular solution. Therefore, an extra condition is needed in order to tell us which member of the family to select, that is, which value to assign to c. For instance, we could ask for the solution of equation (ii) that passes through the point $(0, 3)$. In other words, we want to solve the problem

$$y'(x) = 2y \qquad y(0) = 3$$

Upon substituting this extra condition into the formula for the general solution, we obtain $c = 3$, whereupon the (unique) particular solution of this problem is

$$y(x) = 3e^{2x}$$

We note that equations (iv) and (v) are of second order—since the highest-order derivative involved is second order—and the general solutions contain two arbitrary constants c_1 and c_2. Consequently, two conditions must be given in order to specify a particular solution uniquely. For instance, in equation (iv) we might have

$$y'' = 5y' - 6y \qquad \text{with} \qquad y(0) = 0 \qquad y'(0) = -1$$

Substituting these conditions into the general solution and its derivative, we obtain the system of algebraic equations

$$y(0) = \quad c_1 + \quad c_2 = 0$$
$$y'(0) = -3c_1 - 2c_2 = -1$$

whose solution is $c_1 = 1$, $c_2 = -1$. Therefore, the (unique) solution of this problem is

$$y(x) = e^{3x} - e^{2x}$$

In general, we could be given an mth-order equation—involving derivatives of $y(x)$ up to, and including, mth-order—and an extension of the preceding discussion will show that we need to specify m conditions in order to have a unique solution. We will consider problems in this form, that is, a differential equation plus the required number of conditions so that the problem has a unique solution. There is, of course, the question of the existence of a solution in the first place. However, since this topic is adequately covered in mathematical texts, we will not pursue it here. Instead, we simply assume that the appropriate conditions for the existence of a unique solution are present, and concentrate on the problem of finding it.

So far, we have only discussed differential equations for which we can write down a general formula for the solution. Unfortunately, there are relatively few equations where such a procedure is possible. Therefore, the above method for selecting a particular solution can rarely be used and we must resort to methods of approximating it. The usual approach found in most mathematics books is to construct a series representation for the solution. This technique is universal in that it can be applied to any equation. Therefore, it is worth considering as a basis for a general-purpose subroutine to approximate the solution of a differential equation. However, for many problems, it turns out that the method is not very efficient. To illustrate, we consider the example problem

$$y' = x^2 + y^2 \qquad y(0) = 1$$

in order to construct a series solution about the point $x = a$, we assume an expansion in the form

$$y(x) = b_0 + b_1(x - a) + b_2(x - a)^2 + \cdots$$

where the coefficients b_i are to be determined. To this end, we note that the Taylor series expansion of the solution about the point $x = a$ is

$$y(x) = y(a) + y'(a)(x - a) + \frac{y''(a)}{2!}(x - a)^2 + \cdots$$

and it follows that $b_0 = y(a)$, $b_1 = y'(a)$, $b_2 = y''(a)/2!$, and so on. If, for example, $a = 0$, then successive differentiation (of the differential equation) and substitution gives:

$$y' = x^2 + y^2 \qquad\qquad y'(0) = 1$$
$$y'' = 2x + 2yy' \qquad\qquad y''(0) = 2$$
$$y''' = 2 + yy'' + 2(y')^2 \qquad y'''(0) = 8$$
$$y^{(4)} = 2yy''' + 6y'y'' \qquad y^{(4)}(0) = 28$$

Therefore, the series expansion of the solution about the origin is

$$y(x) = 1 + x + x^2 + \tfrac{4}{3}x^3 + \tfrac{7}{6}x^4 + \cdots$$

One difficulty with trying to use this idea in a computational method is that it requires a symbol manipulation system, or at least an extensive pre-processing step, in order to determine expressions for the higher derivatives, and this can be very expensive. Another disadvantage arises when we want to determine a value of the solution at some point lying outside the radius of convergence of the series. In our example, for instance, the series we constructed cannot be used to find the value of, say, $y(0.1)$ because it only converges within the region $|x| < 0.069$. Now it is true that continuation could be used in this situation but, since this would amount to a repetition of the whole procedure (with the new known value, a, set equal to some point within the radius of convergence), the cost increases significantly. A third disadvantage is the cost of evaluation. Often, the rate of convergence of the series is very slow with the result that a large number of terms must be used in order to attain a required accuracy. Therefore, until a way around these disadvantages can be found, it is quite clear that the series method of solution will not be very useful as a general-purpose computational method so we will not consider it further. Instead, we look at techniques for computing a numerical approximation to the solution.

In discussing the numerical solution of differential equations, we distinguish between *initial-value problems* (IVP's) and *boundary-value problems* (BVP's). Examples of the two types are

IVP: $y''(x) = -y$ with $y(0) = 2$ $y'(0) = -1$

BVP: $y''(x) = -y$ with $y(0) = 2$ $y(3\pi/2) = 1$

The distinction between them lies in the locations where the extra conditions are specified. For an IVP, they are both given at the same value of x, whereas in the case of a BVP, they are given at two different values of x. We note that both example problems have the same solution, that is,

$$y(x) = 2 \cos x - \sin x$$

In each case, the solution is easily determined by taking the formula for the general solution, substituting the conditions, and solving the resulting system of equations for c_1 and c_2. In this situation, it does not matter whether we have an initial-value problem or a boundary-value problem. However, it turns out that the numerical methods for each type of problem are quite different so that they require separate treatment. The subject of boundary-value problems is quite extensive and a good deal of the material is beyond the level of the book. Therefore, we limit our discussion to initial-value problems.

In this chapter, we will consider the problem of solving the mth-order differential equation

$$y^{(m)} = f(x, y, y', y'', \ldots, y^{(m-1)})$$

with initial conditions

$$y(x_0) = y_0 \qquad y'(x_0) = y_0' \ldots y^{(m-1)}(x_0) = y_0^{(m-1)}$$

However, rather than deal with an initial-value problem in this form, it is usual to rewrite the differential equation as an equivalent system of m

first-order equations. Suppose, for example, that we have the third-order initial-value problem

$$y'''(x) = f(x, y, y', y'') = -y'(x)y''(x) + (x + y'(x))^2$$

$$y(0) = 1 \qquad y'(0) = 2 \qquad y''(0) = -1$$

We define new dependent variables $y_1(x), y_2(x), y_3(x)$ by

$$y_1 = y \qquad y_2 = y' \qquad y_3 = y''$$

Then the original problem is equivalent to the system of three first-order differential equations

$$y_1' = y_2 \qquad\qquad = f_1(x, y_1, y_2, y_3)$$

$$y_2' = y_3 \qquad\qquad = f_2(x, y_1, y_2, y_3)$$

$$y_3' = -y_2y_3 + (x + y_2)^2 = f_3(x, y_1, y_2, y_3)$$

with initial conditions

$$y_1(0) = 1 \qquad y_2(0) = 2 \qquad y_3(0) = -1$$

We write such systems in vector form

(6.1) $\qquad \mathbf{y}'(x) = \mathbf{f}(x, \mathbf{y}) \qquad \mathbf{y}(x_0) = \mathbf{y}_0$

where, in this particular case,

$$\mathbf{y}(x) = \begin{bmatrix} y_1(x) \\ y_2(x) \\ y_3(x) \end{bmatrix} \qquad \mathbf{f}(x, \mathbf{y}) = \begin{bmatrix} f_1(x, \mathbf{y}) \\ f_2(x, \mathbf{y}) \\ f_3(x, \mathbf{y}) \end{bmatrix} \qquad \text{and} \qquad \mathbf{y}_0 = \begin{bmatrix} 1 \\ 2 \\ -1 \end{bmatrix}$$

As a general rule, subroutines for solving initial-value problems assume that the problem is in the form (6.1) of a system of first-order equations rather than as a higher-order equation. This is because it is easier to standardize a procedure for a first-order system. In any event, since higher-order equations can easily be reduced to this form in the manner illustrated, the assumption is not a significant restriction. Therefore, we only consider first-order systems (6.1) of differential equations. In fact, to make the analysis as simple as possible, we restrict our discussion to the special case $m = 1$, that is, a single first-order equation

(6.2) $\qquad y' = f(x, y) \qquad y(x_0) = y_0$

There is no loss of generality in doing this because the numerical methods that we discuss for solving (6.2) can be directly extended to the system (6.1).

The exact solution of (6.2) is a curve in the xy-plane passing through the

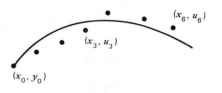

(x_6, u_6)

(x_3, u_3)

(x_0, y_0)

FIGURE 6.1

point (x_0, y_0). We define a *numerical solution* to be a set of points $\{(x_n, u_n)\}_{n=0}^{N}$, where $u_0 = y_0$ and each point (x_n, u_n) is an approximation for the corresponding point $(x_n, y(x_n))$ lying on the solution curve. (For notational convenience, we will henceforth use y_n to denote $y(x_n)$.) The situation is pictured in Figure 6.1. Note that the numerical solution is only a set of points. The process of determining a numerical solution generally proceeds from the initial point (x_0, u_0) and computes, successively, (x_1, u_1), (x_2, u_2), and so on. Again referring to Figure 6.1, this can be viewed as trying to track the trajectory of the true solution $y(x)$.

A subroutine for solving the initial-value problem (6.2) will normally be designed to compute a numerical solution over a specified interval $[x_0, x_{\text{end}}]$ and return the single value u_{end} of the numerical solution at the right-hand endpoint. That is, given the values x_0, x_{end}, and u_0, it will compute u_{end}. A calling sequence for such a routine might therefore be of the form

DEIVP(FCN,X,XEND,U,TOL)

where

FCN is a function subprogram for evaluating $f(x, y)$.

X, XEND are real variables used, on entry, to specify the left and right endpoints, respectively, of the interval of integration and, on return, X will contain the x-coordinate corresponding to the approximate solution returned in U (so that, on a normal return, X = x_{end}).

U is a real variable used to specify the initial value u_0 on entry and to return the approximate solution u_{end} on exit.

TOL is an error tolerance.

Actually, this is a rather simplified calling sequence. As we will see in Section 6.3, it is necessary to have a more elaborate one in order to provide sufficient flexibility to the user. Nevertheless, the above sequence illustrates the basic information that must be provided to a subroutine.

In order to compute u_{end} to within the specified accuracy, a routine subdivides the interval $[x_0, x_{\text{end}}]$ by $x_0 < x_1 < \cdots < x_N = x_{\text{end}}$ and successively applies a formula for advancing the solution a single step from a given point x_n to the next one x_{n+1}. But such a routine consists of more than a straightforward implementation of a particular formula. It must also decide on an appropriate subdivision of $[x_0, x_{end}]$ in order to balance the conflicting goals of reliability and efficiency. We recall that similar ideas were considered in the discussion of quadrature subroutines in Chapter 5. In fact, our treatment of initial-value problems will parallel that of quadrature. In Section 6.2, we discuss some particular formulas and then, in Section 6.3, we consider the design of algorithms for implementation as subroutines. Before proceeding, we comment that, in order to obtain the numerical solution of (6.2) at a prescribed set of points t_j, $1 \le j \le M$, we must call an IVP subroutine M times. Let T and U be $(M + 1)$-vectors and suppose $U(0)$ and $T(j)$, $0 \le j \le M$, are initialized to their specified values. Then a program segment for computing the u_j's with DEIVP is:

```
     UJ = U(0)
     XJM1 = T(0)
     DO 10 J = 1,M
       XJ = T(J)
       CALL DEIVP(F,XJM1,XJ,UJ,TOL)
       U(J) = UJ
  10 CONTINUE
```

After execution of this segment, the vector U will contain the values u_j of the numerical solution at the points t_j.

6.2. NUMERICAL FORMULAS

As in the case of quadrature rules, the literature abounds with a great variety of numerical formulas for solving initial-value problems. Again, rather than selecting a few for close scrutiny, we will try to give an overview of how to derive and assess formulas in general. To assess a formula, we use three criteria, namely, that it must

(6.3)
    i Give a unique (numerical) solution.
    ii Give an accurate approximation.
    iii Be easy to implement.

In order to illustrate these points, we look at a very simple (but not very practical) formula called *Euler's formula*. First, we derive it.

Suppose we have computed the value u_n in the numerical solution. Then an equation for the next value u_{n+1} can be obtained by approximating the derivative in the differential equation (6.2) by a difference quotient, that is,

$$\frac{u_{n+1} - u_n}{x_{n+1} - x_n} = f(x_n, u_n)$$

or

(6.4) $\quad u_{n+1} = u_n + hu'_n$

where $h = x_{n+1} - x_n$ is the *step size*, and $u'_n = f(x_n, u_n)$. This is Euler's formula. We illustrate its use with the example problem

(6.5) $\quad y' = y - 2 \sin x \qquad y(0) = 1$

whose analytic solution is $y = \sin x + \cos x$. Taking $h = 0.2$ and applying (6.4) successively, we obtain

$u_0 = \underline{1.0}$ $\qquad\qquad$ $u'_0 = f(0.0, 1.0) \quad = 1.000$

$u_1 = 1.000 + (0.2)(1.000) \; = \underline{1.200}$ $\qquad$ $u'_1 = f(0.2, 1.200) = 0.8027$

$u_2 = 1.200 + (0.2)(0.8027) = \underline{1.361}$ $\qquad$ $u'_2 = f(0.4, 1.361) = 0.5822$

$u_3 = 1.361 + (0.2)(0.5822) = \underline{1.477}$ $\qquad$ $u'_3 = f(0.6, 1.477) = 0.3477$

$u_4 = 1.477 + (0.2)(0.3477) = \underline{1.547}$ $\qquad$ $u'_4 = f(0.8, 1.547) = 0.1123$

and so on. More results are tabulated in Table 6.1. It is easy to see that, for any fixed $h \neq 0$, this formula satisfies criteria (i) and (iii) of (6.3). In order to check the second criterion, we must first define what is meant when we say that a numerical formula gives an "accurate approximation." To do this, we need to discuss errors.

First of all, we define the difference

(6.6) $\quad E_{n+1} = y_{n+1} - u_{n+1}$

between the true solution and the numerical solution at $x = x_{n+1}$ to be the *global error* in u_{n+1}. Then the value u_{n+1} in the numerical solution will be considered accurate if its global error E_{n+1} is sufficiently small. Of course, our ultimate goal is to compute an accurate numerical solution, but the present concern is to assess the performance of a numerical formula, not the accuracy of a numerical solution. At first glance, these two aspects may appear to be indistinguishable, but there is a difference and it is a very important one. We illustrate with the above example. Consider the step from $x_3 = 0.6$ to $x_4 = 0.8$ and suppose, for the moment, that we want to determine the value of the global error E_4 in u_4. Now, in this particular example, we can use (6.6) to compute the global error directly because the true solution $y(x)$ is known explicitly. We obtain

$$E_4 = y(0.8) - u_4 = 1.414 - 1.547 = -0.133$$

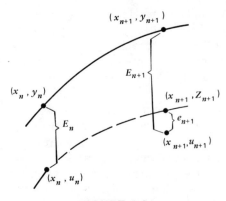

FIGURE 6.2

But since it is not realistic to assume that the true solution is known, we should try to estimate E_4 by some other means. To this end, we consider the one-step, two half-steps idea that was suggested for estimating the error in adaptive quadrature. That is, we compute the value u_{n+1} from u_n using Euler's formula (6.4) with step-size h, and then compute another value $\hat{u}_{n+1}$ using (6.4) twice with step-size $h/2$. The difference $\hat{u}_{n+1} - u_{n+1}$ between the two values will be an error estimate. For our example, we obtain $u_{3.5} = 1.512$ and $\hat{u}_4 = 1.534$, giving

$$\hat{u}_4 - u_4 = -0.013$$

which is not even close to the correct value. Obviously, this is not a good way to estimate the global error. The reason is that the difference $\hat{u}_{n+1} - u_{n+1}$ is only an estimate for the error committed in taking the single step from (x_n, u_n) to (x_{n+1}, u_{n+1}) and takes no account whatever of the error that is already present in u_n. Actually, it is best to view $\hat{u}_{n+1}$ as an aproximation to the solution, at $x = x_{n+1}$, of the *local problem*

(6.7) $\quad z'(x) = f(x, z) \qquad z(x_n) = u_n$

where f is the same function as in the original differential equation (6.2). In Figure 6.2, we illustrate the situation. The point (x_{n+1}, z_{n+1}) is the true solution of the local problem (6.7) at $x = x_{n+1}$. *Consequently, the difference* $\hat{u}_{n+1} - u_{n+1}$ is actually an estimate for the *local error*

(6.8) $\quad e_{n+1} = z_{n+1} - u_{n+1}$

that is, the error that is created by assuming that the value u_n is correct and applying the numerical formula to compute u_{n+1} from it. In other words, the local error e_{n+1} is an indicator of the performance of a numerical formula in taking a single step, rather than a reflection of the overall error in the numerical solution. Hence, recalling criterion (ii) of (6.3), we say that a formula "gives an accurate approximation" if its local error can be made sufficiently small, that is, if it gives an accurate approximate solution to the local problem.

To summarize the foregoing discussion, we have two definitions of error—the local error e_{n+1} and the global error E_{n+1}. The global error has two components, namely, the local error e_{n+1} and the difference $E_{n+1} - e_{n+1}$. The latter component is often called the *propagated error* because, as we see from Figure 6.2, it can regarded as that part of E_{n+1} resulting from the propagation (by the solution of the differential equation) of the global error E_n from the previous step. In the step-by-step computation of a numerical solution of (6.2), we are interested in controlling the global error at each point. However, from our discussion, it is evident that this must be done indirectly through control of the local error in each step. As we will see next, the local errors are relatively easy to control. The difficulty lies in deciding, in advance, how small to make each e_i so that the global errors are within a specified tolerance. We examine this problem in Section 6.3. For the present, we only consider the control of local errors.

An expression for the local error can be obtained by a comparison of the formula for u_{n+1} with the Taylor series expansion of the local solution $z(x)$ of (6.7) about the point x_n. Again, we illustrate the idea with Euler's formula. Assuming continuity of z'', the Taylor expansion is

$$z_{n+1} = z(x_n + h) = z_n + hz_n' + \frac{h^2}{2} z''(\theta_n)$$

$$= z_n + hf(x_n, z_n) + \frac{h^2}{2} z''(\theta_n)$$

$$= u_n + hf(x_n, u_n) + \frac{h^2}{2} z''(\theta_n)$$

where $x_n < \theta_n < x_{n+1}$. Subtracting (6.4) from this and using the fact that z'' is bounded on $[x_n, x_{n+1}]$ (since it is continuous), we obtain

$$(6.9) \quad e_{n+1} = z_{n+1} - u_{n+1} = \frac{h^2}{2} z''(\theta_n) = O(h^2)$$

From this result we see that the local error e_{n+1} in each step of Euler's formula (6.4) can be made as small as we like, provided the step-size h is chosen sufficiently small. Consequently, according to our interpretation, Euler's formula satisfies criterion (ii) of (6.3).

The preceding type of analysis can be applied to other numerical formulas for initial-value problems. In general, we can show that the local error of a formula is $e_{n+1} = O(h^{p+1})$, where p is a positive integer depending on the particular formula under consideration. We say that the formula is *pth-order accurate*. For example, Euler's formula is first-order accurate. The order of accuracy provides us with a means of comparing various numerical formulas. Roughly speaking, if the value of p for one formula is greater than that of another one, then the former will be considered superior on the basis of accuracy.

Another aspect of a numerical formula that we must consider is computational cost. This is usually measured by counting the number of evaluations of the function $f(x, y)$ required to take one step. Actually, we are interested in the total cost of computing u_{end} starting from (x_0, u_0). This is determined by multiplying the cost per step times the number of steps required. The latter factor is dictated by the size of the step-sizes h_n which, in turn, depends on the order of the formula being used. However, this topic is not considered until Section 6.3. For now, we only discuss the cost per step. We define a *step* as the computation of both u_{n+1} and an estimate for the local error e_{n+1}. As we will see in Section 6.3, the latter is important because it is useful for determining an appropriate step size. The usual procedure for estimating e_{n+1} is to compute an additional value $\hat{u}_{n+1}$, which is more accurate than u_{n+1}, that is,

$$|z_{n+1} - \hat{u}_{n+1}| < |z_{n+1} - u_{n+1}|$$

and then use the approximation

(6.10) $e_{n+1} = z_{n+1} - u_{n+1} \doteq \hat{u}_{n+1} - u_{n+1}$

We have already illustrated this idea with respect to Euler's formula. In that example, $\hat{u}_{n+1}$ was generated by taking two half-steps so that the total cost of a step was two functions evaluations—one for computing u_{n+1} and one for $\hat{u}_{n+1}$, assuming that the value of $u'_n = f(x_n, u_n)$ is retained from the computation of u_{n+1}.

We now discuss some other numerical formulas. There are two distinct classes of them—Runge–Kutta and multistep—which we discuss separately.

6.2.1. Runge–Kutta Formulas

We begin by showing how to derive the simplest formulas in this class. These are of the form

(6.11) $u_{n+1} = u_n + (w_1 k_1 + w_2 k_2)$

where

$$k_1 = hf(x_n, u_n)$$

$$k_2 = hf(x_n + ah, u_n + bk_1)$$

The parameters a, b, w_1, and w_2 are chosen in order to make the formula as accurate as possible, that is, to make the order of accuracy as large as possible. To this end, we substitute the true values z_n, z_{n+1} of the local solution into the formula (6.11) and expand about the point x_n. The parameters are then chosen to make the resulting expansion agree as much as possible with the Taylor series for z_{n+1} about x_n. Upon substituting into (6.11), we first obtain the expansion

$$k_2 = hf(x_n + ah, z_n + bk_1)$$

$$= h\left[f + h(af_x + bff_y) + \frac{h^2}{2}(a^2 f_{xx} + 2abff_{xy} + b^2 f^2 f_{yy}) + O(h^3)\right]_n$$

where the subscripts on f denote partial derivatives with respect to the indicated variables, and the subscript n on the square brackets indicates evaluation at the point (x_n, z_n). Hence, the expansion of (6.11) is

$$
\begin{aligned}
z_{n+1} &= z_n + h[w_1 f(x_n, z_n) + w_2 f(x_n + ah, z_n + bk_1)] \\
(6.12)\quad &= z_n + h[(w_1 + w_2)f]_n + h^2 w_2[af_x + bff_y]_n \\
&\quad + \frac{h^3}{2} w_2[a^2 f_{xx} + 2abff_{xy} + b^2 f^2 f_{yy}]_n + O(h^4)
\end{aligned}
$$

The Taylor expansion of z_{n+1} about x_n is

$$
\begin{aligned}
z_{n+1} &= z_n + hz_n' + \frac{h^2}{2} z_n'' + \frac{h^3}{3!} z_n''' + O(h^4) \\
(6.13)\quad &= z_n + hf_n + \frac{h^2}{2}(f_x + ff_y)_n \\
&\quad + \frac{h^3}{3!}[f_{xx} + 2ff_{xy} + f^2 f_{yy} + f_y(f_x + ff_y)]_n + O(h^4)
\end{aligned}
$$

We can make these expressions agree up to, and including, terms in h^2 by equating coefficients of like powers of h. Doing this, we have

$$hf \quad : w_1 + w_2 = 1$$

$$h^2 f_x \quad : \quad aw_2 = \tfrac{1}{2}$$

$$h^2 ff_y : \quad bw_2 = \tfrac{1}{2}$$

This is a system of three (nonlinear) equations in the four unknowns a, b, w_1, w_2, and its solution can be written in the form

$$b = a \qquad w_2 = \frac{1}{2a} \qquad w_1 = 1 - w_2$$

where $a \neq 0$ is arbitrary. Hence, (6.11) defines a one-parameter family of formulas, each of which is second-order accurate. We remark that it is not possible to obtain any better accuracy with formulas of the form (6.11) because it is impossible to equate all of the coefficients of $h, h^2,$ *and* h^3 in (6.12) and (6.13). This is evident from the fact that (6.12) does not contain terms in either $h^3 f_x f_y$ or $h^3 f f_y^2$, which are present in (6.13). Hence, we cannot obtain agreement of (6.11) with the Taylor expansion of z_{n+1} to terms in h^3.

Taking $a = 1$ in (6.11), we get the particular formula

(6.14) $u_{n+1} = u_n + \frac{1}{2}(k_1 + k_2)$

where

$$k_1 = hf(x_n, u_n)$$

$$k_2 = hf(x_n + h, u_n + k_1)$$

Some results from applying this formula to the example problem (6.5) are given in Table 6.1. It is interesting to look at a geometric interpretation of the formula. First, we rewrite it in the form

(6.15) $u_{n+1} = u_n + \frac{1}{2}h[f(x_n, u_n) + f(x_{n+1}, v_{n+1})]$

where $v_{n+1} = u_n + k_1 = u_n + hf(x_n, u_n)$. Hence, u_{n+1} is obtained by taking the previous value u_n and adding h times the average of two values of $f(x, y)$. As shown in Figure 6.3, the point (x_{n+1}, v_{n+1}) where the second evaluation takes place is obtained by moving a distance h, in the horizontal direction, along the line through (x_n, u_n) with slope $m_1 = f(x_n, u_n)$. At this point, we compute another slope $m_2 = f(x_{n+1}, v_{n+1})$. Finally, we determine u_{n+1} by moving a (horizontal) distance h along the line through (x_n, u_n) with slope $m = (m_1 + m_2)/2$, that is, the average of m_1 and m_2.

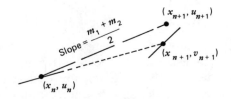

FIGURE 6.3

Higher-order (more accurate) Runge–Kutta formulas can be derived in a similar way. The general form of such formulas is

$$u_{n+1} = u_n + (w_1 k_1 + w_2 k_2 + \cdots + w_s k_s)$$

where

$$k_i = hf(x_n + a_i h, u_n + b_{i,1} k_1 + \cdots + b_{i,i-1} k_{i-1}) \qquad 1 \le i \le s$$

We remark that (6.11) is of this form with $a_1 = 0$ and $a_2 = a$. The parameters a_i, $b_{i,j}$ are chosen to give as high order accuracy as possible. If a pth-order accurate formula is desired, we must take s large enough so that a sufficient number of degrees of freedom (parameters) are available in order to obtain agreement with the Taylor expansion of z_{n+1}, truncated after terms in h^p. A table showing the minimum s for given p is

p	2	3	4	5	6	
s	2	3	4	6	8	$\cdots$

Since s represents the number of evaluations of f, this table shows the minimum amount of work required to achieve a desired order of accuracy with a Runge–Kutta formula. We observe that there is a jump in s from 4 to 6 as p goes from 4 to 5. This means that there is a fourth-order accurate formula that only requires four function evaluations whereas, to get fifth-order accuracy, at least six evaluations are needed. The extra work required (half again as much) to obtain the extra-order of accuracy has traditionally been considered not worth the extra effort so that fourth-order formulas have been quite popular. The classical fourth-order formula is

$$(6.16) \qquad u_{n+1} = u_n + \tfrac{1}{6}(k_1 + 2k_2 + 2k_3 + k_4)$$

where

$$k_1 = hf(x_n, u_n)$$

$$k_2 = hf(x_n + \tfrac{1}{2}h, u_n + \tfrac{1}{2}k_1)$$

$$k_3 = hf(x_n + \tfrac{1}{2}h, u_n + \tfrac{1}{2}k_2)$$

$$k_4 = hf(x_n + h, u_n + k_3)$$

We now turn to the problem of computing a second (more accurate) value $\hat{u}_{n+1}$ in order to estimate the local error e_{n+1}. For Runge–Kutta formulas, using the one-step, two half-steps procedure can be very expensive. Consider, for instance, the fourth-order formula (6.16). The cost of each step would be 11 function evaluations—4 for u_{n+1} and 7 for $\hat{u}_{n+1}$. The following table shows the minimum cost per step for pth-order accurate formulas using two half-steps to compute $\hat{u}_{n+1}$:

p	2	3	4	5	6
No. eval. of f per step	5	8	11	14	17	. . .

A better procedure, known as Fehlberg's[1] method, is to compute $\hat{u}_{n+1}$ using a Runge–Kutta formula of higher-order accuracy than the one used for u_{n+1}. This may seem inefficient but the key is to use a pair of formulas with a common set of k_i's. For example, the Runge–Kutta–Fehlberg fourth-order pair of formulas is

$$u_{n+1} = u_n + \left(\frac{25}{216} k_1 + \frac{1408}{2565} k_3 + \frac{2197}{4104} k_4 - \frac{1}{5} k_5\right)$$

with $e_{n+1} = O(h^5)$

(6.17)

$$\hat{u}_{n+1} = u_n + \left(\frac{16}{135} k_1 + \frac{6656}{12{,}825} k_3 + \frac{28{,}561}{56{,}430} k_4 - \frac{9}{50} k_5 + \frac{2}{55} k_6\right)$$

with $\hat{e}_{n+1} = O(h^6)$

where

$$k_1 = hf(x_n, u_n)$$

$$k_2 = hf\left(x_n + \frac{1}{4} h, u_n + \frac{1}{4} k_1\right)$$

$$k_3 = hf\left(x_n + \frac{3}{8} h, u_n + \frac{3}{32} k_1 + \frac{9}{32} k_2\right)$$

$$k_4 = hf\left(x_n + \frac{12}{13} h, u_n + \frac{1932}{2197} k_1 - \frac{7200}{2197} k_2 + \frac{7296}{2197} k_3\right)$$

$$k_5 = hf\left(x_n + h, u_n + \frac{439}{216} k_1 - 8k_2 + \frac{3680}{513} k_3 - \frac{845}{4104} k_4\right)$$

$$k_6 = hf\left(x_n + \frac{1}{2} h, u_n - \frac{8}{27} k_1 + 2k_2 - \frac{3544}{2565} k_3 + \frac{1859}{4104} k_4 - \frac{11}{40} k_5\right)$$

We remark that, despite the complicated appearance, this pair of formulas is considered easy to implement since it can be coded in a straightforward way. Looking at efficiency, we observe that the formula for u_{n+1} is fourth-order accurate and requires five function evaluations, which is more

---

[1]The idea for the so-called Runge–Kutta–Fehlberg formulas was first proposed by Merson [1957]. It was refined and popularized by Fehlberg [1969, 1970].

expensive than the formula (6.16) for the same-order of accuracy. However, $\hat{u}_{n+1}$ can be obtained at the cost of only one more function evaluation (to compute k_6). Therefore, the total cost of a step using (6.17) is only six function evaluations compared to 11 for (6.16) using two half-steps to compute $\hat{u}_{n+1}$. In addition, since (6.17) gives a $\hat{u}_{n+1}$ that is significantly more accurate than u_{n+1}, we get a more reliable estimate for e_{n+1}. The following table shows the cost per step for a pair of formulas of order p and $p + 1$:

$p, p + 1$	2, 3	3, 4	4, 5	5, 6	
No. eval. of f per step	3	4	6	8	$\cdots$

Comparing this with the previous table, we see that Fehlberg-type pairs of Runge–Kutta formulas are much more efficient than single formulas of comparable accuracy. For this reason, they are the preferred Runge–Kutta formulas for use in subroutines.

6.2.2. Multistep Formulas

This class of formulas is based on the idea of making use of previous values of the solution and its derivative in order to extrapolate to the next one. We begin by discussing a particular subclass called Adams–Bashforth formulas. The general form is

$$(6.18) \quad u_{n+1} = u_n + h \sum_{i=1}^{k} b_i u'_{n-i+1}$$

where $u'_s = f(x_s, u_s)$. This is called a k-*step* formula because it uses information from the previous k steps. We note that Euler's formula (6.4) is of this form—it is a one-step formula ($k = 1$) with $b_1 = 1$. The coefficients b_i in (6.18) are chosen in the familiar way, that is, by assuming that the past values of u are exact, and equating like powers of h in the expansion of the formula (6.18) and of the local solution z_{n+1} about x_n. We illustrate the procedure in the case of a three-step formula

$$u_{n+1} = u_n + h(b_1 u'_n + b_2 u'_{n-1} + b_3 u'_{n-2})$$

Substituting values of z into this and expanding about x_n, we have

$$z_{n+1} = z_n + hz'_n(b_1 + b_2 + b_3) - h^2 z''_n(b_2 + 2b_3) + \frac{h^3}{2!} z'''_n (b_2 + 4b_3) + \cdots$$

The Taylor series expansion of z_{n+1} is

$$z_{n+1} = z_n + hz'_n + \frac{h^2}{2!} z''_n + \frac{h^3}{3!} z'''_n + \cdots$$

and, on equating terms in like powers of h, we obtain the system of (linear) equations

$$hz_n' \ : b_1 + b_2 + b_3 = \ 1$$

$$h^2 z_n'' : \quad b_2 + 2b_3 = -\tfrac{1}{2}$$

$$h^3 z_n''' : \quad b_2 + 4b_3 = \ \tfrac{1}{3}$$

The solution of the system is given by $b_1 = \tfrac{23}{12}$, $b_2 = -\tfrac{16}{12}$, $b_3 = \tfrac{5}{12}$, whereupon the Adams–Bashforth three-step formula is

$$(6.19) \quad u_{n+1} = u_n + \frac{b}{12}(23u_n' - 16u_{n-1}' + 5u_{n-2}')$$

with error $e_{n+1} = O(h^4)$. Some results from applying this formula to solve the problem (6.5) are given in Table 6.1.

A difficulty with multistep formulas is that they are not self-starting. For instance, in (6.19), we need values for u_2, u_0', u_1', and u_2' before we can begin using the formula to compute a numerical solution. Actually, the problem is to compute the "starting values" u_1 and u_2 because, once these are determined, the required derivative values can easily be obtained by

TABLE 6.1
COMPARATIVE NUMERICAL SOLUTIONS OF $y' = y - 2 \sin x$, $y(0) = 1.0$ WITH STEP-SIZE $h = 0.25$

n	x_n	y_n	Euler (6.4)	Runge–Kutta Second-order (6.12)	Adams–Bashforth Three-step (6.19)	Adams–Moulton Three-step PC (6.21)
0	0.0	1.000	1.0	1.0	1.0	1.0
1	0.25	1.216	1.250	1.219	(1.219)	(1.219)
2	0.50	1.357	1.439	1.365	(1.357)	(1.357)
3	0.75	1.413	1.559	1.429	1.412	1.413
4	1.00	1.382	1.608	1.408	1.378	1.381
5	1.25	1.246	1.589	1.304	1.257	1.263
6	1.50	1.068	1.512	1.125	1.057	1.066
7	1.75	0.8057	1.391	0.8837	0.7894	0.8028
8	2.00	0.4932	1.247	0.5974	0.4704	0.4894
9	2.25	0.1499	1.104	0.2867	0.1198	0.1451
10	2.50	−0.2027	0.9910	−0.0255	−0.2418	−0.2089

substituting into the differential equation. The traditional technique for computing starting values has been to use a Runge–Kutta formula (of comparable accuracy) since it would only require the initial value u_0 in order to get started. An alternative procedure, which turns out to be more efficient, is to use a sequence of s-step formulas, with $s = 1, 2, \ldots, k$. The computation is started with the one-step formula in order to provide starting values for the two-step formula. This, in turn, is used to provide starting values for the three-step formula, and so on until the desired k-step formula is reached. (For details, see [28].) This is the kind of procedure currently used in multistep subroutines.

We note that the problem of starting values also arises whenever the step-size h is changed from one step to another. Suppose, in our example, that we want to change the step-size from 0.25 to 0.125 after computing $u_4 = u(1.00)$. Then, order to compute the value $u_5 = u(1.125)$, the formula (6.19) needs the values of $u'(0.75)$, $u'(0.875)$ and $u'(1.00)$. Consequently, we cannot proceed until a value for $u'(0.875)$ is obtained. Again, this problem has traditionally been resolved by using a Runge–Kutta formula to compute $u(0.875)$, and then evaluating f. But the cost of doing this is four function evaluations—three for $u(0.875)$ (assuming a third-order accurate Runge–Kutta formula is used) and one for $u'(0.875)$—which is quite high compared to the cost of a single application of (6.19). As before, there is a more efficient procedure that is used in present-day subroutines. Briefly, the idea is to employ k-step formulas whose coefficients (b_i's) depend on the past step-sizes $h_s = x_s - x_{s-1}$, $s = n, n - 1, \ldots, n - k + 1$. (Again, see [28] for details.) However, while this turns out to be a less expensive procedure, the important point is that step-size changes with multistep formulas will inevitably involve some extra computational cost.

Now we consider the question of how to compute an additional value $\hat{u}_{n+1}$ in order to estimate the local error e_{n+1}. To begin, the one-step, two half-steps procedure seems reasonable since it would only require one extra function evaluation for $\hat{u}_{n+1}$ giving a total of two evaluations per step. However, since this approach compounds the cost of changing the step size, it is not very satisfactory after all. A better procedure is to use a "corrector" formula to compute $\hat{u}_{n+1}$. We consider the class of Adams–Moulton corrector formulas, that is,

$$(6.20) \quad u_{n+1} = u_n + h \sum_{i=0}^{k} b_i u'_{n-1+i}$$

Comparing this with (6.18), we see that the only difference is the additional term $hb_0 u'_{n+1}$ in (6.20). Let us discuss the particular case $k = 2$, that is, the two-step formula

$$u_{n+1} = u_n + h(b_0 u'_{n+1} + b_1 u'_n + b_2 u'_{n-1})$$

As in the derivation of (6.19), we choose the b_i's in order to obtain as much agreement as possible with the Taylor expansion of z_{n+1}. Doing this, we arrive at the formula

(6.21) $\quad u_{n+1} = u_n + \dfrac{h}{12}(5u'_{n+1} + 8u'_n - u'_{n-1})$

with error $e_{n+1} = O(h^4)$. Now a complication with using this formula is the occurrence of $u'_{n+1} = f(x_{n+1}, u_{n+1})$ on the right-hand side. In other words, u_{n+1} is defined implicitly in terms of itself so that (6.21) is not an easy formula to use on its own. Instead, we combine it with (6.19) to form a *predictor-corrector* pair of formulas. We use (6.19) to obtain a "predicted" value $u_{n+1}^{(p)}$ and then compute a "corrected" value $\hat{u}_{n+1}$ using (6.21) with the value of u'_{n+1} on the right-hand side approximated by $(u_{n+1}^{(p)})' = f(x_{n+1}, u_{n+1}^{(p)})$. The combination (6.19) and (6.21) is called an Adams–Moulton predictor-corrector pair of formulas; it has third-order accuracy. We illustrate its use with the example problem (6.5). Taking $h = 0.25$ and computing the starting values u_1 and u_2 as before, we have

$u_0 = \underline{1.0}$

$u_1 = \underline{1.216}$

$u_2 = \underline{1.357}$

$\quad u_3^{(p)} = 1.357 + \dfrac{0.25}{12}[23(0.3981) - 16(0.7212) + 5(1.000)] = 1.412$

$u_3 = \hat{u}_3 = 1.357 + \dfrac{0.25}{12}[5(0.0487) + 8(0.3981) - (0.7212)] = \underline{1.413}$

$\quad u_4^{(p)} = 1.413 + \dfrac{0.25}{12}[23(0.497) - 16(0.3981) + 5(0.7212)] = 1.379$

$u_4 = \hat{u}_4 = 1.413 + \dfrac{0.25}{12}[5(-0.3039) + 8(0.0497) - (0.3981)] = \underline{1.381}$

and so on. Again, more results are tabulated in Table 6.1.

The cost of computing $\hat{u}_{n+1}$ by (6.21) is one extra function evaluation. Therefore, the total cost per step of the formula pair (6.19)–(6.21) is two function evaluations. One can embellish the procedure by using the corrector formula more than once. Initially, we determine a predicted value $u_{n+1}^{(0)}$ using (6.19) and then compute, successively, the corrected values $u_{n+1}^{(s)}$, $s = 1, 2, \ldots$, using (6.21) with $u_{n+1}^{(s-1)}$ on the right-hand side. The process would continue until convergence occurs. We denote the procedure by

PECEC..., where P represents a computation using the predictor formula, E represents an evaluation of f, and C represents a computation using the corrector formula. $\hat{u}_{n+1}$ is taken as the most recent corrected value. For most problems occurring in practice, convergence generally occurs within one or two iterations so that, rather than worry about testing for convergence, a subroutine implementation usually performs a fixed number of corrections. Suppose the number is two. Then, in our notation, a single step with the formula pair (6.19) and (6.21) would consist of the sequence $P(EC)^2$, and the cost per step is three function evaluations.

We have yet to consider the actual computation of an estimate for the local error. We observe that the error in each of the formulas (6.19) and (6.21) is $O(h^4)$. Therefore, the difference $\hat{u}_{n+1} - u_{n+1}$ would appear to be a poor estimate for e_{n+1}. However, it turns out that we can use $\hat{u}_{n+1}$ to obtain a reasonable estimate. Let us see how. It is possible (see Exercise 3) to determine more precise expressions for the errors in each of the formulas (6.19) and (6.21). These are, respectively,

$$(6.22) \quad e_{n+1} = \tfrac{3}{8}h^4 y^{(4)}(\theta_p) \quad \text{and} \quad \hat{e}_{n+1} = -\tfrac{1}{24}h^4 y^{(4)}(\theta_c)$$

where $x_{n-2} < \theta_p$, $\theta_c < x_{n+1}$. Let us assume that, at least for small h, $\theta_p = \theta_c = \theta$. Then, subtracting the two error expressions (6.22), we have

$$\hat{e}_{n+1} - e_{n+1} = \hat{u}_{n+1} - u_{n+1} = -\tfrac{5}{12}h^4 y^{(4)}(\theta)$$

Solving for $h^4 y^{(4)}(\theta)$ and substituting into the expression for $\hat{e}_{n+1}$, we obtain the estimate

$$(6.23) \quad \hat{e}_{n+1} \doteq \tfrac{1}{10}(\hat{u}_{n+1} - u_{n+1})$$

for the local error in $\hat{u}_{n+1}$. Note that this is an error estimate for the more accurate value so that $\hat{u}_{n+1}$ can be used in our numerical solution rather than u_{n+1}. We remark that this type of analysis is not used in the case of Runge–Kutta formulas because the error expressions are very complicated and difficult to manipulate in the above fashion.

The preceding discussion was concerned with various aspects of the three-step Adams–Moulton formula pair (6.19)–(6.21). The same ideas hold for any k-step predictor-corrector pair of formulas, the only difference being that a k-step formula will be kth-order accurate and the formula for estimating $\hat{e}_{n+1}$ corresponding to (6.23) will have a different constant.

Finally, a word about general multistep formulas. These are of the form

$$(6.24) \quad u_{n+1} = \sum_{i=1}^{k} a_i u_{n-i+1} + h \sum_{i=0}^{k} b_i u'_{n-i+1}$$

Both of the Adams k-step formulas (6.18) and (6.20) correspond to the case $a_1 = 1$ and $a_2 = \cdots = a_k = 0$. If $b_0 = 0$, (6.24) is a predictor formula. Otherwise, it is a corrector. Since there are $2k + 1$ parameters (in the case of a corrector), we might expect to obtain a $(2k + 1)$th-order formula. That is, we can obtain agreement with the Taylor expansion of the local solution z_{n+1} up to terms in h^{2k+1}. However, it turns out that we must impose some other restrictions (see [24, p. 181]) on the parameters in order to get a useful formula so that the best we can do is $(k + 1)$th-order accuracy, which is no better than a k-step Adams–Moulton formula. For this reason, along with the fact that their formulas are simpler than (6.24), Adams-type formulas are generally preferred for multistep subroutines.

6.3. SUBROUTINES

We now consider the problem of taking a formula or combination of formulas and designing an algorithm for a subroutine. The basic idea of such an algorithm is to subdivide the interval $[x_0, x_{\text{end}}]$ of integration by the points $\{x_n\}_{n=0}^N$ and apply the formula to compute, successively, the values $u_1, u_2, \ldots, u_N$ of the numerical solution subject to the requirement that the final value $u_N = u_{\text{end}}$ is sufficiently close to the true one $y_{\text{end}} = y(x_{\text{end}})$, that is, the global error E_{end} is sufficiently small. But this is easier said than done. As we have already seen, the global error can only be controlled indirectly through control of the local errors e_n. The difficulty lies in predicting the cumulative effect of the local errors in order to determine appropriate limits for their sizes. Assuming these limits are known, the rest is more or less mechanical. Since the size of e_n depends directly on the step-size $h_n = x_{n+1} - x_n$, we simply have to adjust the step sizes in order to ensure that the estimates for the e_n's are sufficiently small. We consider this aspect first.

6.3.1. Stability and Step-size Control

The mechanism for adjusting the h_n's is called a "step-size choosing algorithm." Such algorithms attempt to strike a reasonable balance between accuracy and efficiency. The step sizes should be such that the local errors are within a given tolerance to ensure accuracy. On the other hand, they should not be too small or else efficiency will be adversely affected by having to take extra steps unnecessarily. Consequently, an algorithm should continually monitor the local error and, by step-size adjustments, attempt to keep its magnitude at a specified level. We describe a typical algorithm. Suppose we want the magnitude of the local errors to be less than a fixed-value TOL. Let $h_{n-1} = x_n - x_{n-1}$ be the step-size used to compute u_n (for which $|e_n| \leq \text{TOL}$) and assume that the formula being used is pth-order accurate. Then the algorithm for selecting h_n is as follows:

1. define $\bar{h} = \min \left[h_{n-1} \cdot \left(\dfrac{\text{TOL}}{|e_n|} \right)^{1/(p+1)}, h_{\max} \right]$
2. IF $\bar{h}/h_{n-1} < 1.25$ THEN
3.   set $\bar{h} = h_{n-1}$
4. compute a trial value $\bar{u}_{n+1}$ using step-size $\bar{h}$ and estimate the local error $\bar{e}_{n+1}$
5. set $h_n = \bar{h}$
6. DO WHILE $(|\bar{e}_{n+1}| > \text{TOL})$
7.   set $\bar{h} = \bar{h} \cdot \left(\dfrac{\text{TOL}}{|\bar{e}_{n+1}|} \right)^{1/(p+1)}$
8.   IF $\bar{h} < h_{\min}$ THEN
9.   RETURN to the calling program with XEND $= x_n + h_n$ and UEND $= \bar{u}_{n+1}$
10.   Compute a new trial value $\bar{u}_{n+1}$ using step-size $\bar{h}$ and estimate the local error $\bar{e}_{n+1}$
11.   set $h_n = \bar{h}$
12. END

The first step (line 1) in the algorithm is to compute a trial value $\bar{h}$ for the new step-size h_n. The reasoning for the particular formula used is as follows. We can write

$$e_{n+1} = O(h^{p+1}) = K_{n+1}h^{p+1} + O(h^{p+2})$$

where K_{n+1} is a constant that is dependent on f. Since we would like to have $e_{n+1} \doteq \text{TOL}$, it follows that we should choose

$$h_n \doteq \left(\frac{\text{TOL}}{|K_{n+1}|} \right)^{1/(p+1)}$$

but now the problem is to estimate K_{n+1}. To this end, we use the analogous expression for e_n:

$$e_n = K_n h_{n-1}^{p+1}$$

which can easily be solved for K_n. Hence, if we assume that $K_{n+1} \doteq K_n$, we obtain the approximation

$$h_n \doteq \bar{h} = h_{n-1} \cdot \left(\frac{\text{TOL}}{|e_n|} \right)^{1/(p+1)}$$

and take the minimum of this value and $h_{\max}$ as the trial step size. Note that, since $|e_n| \leq \text{TOL}$, this is an attempt to increase the step size. We recall that, in the case of multistep formulas, step-size changes are costly. Therefore, the step-size should not be increased unless the resulting savings are at least sufficient to compensate for the additional expense.

This is the purpose of lines 2 and 3, namely, to leave the step size unaltered unless it can be increased by at least 25%. (The precise amount of this minimum increase will vary between subroutines.) On the other hand, for Runge–Kutta formulas, there is no extra cost in changing the step-size. Therefore, lines 2 and 3 will not normally be included in Runge–Kutta subroutines. The DO WHILE loop (lines 6 through 12) is more or less self-explanatory. Its purpose is to find a step-size h_n that satisfies both the reliability and efficiency criteria discussed previously. The formula used in line 7 for modifying $\bar{h}$ is designed to achieve this purpose. Its form, and derivation, is similar to the formula used in line 1. The values h_{max} and h_{min} in lines 1 and 8, respectively, are limits on the permissible size of any h_n. A subroutine will normally give the user the option of either specifying them or using default values set by the routine. The default size for h_{min} is usually in the neighbourhood of machine epsilon. We will discuss the problem of assigning an appropriate value for h_{max} shortly.

Let us now consider the question of controlling the global error. In order to gain some insight, it is instructive to investigate what happens with the simple problem

$$(6.25) \quad y' = cy \qquad y(0) = y_0$$

whose solution is $y(x) = y_0 e^{cx}$. Suppose we use Euler's formula (6.4) with uniform step-size h to compute a numerical solution. From (6.25), each component of the solution will be given by

$$(6.26) \quad u_{n+1} = u_n + hf(x_n, u_n)$$
$$= (1 + hc)u_n = (1 + hc)^2 u_{n-1} = \cdots$$
$$= (1 + hc)^{n+1} u_0$$

In other words, applying Euler's formula to solve (6.25) is equivalent to using the expression $(1 + hc)$ as an approximation for the exponential function e^{hc}.

Let us assume, first, that $c < 0$. Then the true solution of the problem (6.25) satisfies

$$y(x_{n+1}) = y_0 e^{(n+1)hc} \to 0 \qquad \text{as } n \text{ increases}$$

and it is reasonable to require that our numerical solution should exhibit the same behavior. From (6.26), this implies that we must have

$$(6.27) \quad |1 + hc| < 1 \qquad \text{or} \qquad h < \frac{2}{|c|}$$

In Table 6.2, we show some results for the problem (6.25) with $c = -10$ and $y_0 = 1$. In this case, the condition (6.27) requires that $h < 0.2$ and the results verify its necessity.

TABLE 6.2

n	$h = 0.05$	$h = 0.15$	$h = 0.25$
0	1	1	1
1	0.5	-0.5	-1.5
2	0.25	0.25	2.25
3	0.13	-0.13	-3.38
4	0.06	0.06	5.06

The need for h to satisfy (6.27) can be motivated in an alternative way, that is, by showing how the error that is introduced at any stage can propagate as the computation proceeds. Suppose, for example, that the initial value y_0 is not representable exactly as a machine number. Then, as an initial value for the numerical solution, we must use $u_0 = fl(y_0)$, and it will contain some error $e_0 = y_0 - u_0$. Now, from (6.26), we have

$$u_{n+1} = (1 + hc)^{n+1}u_0 = (1 + hc)^{n+1}(y_0 - e_0)$$

so that the global error in u_{n+1} is given by

$$
\begin{aligned}
E_{n+1} &= y_{n+1} - u_{n+1} \\
&= y_0 e^{(n+1)hc} - (1 + hc)^{n+1}(y_0 - e_0) \\
(6.28) \qquad &= [e^{(n+1)hc} - (1 + hc)^{n+1}]y_0 - (1 + hc)^{n+1}e_0
\end{aligned}
$$

Hence, the global error consists of two components. First, there is the error that results from the Euler formula approximation $(1 + hc)$ for e^{hc}. The second component is the propagation effect of the initial error e_0. Quite clearly, if $|1 + hc| > 1$, this component will grow without bound as n increases and, no matter how small e_0 can be made, this term can eventually become the dominant part of E_{n+1}. We remark that the same phenomenon was the subject of Example 5 in Section 1.1.4. There will also be a similar propagation of the local errors introduced in previous steps and it will not take long for these terms to completely swamp the calculations. To avoid such problems, it follows that the step-size h must satisfy the condition (6.27) so that the propagation effects of previous errors will remain bounded rather than be magnified. This condition is called a *stability condition* because, if it is not satisfied, the numerical solution will eventually exhibit unstable behavior such as the results in Table 6.2 for $h = 0.15$ and 0.25.

It is evident from the foregoing discussion that the stability condition should dictate the size of h_{max} in the step-size algorithm. However, this only points out the difficulty in choosing an appropriate value for h_{max}

because the stability condition is both problem dependent (through the parameter c for the problem) and formula dependent. The condition (6.27), for example, was derived from the particular approximation $(1 + hc)$, used by Euler's formula, for e^{hc}. A different condition holds for the Runge–Kutta–Fehlberg formula (6.17) because it corresponds to the approximation

$$e^{hc} \doteq 1 + hc + \frac{(hc)^2}{2!} + \frac{(hc)^3}{3!} + \frac{(hc)^4}{4!}$$

In this case, it is difficult to give an explicit formula for the stability condition, but we can say that it is the set of values h for which the magnitude of the polynomial on the right-hand side is less than 1. We note that it will also depend on the value of c.

Now suppose that $c > 0$ in the problem (6.25). Then, since both $e^{(n+1)hc}$ and the approximation $(1 + hc)^{n+1} \to +\infty$ as n increases, there is evidently no concern about stability. However, this is misleading. It is clear from (6.28) that, since $(1 + hc) > 1$ for *any* $h > 0$, the effect of local errors on subsequent steps will always be magnification. In other words, it is impossible to make the formula stable. But this time the instability is not apparent because the dominant part of the error expression (6.28) will be the first component. No matter how small we choose h, the difference $[e^{(n+1)hc} - (1 + hc)^{n+1}]$ will always be large relative to $(1 + hc)^{n+1}$ once n is sufficiently large. Problems of this sort are said to be *ill conditioned*. The difficulty lies in the problem itself and there is nothing that can be done except to detect its presence.

The preceding analysis carries over to the more general problem (6.2). The constant c in (6.25) corresponds to the partial derivative of $f(x, y)$ with respect to the second variable, that is, $\partial f / \partial y$. Hence, roughly speaking,

$$\text{If } f_y = \frac{\partial f}{\partial y} \begin{cases} < 0 & \begin{array}{l} \text{local errors will decay if the } h_n\text{'s satisfy the} \\ \text{stability condition} \end{array} \\ > 0 & \begin{array}{l} \text{local errors are magnified no matter how small} \\ \text{the } h_n\text{'s are chosen} \end{array} \end{cases}$$

In many problems, f_y changes sign over the interval $[x_0, x_{\text{end}}]$ so that we alternate between decay and magnification of the local errors. It may seem like a good idea to monitor the sign of f_y in order to determine which situation holds. However, in the case of a system of m differential equations, this not very practical. The analogue of f_y for systems is the Jacobian matrix J_y, whose components are

$$(J_y)_{i,j} = \frac{\partial f_i(x, y)}{\partial y_j} \qquad 1 \le i, j \le n$$

and ill conditioning may be present when any of the eigenvalues of J_y has positive real part. Hence, the cost of checking for ill conditioning is quite prohibitive because it involves an eigenvalue calculation each time a check is made.

6.3.2. Stiff Equations

We now turn to a phenomenon called "stiffness" of a differential equation or system of equations. This has to do with the restriction on the size of h imposed by the stability condition. An equation is said to be *stiff* if h must be prohibitively small in order to ensure stability, a situation that arises, for example, in many chemical reaction problems. Again, we use the simple problem (6.25) to illustrate the procedures for dealing with stiff equations. If, for instance, $c = -1000$ in (6.25), the step-size h for Euler's formula would have to be <0.002 so that a considerable amount of effort would be required to advance the solution from $x = 0$ to, say, $x = 1$. We remark that, since the exact solution $y(x) = y_0 e^{-1000x}$ will generally be very close to zero over most of the interval $[0, 1]$, there does not seem to be much point in carrying the numerical solution so far. However, in the case of a system of equations, some components of the system may be essentially zero while others are not, and the integration has to be taken some distance in order to track the latter. Consider, for example, the system

$$\mathbf{y}' = \begin{bmatrix} y_1' \\ y_2' \end{bmatrix} = \begin{bmatrix} -2y_1 - 998y_2 \\ -1000y_2 \end{bmatrix} \qquad \mathbf{y}(0) = \begin{bmatrix} 2 \\ 1 \end{bmatrix}$$

It is easy to verify that the solution is given by

$$y_1(x) = e^{-2x} + e^{-1000x}$$
$$y_2(x) = e^{-1000x}$$

The term e^{-1000x} decays exceedingly fast, but e^{-2x} does not. In computing a numerical solution for such a problem, we want to carry the computations some distance in order to track the component $y_1(x)$. However, the difficulty is that the stability condition is imposed by the second component $y_2(x)$. Even after it becomes essentially zero, the stringent stability requirement must still be enforced. In order to avoid this type of situation, we consider developing a formula that is *unconditionally stable,* that is, one for which there is no condition on h to ensure stability. Consider the following approximation for e^{ch}:

$$(6.29) \qquad e^{ch} \doteq \frac{1 + ch/2}{1 - ch/2} = 1 + ch + \frac{(ch)^2}{2} + \frac{(ch)^3}{4} + \cdots$$

If $c < 0$, this approximation is <1 for *any* $h > 0$, that is, it is unconditionally stable. To translate this approximation into a numerical formula for solving differential equations, we again look at the simple problem (6.25). We take the solution $z_{n+1} = z_n e^{hc}$ of the local problem and, replacing z's by u's and using the approximation (6.29) for e^{hc}, we obtain

$$(1 - \tfrac{1}{2}hc)u_{n+1} = (1 + \tfrac{1}{2}hc)u_n$$

from which we infer the general formula

(6.30) $\quad u_{n+1} = u_n + \dfrac{h}{2} \cdot [f(x_{n+1}, u_{n+1}) + f(x_n, u_n)]$

It is called the *trapezoidal rule* formula because, if we integrate $y' = f(x, y)$ from x_n to x_{n+1}, we have

$$y_{n+1} = y_n + \int_{x_n}^{x_{n+1}} f(x, y(x)) \, dx$$

and approximation of the integral by the trapezoidal rule produces the formula (6.30).

From (6.29), we see that the local error in the trapezoidal rule formula is $O(h^3)$, which is better than Euler but not as good as, say, the Runge–Kutta–Fehlberg fourth-order formula (6.17). On the other hand, (6.30) is stable for *any* $h > 0$, which is a decided advantage. However, the price we must pay for this luxury is quite high in terms of computational cost. We see that (6.30) is a corrector-type of formula, which immediately suggests a predictor-corrector iteration to compute u_{n+1}. But it turns out that convergence considerations reimpose the severe restriction on the step-size h that we were trying to avoid in the first place. To explain, we rewrite (6.30) in the form of a nonlinear equation

(6.31) $\quad F(u_{n+1}) = u_{n+1} - \tfrac{1}{2}hf(x_{n+1}, u_{n+1}) - C = 0$

where $C = u_n + \tfrac{1}{2}hf(x_n, u_n)$ is a constant that is known. Then the predictor-corrector iteration $PECEC\ldots$ with (6.30) as the corrector is equivalent to finding a root of $F(u_{n+1}) = 0$ using the fixed-point iteration (4.8) for non-linear equations. That is, we write $F(u_{n+1}) = u_{n+1} - g(u_{n+1})$ and compute, successively,

$$u_{n+1}^{(s+1)} = g(u_{n+1}^{(s)}) = \tfrac{1}{2}hf(x_{n+1}, u_{n+1}^{(s+1)}) - C$$

In this context, the condition for convergence of the iteration is given by (4.10)(iii), namely,

$$|g'| = |\tfrac{1}{2}hf_y| < 1 \qquad \text{or} \qquad h < \frac{2}{|f_y|}$$

which, in the case of our simple problem (6.25), is precisely the stability condition (6.27). In other words, if we use a predictor-corrector scheme to compute u_{n+1} in (6.30), the advantage gained from the unconditional stability feature of the formula will be lost.

As an alternative method for computing u_{n+1} in (6.30), we consider applying the Newton–Raphson method (4.23) to solve the corresponding nonlinear equation (6.31). The convergence condition for this method is

$$\left| \frac{F \cdot F''}{(F')^2} \right| < 1$$

and, although this still imposes a condition on h, it is not nearly so restrictive. In fact, for our simple problem (6.25), there is no restriction on h at all because $F'' \equiv 0$. Hence, in this particular case, the unconditional stability feature of (6.30) is retained by the Newton–Raphson iteration for computing u_{n+1}.

We recall that the Newton–Raphson method is not very efficient. Moreover, it requires an explicit representation for F'. Consequently, to avoid these difficulties, the usual practice is to use the secant method instead. The method requires two initial guesses and these are normally taken to be the previous value u_n and a value $u_{n+1}^{(p)}$ obtained by using a predictor formula. Normally, these are quite good initial guesses and only two or three iterations are required in order to achieve convergence. The cost per step is one function evaluation for the predictor plus one for each iteration of the secant method. Assuming convergence is achieved in three iterations, the total cost per step is four evaluations of f. This does not seem like much but we must remember that the method is only second-order accurate. Since we have already seen that there are (conditionally stable) second-order formulas which require less work, it is evident that the unconditional stability feature involves some extra expense. In the case of a system of $m > 1$ differential equations, the additional cost is quite significant because each step requires the solution of a nonlinear system of equations. Assuming a quasi-Newton method (see Section 4.3) is used, each iteration requires one function evaluation plus the solution of an $m \times m$ linear system of equations. If, as before, convergence is achieved in three iterations, the total cost of a step is four evaluations of $\mathbf{f}(x, \mathbf{y})$ plus the work required to solve three $m \times m$ linear systems. Quite clearly, then, formulas such as (6.30) should only be used when the differential equation is so stiff that the stability requirement makes "nonstiff" formulas impractical. Unfortunately, there usually is no sure way of detecting stiffness by just looking at a problem. One either knows it will be stiff from the context of the particular application or else finds out by experience in trying to use a nonstiff subroutine.

6.3.3. Calling Sequences

From our discussion, it is evident that the calling sequence for DEIVP described earlier must be expanded in order to include parameters that allow the user some control over the integration process. For instance, we have already seen that there should be provision for specifying the limits h_{min} and h_{max} on the step size. Also, in the case of a nonstiff subroutine, it is useful to have a mechanism for limiting the total number of evaluations of $f(x, y)$ as a safeguard against using a nonstiff routine for a stiff problem. (h_{min} can also be used for this purpose.) As a consequence of the variety of possible parameters, the calling sequences of many routines tend to be long and there is no "typical" sequence. An effective means of avoiding this problem is to combine all of the control information into a *communications vector* so that only one argument is needed. An additional advantage of this approach is that the vector can be turned "on" or "off," giving the user a choice between communicating the control information to the routine or else using default values set by the routine. The former option is useful for experimental purposes, while the latter makes the routine easy to use for "production" work. The subroutine DVERK in the IMSL package makes use of this idea. Its calling sequence is

> DVERK(N,FCN,X,Y,XEND,TOL,IND,C,NW,W,IER)

where, briefly,

> N is the number of equations in the system.
> FCN, X, XEND, TOL are as before.
> IND is used to turn the communications vector on or off.
> C is a communications vector.
> NW is the row dimension of W as specified in the calling program.
> W is a workspace matrix.
> IER is an error indicator.

DVERK will only handle nonstiff problems, but sometimes a routine is designed for both stiff and nonstiff ones. This is done by implementing two different sets of formulas in the routine and adding an argument to the calling sequence for selecting the desired set. While this is convenient, the user is still required to decide whether the problem is stiff or not.

The parameter TOL is a tolerance for the local errors $|e_n|$, whereas we are interested in ensuring that the global error is sufficiently small. Suppose that we want to compute a numerical solution for which $|E_{end}| < $ ERR. Then we must decide how to set TOL in order to achieve this accuracy in u_{end}. As a rough rule of thumb, we should set

> $TOL = h \cdot ERR$

where h is an "average" step size. Again, we use the simple problem (6.25) and Euler's formula with constant step-size h to motivate the reasoning for this statement. Assuming that the stability condition (6.27) is satisfied, we can neglect the second component in (6.28) so that

$$
\begin{aligned}
E_{\text{end}} = E_n &= \{e^{nhc} - (1 + hc)^n\}y_0 \\
&= \{[1 + nhc + \tfrac{1}{2}n^2h^2c^2 + \cdots] \\
&\quad - [1 + nhc + \tfrac{1}{2}n(n-1)h^2c^2 + \cdots]\}y_0 \\
&= \left\{\frac{n}{2}h^2c^2 + \cdots\right\}y_0 \\
&= K_1 h + O(h^2)
\end{aligned}
$$

where K_1 is a constant depending on c (from the problem) and the length nh of the interval of integration. Now we have already seen that each

$$
|e_i| = |[e^{hc} - (1 + hc)]u_i| = K_2 h^2 + O(h^3) \qquad 1 \le i \le n
$$

Therefore, by assuming that $K_1 \doteq K_2$, we have

$$
|e_i| \doteq h \cdot |E_{\text{end}}|
$$

and it follows that we should choose $\text{TOL} \doteq h \cdot \text{ERR}$. We emphasize that this is only a guideline for setting TOL. It will not guarantee that $|E_{\text{end}}| < \text{ERR}$.

EXERCISES

1. Find the series expansions, to terms in x^5, of the solutions of each of the following initial-value problems.

   (a) $y' = 1 - x^2 - y^2$, $y(0) = 0$.
   (b) $y' = x + \sin y$, $y(0) = 0$.
   (c) $y'' + y = 0$, $y(0) = 0$, $y'(0) = 1$.

2. Derive the Adams–Moulton two-step corrector formula (6.21).

3. Derive the error expressions (6.22).

4. Derive the trapezoidal rule formula (6.30) using Taylor expansions in the manner discussed in Section 6.1.2.

5. The general Runge–Kutta formula involving three evaluations of $f(x, y)$ is of the form

$$u_{n+1} = u_n + w_1 k_1 + w_2 k_2 + w_3 k_3$$

where

$$k_1 = hf(x_n, u_n)$$

$$k_2 = hf(x_n + a_2 h, u_n + b_{2,1} k_1)$$

$$k_3 = hf(x_n + a_3 h, u_n + b_{3,1} k_1 + b_{3,2} k_2)$$

(a) Show that, in order to be third-order accurate, the parameters in this formula must satisfy the following system of nonlinear equations.

$$b_{2,1} = a_2$$

$$b_{3,1} = a_3 - b_{3,2}$$

$$w_1 + w_2 + w_3 = 1$$

$$a_2 w_2 + a_3 w_3 = \tfrac{1}{2}$$

$$a_2^2 w_2 + a_3^2 w_3 = \tfrac{1}{3}$$

$$a_2 b_{3,2} w_3 = \tfrac{1}{6}$$

[Hint: Use the expansions (6.12) and (6.13).]

(b) The system in part (a) has six equations in eight unknowns. Let $a_2 = \tfrac{1}{2}$, $a_3 = 1$, and solve the system. Write down the resulting formula.

6. An interesting problem that can be used for experimentation is

$$y' = c[y(x) - g(x)] \qquad y(x_0) = g(x_0)$$

where c is a constant and $g(x)$ is an arbitrary function. The analytic solution is $y(x) = g(x)$.

(a) Let $c = 10$, $x_0 = 0$, and

    i $g(x) = x$
    ii $g(x) = \sin x$
    iii $g(x) = e^{-x}$

In each case, compute a numerical solution at the points $x_n = 0.1n$, $1 \le n \le 50$, and compare with the corresponding values of the analytic solution. Use a tolerance $\text{TOL} = 1.0E - 4$ for the local error. Explain the results.

(b) Repeat part (a) with $c = -10$.

(c) Repeat part (a) with $c = -200$. Use both a nonstiff and a stiff subroutine and compare the respective efficiencies (number of function calls).

A good source of "typical" nonstiff initial-value problems that arise in applications is contained in [20]. The collection of problems in this paper was assembled for the purpose of evaluating algorithms for solving (nonstiff) initial-value problems. Exercises 7 to 16 were selected from this collection. In each case, compute a numerical solution over the interval $[0, 20]$ using a tolerance (for the local error) TOL $= 1000 \cdot$ EPS (machine epsilon), defined by (1.1). [A program segment for computing an approximation for EPS is given by (1.6).] Estimate the global error by computing a new numerical solution using TOL $= 100 \cdot$ EPS and comparing the two solutions. If more than one nonstiff subroutine is available on the local computer system, use each one and compare the respective efficiencies (number of function calls). For more information on the source of each problem, see [20].

7. Oscillatory problems

$$y' = y \cos x \qquad y(0) = 1 \qquad \text{(solution: } y = e^{\sin x})$$

8. Logistic curve

$$y' = \frac{y}{4}\left(1 - \frac{y}{20}\right) \qquad y(0) = 1 \qquad \left(\text{solution: } y = \frac{20}{1 + 19e^{-x/4}}\right)$$

9. Spiral curve

$$y' = \frac{y - x}{y + x} \qquad y(0) = 4 \qquad \text{(solution, in polar coordinates:}$$
$$r = 4e^{\pi/2 - \theta})$$

10. Simple predator-prey model

$$y_1' = 2(y_1 - y_1 y_2) \qquad y_1(0) = 1$$
$$y_2' = -(y_2 - y_1 y_2) \qquad y_2(0) = 3$$

11. Linear chemical reaction

$$y_1' = -y_1 + y_2 \qquad\qquad y_1(0) = 2$$
$$y_2' = y_1 - 2y_2 + y_3 \qquad y_2(0) = 0$$
$$y_3' = y_2 - y_3 \qquad\quad y_3(0) = 1$$

12. Euler equations of motion for a rigid body

$$y_1' = y_2 y_3 \qquad\qquad y_1(0) = 0$$
$$y_2' = -y_1 y_3 \qquad\qquad y_2(0) = 1$$
$$y_3' = -0.51 y_1 y_2 \qquad y_3(0) = 1$$

13. Radioactive decay chain

$$
\begin{bmatrix} y_1' \\ y_2' \\ \cdot \\ \cdot \\ \cdot \\ y_{10}' \end{bmatrix}
\begin{bmatrix} -1 & & & & \\ 1 & -2 & & & \\ & 2 & -3 & & \\ & & \ddots & \ddots & \\ & & & \ddots & -9 \\ & & & & 9 & 0 \end{bmatrix}
\begin{bmatrix} y_1 \\ y_2 \\ \cdot \\ \cdot \\ \cdot \\ y_{10} \end{bmatrix}
\qquad
y(0) = \begin{bmatrix} 1 \\ 0 \\ \cdot \\ \cdot \\ \cdot \\ 0 \end{bmatrix}
$$

14. Orbit equations. Let $x(t)$ and $y(t)$ be the coordinates, at time t, of an object, such as a satellite, orbiting a large body, such as the Earth, that is located at the coordinate origin. Then the position of the satellite with respect to the Earth is determined by solving the following system of differential equations:

$$x''(t) = -\frac{x(t)}{r^3} \qquad x(0) = 1 - \epsilon \qquad x'(0) = 0$$

$$y''(t) = -\frac{y(t)}{r^3} \qquad y(0) = 0 \qquad y'(0) = \sqrt{\frac{1+\epsilon}{1-\epsilon}}$$

where $r^2 = \sqrt{x^2 + y^2}$ and ϵ is the eccentricity of the orbit. The analytic solution is given by

$$x = \cos u - \epsilon \qquad y = \sqrt{1 - \epsilon^2} \sin u$$

where $u - \epsilon \sin u - t = 0$. Consider the cases $\epsilon = 0.1$, 0.5, and 0.9.

15. Bessel's equation of order $\frac{1}{2}$ with the origin shifted one unit to the left

$$(x + 1)^2 y'' + (x + 1)y' + ((x + 1)^2 - 0.25)y = 0$$

$$y(0) = J_{1/2}(1) = 0.6713967071418030$$

$$y'(0) = J'_{1/2}(1) = 0.0954005144474446$$

16. Linear pursuit equation

$$1 + (y')^2 = (25 - x)^2 (y'')^2$$

$$y(0) = 0 \qquad y'(0) = 0$$

17. Consider the orbit equations in Exercise 14. In the case $\epsilon = 0.3$, determine to three significant figures, the time required for the satellite to complete two orbits.

A collection of stiff initial-value problems is contained in [11]. Again, this set of problems was assembled for the purpose of evaluating algorithms.

Problems 18 to 21 were selected from this collection. In each case, compute a numerical solution over the interval $[0, x_{end}]$. Use tolerances $TOL = 1.0E - 3$ and $1.0E - 5$ in order to investigate the global error. Also, try solving the problems using a nonstiff subroutine and compare the respective number of function calls.

18. Simple linear system

$$y_1' = -0.5y_1 \qquad y_1(0) = 1$$
$$y_2' = -y_2 \qquad y_2(0) = 1$$
$$y_3' = -100y_3 \qquad y_3(0) = 1$$
$$y_4' = -90y_4 \qquad y_4(0) = 1$$
$$x_{end} = 20$$

19. Chemical reaction

$$y_1' = -0.13y_1 - 1000y_1y_3 \qquad\qquad y_1(0) = 1$$
$$y_2' = -2500y_2y_3 \qquad\qquad y_2(0) = 1$$
$$y_3' = -0.13y_1 - 1000y_1y_3 - 2500y_2y_3 \qquad y_3(0) = 0$$
$$x_{end} = 40$$

20. Reactor kinetics

$$y_1' = 0.01 - [1 + (y_1 + 1000)(y_1 + 1)](0.01 + y_1 + y_2) \qquad y_1(0) = 0$$
$$y_2' = 0.01 - (1 + y_2^2)(0.01 + y_1 + y_2) \qquad\qquad\qquad y_2(0) = 0$$
$$x_{end} = 100$$

21. Circuit theory

$$y_1' = -1800y_1 + 900y_2 \qquad\qquad y_1(0) = 0$$
$$y_i' = y_{i-1} - 2y_i + y_{i+1} \qquad\qquad y_i(0) = 0 \qquad i = 2, \ldots, 8$$
$$y_9' = 1000y_8 - 2000y_9 + 1000 \qquad y_9(0) = 0$$
$$x_{end} = 120$$

22. Consider the two-point boundary-value problem

$$\mathbf{i} \quad -y'' + y = x \qquad y(0) = 0 \qquad y(1) = 0$$

One way of computing a numerical solution is to use an initial-value or *shooting method*. Briefly, we consider the initial-value problem

$$w'' + w = x \qquad w(0) = 0 \qquad w(1) = s$$

where s is a parameter to be determined. Denoting the solution of this problem by $w(x; s)$, it follows that we want to compute the value s^* for which $w(1; s^*) = y(1) = 0$. In other words, we want to find the root of the function $g(s) = w(1; s) - 0$. For the problem (i), find s^* to within three significant digits and then compute a numerical solution, with the same accuracy, at the points $x_n = 0.1n$, $0 \le n \le 10$. (The analytic solution of the problem is $y = x + e(e^{-x} - e^x)/(e^2 - 1)$.) Also solve the following problems by the shooting method:

ii $-y'' + y = x \qquad y(0) = 1 \qquad y(3) = 1 - e^{-2}$

iii $-(xy')' + (1 + x)^2 y = 2 - e^{-x} \qquad y(0) = 5 \qquad y(1) = -3$

BIBLIOGRAPHY

1. Ahlberg, J. H., E. N. Nilson, and J. L. Walsh, *The theory of splines and their application.* Academic Press, New York, 1967.
2. Anonymous, "American standard Fortran," Report #X3.9-1966, American Standards Assoc., Inc., New York, 1966.
3. Burden, R. L., J. D. Faires, and A. C. Reynolds, *Numerical analysis.* Prindle, Weber and Schmidt, Boston, Mass., 1978.
4. Carnahan, B., H. A. Luther, and J. O. Wilkes, *Applied Numerical Methods.* John Wiley, New York, 1964.
5. Conte, S. D. and C. deBoor, *Elementary numerical analysis: an algorithmic approach,* 3rd ed. McGraw-Hill, New York, 1980.
6. Dahlquist, G., and A. Björck, *Numerical Methods.* Prentice-Hall, Englewood Cliffs, N.J., 1974.
7. Davis, P. J., and P. Rabinowitz, *Numerical integration.* Blaisdell, Waltham, Mass., 1967.
8. deBoor, C., *A practical guide to splines.* Springer-Verlag, New York, 1978.
9. Dennis, J. E., Jr., and J. J. Moré, "Quasi-Newton methods, motivation and theory," *SIAM Review,* **19** (1977), 46–89.
10. Dongarra, J. J. et al., *LINPACK User's Guide,* Society for Industrial and Applied Mathematics, Philadelphia, 1979.
11. Enright, W. H., T. E. Hull, and B. Lindberg, "Comparing numerical methods for stiff systems of ODEs," *BIT,* **15** (1975), 10–48.
12. Fairweather, G., and P. Keast, "An investigation of Romberg quadrature," *TOMS,* **4** (1978), 316–322.
13. Fehlberg, E., "Klassiche Runge–Kutta-formula fünter und siebenter ordnung mit schrittweiten-kontrolle," *Computing,* **4** (1969), 93–106.
14. Fehlberg, E., "Klassiche Runge–Kutta-formula vierter and niedregerer ordnung mit schrittweitenkontrolle and ihre anwendung auf warmeleitungsprobleme," *Computing,* **6** (1970), 61–71.
15. Forsythe, G. E., "Pitfalls in computation, or why a math book isn't enough," *Amer. Math. Monthly,* **77** (1970), 931–956.

16. Forsythe, G. E., and C. B. Moler, *Computer solution of linear algebraic systems*. Prentice-Hall, Englewood Cliffs, N.J., 1967.
17. Forsythe, G. E., M. Malcolm, and C. B. Moler, *Computer methods for mathematical computations*. Prentice-Hall, Englewood Cliffs, N.J., 1977.
18. Hall, A. D., and B. G. Ryder, "The PFORT Verifier," Technical Report No. 12, Bell Laboratories, Murray Hill, N.J., 1973.
19. Hastings, C., Jr., *Approximations for digital computers*. Princeton University Press, Princeton, N.J., 1955.
20. Hull, T. E., W. H. Enright, B. Fellen, and A. E. Sedgwick, "Comparing numerical methods for ordinary differential equations," *SIAM J. Num. Anal.,* **9** (1972), 603–637.
21. Kaplan, W., *Advanced calculus*, Addison-Wesley, Reading, Mass., 1973.
22. Isaacson, E., and H. B. Keller, *Analysis of Numerical Methods*. John Wiley, New York, 1966.
23. Merson, R. H., "An operational method for the study of integration processes" in *Proc. Sym. on Data Processing*, Weapons Research Establishment, Salisbury, South Australia, 1957.
24. Ralston, A., and P. Rabinowitz, *A first course in numerical analysis*. McGraw-Hill, New York, 1978.
25. Rice, J. R. et al., "Numerical computation: its nature and research directions," ACM Report, Association for Computing Machinery, New York, 1979.
26. Romberg, W., "Vereinfachte numerische Integration," *Det. Kgl. Norske Vid. Selsk. Forh.,* **28** (1955), 30–36.
27. Shampine, L. F., and R. Allen, *Numerical computing*. Saunders, Philadelphia, 1973.
28. Shampine, L. F., and M. K. Gordon, *Computer solution of ordinary differential equations: the initial value problem*. Freeman, San Francisco, 1975.
29. Stewart, G. W., *Introduction to matrix computations*. Academic Press, New York, 1973.
30. Stroud, A. H., and D. Secrist, *Gaussian quadrature formulas*. Prentice-Hall, Englewood Cliffs, N.J., 1966.
31. Tee, G. T., "A simple example of an ill-conditioned matrix," *ACM SIGNUM Newsletter,* **7** (October, 1972), 19–20.
32. Wilkinson, J. H., *Rounding errors in algebraic processes*. Prentice-Hall, Englewood Cliffs, N.J., 1963.
33. Wilkinson, J. H., *The algebraic eigenvalue problem*. Clarendon Press, Oxford, 1965.

APPENDIX

SOURCES OF MATHEMATICAL SOFTWARE

In this appendix, we briefly discuss sources where mathematical software can be obtained. First, there are software packages. These are collections of subroutines for solving a variety of mathematical problems that commonly arise in scientific computations. Such packages are distributed in machine-readable form and can usually be obtained for a relatively modest charge to cover development and maintenance costs. Many computer installations acquire this type of mathematical software and make it available, on-line, to their users. This is certainly the most convenient way of making software routines accessible. Hence, before consulting other sources, it is a good idea to determine what packages are available on the local computing system. Listed below are some of the more widely distributed packages.

A second source of subroutines is the scientific literature. A great deal of research activity in recent years has been devoted to software development and, as a result, many excellent subroutines have been written. For the most part, these routines are of a special-purpose nature and it is seldom that they are included in widely distributed packages. Therefore, in order to publicize such work, authors will usually submit it for publication in a scientific journal. One journal that is dedicated to publishing this type of material is *Transactions on Mathematical Software* (*TOMS*), a journal of the Association for Computing Machinery. The high standards imposed by *TOMS* ensures that the algorithms published in it are reliable and well documented. Therefore, *TOMS* is an excellent source of subroutines for solving problems not specifically covered by commercially available packages.

Following is a list of some of the major software packages presently available.

GENERAL-PURPOSE Packages

IMSL (International Mathematical and Statistical Library)

This package contains subroutines for solving problems in each of the areas discussed in this book. Other areas covered are optimization and, as its name implies, statistics. The routines are written in ANSI Fortran.

SOURCE: IMSL Inc., NBC Building, 7500 Bellaire Blvd., Houston, Tex. 77036.

NAG (Numerical Algorithms Group)

The NAG package also covers the basic areas of mathematical and statistical computations. Like IMSL, NAG covers all of the topics discussed in this book. In addition, it contains subroutines for problems in optimization, integral equations and partial differential equations. The package is available in any one of three languages—ANSI Fortran, Algol 60, or Algol 68.

SOURCE: NAG Library Service Co-ordinator, Numerical Algorithms Group Ltd., NAG Central Office, 7 Banbury Rd., Oxford OX2 6NN, United Kingdom. In North America: NAG (USA) Inc., 1250 Grace Court, Downer's Grove, Ill. 60515.

SPECIAL-PURPOSE Packages

In this section, we list some packages that deal with a specified problem area. We have restricted the list to packages that deal with topics discussed in this book.

EISPACK

This package contains subroutines for computing the eigenvalues and/or eigenvectors of a matrix. The routines in EISPACK are written in ANSI Fortran. They have been subjected to rigorous testing at a number of different computer sites and, as a result, the package is regarded as very reliable, high-quality software.

SOURCE: National Energy Software Center, Argonne National Laboratory, 9700 S. Cass Ave., Argonne, Ill. 60439. It is also distributed by IMSL.

LINPACK

A package for solving linear systems of equations and linear least-squares problems. As with EISPACK, the routines in LINPACK have been thoroughly tested at a number of different computer sites so that it is a reliable, high-quality software package. It is written in ANSI Fortran.

SOURCE: National Energy Software Center, Argonne National Laboratory, 9700 S. Cass Ave., Argonne, Ill. 60439. It is also distributed by IMSL.

B-Spline

A package of subroutines for performing calculations with piecewise polynomials (see [8]). It is distributed by IMSL.

MINPACK

A package of subroutines for solving systems of nonlinear equations and nonlinear least-squares problems. It is distributed by IMSL.

QUADPACK

This is a collection of routines for evaluating a definite integral. Many of the QUADPACK routines have been included in the quadrature chapter of the NAG library.

EDUCATIONAL Packages

These packages were developed to provide a vehicle for experimentation and learning how algorithms perform. Since their primary design goal is education rather than efficiency, they are not recommended for "production" computing.

MATLAB (Matrix Laboratory)

This is an interactive facility, intended to be used as a "laboratory" for matrix computations.

SOURCE: Prof. Cleve Moler, Department of Computer Science, University of New Mexico, Albuquerque, N.M. 87131.

TEAPACK (Teaching Package)

A complete package, designed to complement a numerical methods course based on the type of material in this book. It is written in ANSI Fortran.

SOURCE: TEAPACK Co-ordinator, Department of Computer Science, University of Toronto, Toronto, Ont. M5S 1A7, Canada. TEAPACK manual is published by John Wiley.

INDEX